YOU CAN MAKE A DIFFERENCE!

■ ■ ■

You can do something *right now* to help our planet and the people and animals that inhabit it. Whether you are concerned about the homeless, the destruction of the rain forests, saving endangered species, or helping America's youth, this book shows you how to make a difference. A wide-ranging, comprehensive sourcebook, it provides information on:

▶ how to make your own voice heard

▶ the vast resources available to educate you, inform you, and help you to act

▶ practical ways in which to get involved

▶ how to focus your energies on the specific areas and issues that concern *you*

RICHARD ZIMMERMAN left a successful career in 1990 as an institutional bond salesman at a top Wall Street investment firm to write *What Can I Do to Make a Difference?* Now working as a network television executive, he lives in Los Angeles with his wife, Karen, and his young son, Zachary.

WHAT CAN I DO TO MAKE A DIFFERENCE?

A Positive Action Sourcebook

• • •

RICHARD ZIMMERMAN

• • •

A Plume Book

This book is printed on recyclable paper.
PLUME
Published by the Penguin Group
Penguin Books USA Inc., 375 Hudson Street,
New York, New York 10014, U.S.A.
Penguin Books Ltd, 27 Wrights Lane,
London W8 5TZ, England
Penguin Books Australia Ltd, Ringwood,
Victoria, Australia
Penguin Books Canada Ltd, 10 Alcorn Avenue,
Toronto, Ontario, Canada M4V 3B2
Penguin Books (N.Z.) Ltd, 182-190 Wairau Road,
Auckland 10, New Zealand

Penguin Books Ltd, Registered Offices:
Harmondsworth, Middlesex, England

First published by Plume,
an imprint of New American Library,
a division of Penguin Books USA Inc.

First Printing, February, 1992
10 9 8 7 6 5 4 3 2 1

 REGISTERED TRADEMARK—MARCA REGISTRADA

LIBRARY OF CONGRESS CATALOGING IN PUBLICATION DATA:

Zimmerman, Richard, 1960—
    What can I do to make a difference? : a positive action sourcebook /
    Richard Zimmerman.
      p.   cm.
    ISBN 0-452-26632-7
    1. Environmental policy—Citizen participation.   2. Consumer
behavior—Social aspects.   3. Human rights.   4. Humanitarianism.
    5. Social action.   I. Title.
    HC79.E5Z55   1991
    361.6'1—dc20   91-21794
                                                          CIP

Printed in the United States of America
Set in Gill Sans and Sabon
Designed by Kathleen Herlihy-Paoli

To my wife, Karen,
who shares my vision,
and to my son, Zachary,
whose birth inspired me to do everything
I can to make the world a better place
for all of our children.

ACKNOWLEDGMENTS

I would like to thank all the individuals and organizations who helped in this effort, with special appreciation to

My agent, Henry Dunow, of Harold Ober Associates, Inc.
and my editor, Laurie Bernstein
Schelly Reid, Associate Director for Media, and C. Gregg Petersmeyer, Deputy Assistant to the President and Director, White House Office of National Service
Susan Geller, Geller and Associates
Steven B. Dunn, president, Beau-Zac Productions, Inc.
USA Today
The Ceres Coalition
Green Seal
Independent Sector
Co-op America
Council on Economic Priorities
Pennsylvania Resource Council
Clean Water Action News
Mothers and Others for a Livable Planet
Turner Broadcasting Systems, Inc.
American Paper Institute
National Resources Defense Council
Greenpeace
Greenpeace Action
Native Forest Council
Conservation International
Rainforest Action Network
Southern California Metropolitan Water District
Center for Marine Conservation
San Fransisco poster artist Doug Minkler
ASPCA
People for the Ethical Treatment of Animals
United Action for Animals
In Defense of Animals

Compassion for Animals Foundation
Physicians Committee for Responsible Medicine
Earth Island Institute
World Wildlife Fund
National Audubon Society
Humane Farming Association
EarthSave Foundation
Farm Animal Reform Movement
Summit for Animals
Humane Society of the United States
Beauty Without Cruelty, USA
International Society for Animal Rights
Earth Trust
Friends of Animals
United Animal Nation
Wildlife Coservation International
Planned Parenthood
Zero Population Growth
Bread for the World
Hunger Project
Food for the Hungry
World Vision
Ann Landers/Creator's Syndicate
Love Is Feeding Everyone (L.I.F.E.)
Freedom from Hunger Foundation
Childhelp USA
Children's Defense Fund
Girl's Incorporated
Literacy Volunteers of America
PLAN International USA
Amnesty International USA
Abigail Van Buren, Universal Press Syndicate
Southern Poverty Law Center
Mrs. Marva Collins and Ayinde Jean-Baptiste
Gloria Steinem, Ms. magazine

Center to Prevent Handgun Violence
Handgun Control, Inc.
Congress for Racial Equality
PRIDE
United Hospital Fund of New York
America Responds to AIDS, Department of Health and Human Services
AIDS Project Los Angeles
Make A Wish Foundation® of America
American Cancer Society
Braille Institute of America, Inc.
Life Savers Foundation
Cartoonist Don Herron
On Beyond War
Worldwatch Institute
Mothers Embracing Nuclear Disarmament
Youth Ambassadors International
Carnegie Endowment for International Peace
Grandmothers for Peace
SANE/FREEZE Campaign for Global Security
Special Olympics International
Muscular Dystrophy Association
Environmental Defense Fund
United Way
American Red Cross
American Heart Association
Friends of the Earth
National Marrow Donor Program
Guide Dog Foundation for the Blind
Best Buddies

Contents

▪▪▪▪▪▪▪▪▪▪▪▪▪▪▪▪▪▪▪▪▪▪▪▪▪▪

•••

Introduction

■■■■■■■■■■■■■■■■■■■■■■■■■■■■■■■■■■■■■■

Whatever you can do or dream you can, begin it. Boldness has genius, power and magic in it. Begin it now.

—GOETHE

As the title *What Can I Do to Make a Difference?* implies, this book provides information and ideas about what an individual can do to help solve some of the many problems that confront today's world. It focuses on the major issues of the environment, animal rights, human welfare, human rights, health, and peace.

The concept of this book evolved during a period in my life in which I became more aware and concerned about the welfare of the planet. For a while I tried to ignore these weighty matters. They happen elsewhere, I thought, to other people; I have my own life to deal with—my career and my family.

The problems did not disappear, however. In fact, they came closer to home—physically as well as emotionally. Every day I would pass more homeless people on the way to work. The air quality seemed to get worse and the ocean and beaches were more polluted. Alcohol and drug abuse became two of the nation's top concerns. Crime crossed geographic boundaries and extended into all neighborhoods. AIDS became a universal disease, regardless of sex or lifestyle. Watching the news and reading the newspaper often made me angry or depressed.

Nonetheless, I knew that negative emotions would not make these problems go away, so I decided to channel that emotional energy toward useful purposes. I didn't know, however, exactly where to start. I knew about a few of the large organizations, such as the Red Cross and UNICEF, but I didn't realize how many other equally important groups were at my disposal. Moreover, although I thought I was fairly well informed about world issues, in many cases I didn't even know that some problems existed. For instance, I was completely unaware of factory farming or dolphin slaughter. I vaguely knew why Sting and Bruce Springsteen held benefit concerts to increase awareness about political oppression and the destruction of rain forests. I didn't know that in buying certain products I may be contributing to the extinction of an animal.

My search for more information was not easy because there was no single book that would both educate me and lead me to act. I then decided that one way I could contribute to helping the planet was by writing an informative guide intended for someone like me—an individual who is concerned about the many problems in the world today and who wants to help but feels somewhat uninformed, slightly overwhelmed, and, in many cases, powerless.

The premise of *What Can I Do to Make a Difference?* is to give the interested individual a working knowledge of significant global problems and then provide practical ideas about how to help solve them.

You will learn . . .

▶ how you can find out more about these issues

▶ how your own voice can be heard

▶ how you can get involved

▶ different ways to help at home

It provides resources and ideas that will educate, inform, and help you act—without causing you to make a radical change in your life.

Most of all, it will answer the question "What can I do to make a difference?"

YOU CAN MAKE A DIFFERENCE!

• • •

The things to do are the things that need doing that you see need to be done and that no one else seems to see need to be done.

• • •

—R. BUCKMINSTER FULLER

Getting Started

■■■■■■■■■■■■■■■■■■■■■■■■■■■■■■■■

● ● ●

I don't know what your destiny will be, but one thing I do know: the only ones among you who will be really happy are those who have sought and found how to serve.

● ● ●

—ALBERT SCHWEITZER

A journey of a thousand miles begins with a single step.

—An ancient Chinese proverb

If the 1970s and 1980s symbolized the years of "taking," the 1990s will be the decade of "giving back." The message of the present era is to balance your personal life with that of the planet. And that message is being heard. Millions of people give their time and money to various causes, including environmental protection, animal welfare, homelessness, hunger, and AIDS—often with the satisfaction that comes from service as their only payment.

Both young and old are beginning to realize that the planet needs help. And each day more people come to its aid.

You may ask, "How can I help? What can I do?" Well, as Dennis Weaver, actor and social activist, so wisely explains, "We made the situation. We can remake it." What he means is that the world can be helped by you.

The choices are plentiful. Once you start looking you will find more than enough ways to get involved. All you have to do is make the effort.

Those who are giving and volunteering know that they do not have to sacrifice their personal lives to serve others. Business executives, homemakers, senior citizens, and students are among those who balance volunteerism with careers and lifestyle. Their reward: a well-rounded, more fulfilled life.

An ancient Chinese proverb says that "a journey of a thousand miles begins with a single step." Why not take that first, crucial step? Learn what you can do and then do it!

ORDINARY PEOPLE— EXTRAORDINARY ACTIONS

■ ■ ■

Throughout the country ordinary people are doing extraordinary things in an effort to help improve the lives of others:

A grandmother starts a crime telephone hotline to catch drug dealers in her neighborhood. A Mexican immigrant helps feed the homeless with the little money she earns as a cleaning lady. An elderly woman volunteers at a day-care center. A middle-aged man befriends an at-risk youth. A high school class sponsors a needy child. A church group organizes a community litter cleanup day.

These are people like you and me—next-door neighbors, colleagues at work, classmates at school, friends at church. People who spend their free time planting trees in a park, writing to their legislators, collecting trash at the beaches, helping animals that are endangered.

These are people who work by themselves and with others. They belong to organizations and churches and clubs. They inspire their friends and co-workers. And most of all, they bring energy, optimism, and assistance to the many things and people they touch.

Some are recognized for their efforts. Others quietly go about their work. But whether their reward comes from an award, a thank-you, or just a good feeling, more than 80 million Americans volunteer each year in an effort to make a difference in the world.

Volunteering is an act. It's an act of heroism on a grand scale. And it matters profoundly. It does more than help people beat the odds; it changes the odds.

—PRESIDENT GEORGE BUSH

POINTS OF LIGHT

President Bush calls those people who seek to better the lives of others a "Point of Light." The president's Point of Light program recognizes "volunteers who measure life by holding themselves accountable for the well-being of their community." The president awards a Daily Point of Light to an individual or group that "successfully addresses our most pressing social problems through direct and consequential acts of community service."*

The president's Daily Point of Light program identifies the common thread that exists between concerned individuals or

*"A Thousand Points of Light: The First One Hundred," The White House Office of National Service (no date or page).

3

groups across the nation who seek to improve the way of life for others.

There are thousands, even millions, of Points of Light across the land. Each is unique in nature, yet all come from the same brilliant source.

❂ THE DAILY POINT OF LIGHT ❂

Intended as a national tribute of the highest order to every American who makes a positive difference, each day the President recognizes those who are successfully addressing our most pressing social problems through community service. Individuals, families, businesses, groups, and organizations of every conceivable type are taking direct and consequential action to combat drug abuse, illiteracy, inadequate education, environmental decay, homelessness, hunger, AIDS, and other critical ills.

The President urges all Americans to make serving others central to their life and work. "If you have a hammer, find a nail. If you know how to read, find someone who can't. If you're not in trouble, seek out someone who is. Because everywhere there is a need in America, there is a way to fill it. . . . There is no problem in America that is not being solved somewhere."*

*The depictions throughout this book can be found in "A Thousand Points of Light: The First One Hundred," The White House Office of National Service. Reprinted with permission.

WHO IS A DAILY POINT OF LIGHT?

Points of Light are found in all sizes—large, small, short, and tall. Some are old and wise, others are young and energetic. There is no common color, or race, or sex to people who seek to make a difference. Just a similar commitment—to create a better world.

Younger concerned citizens, like the third-grade class of Dian Wurst, and older committed individuals, such as 101-year-old Tero Coleman, prove that age is never a barrier to helping others. Throughout this book are many examples of people to whom the President has bestowed this award. Through their efforts they have made a difference in the lives of others and the community in which they live.

❂ THIRD-GRADE CLASS OF DIAN WURST ❂

Polk, NE
DAILY POINT OF LIGHT RECIPIENT: JANUARY 23, 1990

The third-grade class of Dian Wurst demonstrates that citizens of all ages can make a difference.

For seven years, Ms. Wurst has assigned a "tele-care" program to her third graders. Every morning the students call nineteen homebound seniors, delivering a morning greeting and asking if they need anything. The students meet with the recipients twice a year at a Christmas party and spring tea, and many students visit them after school and on weekends throughout the year. The program gives the seniors and their families the peace of mind that comes from knowing that someone will check daily to make sure that they are safe and well.

❂ TERO MAULDIN COLEMAN ❂

Washington, DC
DAILY POINT OF LIGHT RECIPIENT: DECEMBER 21, 1989

Tero Coleman, 101, comforts 70- and 80-year-olds, telling them to "hang in there" and get better.

She has been a volunteer with the Retired Senior Volunteer Program (RSVP) at the Simpson-Hamline United Methodist Church for 11 years. She calls on elderly homebound worshippers, answers the church telephone, addresses envelopes, and helps out in any way she can. Ms. Coleman's exuberance and sense of humor bring cheer to those around her. She attributes her long life to eating whatever she wants, reading the *Bible* every morning and night, and following the Golden Rule.

VOLUNTEER!

■■■

VOLUNTEERISM IN THE UNITED STATES

The impact of volunteerism in the United States is quite impressive:

▶ According to an Independent Sector Gallup poll, in 1989 98.4 million Americans aged 18 or older volunteered an average of 4 hours a week to such causes and organizations as religious groups, education, health, and social welfare services.

▶ If each of these volunteers was paid for their time and efforts, it would cost as much as $170 billion.*

GETTING STARTED

In order to gain a better understanding of the nature of volunteerism, I spoke with C. Gregg Petersmeyer, the Director of the Office of National Service and Deputy Assistant to the president. The Office of National Service is devoted exclusively to placing direct and consequential community service at the top of the national agenda. Some of its many important

Volunteers are people who get great satisfaction out of giving themselves . . . time, energy and effort. They become dedicated and passionate about giving other people the opportunity to contribute. It serves a meaningful purpose in their lives.

—JONAS SALK

*"Giving and Volunteering in the United States," *The Independent Sector*, 1988.

5

Volunteers In Service To America (VISTA) is a program of ACTION, the federal domestic volunteer agency. Washington, D.C. 20525.

responsibilities are identifying and awarding Points of Light, advising the president on matters of community service, and communicating the president's community service to all the nation.

Mr. Petersmeyer's position as the Director of the Office of National Service allows him a unique vantage point. He not only sees what compels people from all backgrounds to get involved in helping others, but he is also able to better understand the nature and direction of volunteerism in America today.

If you are interested in giving your time and talents to a cause, you should first consider these points:

The reasons for volunteering. More than half the respondents in the Independent Sector's poll said that they wanted to do something useful. Other motivations were enjoyment, benefits to a family member or friend, and religion.

Many people are asked to volunteer. Their church may solicit help for a certain project, a neighbor may need a helping hand, or a group may ask you to donate your time, resources, and effort.

Others may feel obligated to help out in some way and seek opportunities to do so. Disasters tend to bring out the spirit of volunteerism. During Hurricane Hugo and the 1989 San Francisco earthquake, individuals from across the nation lent a hand to help alleviate the suffering of those inconvenienced and injured.

The rewards of volunteering. The reasons for volunteering may differ with each individual, but the rewards are often the same. Mr. Petersmeyer describes these rewards as satisfaction that is experienced by a person involved in meaningful, hands-on engagement in helping to solve the problems of others.

This kind of satisfaction goes beyond the traditional concepts of volunteerism, which emphasize obligation or responsibility. It also includes the highly important element of "enjoyment." In their book, *How Can I Help?* Ram Dass and Paul Gorman explain that "the reward, the real grace, of conscious service, then, is the opportunity not only to relieve suffering but to grow in wisdom, experience greater unity, and have a good time while we're doing it."*

It is this notion of "fun" that is often overlooked when one considers getting involved. Yet, it is the combination of enjoyment and duty that draws millions of Americans to con-

*Ram Dass and Paul Gorman, *How Can I Help?* (New York: Alfred A. Knopf, 1988).

tinue engaging in direct, consequential service to their community. A person may volunteer occasionally to satisfy the urge to "do something good," but that individual will continue to volunteer when he or she realizes that getting involved is both meaningful *and* fun.

Do something you like. Volunteers should have fun, so do something you enjoy. If you like sports, perhaps you can become a big brother or big sister or take your friend to a baseball game. Or you could coach a team in a community sports league. If you like to teach, then help illiterate people learn to read. You may want to work with people, or you might enjoy protecting our wildlife. You may like the lobbying process and spend time calling politicians and their constituents. Or you might prefer traveling to other countries and helping people of poorer nations to improve their lives.

Focus on your talents. If you have special talents, you may wish to offer them to a worthy cause. Gregg Petersmeyer describes these talents as "distinctive competencies." For instance, a doctor can donate some time at a health clinic. A lawyer can provide his or her services to those who cannot afford them. A builder can offer expertise with low-income housing projects. A writer could help with articles, promotional brochures, and press releases.

According to Mr. Petersmeyer, you should not expect to change your own makeup, but instead find a way to utilize what you already enjoy doing in a way that is constructive to someone else. If you do what you like and what you are good at, you will not only enjoy volunteering, you will also be more likely to continue to get involved.

Surround yourself with people you like. Who you get involved with is as important as what you do. For instance, if you love spending time with children, you could volunteer at a day-care center or become a foster parent. If you like working with the elderly, you might want to deliver meals or help out in a nursing home. Many people enjoy working with animals; they spend time helping at shelters or with animal welfare groups. Some love the wilderness and find satisfaction in cleaning up the local landscape, building nature trails, and planting trees. Others feel enriched by working with groups helping to feed the homeless.

Also, make sure you enjoy being with your volunteer

In what areas do people volunteer?

Volunteers work most often for religious organizations (64%), educational activities (44%) and youth organizations (41%). These findings indicate that people who do volunteer are likely to be involved in more than one activity.

Disaster relief and crisis intervention are the two areas in which volunteers are least likely to have volunteered.

	% Yes
Religious organizations	64%
Education	44
Youth organizations	41
Health care	34
Civic improvements	26
Poverty and hunger	23
Disease-related causes	21
Arts and culture	16
Politics	16
Crime prevention	16
The environment	13
Human rights or advocacy issues	12
Humane treatment of animals	11
Drug and alcohol abuse	11
Literacy	10
Crisis intervention	9
Disaster relief	8

Significantly, religious organizations fall to tenth place in interest among nonvolunteers. This indicates that most people who would be interested in working for a religious organization do so. Disaster relief, typically a short-term project, rises to the top

Why do people volunteer?

The vast majority of volunteers do so because they want to help others (97%) and they enjoy the work (93%).

	% Yes
I want to help others	97%
I enjoy the work	93
The specific work or cause interests me	89
I feel a responsibility to volunteer	76
Someone I know asked me to volunteer	59
I have free time on my hands	41
To make new friends	40
To get job experience	15
My employer encourages volunteering	14
Required for membership in an organization; academic responsibility	10
To get freebies such as complimentary tickets, meals, or invitations	7

Giving and Volunteering in America 1990. Independent Sector/Gallup Survey highlights.

7

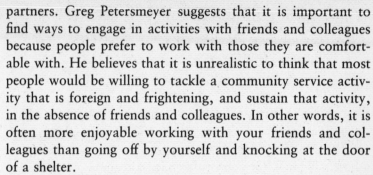

Did you know?

▶ When the San Francisco earthquake disrupted the lives of Bay Area residents, AmeriCares was quick to respond. The relief organization shipped more than 65,000 pounds of nonperishable foods to the homeless in the San Francisco area—helping to make Thanksgiving a little brighter for many.

Coors Brewing Company

partners. Greg Petersmeyer suggests that it is important to find ways to engage in activities with friends and colleagues because people prefer to work with those they are comfortable with. He believes that it is unrealistic to think that most people would be willing to tackle a community service activity that is foreign and frightening, and sustain that activity, in the absence of friends and colleagues. In other words, it is often more enjoyable working with your friends and colleagues than going off by yourself and knocking at the door of a shelter.

So try to join or start service activities that include your friends, family, co-workers, members of the church, and such. For instance, there are Daily Points of Light recipients such as a policeman in Philadelphia who uses his department colleagues to fight illiteracy, a minister in Tampa who got his congregation involved with boarder babies, or a garden club that mentors unwed teenage mothers.

Working with people you know or relate to will make your involvement more fulfilling for you and more beneficial for others.

HOW DOES ONE VOLUNTEER?

There are as many ways to volunteer as there are needs. Here are a few points to think about when you are considering getting involved.

Choose an issue. There are many different issues of concern in today's world. This book addresses just a few. One good first step is to determine what interests you—what issue you would like to address. For instance, perhaps you are most concerned about illiteracy, or drugs, or the homeless. Or maybe you would like to help the environment, save the elephants, or make life a little easier for someone with AIDS. Your next step would be to learn more about some of these problems and then decide which one you would like to "adopt."

Once you reach a decision, you can make that problem, and its solution, your own. Mr. Petersmeyer suggests that you claim one problem, one serious problem, that you want to help solve, then stick to it in a sustained way. Focus on the problem and try to get your friends and peers interested. By getting involved and helping to get others involved, you will be giving power to a growing movement of change.

Think of what you can do. It is important to remember that although some of these issues appear overwhelming, you can help. Instead of focusing on the size of the problem, you must concentrate on what you are capable of providing to its solution. Mr. Petersmeyer explains that sometimes a person tends to think of how large the issue is instead of what he or she could provide to the process. They tend to focus on a major problem like illiteracy or homelessness, and may not realize that they could drive an elderly person to the store once a week, or that they might have a group of colleagues who would be willing to help tutor high school students once a week, or that they could interest a church group in a mentoring program.

Realize that you can make a difference. Mr. Petersmeyer believes that if everyone attempted to espouse the attributes of a Point of Light, many of our nation's problems would be solved:

> The forces that could be unleashed would overwhelm the problems in terms of providing energy and solutions. There are many times more literate people around than illiterate people and there are potentially more adults who would be willing to have a big brother or big sister relationship with an at-risk youth than there are young people who want that kind of help.
>
> So I think that if a Points-of-Light mentality became universally accepted, there would not be enough problems given the amount of people who would contribute to their solutions.

If you focus on what *you* can do, you will be more confident that you can make a difference. And instead of becoming paralyzed by the size of the challenge you will immediately begin to help in a very constructive and beneficial way.

Who to contact. This book is full of ideas of how we can help each other and our environment. It also lists hundreds of organizations that utilize volunteers in many capacities and are extremely appreciative of any support.

Some groups specialize in certain areas, such as protecting dolphins or saving the rain forests. Others are more multifaceted and are active with many different causes. You can contact any of these groups or you can call a volunteer agency. Volunteer agencies match interested volunteers with various

United Way
It brings out the best in all of us.®

Number of United Ways	2,300 local organizations run by volunteers
1988 Dollars Raised	$2.78 billion—6.9% increase over 1987
Volunteers Involved	10.8 million people nationwide—6% of total U.S. adult population
Administrative Costs	10.5% of all funds raised (national average)—kept low by volunteers and by collecting funds through payroll deduction

WHERE THE MONEY COMES FROM

Nonprofit and Government Employees 12.5%
Corporation and Small-Business Employees 51.3%
Small Businesses 2.7%
Noncorporate Foundations 1.4%
Other 6.1%
Professionals 2.6%
Corporations 23.4%

WHERE THE MONEY GOES

More than 40,000 health and human-care groups receive United Way funding

United Way is second only to the federal government in funding health and human-care services

4,625 new agencies have been funded by United Way since 1986

Health 20.2%
Income and Jobs 5.0%
Family Services 21.7%
Other 4.5%
Day Care 6.8%
Public Safety 6.1%
Education 3.2%
Community Development 5.9%
Food, Clothing, and Housing 9.1%
Youth and Social Development 17.5%

Reprinted by permission, United Way of America.

needs in your community. A few of these agencies are listed below.

Organizations and Resources

ACTION
202-634-9108
ACTION is the Federal Domestic Volunteer Agency. More than 440,000 local volunteers serve in ACTION programs in communities across the country. ACTION programs include: the Foster Grandparent Program (FPG), the Retired Senior Volunteer Program (RSVP), the Senior Campaign Program (SCP), Volunteers In Service to America (VISA), the Student Community Service Program, and the ACTION Drug Alliance.

The agency also assists with countless other neighborhood volunteer activities and community projects by providing grants, technical help, and a vast knowledge of volunteer resources, initiatives, and programs.

Goodwill Industries Volunteer Services
(Call your local Goodwill chapter)
More than 75 Goodwill Industries Volunteer Services (GIVS) across the country provide ideas and services to help an interested person volunteer in his or her community.

Independent Sector
202-223-8100
A nonprofit coalition of 675 corporate, foundation, and voluntary organization members with national interest and impact in philanthropy and voluntary action.

Junior League
(Call your local chapter)
There are 272 Junior League groups throughout the United States, Canada, Mexico, and Great Britain representing approximately 180,000 women. The Junior Leagues develop leadership skills in women and address community needs through the development and maintenance of quality volunteer programs.

Kiwanis International
317-875-8755
A worldwide service organization composed of business and professional men and women who are interested in leading and improving their communities.

National Civic League
303-571-4343
A nonprofit, nonpartisan association of individuals and organizations dedicated to the promotion of active involvement of citizens in the governing of their communities.

National Council for Jewish Women
212-645-4048

Peace Corps
800-424-8580
Peace Corps volunteers help people in developing countries learn new ways to fight hunger, disease, poverty, and lack of opportunity.

Retired Senior Volunteer Program (RSVP)
202-634-9108
ACTION's largest program, RSVP matches the interests and abilities of seniors with rewarding part-time opportunities for community service (c/o ACTION).

Rotary International
708-866-3000

Student Community Service Program (SCSP)
202-634-9108
An ACTION program, SCSP encourages students to enroll in volunteer activities in their communities.

"Unsung Americans"
800-228-8813
Initiated by Capital Cities/ABC, Inc., and as part of their commitment to Project Literary U.S. in cooperation with the Public Broadcasting Service, public service announcements on television and radio have been designed to urge adults to call the National Contact Hotline to learn where they can volunteer to help the youth in their own communities.

United States Jaycees
918-584-2481
More than 240,000 members in 5,000 communities actively participate in community projects.

United Way
703-836-7100 (or your local chapter)
Approximately 2,300 local

United Way chapters mobilize over 10 million volunteers to help meet the health and human-care needs of millions of people. In 1987, the United Way raised $2.6 billion to meet health and human care needs. They provide funding to more than 37,000 agencies and programs.

The easiest way to get in touch with the United Way is to call local directory assistance. They will then direct you to a United Way center in your area.

Volunteer—The National Center
703-276-0542
The National Center acts as a referral and information service for those who would like to volunteer in their community. They link interested individuals with local volunteer centers that serve as a clearinghouse for volunteer activities.

Volunteers of America, Inc. (VOA)
800-654-2297
VOA provides a wide variety of services and programs for groups and individuals such as the homeless, the elderly, and substance abusers.

A COMPREHENSIVE LIST OF ASSOCIATIONS

▶ *Encyclopedia of Associations*, Gale Research, Inc. Lists and details almost 22,000 national and international non-profit trade and professional associations, social welfare and public affairs organizations, religious, sports, and hobby groups, and other type of organizations that consist of voluntary members and are headquartered in the United States (found in public libraries).

STARTING A NONPROFIT ORGANIZATION

Here are some references:

▶ *The California Nonprofit Corporation Handbook*, Anthony Mancuso (Nolo Press, 950 Parker St., Berkeley, CA 94710). 415-549-1976

▶ *The Nonprofit Organization Handbook*, Tracy D. Connor, editor (McGraw-Hill Book Co.).

PLAN A VOLUNTEER VACATION

▶ *Volunteer Vacations: Revised and Expanded* (Chicago Review Press), lists useful and fulfilling vacations and weekend projects for interested volunteers. Some ideas include building trails and shelters along the Appalachian trail or repairing and rebuilding low-income housing in Kansas City.

11

BOYCOTTS AND OTHER NONVIOLENT PROTESTS

■ ■ ■

Boycotts and nonviolent protests have been proven highly effective—from large-scale movements led by Mahatma Gandhi and Dr. Martin Luther King, Jr., to individual protests waged by concerned people like homemaker Terry Rakolta, whose protest of a "racy" television show received national attention.

.... Did you know?

► Benetton and Avon felt the pressure of animal rights groups and agreed to stop animal testing.

► Boycotts and shareholder objection of corporate involvement in South Africa influenced many corporations to stop doing business in or with that country.

► The Humane Society's campaign to stop the sale of fur persuaded many consumers to halt their purchases of these luxury items.

► Amnesty International's letter-writing campaigns have brought about the release of many political prisoners throughout the world.

EFFECTIVE CAMPAIGNS

Many organizations utilize the power of boycotts and nonviolent protests to voice their opinions. The media plays a major role in this effort, as national and worldwide news reporting is accessible to almost anyone with a cause. Extensive coverage of activist actions forces corporations and governments to listen, and in many cases to change for the better.

METHODS OF PROTEST

Boycotts and other types of protests are powerful tools for almost any grass-roots movement. These actions take many forms, so it is up to you to decide the extent of your involvement.

For instance, letter writing may appeal to some people, whereas organized marches may interest others. You can carry on your own personal method of protest, such as refusing to eat meat because of cruel treatment of farm animals. Or you might join a large-scale event like the Housing Now! demonstration for the homeless, which brought 250,000 people to Washington, DC, in 1989.

Some types of protest involve more active and somewhat radical actions, such as demonstrators chaining themselves to a fence surrounding a nuclear power plant to protest nuclear power.

Conversely, protest can be done in a calmer fashion through such actions as telling your local grocers that you will not shop at their store unless they offer paper as well as plastic for their shopping bags.

Boycotts and nonviolent protests no longer invoke images of hostility, illegality, and radicalism. For the most part they are well-respected, effective means of change. This country was founded by people who stood up for their beliefs. Do not be afraid to speak out. Remember that you can make a significant impact in creating change.

WRITING LETTERS

▪▪▪

WHY WRITE?

You may ask, "Why should I write a letter? No one will read it!" You are very mistaken if you have that kind of attitude.

Writing letters to support a cause or protest an action is a common and effective means of prompting change. Anyone and everyone can write letters, and it is an action that is easy and productive.

WHO READS LETTERS?

Letter writing can be a very effective way to voice your opinion. For example, a thoughtful and concise message to your political representatives will help them decide important issues. Members of Congress are the first to acknowledge the importance of letters from their constituents:

LETTER WRITING WORKS!

Many organizations urge their members to write letters of protest. These actions have helped bring about many changes:

▶ People for the Ethical Treatment of Animals (PETA) employs letter writing to protest companies that use cruel experiments on animals in order to test their products. This kind of pressure has forced many major corporations to agree to sell only "cruelty-free" products.

▶ According to the National Wildlife Federation, letter writing was instrumental in the passage of the 1988 Endangered Species Act and the Clean Water Act.

My mailbag is my best "hot line" to the people back home. On several occasions a single, thoughtful, factually persuasive letter did change my mind . . .

—MORRIS UDALL, Representative from Arizona*

Someone who sits down and writes a letter about hunger . . . almost literally has to be saving a life . . .

—PAUL SIMON, Senator from Illinois*

*From "A Guide to Effective Letter Writing on Hunger Issues," a pamphlet published by Bread for the World.

▶ Greenpeace constantly reminds its constituents to write letters to corporations and politicians to express concern about environmental problems, ranging from the greenhouse effect to ocean dumping.

▶ Amnesty International emphasizes the importance of letter writing to help bring about the release of political prisoners in other countries. Their letter-writing programs have proved highly effective in improving conditions and securing the release of political prisoners throughout the world.

You do not have to be a "career activist" to write a letter. You just have to care.

▶ Terry Rakolta felt that a certain television show was too "racy" for her children. So she began a letter-writing campaign to the show's advertisers, expressing her concern about their involvement with the show. Her protests prompted those businesses to pull their advertisements and her actions caused many corporations to review their policies toward advertising.

▶ In 1983, 10-year-old Samantha Smith wrote a letter to the Soviet government about peace between our nations. As perhaps our youngest goodwill ambassador she went to a Soviet youth camp at the invitation of Premier Yuri Andropov, thus paving the way for many other peace activists to visit and learn about other countries and their citizens.

Letter writing works! It does not matter who you are or what you do—just express your feelings and show your concern.

WHO ELSE TO WRITE

Besides writing letters to the legislators and corporations you can also write to members of the media. Letters written to a newspaper may be printed in the letters to the editor section, or may inspire an opinion editorial by that paper. A television or radio station might use your letter or your ideas during an editorial. The media is very interested in your views, regardless of whether you're an expert or not.

To get in touch with the media contact the station, paper, or magazine and ask how to address letters to the editor. A good resource is:

▶ *The News Media Yellow Book,* which is an updated directory of those who report, write, edit, and produce the news

THE ASPCA'S DOLPHIN T-SHIRT

Permission courtesy of the American Society for the Prevention of Cruelty to Animals (ASPCA) 800-395-ASPCA in Washington, DC, and New York. Subscription available from Monitor Publishing Company, 104 Fifth Ave., 2d floor, New York, NY 10011 (212-627-4140).

Reprinted with permission of Joe Heller. *Green Bay Press-Gazette*.

WRITING AN EFFECTIVE LETTER

There is no single formula for writing effective letters. The most important thing is to state your opinion in a clear and concise manner.

The contents of your letter may differ slightly, depending on whom you are writing. For instance, a letter to a politician should contain different information than a letter to a corporate manager.

SANE/FREEZE: Campaign for Global Security, a leading peace advocacy group, has been very effective in persuading its members to write letters to political representatives. They suggest a few simple steps to follow when writing a politician:

▶ Keep it short and simple.

▶ Use your own words and thoughts, and personally sign the letter.

▶ When writing to a politician, focus on current pending legislation. Cover only one issue.

▶ Use a bill number, if possible, or the names of the sponsors of that bill.

▶ Be specific about what you want your representative to do.

15

·········· Did you know?

▶ Greenpeace's ship of protest, *Rainbow Warrior*, has effectively blocked and halted the dumping of toxic waste in parts of the ocean.

▶ PETA's "Fur Is Dead" campaign, Trans-Species Unlimited's nationwide Fur-Free Friday, and the Humane Society's "Shame of Fur" messages, together with pressure from many other organizations and individuals, prompted some major retailers to halt the sale of fur coats in their stores.

▶ Give brief reasons for your positions.

▶ Ask your legislator a direct question about his or her position.

▶ Write as an individual, not as a member of an organization.

▶ Don't threaten your legislator, and always be polite.

▶ Handwritten or typed letters are most effective. Postcards are less effective.*

SAMPLE LETTER WRITTEN TO A POLITICAL REPRESENTATIVE

The Hon. (Your Rep's Name)
House of Representatives
Washington, DC 20515

Dear Rep (Your Rep's Name):

I urge you to vote for bill (Bill number)—the Child Safety Bill—sponsored by Rep.'s Mr. Smith and Mr. Jones. I fully believe in legislation to improve the welfare of our children and I think that this bill effectively supports child safety.

What is your stance on this issue?

Sincerely,
(Your name and address)

WHEN AND HOW TO CONTACT YOUR LEGISLATOR

▶ Send a letter several weeks before the vote, or make a phone call a few days before the vote.

▶ You can also send a telegram or Mailgram. Contact Western Union about their overnight Public Opinion Message to elected officials for $7.95. (20 words) 800-325-6000.

▶ To find out who your state representatives are, look in the phone book under your state's governmental listings or contact your local League of Women Voters.

*Reprinted with permission of SANE/ FREEZE: Campaign for Global Security.

WRITE:

The Hon. _____
U.S. House of Representatives
Washington, DC 20515

The Hon. _____
U.S. Senate
Washington, DC 20510

President George Bush
The White House
1600 Pennsylvania Avenue
Washington, DC 20515

Did you know? ∎∎∎∎∎∎∎∎∎∎∎∎

▶ The American Paper Institute receives 500 requests a week for information on recycling, including how to start office recycling programs.

▶ The average office worker disposes of 130 pounds of paper a year. If recycled this trash would be enough to save a 35-foot tree.

Call:

The Capitol Hill switchboard number is (202) 224-3121.
Ask for your representative or senator's office.

Organizations and Resources

Amnesty International
212-807-8400
Amnesty International uses letters as one of its primary tools in aiding prisoners of conscience throughout the world. Since it was founded in 1961, Amnesty International has worked on behalf of more than 25,000 prisoners around the world.

Bread for the World
800-82-BREAD
BFW is a grass-roots lobbying movement that uses letters as an important means of shaping legislation. For example, an estimated 250,000 letters were generated in support of the Right-to-Food bill by the efforts of BFW. Ask for a copy of "A Guide to Effective Letter Writing on Hunger Issues."

SANE/FREEZE
202-862-9740
One of America's largest peace organizations, Sane/Freeze's work involves national lobbying, local organizing, and public education. Ask for their flyer on letter writing.

Seeds
404-378-3566
A magazine about hunger. Ask them for a copy of their *Hunger Action Handbook* and refer to the "Influence Public Policy through Congress" and "Use the Media" sections.

20/20 Vision National Project
415-528-8800 / 413-253-2939
Offers information on how an individual can write letters to members of Congress to advocate the end of the arms race.

YOUR POLITICAL REPRESENTATIVE WORKS FOR YOU!

∎∎∎

·········· Did you know?

▶ Consumer-led boycotts of products from cosmetic giant Avon Products influenced that company and others to halt animal testing.

▶ Pressures from environmental organizations caused major fast-food chains to cancel purchases of beef from rain-forest regions and reassess their policies toward Styrofoam packaging.

▶ Major stockholders protested and divested holdings of companies that did business in South Africa, leading to massive withdrawals of American corporate investments in that country.

KEEP INFORMED

The political process is highly important to creating change. Politics and the law are connected in one way or another to almost every issue and cause. Bills are introduced and passed in the state and federal government, covering affairs ranging from clean air to the war on drugs.

Often, the ability to solve a particular issue of concern may depend largely on political support. For that reason most organizations are well aware of the political process, and some groups spend much of their time and energy educating their members about legislative issues and mobilizing them to contact their legislators to express their views.

Enacting legislation involves tough battles because often many competing special interests complicate the decision-making process. A ban on drift nets may help save the dolphins but hurt the fishing industry. One version of the Clean Air Bill will help affected coal miners, whereas another version ignores them. Also, certain areas of the country have different requirements, which can sometimes create disparate laws. One state may have tougher abortion laws than another—one city may enact more stringent pollution standards than another. Thus it is very important to realize that each individual's voice counts.

CONTACT YOUR POLITICAL REPRESENTATIVE

Throughout this book you will find examples of legislation enacted to help protect the environment, preserve wildlife, and to provide for the welfare of our citizens.

Many of these laws are prompted by individual actions. Letter writing, telephone calls, and meetings are all effective measures you can take to participate in the political process.

Lawmakers listen to their constituents, so keep informed of upcoming legislation by contacting one of the many groups listed throughout this book and by referring to the sources listed below.

▶ For information about how to contact your legislators refer to the letter-writing section.

Organizations and Resources

• •

Listed here are a few groups that utilize their energy and resources toward political change.

Bread for the World (BFW)
800-82-BREAD / 202-269-0494
BFW is one of the nation's most effective hunger-lobbying groups. They mobilize their members to contact politicians on pending hunger legislation. They track the voting record of politicians and provide a breakdown of government organizations. Their "Issue Update" line provides recorded updates on current legislation regarding hunger and hunger-related issues.

Common Cause
202-833-1200
Founded in 1970, Common Cause is a nonprofit, nonpartisan citizens' lobby with more than 275,000 members. They publish *Common Cause Magazine,* which features investigative articles, in-depth interviews, legislative updates, and Action Alerts that explain issues and suggest lobbying actions to take. Archibald Cox, former Watergate Special Prosecutor, is chairman.

Congress Watch
202-546-4996
A lobbying group that monitors how Congress represents consumer interests.

Council for a Livable World
202-543-0006 (Hotline on Political Arms Control Issues)/ (Headquarters) 617-542-2282
A nonpartisan political action committee devoted solely to the prevention of nuclear war. The Council publishes profiles of political officials and candidates and lobbies extensively for peace issues. Ask for a copy of *How to Lobby Congress for an End to the Nuclear Arms Race,* a citizen's guide to lobbying Congress, which provides practical advice on the most effective methods of constituent lobbying and describes how Congress acts on the military budget and shapes nuclear arm policies.

Friends Committee on National Legislation
202-547-6000

Interfaith Action for Economic Justice
800-424-7290
Recording which gives legislative updates on a variety of issues.

League of Conservation Voters
202-785-VOTE
A Political Action Committee with membership support, the League seeks to influence elections to get pro-environmental candidates into office. They publish an annual scorecard, which tracks the environmental voting record of politicians. They have drafted the Survival Agenda, which addresses the minimum course of action that Congress must take to reverse the growing environmental crisis.

The League of Women Voters
202-429-1965
A multifaceted organization with more than 100,000 members, the League works through the political process and with citizens to bring about constructive change. They lobby, mobilize people to register to vote, and educate citizens about issues and their rights.

National Association of Realtors
202-383-1000
Ask for a free copy of *The 1990 U.S. Congress Handbook,* which lists the names and addresses of all political representatives and also gives tips on writing a member of Congress, explains how legislation is passed, etc.

National Wildlife Federation's Legislative Hotline
202-797-6655
Status report on Congressional happenings each week, including hearing dates, the status of legislation, and federal agency regulation proposals.

OMB Watch
202-234-8494
Disseminates information about the Office of Management and Budget especially concerning nonprofit and community-based groups.

People for the American Way

202-467-4999

Their *Congressional Directory* gives the names, addresses, political affiliation, and committee memberships of every member of Congress, plus valuable tips on the most effective ways to voice your opinion. $6.95 member/$7.95 nonmember.

Public Citizen

202-833-3000

Founded by Ralph Nader, Public Citizen's Clean Up Congress Campaign serves as a watchdog over the actions of Congress.

Sierra Club Public Information

415-776-2211/202-547-1141

Tracks the environmental profiles of members of the U.S. Senate and House of Representatives.

OTHER RESOURCES

▶ "Congress in Committee." Describes how Congress works: its committees, how a bill is introduced, and how to influence a member of Congress. Contact BFW, background paper #32, March 1979.

▶ "Congressional Committees." Provides a list of current committee assignments of all members of Congress. Contact Bread for the World.

▶ "Visiting With Your Members of Congress." Describes the best ways to organize a meeting with a Congressional representative. Contact Bread for the World.

▶ *How Our Laws Are Made.* A 70-page document available from your Congressional rep. (free) or for $1.50 from the Government Printing Office, Washington, DC 20402.

▶ *Interaction.* A publication of Global Tomorrow Coalition, which provides a series of articles written by member organizations, updating and discussing legislation. 202-628-4016.

▶ *Tell It to Washington: A Guide for Citizen Action Including Congressional Directory* (1982–83), 24 pages. Contact the League of Women Voters. $1.00.

▶ *Congress and the Budget,* 6 pages. Contact the League of Women Voters.

▶ *How a Bill Becomes Law,* pp. 145–50 of the *Congressional Quarterly of Current American Government,* Spring 1977. Available at most public libraries.

▶ *The Federal Yellow Book.* An updated directory of the federal departments and agencies, including more than 35,000 names. Monitor Publishing Company, 104 Fifth Ave., 2d fl., New York, NY 10011   212-627-4140.

▶ *The Congressional Yellow Book.* An updated directory of members of the Congress including their committees and key staff aides. Subscription available from Monitor Publishing Company, 104 Fifth Ave., 2d fl., New York, NY 10011   212-627-4140.

▶ *The State Yellow Book.* An updated directory of the Executive, Legislative, and Judicial branches of 50 state governments. Subscription available from Monitor Publishing Company, 104 Fifth Ave., 2d fl., New York, NY 10011   212-627-4140.

For further information on Congress and federal agencies:

▶ *"Congressional Staff Directory,"* P.O. Box 62, Mount Vernon, VA 22121 ($35).

▶ *"Politics in America,"* Congressional Quarterly Inc., 1414 22nd St., NW, Washington, DC 20037 ($29.95).

CORPORATE ACCOUNTABILITY

■ ■ ■

YOU CAN RUN BUT YOU CAN'T HIDE

Increasing numbers of corporations are being held account-able for their policies and actions that endanger or are oth-erwise harmful to society. Businesses no longer have the luxury of hiding from their misbehavior. Tragedies such as the Exxon *Valdez* oil spill and the Hooker Chemical Com-pany's Love Canal have brought to public attention corporate activities in areas such as environmental pollution, animal testing, and the endangerment of marine animals.

Consumers and investors are emphasizing their impor-tance and influence through boycotts, protests, and divest-ment. Social, animal, and environmental welfare agencies, with assistance from the media and politicians, have joined with governmental supervisory agencies such as the Federal Trade Commission and the Consumer Product Safety Com-mission to ensure that big business stays honest.

CORPORATE AMERICA LISTENS

To some extent corporate America is listening. Rafael D. Pa-gan, Jr., chairman of Pagan International, a company that specializes in resolving conflicts between corporations and ac-tivist groups, notes activists' growing influence. "Activists are becoming increasingly influential in their efforts to force cor-porations to cooperate in their vision of social change, and the governments are left in the ineffectual middle."* Pagan points out that "activists are not overzealous adolescents hav-ing a go at the adults. They are for the most part serious-minded people whose purpose is to work for a cleaner, safer, healthier, saner world."**

DISASTERS—PLACING CORPORATIONS IN THE SPOTLIGHT

How does one know which companies are doing a good job and which need to reform? Unfortunately, tragedies highlight

The '90s will make the '60s pale into insignificance in terms of the reform drive to clean up the fraud, waste, abuse and crimes of many corporations.

—RALPH NADER, Consumer Advocate, in *Time* magazine, July 3, 1989

*"A New Era," *The Futurist,* May/June 1989.
**"A New Era."

21

▶ The Bhopal, India, chemical leakage disaster led to a review of the chemical industry's safeguards.

▶ The *Valdez* oil spill caused the oil industry to set up a special $250-million oil-spill fund and sparked the debate over twin-hull ships, crew competence, and overall shipping standards.

▶ Hazardous waste pollution in the Love Canal helped bring about the federal toxic Superfund.

corporate irresponsibility, but they also serve to reveal how industry and government create and follow policy. The intense exposure that disasters create usually serves to create reform.

SHAPING CORPORATE POLICY

People are no longer waiting for tragedy to strike to fuel the fire of change. Public outcry has been instrumental in policing, educating, and shifting businesses and their policies toward greater responsibility.

Shareholders, especially large pension funds, now realize that they have considerable leverage on corporate policy. In many cases they demand change in terms of the way corporations deal with environmental and social concerns. For instance, a coalition of concerned shareholder groups, the Coalition for Environmentally Responsible Economies, was formed to address the corporate role in the environment and to mobilize shareholder action. This type of pressure on corporations is on the rise and is proving very effective:

▶ The Sullivan Principles guided many U.S. businesses to practice humane, antiracial policies in South Africa and were endorsed by major shareholders.

▶ The Valdez Principles are 10 clear-cut guidelines that define exactly what businesses must do to protect the endangered planet. In 1989 more than 20 major corporations, including all major oil companies, received shareholder resolutions asking them to report on their progress toward compliance with the Valdez Principles.

▶ In that same year record-numbers of resolutions on social issues were filed for consideration at corporate annual meetings, including 40 resolutions on environmental subjects versus almost none the previous year.

When profits get in the way of ethics, concerned individuals become activists, and boycotts, protests, and financial leverage become their instruments of change. Citizens, shareholders, and organizations now realize that they not only have the right, but also the power, to influence corporate policy.

WATCHDOG GROUPS

Many organizations act as a type of watchdog in order to influence corporate action, such as the the Natural Resources

THE VALDEZ PRINCIPLES

1. Protection of the Biosphere
Minimize the release of pollutants that may cause environmental damage.

2. Sustainable Use of Natural Resources
Conserve nonrenewable natural resources through efficient use and careful planning.

3. Reduction and Disposal of Waste
Minimize the creation of waste, especially hazardous waste, and dispose of such materials in a safe, responsible manner.

4. Wise Use of Energy
Make every effort to use environmentally safe and sustainable energy sources to meet operating requirements.

5. Risk Reduction
Diminish environmental, health, and safety risks to employees and surrounding communities.

6. Marketing of Safe Products and Services
Sell products that minimize adverse environmental impact and that are safe for consumers.

7. Damage Compensation
Accept responsibility for any harm the company causes to the environment; conduct bio-remediation, and compensate affected parties.

8. Disclosure
Public dissemination of incidents relating to operations that harm the environment or pose health or safety hazards.

9. Environmental Directors and Managers
Appoint at least one board member who is qualified to represent environmental interests.

10. Assessment and Annual Audit
Produce and publicize each year a self-evaluation of progress toward implementing the principles and meeting all applicable laws and regulations worldwide. Environmental audits will also be produced annually and distributed to the public.

For the 1990 CERES Guide to The Valdez Principles which explains the Principles in complete detail, send a self-addressed 9x12 envelope with 65¢ postage attached to: CERES, 711 Atlantic Ave., 5th floor, Boston, MA 02111

▪▪▪▪▪▪▪▪▪ **Did you know?**

▶ U.S. corporations donated $5.6 billion to charities in 1989, according to the Council for Aid to education.

▶ Many companies have established day-care centers, health facilities, and substance abuse programs for their employees.

▶ Others recycle office trash and are now developing more efficient waste-disposal policies.

Defense Council. Their "Citizen Enforcement Project" organizes citizen lawsuits against the nation's top polluters.

There are also organizations that publish newsletters and others materials that rate business policy and document corporate actions—positive and negative.

▶ The Council on Economic Priorities rates corporate performance in policy areas such as fair employment practices and environmental impact.

▶ Action for Corporate Accountability, a coalition of 110 community and religious groups, serves as a corporate watchdog and organizes consumer-led boycotts.

▶ The Council of Better Business Bureaus works with local Better Business Bureaus to assist consumers, encourage the effective self-regulation of business, and promote confidence in the private enterprise system.

▶ Co-op America publishes a *Directory of Responsible Businesses* and keeps members informed of current boycotts.

These groups and others have been instrumental in helping individuals and organizations monitor and adjust business actions. For more information consult "Organizations and Resources" at the end of this section.

NOT ALWAYS THE BAD GUYS

It should not be assumed that all corporate policies are negative and destructive. For the most part, businesses attempt to do the right thing. In fact many businesses take the lead in the protection of the environment and the welfare of our society.

Activist groups are now finding that working with corporations can be more effective than working against them. Craig Smith, publisher of the *Corporate Philanthropy Report,* says that in terms of effectiveness, it is faster and cheaper to go directly to the companies.* The Environmental Defense Fund followed that advice when they wrote McDonald's Corporation and said, "Let's talk." The fast-food giant then worked with the environmental group to phase out foam packaging and replace it with paper.

Businesses and groups are beginning to realize that the enemy is not each other but rather the destruction of our environment and society.

*From the *Wall Street Journal,* 6 July 1989, p. 1.

Organizations and Resources

Action for Corporate Accountability
612-332-6411
Ask them about their infant Health Campaign and their boycott of companies that promote infant formula in poor countries. The group believes that formula feeding reduces the amount of breast-feeding, which they consider more beneficial for babies.

Ceres Coalition
617-451-0927
A coalition created by the Social Investment Forum, which encourages environmental groups to challenge corporate behavior.

Co-op America
202-872-5307/800-424-2667
Contact them for a copy of *Co-op America's Directory of Responsible Businesses* and their quarterly publication, *Building Economic Alternatives*.

The Council of Better Business Bureaus
703-276-0100
Works with local Better Business Bureaus to assist consumers, encourage the effective self-regulation of business, and promote confidence in the private enterprise system.

The Council on Economic Priorities
212-420-1133/800-822-6435
Founded to promote corporate responsibility, they rate corporate America on its performance in such policies as environmental impact, military weapon involvement, and community participation. Ask about their publications *Shopping for A Better World* and *Rating America's Corporate Conscience*.

INFACT
617-742-4583

Interfaith Center on Corporate Responsibility
212-870-2936
A coalition of churches that monitors corporate responsibility, especially in terms of social justice issues.

Public Citizen
202-833-3000
Founded by Ralph Nader, Public Citizen is a public interest group that fights for consumer protection and corporate accountability.

TRUE, YOU TRUSTED US TO DELIVER OIL SAFELY AND WE MESSED UP...

YOU COUNTED ON US TO BE READY FOR AN OIL SPILL AND WE WEREN'T...

WE SAID WE'D CLEAN IT UP AND WE BOTCHED IT...

OF COURSE WE'LL BE LIABLE FOR ALL CLEAN-UP COSTS + FINES (WHICH WE'LL PASS ON TO YOU)...

BUT REMEMBER THE REASON WE'RE DOING THIS—

BECAUSE YOU CANT <u>DEPEND</u> ON FOREIGN OIL PRODUCERS!

Reprinted with permission of Joe Heller. *Green Bay Press-Gazette*.

The Power of the Purse

■■

DONATE!

■ ■ ■

■■■■■■■■■ **Did you know?**

According to the Independent Sector, in 1989 Americans gave more than $104 billion to charitable causes.

WHO GIVES TO CHARITY?

To answer that question the Independent Sector commissioned the Gallup organization to conduct a national survey on the number of Americans who contributed and volunteered. The 1990 survey "Giving and Volunteering in the United States" discovered that:

▶ Approximately 75 percent of all households, or 71 million households, contributed to charity in 1989.

▶ Each household gave an average of $734 or almost 2 percent of their income to charitable causes.

It is interesting to note that the households with less income gave a greater percentage of that income than wealthier households. In 1989, households with incomes of $10,000 or less donated 5.5 percent of their total income, whereas those who made over $100,000 gave an average of 2.9 percent, according to the Independent Sector.

WHAT INDUCES PEOPLE TO GIVE TO CHARITY?

According to the same survey, the top three motivating factors for giving and volunteering among those asked are:

▶ Feeling that those who have more should help those with less (53 percent)

▶ Gaining a sense of personal satisfaction (49.6 percent)

▶ Meeting religious beliefs or commitments (43.3 percent)

Those who give and volunteer were also highly motivated by a few other reasons, including a sense that the continuation of certain activities or institutions will benefit themselves or their families; a feeling that one should give back to society; and a belief that charitable behavior is a good example to set for others.

The way a person has been raised also helps determine his or her charitable behavior. The three most common background influences cited for giving and volunteering were personal values (64 percent), religious beliefs (51 percent), and parents' example (40 percent). With this in mind, it makes sense that the survey found that religious organizations receive almost two-thirds of all individual donations. The remaining contributions are divided among organizations involving service, arts and humanities, education, social welfare, environmental and animal welfare, and health.

CORPORATE AND FOUNDATION GIVING

According to the Council of Better Business Bureaus (CBBB), more than 80 percent of the money raised by charities in this country comes from individuals. Corporations and foundations donated the rest. The Council for Aid to Education estimates that in 1989, U.S. corporations gave about $5.6 billion to charitable organizations. Approximately 39 percent of those contributions went to education, 27 percent for health and human services, and 14 percent for civic and human services.

Private foundations distribute income from an endowment usually started by a large gift. There are more than 30,000 foundations in the United States and in 1989 they donated more than $7 billion to charitable causes.

Community foundations are established by contributions from a wide range of donors. The donations form an endowment which uses its funds to finance grants to worthy causes in a city, county, or state. In 1989, there were almost 400 community foundations with assets exceeding $3 billion. The New York Community Trust has the largest foundation with approximately $800 million in assets. Donations to community foundations are tax deductible.

Free

BETTER BUSINESS BUREAU®

TIPS
ON
CHARITABLE
GIVING

Published by
COUNCIL OF BETTER
BUSINESS BUREAUS, INC.

4200 Wilson Boulevard
Arlington, Virginia 22203

YOUR MONEY: WHERE IT GOES AND HOW IT IS USED

Most of the money donated to charity goes directly toward its cause. Of course, some of the moneys a charitable organization receives must be used to maintain the organization. Charities are like most businesses in the sense that they must pay for certain expenses such as advertising and promotion, and salaries and general administrative costs. The majority of their income is derived from donations or grants rather than the sale of goods or services.

If you give $100 to a group that helps the homeless, some portion of that money will be spent maintaining the organization itself, including salaries of employees and rent. Other money may go toward fliers, mailings, newsletters, and other promotional items to solicit funds. Finally, some of your $100 will be spent to buy food, clothing, blankets, and other necessities for the homeless.

The spirit of giving

U.S. citizens increased their contributions to charity in 1989 over 1988.

Individuals +11.7%

Foundations +8.9%

Corporations +4.2%

Source: American Association of Fund-Raising Counsel

Copyright 1990 *USA Today*. Reprinted with permission.

WILL MY MONEY BE PROPERLY SPENT?

One of the most common questions people ask before donating money to organizations is whether it will be properly spent. Perhaps you may fear that only $20 of your $100 donation will be spent on actual necessities for the homeless, with most of the rest going to excessive salaries of management or lavish fund-raisers.

These questions are well-founded because your contribution is, in a sense, an investment. If you buy stock in a company, you expect that company to practice sound business policies. You hope your reward will be an increase in the value of your investment. If you give to a charity, you also hope that your money is spent wisely. Your reward comes from knowing that someone or something benefited from your contribution. (Of course, you may receive a tax deduction as well.)

"Watchdog" groups. Certain groups consult charitable organizations and monitor and report their activities to ensure that donations are properly utilized. For instance, how much of your $100 goes toward promotion and other fund-raising expenses? And how much actually goes toward the actual program?

The National Charities Information Bureau (NCIB) and the Better Business Bureau's Philanthropic Advisory Service (PAS) serve as watchdogs over the activities of charities and nonprofit groups. They collect data and make recommendations concerning the amount of money that is spent in administration, fund-raising, and the actual program. For instance, NCIB recommends that 60 cents of every dollar be spent on the actual program and that no more than 30 cents go toward fund-raising. PAS feels that at least 50 cents should be allocated to the actual program and up to 35 cents can go to fund-raising.

Both organizations offer summaries of their findings:

▶ NCIB publishes detailed reports and a list called "Wise Giving Guide."

▶ PAS publishes "Give But Give Wisely." (For additional information about NCIB and PAS refer to the "Organizations" and "Resources" sections at the end of this chapter.)

Consultants. Many charities employ special consultants to aid in the fund-raising process. The American Association of Fund Raising Counsel (AAFRC) ensures that these fund-raising counseling firms contribute positively and ethically to their clients' fund-raising activities. Members of AAFRC must adhere to a strict Fair Practice Code, which states that "member firms do not engage in methods which are misleading to the public or harmful to their clients; do not make exaggerated claims of past achievement; and do not guarantee results or promise to help clients achieve unrealistic goals."

Doing your own homework. Besides consulting some of the experts listed previously, you should ask a few questions: What is the stated purpose of the organization and

The COUNCIL of
BETTER BUSINESS
BUREAUS'

**STANDARDS
FOR
CHARITABLE
SOLICITATIONS**

Published by
COUNCIL OF BETTER
BUSINESS BUREAUS, INC.

what are its activities? Who leads the group? What are the credentials of the officers and the members of the board of directors? Who employs the funds and how are they employed?

Some of these questions can be answered by obtaining the latest financial report or an information brochure. Others may require more research.

The amount of time you should spend researching an organization depends mostly on how much time you have and how much money you are giving. If you give a few dollars to a homeless welfare group that solicits funds outside your supermarket, perhaps you might just ask to see a community or state certification document. If you donate $1,000, you might want to request more information.

HOW TO GIVE

Because fund-raising is essential to the well-being of an organization, more often than not they will approach you for a contribution. Methods of raising funds vary from direct mailings to special events. You might receive a letter in the mail asking for a donation. That donation may entitle you to membership in that organization, and you may receive newsletters and other publications from them.

Your office may ask for donations. For example, many companies now sponsor United Way campaigns. Or if you are an active federal employee, you are probably aware of the Combined Federal Campaign (CFC). The CFC collects donations from federal employees and distributes the money to chosen organizations. During a six-week period in the fall, the CFC distributes a list of national and local organizations to all employees. The employees then donate money to groups of their choice.

The CFC is administered regionally by 536 local campaigns across the country and throughout the world. The Office of Personnel Management (OPM) is responsible for the CFC and determines what organizations will be listed. Groups that apply and meet certain standards will appear on the CFC list. The fall 1988 campaign raised $170 million, and the 1989 campaign raised close to $200 million.

"Mega" media events have been very successful in raising money for causes during the past few years. Proceeds from concerts and record sales such as "Do They Know It's Christmas" and "Live Aid" netted millions of dollars for African famine relief. Other "special events" have also become more common methods of fund-raising. *The Jerry Lewis Telethon for Muscular Dystrophy* is an annual event that raises millions of dollars. More than five million people participated in "Hands Across America," raising more than $30 million for hungry and homeless Americans.

On a smaller scale, local walks or runs, bake sales, car washes, and parades are good ways to raise money for causes. Or you may buy a ticket for a dinner or a concert in which the proceeds will go toward helping a certain charity.

NONCASH CONTRIBUTIONS

Money is not the only type of donation available. Many charitable organizations receive noncash contributions as well. In fact, in 1989 corporations that responded to the Council for Aid to Education's survey reported giving 15 percent of their total contributions in noncash donations, such as securities, company products, and other property.

Many businesses will donate equipment and other resources, ranging from pens and pencils to computers. Others may donate their services. The National Association for the Exchange of Industrial Resources and the United Way-affiliated Gifts in Kind, Inc., link donors with groups in need of equipment.

Individuals can give noncash contributions as well. Many donations to groups such as Goodwill and the Salvation Army come from private homes. Clothing, appliances, dishes, utensils, and furniture are a few of the items that can be donated to charity. Canned-food drives and Toys for Tots are common during the holiday season.

Check with a tax consultant to determine the deductible value of noncash gifts.

From "A Thousand Points of Light: The Second Hundred," the White House Office of National Service.

❂ JACK L. POWELL ❂

Salisbury, MD
DAILY POINT OF LIGHT RECIPIENT: DECEMBER 16, 1989

Jack Powell annually organizes his community to gather food and clothing for economically disadvantaged individuals.

Each year empty grocery bags are placed on doorsteps in various neighborhoods to be filled with nonperishable food and clothing. Neighborhood children distribute the bags to area homes and then collect the full bags. The food is then distributed to local needy people by the Joseph House, a private Salisbury emergency relief organization that provides counseling as well as food. Since 1986, the Joseph House drive has raised more than 25 tons of food and clothing for impoverished families. Contributors have ranged from elementary-school students to the governor of Maryland.

DONATIONS AND YOUR TAXES

Donations to many charities can be used as tax deductions. If you wish to deduct your donation, you must determine the status of the organization to which you are giving.

Donating to an organization that advertises itself as tax-exempt may not mean that your contributions are tax deductible. According to the Philanthropic Advisory Service of the Better Business Bureau, "Tax exempt simply means that the organization does not have to pay taxes. Tax deductible means the donor can deduct contributions to the organization on his or her federal income tax return. The Internal Revenue Code defines more than twenty different categories of tax-exempt organizations, but contributions to only a few of these categories are also tax deductible. Principal among 'tax deductible' groups is the 501(c)(3) category, broadly termed 'charitable' organizations."

To ensure that your contribution is deductible, consult a tax adviser or your local tax agency. For other tax-related information contact:

▶ The Independent Sector for a copy of "How Much Really Is Tax Deductible?—A User's Guide to IRS Publication 1391."

▶ The AAFRC for "Strategies for Individuals Contributing to Charitable Organizations under the Old Tax Law as Compared with the New Law in 1987." For additional information about The Independent Sector and the AAFRC, refer to "Organizations and Resources," at the end of this section.

HOW MUCH TO GIVE

Another important consideration is how much to give. Only you can answer this question, because charity is a matter often determined by your own personal financial situation.

The first step is to determine how much and what percentage of your income you have donated in the past. This will give you a reference point.

▶ In 1989, households that contributed to charitable causes gave an average of $934, or 2.5 percent of their income.

▶ 24 percent of the givers, or about 17 million households, donated more than $1,000. 15 percent of the household contributors gave 5 percent or more of their income to charity.*

*The Independent Sector, "Giving and Volunteering in the United States," 1990.

The second step is to determine how much you can afford to contribute. Perhaps you cannot afford to give much this year, or maybe you can give more than you have in the past. You should donate only as much as you can afford.

Also, as we will discuss, there are many different ways to contribute to the world. If you cannot give much money, you can donate your time instead. Sister Clare of the Lakeview Shepherd Center in New Orleans reminds us that "you do not have to be donating $1,000 to be making a viable contribution to humanity." (Her center received a Daily Point of Light award for its service for the elderly.)*

The important thing is to review your finances and your charitable behavior, and then set realistic goals.

"GIVE FIVE"—A GUIDELINE TO GIVING

The Independent Sector's "Give Five" campaign outlines a program to set generous goals for donating your money and time. In 1989, more than 20 million people gave 5 percent of their income to charitable causes and volunteered five hours a week.

This is a great program to undertake. If every household met these monetary goals, the results for our society would be fantastic.

For more information contact the Independent Sector at 202-223-8100.

GIVE WITH YOUR MIND, WALLET, AND HEART

You should make sure that your donation goes to an organization that contributes to a cause which you support. This sounds rather simplistic, but many groups have similar names and it is easy to get confused.

Also, how does the group achieve its purpose? Some organizations act more aggressively in reaching certain goals. For instance, their methods of protest may involve breaking

*From "A Thousand Points of Light: The Second Hundred," the White House Office of National Service.

By permission of Johnny Hart and NAS, Inc.

the law in some fashion. This fact may or may not bother you, but it is worth considering.

Finally, it is important to remember why you are giving. Ultimately, your contribution is going to a worthy cause, and someone or something in need will benefit from your charity.

The following serves only as an example of how your donation helps an organization carry out its programs. In no way does it represent a solicitation of funds from these groups.

WHAT WILL MY DONATION PAY FOR?

Your generosity:

▶ Will help keep the Contact Center's national toll-free literacy hotline open to assist the 26 million functionally illiterate adults in this country.

▶ Will enable you to become a Citizen Sponsor of Earth Day.

▶ Will help fund the Natural Resources Defense Council historic pact with the Soviet Academy of Sciences to combat global warming.

▶ Will help SANE/FREEZE build a strong movement for peace and nuclear sanity.

▶ Will help the Life-Savers Foundation expand the much needed bone marrow registry, saving the lives of those with Leukemia and other types of cancer.

▶ Will help support PETA's direct action Compassion Campaign aimed at stopping ruthless and unnecessary product testing on animals.

Here is an inspiring story of an individual who contributed to victims of Hurricane Hugo.

USA Today news clipping; Jan. 11, 1990:

MYSTERY DONATION: The American Red Cross in Charleston, South Carolina, wants to thank a Pennsylvania child who, for 17 weeks, has sent $1 to help Hurricane Hugo victims. But they can't find the child. Money arrives in an envelope addressed in a child's hand, but without a name. Clue: the postmark is Rossiter, 65 miles northeast of Pittsburgh.*

USA Today news clipping; Jan. 15, 1990:

SPECIAL THANKS: American Red Cross Officials say they will honor Dalbey Marsh, 54, of Rossiter, Pa., for donating $17 for victims of Hurricane Hugo. Before discovering his identity, officials were baffled about the $1 weekly donations in an envelope addressed in a child's hand. "I try to be kind," said Marsh, who is mentally handicapped.*

*Copyright 1990, *USA Today*. Reprinted with permission.

Organizations and Resources

American Association of Fund-Raising Counsel (AAFRC)
212-354-5799
An organization created to advance the philanthropic cause and the ethical approach to fund raising. Their Fair Practice Code sets ethical standards for members to follow. They publish *Giving USA* and *Giving USA Update*, which are recognized as leading information sources for counseling firms, fund-raising and development officers, volunteer leaders, government officials, trustees of not-for-profit organizations, the media, students, and the general public. (*Giving USA*, $45.00)

Fund for the Environment
800-673-8111
Sponsored by The Environmental Federation of America, the Fund acts much like the United Way by raising money through corporate and government payroll deductions. Money is then donated to 18 environmental groups.

Independent Sector
202-223-8100
A nonprofit coalition of 675 corporate, foundation, and voluntary organization members with national interest and impact in philanthropy and voluntary action. The organization's mission is to create a national forum capable of encouraging the giving, volunteering, and not-for-profit initiative that helps all of us better serve people, communities, and causes. Contact them about their Give Five campaign and a copy of "Giving and Volunteering in the United States."

National Center for Charitable Statistics (NCCS)
202-223-8100
NCCS provides statistical information on philanthropic and voluntary organizations. They developed the National Taxonomy of Exempt Entities, a common language for describing different types of organizations, programs and

services in the nonprofit sector. They also publish a series of state directories that make available fund-raising and expense information as reported by charitable, civic, health, fraternal, and other nonprofit organizations.

National Charities Information Bureau (NCIB)

212-929-6300

NCIB regularly publishes listings and reports on charities, monitoring which groups meet their standards. Ask for a copy of their "Wise Giving Guide." Individual contributions of $25 or more and corporations and foundations contributing $100 or more will be sent the "Wise Giving Guide" for one year. NCIB also publishes detailed evaluations about organizations. As many as three reports at a time are available without charge.

Philanthropic Advisory Service (PAS) of the Council of Better Business Bureau (CBBB)

703-276-0100

The Council and its Philanthropic Advisory Service (PAS) promote ethical standards of business practices and protect consumers through voluntary self-regulation and monitoring activities. They publish a bimonthly list of philanthropic organizations that meet the Council of Better Business Bureau's (CBBB) Standards for Charitable Solicitations. The standards include: Public Accountability, Use of Funds, Solicitations and Informational Materials, Fund Raising Practices, and Governance. Ask for a copy of "Give But Give Wisely" ($1.00).

Salvation Army

Call your local chapter. Founded in 1865, the Salvation Army is an international religious and charitable movement organized and operated on a quasi-military pattern; it is a branch of the Christian church. They help people of all ages, races, and cultural backgrounds, including the elderly, families, young people, and drug/alcohol abusers. They operate programs around the world, such as emergency lodges, social service centers, counseling for unwed mothers, and employment services. They also provide aid in times of disaster. Most of the Army's more than 10,000 national and 14,000 international programs are administered through the local corps community centers. They are often recognized for their Christmas Kettles, used to raise funds for the needy.

United Way

703-836-7100 (or your local chapter)

More than 2,300 local United Way chapters mobilize approximately 10 million volunteers to help meet the health and human-care needs of millions of people. In 1987, the United Way raised $2.6 billion to meet health and human-care needs. They provide funding to more than 37,000 agencies and programs. The easiest way to get in touch with the United Way is simply to call local directory assistance. They will then direct you to a United Way center in your area.

United Way-affiliated Gifts in Kind

703-836-2121

Helps corporations give noncash donations such as office equipment to charity and nonprofit groups nationwide.

OTHER COMMITTED ORGANIZATIONS

Council on Foundations, Inc.

Goodwill

Toys for Tots (sponsored by the Marine Corps Reserve)

SHOPPING WITH YOUR CONSCIENCE
■ ■ ■

When you decide to buy a certain product, do you think only about whether that item will fit your immediate needs, such as taste, nutritional value, and price? Or do you wonder how that product was made, who made it, and what will happen when you are through with it?

More and more people are realizing that a good product is not enough. They want to purchase items that have been made by a company that adheres to policies that are socially and ecologically beneficial. They seek products that do not harm the environment and that are recyclable. And they want cosmetics and other household goods that have not been tested on animals.

Consumers are realizing that they carry more than money in their wallet—they also carry a bit of their conscience.

PETA, People for the Ethical Treatment of Animals

SHOPPING LIST

· ·

Remember to learn about the company behind the product!

▶ Is this company generous with charitable causes?

▶ Does this company advance women and minorities?

▶ Does this company have ties to South Africa?

▶ Is this company involved with the community?

Don't Forget!

▶ Bring *Shopping for a Better World* or another good socially responsible shopping guide when you shop.

▶ Ask the store manager to stock more products from socially conscious companies.

WHAT DO YOUR PURCHASES SUPPORT?

Businesses pursue activities and policies in the course of creating their products and services. These policies range from waste disposal and product testing to community involvement and minority participation.

When you buy a product, you support the entire operations of that company. Your purchase rewards a business for the creation of a fine product; however, your dollar spent may also support policies that you oppose.

For instance, how would you feel if you knew that you buy items from a corporation that is continually being fined for polluting the environment? Or a business that invests in South Africa? Conversely, what if you could buy products from a company that practices sound recycling policies, offers excellent opportunities for women and minorities, or gives extensive time, resources, and money to community programs?

COUNCIL ON
ECONOMIC
PRIORITIES

Company or Product	Abbr.	$	♀	‖	🐰	✍	🐷	🐱	🌲	🏠	🏭	ALERT
Special K	K	✔	✔	✔	✔*	✔	✔	YesIN	✔	✔	✔	
Spoon Size Shr. Wht.	RJR	?	✓	?	?	✖	✓	Yes	✖	?	✓	cigarettes
Sun Flakes	RAL	✓	✖	✖	✔	✔	✓	No	✓	✓	?	✈
Super Golden Crisp	MO	?	✔	✔	?	✖	?	Yes	?	?	?	cigarettes; Salvadoran coffee

✔ = Top Rating ✓ = Middle Rating ✖ = Bottom Rating ? = Insufficient Information	
For a more detailed explanation see key on page 13	**Page 107**

CEREAL

Shopping for a Better World: The Quick and Easy Guide to Socially Responsible Supermarket Shopping 1991 Edition by the Council on Economic Priorities.

BELIEVE IN THE PRODUCT *AND* THE COMPANY!

As a socially responsible shopper it is as important to support the company behind the product as it is to support the product itself.

Therefore, one should know how corporations rate in areas such as giving to charity, minority and women's advancement, military contracts, animal testing, nuclear power, apartheid and other social policies, the environment, labor policies, and community involvement.

You may wonder how you can find out so much about a company—it is hard enough to determine the nutritional value of a product, much less its social or environmental policies. Two excellent services offer easy-to-read detailed information about corporate policies:

▶ The Council on Economic Priorities publishes "Shopping for a Better World," which rates companies in the categories of animal testing, community outreach, nuclear power, and apartheid, to name just a few.

▶ Co-op America offers information about corporate policies and provides lists of socially responsible organizations that care about consumers, workers, their community, and the environment.

Organizations and Resources

SOCIALLY RESPONSIBLE SHOPPING

The Council on Economic Priorities (CEP)

(800) 822-6435/(212) 420-1133
Since December 1988, more than 250,000 copies of "Shopping for a Better World" have been sold by CEP.

Co-op America

202-872-5307/800-424-2667
A nonprofit, member-controlled, worker-managed association linking socially responsible businesses and consumers in a national network—a new alternative marketplace. Co-op America's services include catalogs for socially responsible products and access to networks of socially responsible financial services.

Courtesy of CO-OP America

ENVIRONMENTAL SHOPPING

∎∎∎

The years 1989 and 1990 marked a revolution in manufacturing and marketing of consumer products. Consumers became aware that the production, use, and disposal of many products damage the environment. These concerns led to the "green movement"—consumers demanding products that are not harmful to the environment. Ultimately, the advent of "green consumerism" prompted many companies and advertisers to create and promote environmentally "safe" products.

CONSUMERS LEAD THE CHARGE

Consumer opinion is the lifeblood of a corporation. If a consumer boycotts a product because it is unsafe for the environment, the manufacturer suffers. Results of numerous surveys reveal that many consumers are concerned about the environmental impact of the products they buy. Many say that they will choose a product deemed environmentally safe over one that pollutes or otherwise hurts the environment. Moreover, they are willing to pay more for these products.

Many businesses quickly jumped on the ecological bandwagon by creating and promoting products that are not harmful to the environment. "Green" products flooded the shelves, ranging from degradable diapers and plastic bags to sprays that will not damage the ozone and detergents that do not pollute the water. Retailers also joined in by offering and highlighting "green" products.

For more information about consumer products and their impact on the environment consult "Our Pollution Problem," on page 58.

Praise from the Nation's Press for "SHOPPING FOR A BETTER WORLD"

MAKING SURE

Environmental groups caution that many products deemed safe for the environment are really only polished marketing ploys devised by corporations and their advertisers. For example, they claim that the degradability of plastics has not been perfected. Furthermore, promotion of some items diverts attention from the importance of recycling and waste reduction. As a matter of fact, the Federal Trade Commission is investigating advertising claims of products that bill themselves as environmentally safe. The FTC has asked many companies to substantiate their environmental claims and will actively pursue cases of deceptive advertising on a variety of fronts. Greenpeace publishes a report discussing this issue and debating the ecological "safety" of certain products.

THINK BEFORE YOU BUY

Environmental shopping requires making conscious choices at the supermarket to avoid products that contribute to environmental problems, such as excess and harmful waste in our landfills and groundwater. As a shopper, you have the opportunity to select products that will protect the environment, conserve energy, alleviate trash disposal problems, and still be nutritious and affordable.

RESEARCH YOUR PURCHASES

How do you know what products are acceptable and who to believe about "green" claims? According to Janet D. Steiger, FTC Chairman, "Consumers who buy 'environmentally friendly' products in hopes of bettering the environment cannot themselves judge whether such products will deliver the promised benefits." Should that dissuade you from caring about the environmental effects of your purchases? Absolutely not. But just like anything else, choosing "safe" items requires some research and a lot of trust.

Many books and services offer information about how to become an environmental shopper. The Pennsylvania Resources Council (PRC) offers a handy guide entitled *Become an Environmental Shopper,* which outlines ideas to help you shop for the needs of your family and the environment. They also list numerous products packaged in recycled or recyclable packaging. In this guide the PRC outlines the four R's of Environmental Shopping:

Reduce the amount of trash discarded.

Reuse containers and products.

Recycle as much as possible.

Reject excessive packaging, non-recyclable packaging and products harmful to the environment.

Did you know? ••••••••••

▶ Wal-Mart Stores, Inc., the nation's third largest retailer, encourages its suppliers to create environmentally friendly products by displaying them in their stores.

▶ Many grocery stores have either introduced their own brand of ''green'' products or specially advertise other safe brands.

▶ A coalition of grocery stores agreed to phase out selling produce tainted with cancer-causing pesticides by 1995. Pesticides pollute the environment as well.

Some other suggestions include using paper instead of plastic, buying in bulk, and avoiding disposable items such as razors and diapers. Many of the other sources listed at the end of this section offer excellent information about environmental shopping.

LOOK FOR THE GREEN SEAL OF APPROVAL

One way to make sure a product is environmentally "safe" is to look for the Green Seal of Approval. Green Seal is an independent, nonprofit environmental labeling organization which seeks to identify those products that "produce the least harm and provide the most benefit to the environment."

A Green Seal will assure the consumer that the product has met the strict criteria established by the Green Seal organization. The criteria are based on a review of "the impact of the product on the environment over its entire lifecycle, from its 'cradle to its grave.' " Green Seal will review all types of products—such as light bulbs, toilet paper, facial tissues, cleaners and paints.

Excerpted from the Green Seal brochure, September 1990.

WHERE DID IT COME FROM?

Another facet of environmental shopping is the concern about the origin of a product. Many products and souvenirs are made from the hides, shells, teeth, or feathers of endangered species. If you buy these items, your purchase will support the illegal and unethical use of endangered species for consumer products and you may face a fine and risk seizure.

Illegal wildlife products frequently appear in the form of jewelry, clothing, and even furniture. Any product that is made of skin from spotted cats, sea turtles, lizards, snakes and crocodiles, birds and feathers, ivory, furs, coral, and plants could be from an endangered species.

Not all products within these categories are prohibited imports; however, a large percentage of the wildlife trade still involves endangered species. In fact, more than one-third of "exotic" leathers come from endangered, poached animals.

SHOPPING LIST

Canned tuna	Is it "dolphin safe"?
Fruit and vegetables	Buy organic—reduce pesticide intake.
Soda	Remember to recycle!
Deodorant/Hair spray	Not spray—it harms the atmosphere.
Plastic bags	Degradable—or get paper instead.
Light bulbs	Use low watt or fluorescent.
Razor	Don't use disposables.
Detergent and soap	Use phosphate free/biodegradable.
Diapers	Use cloth as much as possible.

▶ For more information contact the Division of Law Enforcement of the U.S. Fish and Wildlife Service and TRAFFIC (USA) of the World Wildlife Fund.

▶ Don't Forget:

▶ Take used paper or plastic bags when you shop. Better yet, bring canvas shopping bags.

▶ Precycle—cut down on unnecessary items and avoid over-packaged items.

▶ Ask store managers to stock environmentally "friendly" products.

Organizations and Resources

Green Seal
202-328-8095
An independent, nonprofit environmental group that labels products with a GREEN SEAL to insure that they are environmentally "safe."

Division of Law Enforcement of the U.S. Fish and Wildlife Service
Division of the U.S. government that protects endangered species. P.O. Box 28006, Washington, DC 20005

The Pennsylvania Resources Council (PRC)
215-565-9131/800-GO TO PRC
The PRC offers a handy guide, entitled *Become an Environmental Shopper,* which outlines ideas to help you shop for the needs of your family and the environment. They also list numerous products packaged in recycled or recyclable packaging. For a copy, send $2.00 to PRC, P.O. Box 88, Media, PA 19063.

The Seventh Generation
800-456-1177
Mail-order business that sells environmentally safe household products.

TRAFFIC (USA), World Wildlife Fund
800-634-4444

Ask for *Buyer Beware,* a free booklet telling how to recognize products from endangered species. 1255 23d St., NW, Washington, DC 20037.

OTHER RESOURCES

110 Things You Can Do for a Healthy Environment, Seventh Generation, 800-456-1177 ($2.00).

NonToxic and Natural: How to Avoid Dangerous Everyday Products or Buy Safe Ones, Debra Lynn Dodd, P.O. Box 1506, Mill Valley, CA 94942. $11.95.

The Earthwise Consumer, Debra Lynn Dodd—expert on toxics in the home, P.O. Box 1506, Mill Valley, CA 94942. $20 for eight issues.

The Green Consumer Letter, Joel Makower, a monthly newsletter on "green products," 800-955-GREEN. $27.

Toxics Stepping Lightly on the Earth: Everyone's Guide to

Toxics in the Home, Greenpeace, Box 3720, Washington, DC 20007 202-462-8817.

"The Earth's Future Is in Your Shopping Cart," c/o National Consumers League, Suite 516, 815 15th St., NW, Washington, DC 20005. Attn: Shopping Guide.

The Green Consumer, J. Elkington, J. Hailee, and J. Makower, Penguin Books, NY, 1990. $8.95.

"CRUELTY-FREE" SHOPPING

■ ■ ■

▪▪▪▪▪▪▪▪▪ Did you know?

According to People for the Ethical Treatment of Animals:

▶ The cosmetics you use may have been tested in the eyes of rabbits, causing them excruciating pain and eventual blindness.

▶ The detergent you use might have been force-fed to a dog until it gets so violently sick it dies.

▶ An estimated 14 million animals suffer and are killed each year by cosmetics and household products companies during the testing process.

PRODUCT TESTING

In many cases of consumer product testing, unanesthetized animals are burned, blinded, get violently ill, and eventually die. Many common household products are tested for consumer safety by being force-fed to animals or dropped into their eyes during tests called the lethal dose tests and Draize Eye irritancy tests.

These tests are intended to check for poisoning and irritancy of skin and eyes, but in many cases they are both cruel and unnecessary. In fact, the Consumer Product Testing Commission states that the law does not require the testing of animals to determine the toxicity or irritancy of products.

The products being tested on animals are common household items manufactured and sold by major corporations. These include toothpaste, soap, deodorants, and cosmetics such as makeup, skin-care lotions, and perfume. Your purchase of such products supports the vicious and unnecessary testing on rabbits, dogs, cats, and other animals.

"CRUELTY-FREE" ALTERNATIVES

There are, however, alternatives to "cruel" products. Cruelty-free items are safe and effective products, which, when produced, do not hurt or kill animals. Until recently, most cruelty-free products were made by smaller, specialized manufacturers, but due to increasing public pressure, major national and international businesses have stopped product testing on animals and offer cruelty-free products.

DETERMINING "CRUELTY"

How does one know if a product he or she purchases has been tested on animals, and where does one find cruelty-free products?

Certain animal rights groups lead the fight against animal testing. Many organize highly effective boycotts against large corporations that test on animals. For instance, due to pressure from People for the Ethical Treatment of Animals and other animal welfare organizations, companies such as Avon, Benetton, Revlon, and Mary Kay have halted animal testing. These groups also publish reports that document their progress and provide alternative products that are cruelty-free.

BUYING CRUELTY-FREE PRODUCTS

Companies and businesses also have been formed that sell cruelty-free products. Most are mail-order companies although some sell these products in their stores. The Body Shop, a London-based company with 14 stores in the United States, sells cosmetics and other products that are cruelty-free.

An increasing number of companies use ingredients that are natural and known safe, and do not use animals in the testing of their products. As a compassionate consumer you can buy cruelty-free products ranging from perfumes and colognes to skin cleaners, soaps, and deodorants.

For additional information concerning the welfare of animals in product testing see "The Debate Over Animal Experimentation" in the Animal Rights section.

NOT TESTED ON ANIMALS

NO ANIMAL INGREDIENTS

People for the Ethical Treatment of Animals

SHOPPING LIST

Are these products cruelty-free?

Shampoo
Detergent
Cosmetics
Mouthwash
Toothpaste
Oven cleaners

Don't add animal suffering
to your shopping list.

Organizations and Resources

Compassion for Animals Foundation, Inc.
800-82-VOICE
Look for the cruelty-free "seal of approval," which shows consumers at a glance that the product is cruelty-free. For more information about the Seal of Compassion write P.O. Box 341347, Los Angeles, CA 90034. Enclose a SASE.

People for the Ethical Treatment of Animals (PETA)
301-770-7444
PETA's Compassion Campaign is well known for its effective boycotts of corporations that product test on live animals and its "cruelty-free" solutions to shopping. Ask for their wallet-sized *Cruelty-Free Shoppers' Guide,* P.O. Box 42516, Washington, DC 20015. $2.00

The Council of Economic Priorities (CEP)
800-822-6435/212-420-1133
Ask for *Shopping for a Better World,* which rates companies on matters of social concern, including animal testing.

In Defense of Animals
415-453-9984

Ask them about their boycott campaign and for their list of cruelty-free companies.

COMPANIES THAT SELL CRUELTY-FREE PRODUCTS

Allens Cruelty Free Naturally, P.O. Box 339, Farmington, MI 48332-0339, 313-453-5410.

AVEDA,
2125 Broadway St., NE, Minneapolis, MN 55413, 800-328-0849.

Beauty Without Cruelty, 175 W. 12th St., New York, NY 10011. Send $2.00 for an extensive list. Ask about "The Compassionate Shopper" a newsletter about animal testing and cruelty-free products.

The Body Shop,
Retail stores, that sell cruelty-free cosmetics and other products. 45 Horsehill Rd., Cedar Knolls, NJ 07927.

The Compassionate Consumer,
P.O. Box 27, Jericho, NY 11753, 718-445-4134.

Humane Alternative Products,
8 Hutchins St., Concord, NH 03301, 603-228-1929.

PURL Unlimited,
361 New Bridge Rd., Dept. TAV389, Bergenfield, NJ 07621, (201) 387-1302.

Ecco Bella,
125 Pompton Plains, Crossroad, Wayne, NJ, 07470, 201-256-3201 (send $1.00).

Tom's of Maine,
Railroad Ave., Kennebunk, ME 04043.

FOR A MORE EXTENSIVE LIST CONTACT:

National Anti-Vivisection Society,
312-427-6065

In Defense of Animals,
415-453-9984

(A list of approximately 100 companies can be found in

Animal's Voice Magazine
April 1989, 1-800-82-VOICE.)

SOCIALLY RESPONSIBLE MONEY FUNDS

■ ■ ■

THE ETHICAL INVESTOR

Many investors are concerned with more than a positive return on their money. They also want to make sure that the companies in which they invest follow policies and create products that are constructive rather than destructive to society.

These "ethical" investors research and invest in companies and industries that help seek solutions to current problems, such as today's health, the environment, and urban decay. They seek out companies that promote policies geared toward consumer and environmental protection, occupational safety, and make products that have a positive social use. For instance, an ethically minded person may invest in companies that do not trade with South Africa, or in environmental companies that produce pollution control products and recycle waste.

SOCIALLY RESPONSIBLE MONEY FUNDS

Socially responsible money funds provide an opportunity for individuals to invest in the stocks and bonds of companies that produce goods and services which help to improve the quality of the planet and its inhabitants. In the past few years, billions of dollars have been directed to such funds. Experienced portfolio managers purchase the securities of companies that meet ethical as well as economic criteria.

▶ The Pax World fund invests in companies that produce life-supportive goods and services.

▶ The Working Assets Money Fund buys short-term commercial paper of companies with good environmental and labor records, without involvement in defense, nuclear power, or South Africa.

▶ The Fidelity Environmental Services Portfolio invests in businesses engaged in the development, manufacture, and distribution of products, processes, and services related to waste management and pollution control.

Author's Note
It is important to remember that investing in such funds will not guarantee you a return on your money greater than or even equal to other methods of investing.

47

Socially Responsible
Investment Services and Publications

The Catalyst Group
802-254-8144

Catalyst Newsletter
802-223-7943

Clean Yield Publications
802-533-7178

Co-op America
800-424-COOP/202-872-5307

Council on Economic Priorities
800-822-6435/212-420-1133

First Affirmative Financial Network
800-422-7284/719-636-1045

GOOD MONEY Publications, Inc.
802-223-3911

Insight
617-423-6655

Investor Responsibility Center
202-234-7500

Economics As If the Earth Really Mattered: A Catalyst Guide to Socially Conscious Investing, Susan Meeker-Lowry, New Society Publishers, $10.95.

Socially Responsible Money Funds

Affirmative Investments, Inc.
617-350-0250

Calvert Social Investment Fund
800-368-2748

Clean Yield Asset Management
207-439-3922

Dreyfuss Third Century Fund
800-645-6561

Fidelity Environmental Services Portfolio
800-544-6666

New Alternatives Fund
516-466-0808

PAX World Fund
603-431-8022

Social Investment Forum
617-451-0927

Working Assets Money Fund
415-989-3200/800-533-3863

Social Investment Forum
612-333-8338

SOCIALLY RESPONSIBLE CREDIT CARDS

...

CARDS "WITH A PURPOSE"

You now have the option of using a VISA or MasterCard to help save the planet. Many socially conscious environmental and animal welfare organizations now offer their members credit cards "with a purpose." A percentage of fees and annual dues charged by an affiliated bank is donated to a concerned organization, which then appropriates the money to a worthy cause.

For example, the International Wildlife Coalition offers VISAs and MasterCards through Monogram Bank, USA. Card users pay Monogram Bank interest fees and annual dues, Monogram Bank donates a portion of this money to IWC, which then uses the money for general purposes or special programs. IWC MasterCard proceeds help protect all endangered wildlife, whereas IWC VISA proceeds are used to protect marine animals.

HOW TO ENROLL

If there is an organization you would like to help, call them and ask if they offer credit card programs. Then each time you use their card (which often has the group's logo imprinted upon it), you will be contributing to a worthy cause. The money raised for these groups has been substantial, in the hundreds of thousands of dollars for some organizations.

WORKING ASSETS VISA—A CARD FOR MANY CAUSES

If you like the idea of using your credit card purchases to help the planet but do not want your proceeds to go to just one group, you should contact Working Assets VISA. Working Assets Visa is a credit card offered by First Financial Savings, a financial institution that works in conjunction with Working Assets, a socially responsible money fund. When you sign up for and use the Working Assets Visa card, Working Assets contributes money to nonprofit organizations that work with one of four areas of concern: peace, human rights, the environment, and hunger/economic justice. Upon enrollment Working Assets donates $2.00, and with each subsequent purchase made on your card they will contribute 5 cents.

In 1990, Working Assets donated $560,000 to 36 worthy, time-tested organizations, including Amnesty International, Oxfam America, and Greenpeace. As a cardholder, you vote on how to allocate funds among the groups each year.

OTHER WAYS TO SPEND ETHICALLY

It is likely that organizations will devise many other methods to raise money for their causes. For instance, Greenpeace now offers socially responsible checks for your personal checking

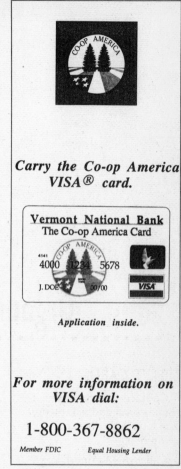

Carry the Co-op America VISA® card.

Vermont National Bank
The Co-op America Card

4141
4000 1234 5678
J. DOE   00/00

Application inside.

For more information on VISA dial:

1-800-367-8862

Member FDIC   Equal Housing Lender

Revolving Credit Department—Valid for U.S. Citizens Only

account. The Greenpeace checks contain the same information as your normal banking checks with one difference—they carry an important message. Imprinted on the checks is a picture of the Greenpeace *Rainbow Warrior* or a dolphin swimming in the sea, along with the Greenpeace name. For every batch ordered Greenpeace receives $1.50 and you get to advertise a worthy cause.

Another concept of Working Assets Money Fund is to encourage long-distance phone dialers to use U.S. Sprint, which will donate 1 percent of your phone charges to Working Assets, which will in turn donate that money to nonprofit organizations.

And for the ultimate donation, Greenpeace advises people on the construction of their will, with some suggestions about bequests to their organization.

Organizations and Resources

CREDIT CARDS

▶ Contact your favorite organization and ask them if they have a credit card program.

▶ Call MBNA America, a company which specializes in credit cards for over 2,000 organizations, including National Wildlife Federation, ASPCA, and National Audubon Society. (800-847-7378)

▶ Call Working Assets Funding Service, to sign up for a socially responsible VISA card for your personal use, or a MasterCard for your business. (800-52-APPLY)

OTHER SOCIALLY RESPONSIBLE RESOURCES

Greenpeace
"How to Protect Your Rights with a Will" (free)
PO Box 3720
Washington, DC 20007

Message!Check
206-324-7792
Message!Check imprints the logo of a socially conscious nonprofit organization such as MADD, Greenpeace, CO-OP America, and others on your bank check.

Working Assets Long Distance
c/o U.S. Sprint
800-877-2100, Ext. 222 (to sign up)
800-52-APPLY (for more information)

ORGANIZATIONS

ACTION
The Federal Domestic Volunteer Agency
Washington, DC 20525
202-634-9108

Action for Corporate Accountability
212 Third Ave. North,
Suite 300
Minneapolis, MN 55401
612-332-6411

American Association of Fund-Raising Counsel (AAFRC)
25 West 43rd St.
New York, NY 10036
212-354-5799

Ceres Coalition
711 Atlantic Ave.
Boston, MA 02111
617-451-0927

Chronicle of Philanthropy
P.O. Box 1989
Marion, Ohio 43306-4089

Common Cause
2030 M St., NW
Washington, DC 20036
202-833-1200

Congress Watch
215 Pennsylvania Ave., SE
Washington, DC 20003
202-546-4996

Consumers Union
101 Truman Ave.
Yonkers, NY 10703
914-378-2000

Co-op America
2100 M St., NW, Suite 310
Washington, DC 20063
800-424-COOP/202-872-5307

Council of Better Business Bureau (CBBB)
4200 Wilson Blvd.
Arlington, VA 22203-1804
703-276-0100

Council on Economic Priorities
30 Irving Place
New York, NY 10003
212-420-1133
800-822-6435

Council on Foundations, Inc.
1828 L St., NW
Washington, DC 20036
202-466-6512

Foundation News
c/o Council on Foundations,
  Inc.
P.O. Box 2029
Langhorne, PA 19047
215-547-2541

Friends Committee on National Legislation
245 2d St., NE
Washington, DC 20002
202-547-6000

Fund for the Environment
c/o The Environmental
Federation of America
3007 Tilden St., NW, Suite 4L
Washington, DC 20008
800-673-8111

Goodwill Industries Volunteer Services
9200 Wisconsin Ave.
Bethesda, MD 20814
301-530-6500

Green Seal
1733 Connecticut Ave., NW,
Suite 300
Washington, DC 20009
202-328-8095

In Defense of Animals
21 Tamal Vista Blvd.
Corta Madera, CA 94925
415-453-9984

Independent Sector
1828 L St., NW
Washington, DC 20036
202-223-8100

INFACT
256 Hanover St., 3d floor
Boston, MA 02113
617-742-4583

Interfaith Center on Corporate Responsibility
475 Riverside Drive,
Room 566
New York, NY 10115
212-870-2936

Junior League
660 First Ave.
New York, NY 10016
212-683-1515

Kiwanis International
3636 Woodview Trace
Indianapolis, IN 46268
317-875-8755

League of Conservation Voters
2000 L. St., NW, Suite 804
Washington, DC 20036
202-785-VOTE

The League of Women Voters
1730 M St., NW
Washington, DC 20036
202-429-1965

National Anti-Vivisection Society
53 West Jackson, #1550
Chicago, IL 60604
312-427-6065

National Association of Realtors
777 14th St., NW
Washington, DC 20005-3271

National Center for Charitable Statistics (NCCS)
1828 L St., NW
Washington, DC 20036
202-223-8100

National Charities Information Bureau (NICB)
19 Union Square West
New York, NY 10003

National Civic League
1445 Market St., Suite 300
Denver, CO 80202-1728
303-571-4343

National Council for Jewish Women
53 W 23rd St.
New York, NY 10010
212-645-4048

OMB Watch
20001 O St., NW
Washington, DC 20036
202-234-8494

Peace Corps
P-301
Washington, DC 20526
800-424-8580

People for the American Way
2000 M St., NW, Suite 400

Washington, DC 20036
202-467-4999

Philanthropic Advisory Service (PAS)
c/o Council of Better Business Bureau (CBBB)
4200 Wilson Blvd.
Arlington, VA 22203
703-276-0100

Public Citizen
2000 P St., NW, Suite 300
Washington, DC 20036
202-833-3000

Rotary International
1560 Sherman Ave.
Evanston, IL 60201
708-866-3000

Salvation Army
National Headquarters
799 Bloomfield Ave.
Verona, NJ 07044

Sierra Club Public Information
730 Polk St.
San Francisco, CA 94109
415-776-2211

Toys for Tots
c/o USMCR
4th Marine Division, JPAO
440 Dauphine St.
New Orleans, LA 70146
504-948-1227

United States Jaycees
P.O. Box 7
Tulsa, OK 74121
918-584-2481

United Way
National Headquarters
701 N. Fairfax St.
Alexandria, VA 22314-2045
703-836-7100

United Way-Affiliated Gifts in Kind
700 North Fairfax St.,
Suite 300
Alexandria, VA 22314
703-836-2121

Unsung Americans
77 W. 66th St.
New York, NY 10023-6298
212-456-7079
800-228-8813
(National Literacy Hotline)

Volunteer—The National Center
1111 North 19th St.,
Suite 500
Arlington, VA 22209
703-276-0542

Volunteers of America
3813 North Causeway Blvd.
Metiarie, LA 70002
504-837-2652

Volunteers Under 30
P.O. Box 1987
Denver, CO 80201
303-277-5968

THE ENVIRONMENT

• • •

**The most alarming of all man's assaults
upon the environment is the
contamination of air, earth, rivers and sea
with dangerous and even lethal chemicals.**

• • •

—RACHEL CARSON, *SILENT SPRING*

Environimental Action

Greenpeace USA

Environmental concerns topped the list in news story coverage during the late 1980s. The greenhouse effect, a thinning ozone layer, deforestation, and pollution of our oceans and air all became major headlines.

These problems were not unforeseeable and they did not just appear without warning. But the most shocking aspect is how quickly they became significant dilemmas with enormous consequences.

CITIZENS ARE CONCERNED

Many people have become increasingly aware of our planet's ecological plight.

▶ In a Gallup poll, three out of four Americans consider themselves environmentalists.

▶ Results from a Union of Concerned Scientists poll reveal that atmospheric pollution, water quality, and waste disposal are the most pressing environmental issues for Americans.

▶ Many other studies have determined that Americans want a greater selection of environmentally safe products and are willing to make lifestyle changes such as recycling and conservation in order to help.

ENVIRONMENTAL GROUPS FOSTER

During the 1980s these "ecological" anxieties led to action, as many concerned individuals joined or formed environmental organizations.

▶ The Nature Conservancy almost doubled in size, and the World Wildlife Fund grew by 400,000 people between 1986 and 1991.

▶ In 1989, membership in Greenpeace increased by 50 percent to 1.4 million.

54

▶ The Environmental Defense Fund's membership jumped about 30 percent, and the Wilderness Society added 27,000 new members in one month alone.

Environmental groups quickly took advantage of this burgeoning ecological interest. More money, greater media attention, and a growing membership increased the clout of the protesters, lobbyists, and activists. The organizations pressured legislators to enact and strengthen environmental policies. Businesses that polluted could no longer hide as negative publicity, boycotts, and lawsuits forced them to reassess the ways they produce and discard waste.

SAVE OUR HOME EDF

Environmental Defense Fund, Box 96969, Washington, DC 20090, 1-800-CALL EDF.

POLITICIANS REACT

Politicians soon realized that environmental concerns are now highly significant issues for their constituents, so they began to reevaluate government policy.

▶ Legislation to protect and improve the environment has been proposed and passed throughout the country, from measures to protect the earth from global warming to community and state recycling programs.

▶ President Bush endorsed legislation to elevate the Environmental Protection Agency to a Cabinet-level position and noted that environmental issues "are so important that they must be addressed at the highest level of government." He also made the amendment of the Clean Air Act his highest priority.

In a *Time* magazine article, Hugh Sidey observes the political and environmental movement:

> With the Berlin Wall down, the cold war over, the drug battle stuck in stalemate, almost everybody in the political world is waking up to the fact that the preservation and care of the land, air and water may rise and dominate all other issues. It links hearts and minds across continents, obliterates old barriers that kept people apart, banishes ideology. . . . The environmental political flood is about to break over us all.*

Citizens and politicians alike must continue to keep their concern for the environment at the top of their priority list.

*Hugh Sidey. "The Presidency: The Issue That Won't Wash Away." *Time,* 26 March 1990, 21.

.... Did you know?

▶ Pressure from concerned individuals helped generate corporate and government support of the reduction of CFCs, which cause the depletion of the ozone layer.

▶ Consumer protests of the pesticide Alar forced companies to discontinue production of that dangerous chemical.

▶ Recycling and natural resource conservation are becoming a matter of public and private policy.

BUSINESS FOLLOWS

Pressure from consumers, investors, activists, and legislators made businesses realize that cleaning up the environment is necessary and profitable.

Here are some things that are being done:

▶ Concerned citizens ask for environmentally safe products, which are made from recycled or biodegradable materials and which do not pollute the environment when they are produced, used, or discarded.

▶ Activists boycott products and divest the stock from companies that pollute. Many invest only in companies that are ecologically minded.

▶ An EPA report on businesses that produce toxic waste prompted many companies to review and change their waste-disposal policies.

▶ Many businesses are reevaluating their energy policies and finding that they can save money through conservation measures.

Some businesses have actually been created as a result of the environmental movement. These include natural resource conservation advisers, environmentally "friendly" product manufacturers, recycling companies, and toxic waste disposers. As the environmental movement grows the need for such business will increase tremendously.

THE MEDIA JOINS IN

The environment became one of the top news stories in the late 1980s.

▶ *Time* magazine featured Earth as the Planet of the Year.

▶ Every major TV network featured ecological issues in special segments or as a part of their normal broadcast agendas.

▶ Cable TV airs documentaries and weekly shows about the environment, such as National Geographic and Cousteau Society specials.

▶ Regular programming also incorporates the environment. A *Murphy Brown* show dealt with recycling and environmentally safe products; *thirtysomething* characters often discuss environmental issues; Kevin Costner and Barbra Streisand

56

hosted an Earth Day special to help the planet; TBS introduced a children's cartoon called *Captain Planet*.

Many celebrities also champion environmental causes. Olivia Newton-John has been chosen goodwill ambassador for the United Nation's Environment Program. Ted Danson gives talks on saving our oceans, Sting and Madonna publicize the destruction of rain forests, and Robert Redford speaks out on global warming.

TIME TO ACT

The events of the 1980s helped assemble all the forces necessary for environmental change. Citizens, organizations, politicians, businesses, celebrities, and the media are now assembled to aid a single cause—the protection of our planet. With an all-star lineup like this we now have the ability to win. However, everyone must work together.

Your actions are most important because you serve as a vital first link in this chain of action. As Jay Hair, president of the National Wildlife Federation once observed, "when people lead eventually leaders follow." The concerned individual contributes to organizations that promote action. Politicians listen to their constituents. Businesses live and die by the needs of the consumer. The media helps publicize the issues so everyone can be kept aware.

This section is designed to mobilize and educate. It outlines major environmental problems facing the world today. More significantly, it demonstrates that there is much that each individual can do to help protect and save the environment.

We all contribute to smog, pollution—even the greenhouse effect. There is no reason why we cannot also work to solve these problems. Individual action is easy and fun to do and, most important, it works!

22 APRIL 1990

Many of the services performed by Earth Day 1990 have been turned over to Earth Day Resources, 800-727-8619.

Reprinted with special permission of North American Syndicate, Inc.

Our Pollution Problem

■■■■■■■■■■■■■■■■■■■■■■■■■■■■■■■■■■■■■■

• • •

There is not a single nation or individual on Earth whose well-being is not fully dependent on its biological resources; its seas and rivers, grasslands, forests, soil and air. Unless all nations [mount] a massive and sustained effort into safeguarding their shared living resources, we could face a catastrophe on a scale rivaled only by nuclear war.

• • •

—MOSTAFA K. TOLBA, Executive Director of the United Nations Environmental Program

TOXIC POLLUTION

■ ■ ■

In 1987, America's factories emitted 7 billion pounds of toxic waste into the environment. Another 3 billion pounds were sent to facilities for treatment, reclamation, or disposal. Of the 7 billion pounds of toxic waste, 5 percent went into the water; 26 percent in the air; 15 percent underground; 23 percent off-site disposal; 23 percent to landfills; and 8 percent to sewage plants.*

These numbers do not include the huge amounts of toxins released into the environment from sources such as power plants, automobiles, sewage runoff from farms and cities, the military, and nuclear waste disposal. According to the Worldwatch Institute, the United States as a whole disposes of 290 million tons of toxic waste a year.

*USA Today analysis of 1987 EPA Toxic Release Inventory Report, 31 July 1989.

DANGEROUS TOXINS THREATEN THE ENVIRONMENT

The release of such dangerous toxins threatens the planet by poisoning ecosystems, polluting the air, and endangering the welfare of animals and humans. A poisonous gas leak in Bhopal, India, injured thousands of residents. The Love Canal area in upper New York State became America's first toxic waste crisis when 43 million pounds of toxins deposited by Hooker Chemical into a nearby dump seeped into the land and water system. A health disaster resulted with incidents of birth defects and cancer occurring far above normal levels.

The EPA now lists approximately 180 industrial plants in 34 states that release enough toxic pollutants to give residents a much higher than acceptable risk of cancer.

NUCLEAR WASTE

Military and nuclear power facilities produce large amounts of hazardous substances. According to Citizen's Clearinghouse for Hazardous Waste, the Pentagon has more toxic sites than Superfund and produces more toxic waste than the five biggest chemical companies. The United States receives 18 percent of its electricity from 110 nuclear power plants, which produce large amounts of radioactive waste.

Nuclear waste is highly toxic and remains radioactive for hundreds of years. Currently, 18,000 metric tons of used nuclear fuel and 9,000 metric tons of nuclear weapons waste await disposal in the United States. According to a report by Public Citizen, "the amount of high-level radioactive waste from nuclear weapons plants is up 24% since 1980; high-level waste from commercial nuclear power plants

Did you know? ⬛⬛⬛⬛⬛⬛⬛⬛⬛⬛

▶ Karen Schroeder was pregnant at the time she lived in the infamous Love Canal, home to one of America's most tragic toxic waste disasters. Her daughter, Sheri, was born with numerous deformities, including a cleft palate, deformed ears, and impaired learning ability. Many other children who were born and grew up in the area developed cancer and had birth defects.

Atlantic Monthly, July 1989.

ORDINARY PEOPLE—EXTRAORDINARY ACTIONS

In 1978, Lois Gibbs, a homemaker and mother of two in the Niagara Falls area, learned about the Love Canal—a toxic waste dump that sat right in the middle of her neighborhood. In the early 1950s, Hooker Chemical, a subsidiary of Occidental Petroleum, dumped 20,000 tons of chemical poisons on a 24-acre site. The company later sold the land to the city of Niagara Falls, which then developed residential properties and a school around it.

Lois became extremely concerned about the welfare of her children, who often became very sick. She asked city leaders to explore the issue, but her concerns and protests fell on deaf ears. So Gibbs knocked on the doors of her neighbors and organized the Love Canal Homeowners Association (LCHA).

From the resolve of one came the strength of many as the LCHA forced officials to confront the problem. Test results showed alarming levels of contamination in the homes surrounding the site, indicating danger for the residents. After a period of much debate then Governor Hugh Carey ordered the evacuation of the 239 families closest to the dump, and Gibbs and the LCHA won a milestone victory for citizen activism in this country.

Lois Gibbs went on to form the Citizen's Clearinghouse for Hazardous Wastes, one of America's best known and most efficient environmental organizations.

Did you know?

▶ Charles Zinser believes that his two sons developed cancer by breathing contaminated emissions from a nuclear weapons plant that stood near a family vegetable garden. One son got leukemia, the other had to have part of his leg amputated.*

*Michael H. Brown, "A Toxic Ghost Town," *Time,* 31 October 1988, 61.

has nearly tripled and is expected to increase by another 225% by the year 2000."*

Questions concerning the safe storage of the waste from these sources has provoked quite a debate. Some states, such as Nevada, have vast unpopulated areas, and may serve as dumps for radioactive waste. Residents, however, fear that the waste may leak and contaminate underground water sources.

Across the country the health of residents has been endangered by leakage of radioactive waste disposal. Cancer cases far above normal levels have been found in areas near nuclear weapons plants, where residents breathed air, ate foods, and drank milk and water contaminated by radioactive waste.

The controversy continues as the Department of Energy tries to determine how to dispose of thousands of metric tons of nuclear waste.

OTHER HARMFUL WASTE

Although it is easy to point the finger at industry and the government for the dangerously high levels of waste emitted into the environment, individuals also contribute to this growing dilemma. Automobile emissions, chemical "runoff" from farms and suburban yards, and household pollution all add to the toxic pollution problems.

Just as we all contribute to the problem of toxic waste, we can also share the responsibility of changing our habits in order to help protect the environment.

WHAT IS BEING DONE?

Public Sector

▶ The Love Canal became one of many toxic pollution problems nationwide that led to the creation of the federal toxic Superfund. The Superfund, now valued at more than $10 billion, has examined over 31,500 hazardous waste dumps, putting 1,224 sites on a priority cleanup list.

▶ The Federal Right to Know Act, passed as part of Superfund, is central to the effort of helping citizens and industries learn about and combat toxic hazards.

USA Today analysis of Public Citizen Report, 19 September 1989.

► The EPA issues a Toxic Release Inventory report, which records the amount of toxins released into the environment and which companies emit them.

Private Sector

► As a result of publicity from the EPA Toxic Release Inventory report, Monsanto set a goal of cutting toxic waste 90 percent by 1992. Dow and Upjohn have instituted similar programs to reduce hazardous waste.

► Actions from groups such as Citizen's Clearinghouse for Hazardous Waste and Greenpeace have been effective in limiting toxic waste dumping throughout the world.

► In 1983, 1986, and 1987, Greenpeace campaigners entered the U.S. nuclear testing site in Nevada. These actions focused international attention on the U.S. nuclear testing program and the environmental and health hazards of weapons manufacture.

WHAT CAN I DO?

► **Order a copy of *USA Today*'s "The Chemicals Next Door" report.** It analyzes the EPA Toxic Inventory Release. Write: USA Today Back Issues Dept., P.O. Box 4179, Washington, DC 20904 ($6.00).

► **Contact the EPA (800-535-0202) for information about toxic dumping in your area.**
　► For detailed information through a computer call (301-496-6531).
　► To purchase the database call the National Technical Information System in Springfield, VA (703-487-4650).

► **Toxic pollution begins at home!** In fact, each American generates an average of 160 pounds of household hazardous wastes every year. Many common household products, such as paint, detergents, cleaners, and motor oil will pollute the land and the water if not disposed of properly. For instance:
　► One gallon of motor oil will contaminate as much as 65,000 gallons of water.
　► Americans discard 2.5 billion household batteries each year—the acid leaks into the land and groundwater sur-

Copyright 1989, *USA Today*. Reprinted with permission.

rounding a landfill, significantly contributing to background levels of mercury.

▶ Phosphates from detergents create an overabundance of chemical food in the water, causing plants to grow rapidly and use up all the oxygen. This depletes the oxygen supply for fish.

Refer to air pollution, water pollution, and pesticide sections for additional information about toxic pollution and what you can do to help. Call your local authorities and ask where you can dispose of hazardous waste in your area.

Organizations and Resources

Citizen's Clearinghouse for Hazardous Waste (CCHW)
703-276-7070
A nonprofit environmental crisis center that focuses primarily on grass-roots environmental organizations across the nation. Its Grassroots Movement Campaign works for waste reduction and recycling and protests toxic waste. Ask for a copy of *Making A Difference* ($1.50) and request their newsletter, *Everyone's Backyard*.

Clamshell Alliance
603-224-4163
Antinuclear organization best known for its protests against the Seabrook nuclear power plant in New Hampshire.

Critical Mass Energy Project
202-546-4996
A division of Public Citizen. Ask them about their status report on nuclear waste.

Environmental Hazards Management Institute
Order their Hazardous Waste Wheel to learn what products contain toxics and their

environmentally safe alternatives ($3.95).

Environmental Action, Inc./Environmental Action Foundation
202-745-4870
Helps citizens threatened or harmed by toxic pollutants and works to protect the safety of our drinking water.

Environmental Research Foundation
Ask for *Rachael's Hazardous Waste News,* a weekly report on toxic substances ($25/yr.).

Greenpeace
202-462-1177
Their Toxics Campaign seeks to solve the toxic pollution problem through waste prevention. Greenpeace takes direct action against the polluters, fighting to cut off toxic substances at their source. Ask for a copy of *Toxics: Stepping Lightly on the Earth: Everyone's Guide to Toxics in the Home* (free).

Household Hazardous Waste Project
417-836-5777
Ask for a copy of their *Guide to Hazardous Products Around the Home* ($9.95).

OTHER COMMITTED ORGANIZATIONS

Center for Hazardous Materials Research
800-334-CHMR

Natural Resources Defense Council
212-727-2700

National Toxics Campaign
202-291-0863/617-232-0327

TOXIC WASTE DUMPING INFORMATION HOTLINES

EPA Superfund Hotline
800-424-9346
Contracted by GEO Resources. Answers questions about Superfund regulations and how to comply with them; also provides information about securing funding for cleaning up hazardous waste sites.

Safe Drinking Water Hotline
800-426-4791
Contracted by GEO Resources, answers questions and provides publications about the safety of our drinking water.

S.A.R.A. Emergency Planning and Community Right to Know
800-535-0202
Contracted by GEO

Resources, it answers questions and provides publications to those concerned about toxic spills.

Toxic Substance Control Act Hotline
202-554-1404
Answers questions about toxic substances and regulations.

PESTICIDE POISONING

■■■

Each year, the United States uses an astounding 1.1 billion pounds of pesticides—or 5 pounds for each citizen.

PESTICIDES—THE GOOD AND THE BAD

Pesticides are chemicals developed to kill insects that attack and eat fruits and vegetables; they have helped our farmers grow bumper crops. However, some of these chemicals are deadly substances—excess amounts can be lethal to humans, animals, and the environment.

KNOWN CARCINOGENS

Many pesticides are known to be cancer causing. According to the Natural Resources Defense Council, the EPA has identified 66 of the 300 pesticides used on food as known or suspected carcinogens. The NRDC reports that as a result of the exposure to only eight pesticides during their preschool years alone, as many as 6,200 children may develop cancer at some time in their lives.

POLLUTING OUR ENVIRONMENT

Pesticides also pollute our waters and deplete our topsoil. The application of synthetic fertilizers and pesticides on our farmland is responsible for more than half of the water pollution in the United States. More than 110 million pounds of DDT (a deadly pesticide banned many years ago) have ended up in the oceans of North America. And U.S. farmlands have lost

In McFarland, Calif., a town of 6,000, a rare cancer has stricken 16 children. Nine have died. The town lies in the state's heavily-farmed Central Valley region. Seven percent of the 500 million tons of pesticides used annually in the United States are applied here—on one percent of the nation's farmland. One-third of the area's wells are contaminated with pesticides.

—Excerpt from *Clean Water Action News,* Spring 1989.

63

WE do mind dying.

Reprinted with permission of San Francisco artist Doug Minkler.

75 percent of their topsoil; much of this loss is caused by fertilizer and pesticide applications.

IN THE FOOD CHAIN

Pesticides do not disappear easily. After they enter the soil and water, they make their way into the food chain, and their deadly effects can be felt for years. Michigan residents consumed more than 5 million pounds of hamburger contaminated with PBB's, a toxic chemical, years after the pesticide had been applied and subsequently banned.

And the farther up on the food chain, the higher the concentration of pesticides and thus the greater risk to the public. In *Diet for a New America,* John Robbins discusses the risk of pesticides in the food chain:

> . . . a cow or chicken or pig will retain in its flesh all the pesticides it has ever consumed or absorbed. . . . These poisons are retained in the fat of the animals. . . . Recent studies indicate that of all the toxic chemical residues in the American diet, almost all, 95% to 99%, comes from meat, fish, dairy products and eggs.*

Because humans are at the top of the food chain, they face the greatest risk of being poisoned by these pesticides.

WHAT IS BEING DONE?

● ●

▶ In 1989, public outrage arose over the use of the cancer-causing pesticide Alar. Alar regulated the growth of apples, helping them to turn a beautiful shade of red. Protests such as school system apple and apple-juice bans led to the withdrawal of Alar from any such use.

The controversy spread to similar pesticides, and soon after the demise of Alar, EBDC, a fungicide 10 times more toxic than Alar and used on 30 percent of all fresh fruits and vegetables, was withdrawn by its major manufacturers.

▶ The National Toxic Campaign Consumer Pesticide Project prompted a consortium of supermarkets to phase out selling produce tainted with cancer-causing pesticides by 1995. More

*John Robbins, *Diet for a New America* (Stillpoint Publishing, 1989).

than 1,000 supermarkets with annual sales over $8 billion agreed to support the project.

MOTHERS AND OTHERS FOR A LIVABLE PLANET

···

Here are some of the pesticides that the NRDC found to pose the greatest risks to children:

▶ Daminozide is sprayed on apples and other fruits to improve their appearance, increase their shelf life, and make harvesting easier. It breaks down into UDMH when the fruit is processed into products like applesauce and apple juice. UDMH is a potent carcinogen.

▶ Mancozeb is a fungicide used primarily on tomatoes, potatoes, and apples. During processing it breaks down into ETU, which is carcinogenic and otherwise toxic.

▶ Captan is a carcinogenic fungicide used on strawberries and other fruits.

▶ Methamidophos, parathion, methyl parathion, and diazinon are all "organophosphate insecticides that can cause nervous system damage.

"As a result of this exposure to only eight pesticides during their preschool years alone, as many as 6,200 children may develop cancer at some time in their lives."

▶ For more information contact:
Mothers and Others for a Livable Planet/NRDC
40 West 20th Street
New York, NY 10011
212-727-4474

In this country, major reforms occur only when substantial public pressure is applied to the government and Congress in order to counteract the lockhold of special interests.

—JOHN H. ADAMS, Executive Director, Natural Resources Defense Council

WHAT CAN I DO?

●●●

▶ Contact your elected representatives. Let them know that you are concerned about the pesticide problem. Press them for reforms and ask them what they are doing to help solve the problem.

Mothers and Others for a Livable Planet, a project of the Natural Resources Defense Council, suggests reforms to solve

the pesticide problem. Their suggestions include:
- ▶ Revising legal limits on pesticide exposures to protect children.
- ▶ Better regulation of testing and removing dangerous chemicals.
- ▶ Financial assistance for new, safer methods.

▶ **Ask your legislators to budget more money for organic and Integrated Pest Management (IPM) research.** According to Robert Scowcroft, executive director of California Certified Organic Farmers, in 1987 California had only $400,000 in research money for nonchemical agricultural research. That is a very small amount of money considering California is one of the largest produce-growing states.

▶ **Buy organic produce!** Urge your supermarkets to stock organically grown produce and to label imported produce, which often contains more pesticide residue than domestically grown produce.

Note: Organic produce can cost more than normal goods. Consumer Alert organization reports that shopping at organic grocers may increase your grocery bill by as much as 25 percent. However, if your traditional supermarket could buy organic goods in bulk quantities, they probably would be able to sell them at lower prices than specialty stores.

▶ **Don't judge an apple by its cover.** As much as 60 percent of the pesticides applied on fruits and vegetables are used solely for cosmetic purposes. After harvest a wax coating often mixed with pesticides is applied to fruits and vegetables to preserve their appearance. This coating will not wash off easily. Organic produce may not look perfect on the outside, but it tastes better and is less harmful.

▶ **Wash your produce carefully, especially your children's food.** Mothers and Others for Pesticide Limits states that children are exposed to more pesticides in their food than adults are—at a time when they may be particularly vulnerable to the harmful effects of pesticides.

▶ **Watch what you eat.** Animals higher on the food chain contain larger percentages of pesticides. John Robbins suggests that the most effective way of reducing your intake of toxic chemicals is to cut down on or eliminate your intake of meats, fish, dairy products and eggs.*

·········· Did you know?

▶ U.S. homeowners use 70 million pounds of pesticides a year on their lawns—or up to 10 pounds per acre.

▶ We spread 500 million pounds of chemical fertilizers on our gardens and yards each year.

▶ Each year 50,000 cases of pesticide poisoning are reported in the United States.

*John Robbins, *Diet for a New America.*

Pesticide residues in the U.S. diet supplied by:

Meat	55%
Dairy products	23%
Vegetables	6%
Fruits	4%
Grains	1%

▶ **Be careful about the fertilizers and pesticides you put on your own lawn.** These chemicals run off into our water supply and otherwise pollute the environment. The EPA has fully examined only 2 of the 34 most popular lawn pesticides.

Did you know? ··········

According to pesticide expert Lewis Regenstein, meat contains approximately 14 times more pesticides than plant foods; dairy products contain 5½ times more.

John Robbins, *Diet for a New America.*

©D. MINKLER 1986

CIRCLE OF POISON
WHAT GOES AROUND, COMES AROUND

Banned and restricted pesticides are being produced and shipped from the United States by companies like Velsicol, Monsanto, ICI Americas, and others. These deadly poisons are used on export crops like coffee, bananas and pineapples destined for markets in the United States and Europe. Workers producing and applying these chemicals are being poisoned — and so are we. For more information, contact:

Pesticide Action Network
965 Mission St., Suite 514, San Francisco, CA 94103
415-541-9140

Reprinted with permission from San Francisco poster artist Doug Minkler.

Organizations and Resources

Better World Society
202-331-3770
Become a BWS video advocate and obtain *Profits from Poison,* a documentary about the dangerous misuse of pesticides in developing countries.

Rachel Carson Council, Inc.
301-652-1877
Acts as a clearinghouse on environmental information, especially pesticide contamination.

EarthSave
408-423-4069
Ask for a copy of John Robbins's *Diet for A New America* and refer to sections on pesticides and fertilizers.

Friends of the Earth
202-544-2600
Ask about their Pesticide Project.

Greenpeace
202-462-1177
Ask for a copy of "Toxics," a leaflet about pesticide dangers and alternatives.

Mothers and Others for a Livable Planet
212-727-4474
A project of the Natural Resources Defense Council, they work nationwide to call attention to the problem of pesticides in children's food; press reforms in pesticide regulations and enforcement; and ensure that safe produce is widely available around the country. Ask them for a copy of "For Our Kid's Sake: How to Protect Your Child Against Pesticides in Food."

National Pesticide Telecommunications Network (NPTN)
800-858-PEST / 800-858-7378
A toll-free telephone service that provides a variety of impartial information about pesticides to anyone in the contiguous United States, Puerto Rico, and the Virgin Islands.

The National Resources Defense Council
212-727-2700
Ask for a copy of "Intolerable Risk: Pesticides in our Children's Food."

National Coalition Against the Misuse of Pesticides
202-543-5450
Focuses public attention on serious public health, environmental, and economic problems associated with the misuse of pesticides. Ask for a copy of "Pesticide Safety: Myths & Facts" and "Pest Control Without Toxic Chemicals" (.50 each).

OTHER COMMITTED ORGANIZATIONS

Americans for Safe Food
c/o Center for Science in the Public Interest
202-332-9110

Consumer Pesticide Project of the National Toxics Campaign
202-291-0863 / 617-232-0327

Pesticide Action Network
415-541-9140

Sierra Club Toxics Committee
415-776-2211

Cartoon by Tom Chalkey, from Clean Water Action News, Spring 1989 issue. Reprinted with permission by Clean Water Action, Washington, DC.

OUR POLLUTED AIR

■ ■ ■

A WORLDWIDE PROBLEM

There is hardly a place on earth that does not suffer some ill effects from air pollution. Factories, power plants, and automobiles release enormous amounts of dangerous compounds into the atmosphere, threatening the health of the planet and its inhabitants.

Highly industrialized nations account for much of the air pollution problem. In fact, according to the World Resources Institute, five nations contribute to more than 60 percent of the world's carbon dioxide emissions. The United States emits the most, contributing 23 percent, and the USSR is second with 19 percent—with China, Japan, and West Germany making up the remaining 18 percent.

AIR POLLUTION IN THE UNITED STATES

Although the United States provides much to the world in terms of productivity and resources it also is a major polluter. In 1987, 1.8 billion pounds of toxic substances were emitted

Did you know? ∙∙∙∙∙∙∙∙∙∙

▶ In 1987, U.S. manufacturers released 2.6 billion pounds of toxic pollutants into the air according to the EPA.

▶ Throughout the country more than 150 million people breathe air deemed unfit by the EPA.

❖ JOSEPH ZISKOVSKY ❖

Shoreview, MN
DAILY POINT OF LIGHT RECIPIENT: MARCH 15, 1990

Joseph Ziskovsky, 14, has committed his young life to making the community a better place.

Mr. Ziskovsky, an active Boy Scout, was only 12 years old when he became concerned about the dangers of pollution. He had experienced firsthand the effects of a drought on his hometown and had learned that planting trees could help solve environmental problems. He initiated a community-wide project to address these issues. He persuaded nursery owners to donate nearly 3,500 trees and the National Arbor Day Foundation to provide educational brochures on the importance of trees for a healthy environment. He then mobilized area organizations to distribute the trees, planting instructions, and educational materials to every child in three local elementary schools.

Reprinted with permission from the White House Office of National Service.

.... Did you know?

▶ In the United States, cars and light trucks use 30 percent of the country's total petroleum resources.

▶ Automobiles throughout the world produce about 13,000 billion cubic yards of exhaust fumes every year.

▶ An American car run for 10,000 miles will emit its own weight in carbon as carbon dioxide.

Copyright 1989, *USA Today*. Reprinted with permission.

*EPA, Toxic Chemical Release Inventory Report, 1987.
**Hilary French, "Clearing the Air: A Global Agenda." Worldwatch Institute, January 1990, 16.
†French, "Clearing the Air," 19.

through smokestacks; the rest were released through evaporation and leakage during storage and from vents and windows.* *Note:* This number does not include the billions of pounds of toxins released from government facilities, power plants, small businesses, and automobiles.

Some U.S. cities have the world's most polluted air. In Los Angeles, the air quality does not meet federal standards, in two out of three days, and the number of days of unhealthy ozone levels is nine times that of any other city in the nation.

HEALTH EFFECTS

Air pollution has a severe impact upon both personal and environmental health. Toxic metals and gases in the atmosphere cause health problems, ranging from breathing difficulties and lung damage to cancer. Sulfur dioxide, found in acid rain, is thought to cause as many as 50,000 deaths each year in the United States. In West Virginia's Kanawha Valley, 250,000 people live near 13 chemical plants. One study reports that between 1968 and 1977 the incidence of respiratory cancer in that region was more than 21 percent above the national average.**

Other reports have determined that children living in air-polluted areas have decreased lung capacity and suffer more respiratory infections and asthma attacks than those raised in clean-air regions. Ironically, the costs of health care and lost productivity exceed proposed plans to clean the air. According to Thomas Crocker of the University of Wyoming, air pollution costs the country as much as $40 billion in health care and lost productivity.†

ENVIRONMENTAL IMPACT

Air pollution's toll on the environment is equally as detrimental. The billions of pounds of toxic substances emitted into the atmosphere cause major environmental problems, such as acid rain, smog, the greenhouse effect, and the thinning of the ozone layer. All of these ecological responses to air pollution have devastating repercussions.

Acid rain. Acid rain is created when coal-burning power plants release sulfur and nitrogen oxides into the atmosphere; automobiles emit nitrogen oxides as well. These substances then change chemically and fall to the earth as acidified rain or snow. This "acid rain" destroys plant and animal life in streams, damages forests, and erodes buildings. Like other air pollution, it also causes respiratory problems, sometimes leading to permanent disability or death.

Evidence of acid rain is found throughout much of Europe and North America. Almost one-quarter of Europe's forests have been damaged by acid rain. In West Germany alone, more than 30 percent of the forests show signs of acid rain destruction. Symptoms include thinning of leaves and needles, deformed and reduced growth, and in some cases death. The acid rain also enters lakes and rivers, polluting the water and poisoning fish and animals.

In North America, areas affected by acid rain range from Canada through New England and the Appalachians, as well as in California. Acid rain is particularly disturbing, because it is carried in the atmosphere and no area is completely exempt from its destruction. New Hampshire's White Mountains receive acid rain from both directions—sulfur dioxide emissions from Midwest power plants and nitrogen oxides from automobile exhaust on the East Coast.*

Ozone. Ozone is the prime ingredient of smog. Ozone forms when sunlight mixes with auto exhaust and smoke from factories and power plants. Scientists believe that prolonged breathing of ozone can cause coughing, chest pain, and respiratory ailments—sometimes permanent. It also damages trees and crops. In 1988, approximately 100 urban areas failed to meet federal ozone or carbon monoxide standards. Ground-level ozone pollution is predicted to increase by as much as 50 percent in the next 30 years throughout the United States and by 21 percent throughout the world by the year 2030, according to a report in *Nature* magazine.**

Motor vehicles are a major contributor to ozone pollution. In 1985, there were 520 million motor vehicles in the world, almost double the amount ten years earlier; 350 million of these vehicles are automobiles. The amount of energy used to fuel these vehicles and the amount of pollution they emit into the atmosphere are astounding.

These pollutants contribute to the greenhouse effect and smog, greatly affecting our health and the welfare of the planet.

Greenhouse gases: Air pollution contributes to the greenhouse effect and the thinning of the ozone layer. Carbon

Did you know? ··········

▶ Each year 450,000 tons of lead are released into the air—more than half from automobiles.

▶ Each year the world emits almost 22 billion metric tons of carbon dioxide. The U.S. share is approximately one-quarter, or about 5 billion metric tons.

*Sandra Postel, Publication #58, Worldwatch Institute; and Hilary French, Publication #94, Worldwatch Institute.
**Analyzed in *USA Today*, 12 April 1990.

dioxide, chlorofluorocarbons, and methane form a blanket in the atmosphere, trapping in the earth's heat and causing the greenhouse effect. Warming of the earth's surface may have devastating results, including droughts, ocean level increases, and coastal flooding.

Ozone thinners: Chemicals such as chlorofluorocarbons and halons destroy the protective ozone layer, allowing an excess of ultraviolet radiation to penetrate the planet's atmosphere. Overexposure to UV rays can cause greater incidence of skin cancer, weakened immune systems, and damage to the retina of the eye. Ozone depletion also can decrease crop yields and kill ocean plankton, which are key links in the earth's food chain.

> The ultimate solution to air pollution is not to control it but to act in ways that prevent it in the first place.
>
> —HILARY F. FRENCH, Worldwatch Institute

ALTERNATIVE FUELS

....

Alternative fuels for motor vehicles may be one answer to cutting air pollution. Many companies are experimenting with fuels that will burn cleaner than regular gasoline. Some of the alternatives include natural gas, electricity, methanol, ethanol, and reformulated gasoline.

Natural gas can reduce nitrogen oxide emissions and hydrocarbon emissions by as much as 25 percent and 13 percent, respectively. Both pollutants contribute to smog and ozone. Reformulated gasoline changes the content of normal gas by reducing lead and other elements.

The car makers push for reformulated gasoline as one of the top alternatives because it is easier to implement than other potential fuels. Cars do not have to be redesigned and new fuel pumps and stations do not have to be built.

In a nationwide poll, 68 percent of the consumers who replied felt that automobile manufacturers should be required to build cars that run on alternative fuels. At least a quarter of the respondents said they would pay more than $1,000 more for such automobiles.

Sources of Carbon Dioxide Emission in the United States*

11 percent—Home heating
24 percent—Industrial uses

30 percent—Motor vehicles
35 percent—Electricity production

*World Resources Institute, 1988 data.

WHAT IS BEING DONE?

Public Sector

▶ In 1989, President Bush imposed major amendments to the Clean Air Act, designed to reduce acid rain emissions by 50 percent, cut tailpipe emissions by 40 percent and toxic chemicals emitted by factories by 75 percent. The plan also called for a major push for alternative fuels for automobiles.

▶ Los Angeles proposed a bold air-quality plan to clean up its dirty air. Elements of the plan include discouraging automobile usage, increasing public transportation, and curbing pollution from factories and households. It sets a goal of an 80 to 90 percent reduction of noxious emissions from all sources by the year 2007.

▶ In an effort to halt acid rain, members of the European Economic Community (EEC) committed to a plan that will reduce acid rain emissions significantly. The directive will decrease emissions of sulfur dioxide and nitrogen oxides substantially.

Private Sector

▶ The Natural Resources Defense Council and the Rocky Mountain Institute are working with the Soviet government to devise policies that will improve energy efficiency.

▶ General Motors developed a prototype for an electric car that may be suitable for daily commuting. The Los Angeles Initiative, a program of So Cal Edison and LA Department of Water and Power, will put 10,000 electric vehicles on the road by 1995.

▶ UPS is participating in a two-year experiment testing natural gas as a substitute to gasoline to fuel their trucks. Currently, about 30,000 vehicles in the United States are powered by natural gas.

▶ The oil industry and auto makers have established a research consortium to develop low-pollution cars using alternative and reformulated fuels. Many oil companies, including Shell, ARCO, Marathon Oil, Phillips Petroleum, and Conoco, are testing and/or marketing cleaner-burning gasoline at the pump.

USA SNAPSHOTS®
A look at statistics that shape your finances

Drivers want fuel choices
68% of consumers say carmakers should be required to build cars that run on alternative fuels. How much more they're willing to pay for such a car:

Nothing 27.5%
Less than $200 9.6%
$200–$599 13.5%
$600–$999 2.1%
$1,000 or more 26.2%
Don't know 21.1%

Source: Maritz Marketing Research poll of a national representative sample of 1,000 adults

Copyright 1989, *USA Today.* Reprinted with permission.

73

WHAT CAN I DO?

▶ **Write your legislators.** Tell them that you would like to see strong enforcement of the Clean Air Act. Proposed changes to the act include: imposing tough tailpipe emission standards, cutting industrial emissions, phasing out ozone-destroying chemicals, reducing acid rain emissions, and setting standards for toxic pollutants.

▶ **Remember, every time you drive you contribute to air pollution.**

    ▶ **Buy alternative fuels for your car if possible.** Reformulated gasoline with oxygenated additives such as ethanol and MTBE are becoming more widely available. Denver and Phoenix both offer such fuels. In California, cars using methanol, natural gas, and other alternative fuels may become more commonplace as manufacturers strive to meet strict emission standards. Most of Brazil's 13 million motor vehicles run on ethanol, either pure or mixed with gasoline.

    ▶ **Car pool!** Cars account for one-quarter of all U.S. energy usage. If one more person on average joined car pools, the nation would save 600,000 barrels of oil and avoid emitting 6,000 tons of carbon dioxide a day.

    ▶ **When you buy a car, consider its fuel efficiency.** Ask your dealer for a free copy of the latest EPA/DOE Gas Mileage Guide (or write: EPA Public Affairs Office, 401 M St., PM211B, Washington, DC 20460).

    ▶ **Buy cars with catalytic converters and which use unleaded gasoline.** Make sure your car is well maintained. Have it tuned regularly, use the correct gasoline octane and oil grade, check the tire pressure, and keep the engine filters clean.

    ▶ **Write to automakers and oil companies.** Ask them what they are doing to combat air pollution. Contact Shell Oil for a free copy of *Protect Your Car and Your Environment.* P.O. Box 4681, Houston, TX 77210.

▶ **Consider riding a bike when possible.** Encourage your community leaders to build bike lanes and other facilities to make biking easier. A bike-and-ride commuter transit system is one of the best ways to reduce hydrocarbon and carbon monoxide emissions.

Halstead Hannah—Originally for "Citizens for a Better Environment."

There are more than 800 million bicycles in the world today, but most are used in foreign countries, especially in Asia.

In many U.S. communities, biking is becoming more commonplace. Palo Alto and Davis, California, lead the nation in bicycle policies. Palo Alto has spent more than $1 million to create a 40-mile system of bikeways and other bicycle facilities. According to Marcia D. Lowe in *The Bicycle: Vehicle for a Small Planet* (Worldwatch Institute, 1988) one-quarter of the total travel in Davis is by bike.

▶ For additional information about bike riding contact the Institute for Transportation & Development Policy (ITDP).

▶ **Stop using aerosol sprays and other household products that cause pollution.** The propellants that push the formula out of pressurized cans are the primary cause of concern. Consumer products, ranging from hair sprays to barbecue lighter fluids, emit chemicals that contribute to smog.

Did you know? ....

Every day in California aerosol antiperspirant and deodorant containers spew up to 5 tons of smog-causing volatile compounds in the atmosphere—an amount equal to the emissions from a typical oil refinery.

Organizations and Resources

Air Resources Information Clearinghouse (ARIC)
716-271-3550

Citizen's Clearinghouse for Hazardous Waste, Inc.
703-276-7070
A nonprofit environmental crisis center that focuses primarily on grass-roots environmental organizations across the nation.

Clean Water Action
202-457-1286
A national citizen's organization that works for clean and safe water at an affordable cost, control of toxic chemicals, and the protection of our nation's natural resources. Has more

than 400,000 members and 18 offices in 10 states and the District of Columbia. Publishes *Clean Water Action News.*

Fossil Fuels Policy Action Institute
703-371-0222
Represents an alliance of two dozen environmental groups nationally.

Institute for Transportation & Development Policy (ITDP)
202-387-1434
ITDP's Transportation Alternatives Project challenges transportation policies in Congress, the World Bank,

and elsewhere to promote affordable nonmotorized transportation for development.

National Clean Air Coalition
202-624-9393
An alliance of environmental, public health, and consumer groups.

National Audubon Society
212-832-3200
Ask for a copy of "The Audubon Activist Carbon Dioxide Diet," a worksheet that tells you how to reduce your household's production of carbon dioxide, CFCs, and trash. $2.00

Natural Resources Defense Council
212-727-2700
Their Citizen Enforcement Project successfully institutes citizen lawsuits against the nation's largest and worst polluters.

Worldwatch Institute
202-452-1999
Ask for publications such as "Clearing the Air: A Global Agenda," "Air Pollution, Acid Rain, and the Future of Forests," and "The Bicycle: Vehicle for a Small Planet."

THE GREENHOUSE EFFECT

■ ■ ■

"Copyright 1989, *USA Today*. Reprinted with permission."

THE FORECAST: HOT— AND GETTING HOTTER

The year 1988 was the hottest on record. The four hottest years of the last 130 years have occurred since 1980. Some climatologists estimate that the earth's surface temperature has already increased by .5 to 1.25 degrees since 1850 due to the greenhouse effect.

And it may get hotter still. An article in *Good Housekeeping* magazine (October 1990) reports that "a UN commission of more than 300 climate experts recently concluded that if global warming continues unchecked, the earth's temperature will rise 2 degrees in the next 35 years, and 6 degrees by the end of the 21st century." If these predictions come true, we will face dire consequences in the years ahead.

GLOBAL WARMING

Normally sunlight travels through the atmosphere and heats the planet's surface. Infrared heat then radiates back into space. However, proponents of the greenhouse effect theorize that trace gases such as carbon dioxide, chlorofluorocarbons, and methane form a blanket in the atmosphere and trap the infrared heat instead of allowing it to escape into space.

Thus, the earth's atmosphere acts much like a greenhouse, which results in a greater heating of the earth's surface.

.... Did you know?

In the past century, the airborne CO_2 level has increased by 30 percent. Within another century it is predicted to double.

GREENHOUSE GASES

Carbon Dioxide: The burning of trees and fossil fuels, such as coal and oil, releases carbon into the air where it joins with oxygen to create CO_2, a gas that contributes to global warming. Carbon is normally absorbed by oceans, forests, and other biotic systems. However, because of the increased use of fossil fuels, an excess of carbon is created, causing an imbalance.

Chlorofluorocarbons: CFCs are artificial industrial compounds that are also responsible for ozone depletion. They are used in refrigerators, air conditioners, foam insulation, and food packaging (e.g., Styrofoam containers).

Methane: Methane is produced by a variety of sources, including landfills, compost piles, jet plane exhaust, and emissions from cows and termite mounds.

DIRE CONSEQUENCES

Many scientists believe that global warming due to the greenhouse effect can cause a marked change in weather patterns, including a northward shift of precipitation, droughts, and melting of the polar ice caps, resulting in an increase in coastal flooding.

According to one report in *Whole Life Times* by Don Strachen, "Just a three-foot surge—which is likely to occur

A polar bear, clinging ever more desperately to a shrinking ice floe, gradually sinks in the sea. The streets of London and East Coast American cities are slowly inundated by the ever-rising tide. Fertile grain fields are transformed into parched arid deserts. China becomes the lead country in terms of greenhouse gases.

—Images from *Can Polar Bears Tread Water?* a documentary produced by the Better World Society.

The "Green" house effect explained:

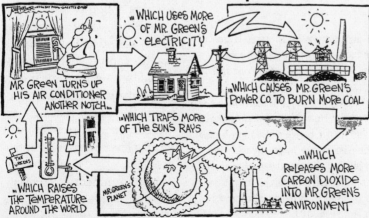

...WHICH USES MORE OF MR. GREEN'S ELECTRICITY

MR. GREEN TURNS UP HIS AIR CONDITIONER ANOTHER NOTCH...

...WHICH CAUSES MR. GREEN'S POWER CO. TO BURN MORE COAL

...WHICH TRAPS MORE OF THE SUN'S RAYS

...WHICH RELEASES MORE CARBON DIOXIDE INTO MR. GREEN'S ENVIRONMENT

THE WRENS

MR. GREEN'S PLANET

...WHICH RAISES THE TEMPERATURE AROUND THE WORLD

Reprinted with permission of Joe Heller, *Green Bay Press-Gazette*.

··········· Did you know?

- ▶ Estimates of damages caused by smog are about $2 billion annually in the United States.

- ▶ Losses associated with increases of ultraviolet light from ozone depletion are estimated at $2.5 billion a year.

- ▶ The drought of 1988 cost the United States billions of dollars.

- ▶ If polar ice caps begin to melt, ocean levels could threaten homes of coastal residents worldwide by 2050.

Reprinted with permission from the White House Office of National Service.

within 50 years—will drown southern Florida, New Orleans, the Sacramento River delta, Cairo, the Netherlands, and all the rice floodplains in southern Asia. Saltwater will bleed into freshwater, destroying irrigation sources and urban drinking water supplies throughout the world.

Any or all of these consequences could prove disastrous to the world and threaten human existence.

STOPPING GLOBAL WARMING

A number of immediate steps can be taken to help stop global warming. One of the most important is to learn to use fewer fossil fuels. The United States and the Soviet Union are responsible for nearly 50 percent of the carbon dioxide buildup in our atmosphere. By working together, however, these two countries could cut the use of fossil fuel in half in just 25 years, simply by improving the energy efficiency of cars, houses, appliances, and mass-transit systems.

Another way to help cure the greenhouse effect is to slow the rate of deforestation in the world. Trees actually absorb carbon, thus acting to decrease the amount of that deadly greenhouse gas, which is why people are being urged to plant more trees. Also, the burning of forests actually releases carbon into the atmosphere, further aggravating the greenhouse problem.

We must also work on further developing renewable energy resources. Wind power, solar power, and biomass energy have proven viable energy alternatives. Methods such as these are creatively exciting. *Good Housekeeping* (November 1990) states that "Now scientists have found a way to capture methane produced by landfills, pipe it out, and burn it to produce electricity." More reliance on cleaner energy sources will mean a less-severe greenhouse problem.

Environmental energy experts agree that major changes must be made to attack this problem. This

❂ FRANK H. LOCKYEAR ❂

Wilsonville, CA
DAILY POINT OF LIGHT RECIPIENT: APRIL 16, 1990

"Trees give us many things . . . To plant and nurture forest trees is one of the most noble things a person can do for the future of the human race."

Mr. Lockyear, 73, is a latter-day Johnny Appleseed. More than one million trees have been planted because of his tireless work.

Over 50 years ago, while working for a large nursery, Mr. Lockyear saw boxes of cedar seedlings headed for the burn pile. He requested permission to plant the trees that were to be discarded, and he has been involved in planting trees ever since. In 1980, Mr. Lockyear founded Retree International, a non-profit group with three goals: to plant trees, to educate the public on the importance of planting trees, and to assist in forestry research. In addition, Retree plants trees in honor of individuals or events, including a memorial in Lockerbie, Scotland, for the victims of Pan Am Flight 103.

means that change must be implemented by the government of every country throughout the world.

WHAT IS BEING DONE?

Public Sector

▶ In 1988, representatives from 35 nations attended the Global Greenhouse Network First International Conference in Washington. They concluded that global warming is a crisis that requires massive scientific and political coordination to stem the burning of fossil fuels and halve the emissions of carbon dioxide by the year 2030.

WHAT CAN I DO?

Everyone on an individual and global basis can help. Here are some suggestions:

▶ **Simple energy conservation is necessary.** That means better automobile efficiency and greater conservation of energy at home and at work. Dr. George Goodwell, director of the Woods Hole Research Center, in testimony on the greenhouse effect given to the U.S. Senate Committee on Energy and Natural Resources (June 23, 1988), recommends that the government establish policy immediately to reduce our emissions of fossil fuels by 50 percent over the course of the next years, possibly a decade or so. This can be done simply by conservation, changing standards such as automobile efficiency and by building houses that are more energy efficient.

According to the World Resources Institute, vehicles and residences account for 31 percent and 12 percent of total carbon dioxide emissions, respectively. Because most of us drive cars and live in houses, conserving less energy in these areas would be highly beneficial.

Refer to "Energy and Water Conservation" for ideas on how you can conserve.

▶ **Protest the destruction of our forests.** Trees store carbon. When they are burned, carbon is released into the atmo-

Did you know? ⬤⬤⬤⬤⬤⬤⬤⬤⬤⬤⬤

It is estimated that 1 to 3 billion tons of carbon are released each year due to the destruction of the rain forests.

·········· Did you know?

According to the Worldwatch Institute, 100 million newly planted trees can store approximately 600,000 tons of carbon and save American homeowners and businesses more than $4 billion in yearly energy bills by cooling streets and buildings.

sphere, combining with oxygen to make CO_2, which causes the greenhouse effect.

Refer to "Our Disappearing Rain Forests" to learn more about this problem and what you can do to help.

▶ **Avoid buying products that contain CFCs (chlorofluorocarbons).** CFCs are artificial gases that collect high in the atmosphere and break down the protective ozone layer. CFCs are also potent greenhouse gases, acting much like CO_2 by trapping ultraviolet light. In fact, CFCs are much more potent than CO_2.

Refer to "Ozone Thinning" to learn more about CFCs and what you can do to help reduce them.

▶ **Write to those in our government who are working on this problem.** Voice your concern, ask what is being done, and ask what you can do to help.

▶ **Join a local or national environmental group.** Ask for their advice and help them with their efforts. Here are few examples of such programs:

  ▶ The Natural Resources Defense Council signed an agreement with the Soviet Academy of Sciences, calling

---

SOYLENT GREEN

··

Do you remember the movie *Soylent Green,* starring Charlton Heston? This visionary tale of the future depicts New York City in the year 2022. The vision is hardly positive. The population of the city is 40 million, with one-half unemployed. The daily temperature is above 90 degrees, the air is virtually unbreathable, and food is in such short supply that a jar of strawberry jam costs $150.

The environmental erosion is so immense that people must eat waferlike food called Soylent, which supposedly comes from plankton. What Charlton Heston discovers, however, is that Soylent is actually reprocessed humans.

In 1973, this movie appeared a bit far-fetched. What could ever cause the planet to be like this in a short fifty years? In the movie the characters attribute their current dismal ecological condition to a heating of the earth's surface caused by massive releasing of pollutants into the air, which trap in warmer ultraviolet rays. *They called this condition the greenhouse effect.*

---

for American and Soviet scientists to work together to curb global warming.

▶ The American Forestry Association has launched a nationwide campaign "Global ReLeaf" to encourage Americans to plant 100 million trees in their communities by 1992 to combat global warming. As part of the "America the Beautiful" initiative the Bush administration plans a national tree-planting campaign to combat the greenhouse effect. Australia plans to plant 1 billion trees during the next decade.

▶ The League of Conservation Voters has drafted the Survival Agenda, which addresses the minimum course of action that Congress must take to reverse the growing environmental crisis.

▶ **Plant trees!** Trees combat the greenhouse effect by soaking up excess carbon dioxide in the atmosphere.

Tree planting is especially important in cities, because urban trees consume 15 times more carbon dioxide than trees in rural areas. For more information contact: Tree-People, National Arbor Day Foundation, Friends of Trees, Philadelphia Green, Trees Atlanta, Trees for Houston, or the American Forestry Association. (Addresses and phone numbers are at the end of the Environment section.)

Did you know? ┅┅┅┅┅┅

One study reports that CFCs are as much as 20,000 times as effective as carbon dioxide in trapping the Earth's heat.

ORDINARY PEOPLE—EXTRAORDINARY ACTIONS
EUDORA RUSSELL, CITIZEN FORESTER

Eudora Russell organized a community get-together and planted 23 trees in a rundown section of La Brea Avenue in Los Angeles. The following year, she planted 300 trees on a seven-mile stretch of Martin Luther King Boulevard in Crenshaw.

TreePeople, of Los Angeles, organizes the Citizen Forestry projects. Contact TreePeople to find out how you can start a similar program in your community.

For more information call TreePeople at 818-753-4600.

Organizations and Resources
• •

American Forestry Association (AFA)
202-667-3300/(To donate $5.00 for Global ReLeaf call 900-420-4545)
To plant trees contact their Global ReLeaf Campaign.

Better World Society
202-331-3770
Ask BWS for their documentary on global warming: *Can Polar Bears Tread Water?*

Environmental Defense Fund (EDF)
800-Call-EDF
Sponsored meetings that led to the Bellagio report, an influential report on the greenhouse effect presented to Senate hearings on global warming.

Friends of the Earth (EPI/FOE)
202-544-2600
Ask for a poster that details 10 simple ways you can help forestal global climate change. Send $10.00 + $2.00 shipping to the Environmental Policy Institute.

Greenpeace
202-462-1177
Ask for a copy of *Global Warming: The Greenhouse Report.*

National Audubon Society
212-832-3200
Ask for a copy of "The Audubon Activist Carbon Dioxide Diet," a worksheet that explains how to reduce your household's production of carbon dioxide, CFCs, and trash. $2.00

NASA's Goddard Institute for Space Studies
This institute studies Global Change, which is an interdisciplinary research initiative addressing natural and man-made changes in our environment, which occur on time scales of decades and affect the habitability of our planet.

Natural Resources Defense Council (NRDC)
212-727-2700
One of the most effective environmental action groups in the nation, NRDC is backed by 125,000 members working to protect the environment through strategic lobbying, litigation, public education, and research.

Environmental Protection Agency
Ask for a copy of *The Potential Effects of Global Climate Change on the United States* (Oct. 1988).

Union of Concerned Scientists
617-547-5552
Ask for their resources on global warming such as "How You Can Fight Global Warming: An Action Guide" and "How You Can Influence Government Energy Policy."

Worldwatch Institute
202-452-1999
Ask for a copy of "Slowing Global Warming: A Worldwide Strategy."

World Resources Institute
202-638-6300
Ask for a copy of "Changing Climate: A Guide to the Greenhouse Effect" and "A Matter of Degrees: The Potential for Controlling the Greenhouse Effect."

OTHER COMMITTED ORGANIZATIONS

Air Resources Information Clearinghouse
716-271-3550

Environmental Action Foundation
202-745-4870

Climate Change Activist Program
c/o National Audubon Society
212-832-3200

Greenhouse Crisis Foundation
202-466-2823

Rocky Mountain Institute
303-927-3128

United Nations Environment Program (UNEP)
212-963-8093

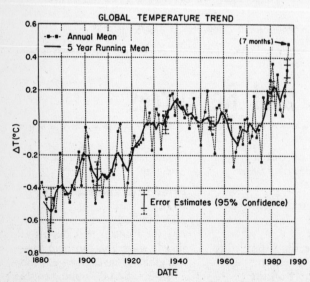

NASA Goddard Institute for Space Studies

OZONE THINNING

■ ■ ■

WHAT IS THE OZONE LAYER?

The ozone layer, located 10 to 35 miles above the earth in the stratosphere, protects the planet from destructive effects of ultraviolet rays. Robert Watson, chief of Ozone Research at NASA, claims that ozone is the only atmospheric gas that effectively absorbs UV rays from the sun.

CAUSES OF OZONE DEPLETION

What is causing the ozone layer to thin? Synthetic chlorine chemicals released into the atmosphere destroy ozone gases. The chemicals most responsible for causing this reaction are chlorofluorocarbons (CFCs), which are used in refrigerators, air conditioners, foam insulation, and food packaging; and halons, which are the chemicals found in fire extinguishers. These ozone-depleting chemicals are emitted into the atmosphere during production, through normal use, and by leakage.

As CFCs rise to the ozone layer, sunlight decomposes them and releases chlorine. The chlorine then attacks and destroys the ozone molecules. In the area of the ozone hole above Antarctica, the scientists determined that about half the planet's normal ozone level had been destroyed, and found chlorine compounds at 20 to 50 times above expected levels.

CFCs also contribute to the greenhouse effect, because

Did you know? ．．．．．．．．．．．

Worldwide attention to the problem of ozone depletion increased dramatically when scientists in 1985 discovered a hole the size of North America in the ozone layer over Antarctica.

Reprinted with special permission of North American Syndicate, Inc.

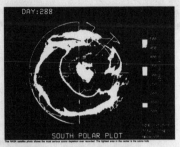

GLOBAL EMERGENCY

High above our heads a fragile, invisible layer of ozone shields the earth's surface against dangerous solar ultraviolet radiation. The ozone layer has been there for eons. Indeed without it, life on dry land simply could not have gotten started.

But now man is destroying this protective shield. Chlorofluorocarbons (CFCs), halons, and other man-made chemicals are wafting up to the stratosphere, six to 30 miles overhead. There they break down, releasing chlorine and bromine atoms that destroy

Natural Resources Defense Council
122 East 42nd Street
New York, NY 10168

The light color area in the center of this 1987 NASA satellite photo is the ozone hole—which measures nearly half the size of the Antarctic continent, an area covering approximately 2.5 million square miles.

they are 20,000 times as effective as carbon dioxide in trapping the earth's heat. Moreover, they do not dissipate easily. They last for years in the atmosphere, causing continuous damage. According to EPA Administrator Lee M. Thomas, they can persist for up to 100 years, building up their concentrations 10 to 30 times their present levels. Therefore, even if all production of CFCs was halted, the present level of these ozone-destroying substances would affect the ozone for years to come.*

CONSEQUENCES OF A THINNING OZONE LAYER

Without an adequate ozone layer an excess amount of ultraviolet rays will reach the earth, adversely affecting the planet and its inhabitants.

Health effects. Overexposure to UV rays causes a greater risk of skin cancer, weakened immunity systems, and damage to the retina. For each 1 percent increase in ultraviolet radiation, the likelihood of contracting melanoma (a deadly skin cancer) increases at approximately the same percentage. The rate of skin cancer in the United States is already increasing at a "near epidemic" pace, according to researchers. In an April 1991 report, the Environmental Protection Agency estimated that more than 200,000 people will die over the next 50 years from skin cancer. That is 20 times earlier estimates.

OZONE BUSTERS

Ozone-eating Chemicals	Sources of Ozone-eating Chemicals
▶ CFC's (chlorofluorocarbons)	▶ Air-conditioner and refrigerator substances
▶ Halons	▶ Fire extinguishers that use halon chemicals
▶ Methyl chloroform (TCA)	▶ Foam plastic products used for food packaging, cushions, and insulation
▶ Carbon tetrachloride	▶ Industrial agents for cleaning microelectronic circuitry
	▶ Medical industry sterilants

---

*Sarah Glazer, "The Ozone Mystery," Editorial Research Reports, 24 March 1987.

Environmental damage. Ozone depletion can also decrease crop yields and kill ocean plankton, which are key links in the earth's food chain. Plankton generates 50 percent of the world's oxygen. A Scripps Institute study conducted in Antarctic waters, found that plankton photosynthesis, and the resulting food supply within the plankton chain, had decreased by 25 percent, according to Don Strachen of the *Whole Life Times.*

An increase in intensity of ultraviolet rays can destroy crops, especially soybean and cotton. Laboratory experiments on soybeans have shown that every 1 percent decrease in ozone would reduce crop yields by about the same percent from a normal year's yield.* Obviously, a thinning ozone layer would wreak havoc on our ability to produce food.

Ozone-layer depletion is one of the world's most pressing environmental dilemmas. The thinning of this life-saving atmospheric shield could lead to the destruction of the planet. And this problem will not go away on its own. In fact, ozone loss is even worse than expected. In April 1991, William K. Reilly, administrator of the Environmental Protection Agency, reported that recent NASA studies indicate that the protective ozone layer over the United States has diminished by 4 to 5 percent. Previous reports estimated the loss to be 1 to 3 percent.

HOW TO SOLVE THE PROBLEM

Phasing out and replacing CFCs and other ozone depleting chemicals seems to be the natural course of action. Doing so, however, will take some time. CFCs are highly versatile and because they are nontoxic and nonflammable, they are found in a variety of products, including home insulation, coolant for refrigerators and air conditioners, cleaning solvents and seat cushions.

The extent of CFC use in the United States alone is astounding. According to The Alliance for a Responsible CFC Policy, CFCs are used in:

▶ More than 85 million household refrigerators.

▶ More than 40 million home air conditioners.

▶ More than 70 million motor vehicles.

▶ In the air-conditioning systems of most public buildings.

*Glazer, "The Ozone Mystery."

85

The installed equipment that relies on CFCs in the United States is approximately $135 billion. It is not realistic to halt production on the 20,000 refrigerators produced in the United States each day; however, the environment cannot wait too long for new technology to replace these chemicals.

WHAT IS BEING DONE?

B.C.   **BY JOHNNY HART**

By permission of Johnny Hart and Creators Syndicate, Inc.

Public Sector
▶ A landmark treaty called the Montreal Protocol has been signed by more than 90 countries, pledging a 50 percent reduction in CFCs by 1999. Major corporations such as Du Pont and Union Carbide have supported such phaseouts and are working on safer substitutes.

Private Sector
▶ Virtually all of the major American and Japanese car manufacturers announced plans to redesign car air conditioners to omit the use of CFCs as coolants. Automobile air conditioners account for 20 percent of the CFC emissions in the United States. According to the EPA, automobile air conditioners released 120 million pounds of CFCs into the atmosphere in 1985.

▶ Four national grass-roots organizations, Clean Water Action, Greenpeace, the National Toxics Campaign, and the U.S. Public Interest Research Group, formed a national campaign to protect the ozone. The Campaign for Safe Alternatives to Protect the Ozone Layer promotes comprehensive legislation to protect and restore the earth's ozone layer.

WHAT CAN I DO?

▶ **Write to your political representatives.** More extreme legislation must be passed to halt all ozone thinning substances now. One very involved person is Congressman Henry Waxman, Chairman of the Energy and Commerce Subcommittee on Health and Environment. Here is an example of the type of letter to write your representatives: (Note: Some of the issues in this letter have been passed and/or are outdated.

Contact Greenpeace Action or another dedicated organization to find out current legislative issues regarding ozone depletion.)

The Honorable Henry Waxman
U.S. House of Representatives
Washington, DC 20515

Dear Rep. Waxman:

The very survival of life on Earth is threatened by the destruction of the ozone layer. Action on this issue cannot wait until it is politically expedient.

I urge you to support and assist legislation to save the ozone shield. Such a bill must provide for:

—an immediate phase-out of ozone depleters

—safe alternatives that will not harm human health and the environment in other ways

—required recycling and destruction of existing stocks of ozone destroying chemicals

—assistance for workers whose jobs are lost because of the phase-out
....

You may also call Rep. Waxman in Washington, DC at 202-225-3976 or at his home district office at 213-651-1040.

A copy of your letter would be greatly appreciated. Please send it to Lynn Thorp at Greenpeace Action; 1436 U Street, NW, Washington DC 20009 (202) 462-8817. Also feel free to call for more information.

Greenpeace Action

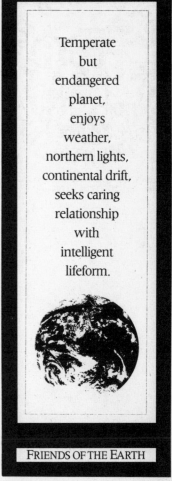

Temperate but endangered planet, enjoys weather, northern lights, continental drift, seeks caring relationship with intelligent lifeform.

FRIENDS OF THE EARTH

Copyright 1991 by Friends of the Earth. Used by permission.

▶ **Write the president, the head of the EPA, and your congressional representative.** The Natural Resources Defense Council suggests that you urge them to enact and support legislation to phase out CFCs and halons worldwide. The NRDC's five-part phaseout program includes the following steps:
  ▶ Phase out CFCs and halons by 1995
  ▶ End unnecessary uses and wasteful practices of these substances immediately

Citizen's Clearinghouse for Hazardous
Wastes, Inc. 703-237-CCHW

▶ Require labels on products made with CFCs and halons

▶ Tax away the CFC and halon producers' multibillion-dollar windfall profits

▶ Prohibit imports of ozone-depleting chemicals and products that use them

▶ **You can help stop ozone depletion in your car!** Leaky auto air conditioners are the single largest source of CFC emissions to the atmosphere in the United States. When an air conditioner is refilled, the coolant is vented and replaced. Refilling car air conditioners is responsible for about 100 million pounds of emissions each year, according to Kevin Fay, executive director of Alliance for Responsible CFC Policy. Follow these easy steps to protect the ozone:

▶ Vampire equipment captures CFCs that are released from leaks and flushing of auto air conditioners. Patronize only those service stations that have such equipment; do not allow unnecessary flushing of fluid from air conditioners; and repair leaks rather than recharging your system. This applies to home air conditioners as well.

▶ If you plan on junking your car or your home air conditioner, make sure the fluid has been properly drained. Otherwise, it will leak into the atmosphere while sitting in the junkyards.

▶ **Boycott foam packaging.** Wait until CFCs have been completely phased out. Consider using paper or other packaging materials instead.

▶ **Check your fire extinguisher.** Make sure it does not contain halon chemicals. These ozone-depleting substances will eventually leak into the air even if you do not use the extinguisher.

▶ **Write to the manufacturers of CFCs and Halons.** Ask them to commit to a crash program of eliminating these chemicals.

▶ According to the Natural Resources Defense Council, more than 200 million pounds of three ozone-destroying chemicals have been released into the atmosphere by more than 3,000 companies.

▶ Contact NRDC for a list of the names and addresses of the major manufacturers.

Organizations and Resources

Alliance for Responsible CFC Policy
202-429-1614
A coalition of U.S. companies and trade associations representing businesses that use or produce CFCs. The Alliance is a key supporter of the Montreal Protocol On Substances that Deplete the Ozone Layer.

Clean Water Action
202-457-1286
Ask for *As the World Burns* and other reference information.

Environmental Defense Fund (EDF)
800-CALL EDF
Ask for "Protecting the Ozone Layer: What You Can Do."
$2.00

Environmental Policy Institute
202-544-2600
Ask for *Saving our Skins,* which documents alternatives to CFCs.

Friends of the Earth
202-544-2600
A multifaceted environmental group, FOE's consumer campaign focuses attention on products that deplete the ozone layer.

Greenpeace Action
202-462-8817
Division of Greenpeace that provides "action" memorandums promoting citizen involvement in issues such as ozone thinning. (c/o Lynn Thorp)

National Audubon Society
212-832-3200
Ask for a copy of *The Audubon Activist Carbon Dioxide Diet,* a worksheet that tells you how to reduce your household's production of carbon dioxide, CFCs, and trash. $2.00

Natural Resources Defense Council
212-727-2700
Publications Dept. S. Ask for list of CFC-producing companies and *Saving the Ozone Layer: A Citizen Action Guide.*

Worldwatch Institute
202-452-1999
Ask for a copy of "Protecting Life on Earth: Steps to Save the Ozone Layer."
($4.00 + postage)

OTHER COMMITTED ORGANIZATIONS

The National Toxics Campaign
202-291-0863/617-232-0327

World Resources Institute
202-638-6300

THE WIZARD OF ID   BY BRANT PARKER AND JOHNNY HART

READ ME THE DISTANT FUTURE / OKAY

...IT'S THE TWENTIETH CENTURY...

...SCIENTISTS MAKE A HORRIFIC DISCOVERY!

THE PUBLIC PANICS!.. INDUSTRY COMES TO THE RESCUE!....

THE HORSE-AND-BUGGY ERA IS OFFICIALLY OVER!

...AS THE INTERNAL-COMBUSTION ENGINE SAVES THE DAY!

..WHAT WAS THE HORRIFIC DISCOVERY?

HORSE MANURE WAS DESTROYING THE OZONE LAYER

By permission of Johnny Hart and NAS, Inc.

OUR DISAPPEARING RAIN FORESTS

∎ ∎ ∎

.... Did you know?

▶ According to a 1990 FAO report, each year approximately 42 million acres of tropical rain forests equal to an area larger than Nevada are destroyed worldwide by landless peasants, cattle ranchers, and giant corporations.

▶ That works out to be about 80 acres a minute!

The world's tropical rain forests are located close to the equator, concentrated mainly in Amazonia, Southeast Asia, and West Africa. Half of the world's rain forests are found in Brazil, Indonesia, and Zaire, with Brazil having the largest concentration. Currently, 2.4 billion acres, or only half of the world's original acreage survives from this destruction.

CAUSES OF DEFORESTATION

Why are the world's rain forests disappearing? The Rainforest Action Network claims that the main causes of deforestation are cattle ranching, logging, road-building, and agriculture and industrial developments such as hydroelectric dams and mines. In Latin America, the chief cause has been raising cattle; in Southeast Asia, Oceania and Africa, logging and peasant agriculture are the biggest culprits.

▶ **Governmental policies and developing world poverty** have aided the demise of the rain forests. Many of the world's poorest people live in or near tropical rain forests, and they cut down the trees to clear land for farming. Ironically, the land is not suitable for proper farming and it runs out of nutrients within a season or two. Thus, the cycle continues as the farmer clears a new piece of land to farm.

▶ **Cattle ranchers** also cut down the trees to create pastureland for their cattle. According to the Rainforest Action Network, each year the United States imports more than 130 million pounds of fresh and frozen beef from Central American countries. Two-thirds of these countries' rain forests have been cleared to raise this cattle.

▶ Finally, **large-scale private and governmental development projects,** such as dams, highways, and mines, sacrifice huge sections of the rain forests.

IMPORTANCE OF RAIN FORESTS

Tropical rain forests are highly important to our planet for a number of reasons:

▶ **Rain forests provide a home to as many as five million species of plants, animals, and insects** (40 percent to 50 percent of all types of living things). A 1982 U.S. National Academy of Sciences report estimates that a typical 4 square mile patch of rain forest may contain 750 species of trees, 125 kinds of mammals, 400 types of birds, 100 of reptiles, and 60 of amphibians. Each type of tree may support more than 400 insect species. Alarmingly, Conservation International notes that at the current rate of deforestation, as many as one-fourth of all species of life on earth could vanish in the next 25 years!

▶ **At least 25 percent of our prescription drugs were originally derived from tropical plants.** These drugs are used in treating diseases such as childhood leukemia, arthritis, some types of cancer, heart disease, and malaria. Approximately 70 percent of all plants identified as having anticancer properties by the National Cancer Institute exist only in the rain forest. Yet, less than 1 percent of the tropical species have been noted and many will be destroyed before scientists have a chance to examine them.

▶ **The world's rain forests help regulate global climate.** As they are destroyed they will emit less oxygen and more carbon. Scientists fear that the amount of carbon released from the burning of the rain forests will accelerate global warming. Greenhouse-effect theorists believe that global warming will cause polar ice caps to melt and will disrupt the temperature cycles throughout the planet, creating floods in some areas and droughts in others.

▶ **Deforestation also endangers many people who live in and around the rain forests.** Hundreds of thousands of indigenous tribal people live in the rain forests and are now being threatened with their own extinction. The Malaysian Iban and Penan tribes are fighting to save the oldest rain forest in the world, which has been their home for centuries. Today they inhabit only 18 percent of the land they lived on just 20 years ago.

RAIN FORESTS AND ECONOMICS
Like many of the other environmental problems confronting the world today, the causes of deforestation—and its solutions—are economic in nature.

Did you know? ▪▪▪▪▪▪▪▪▪▪▪▪▪
According to the Rainforest Action Network, at present rates all the planet's tropical rain forests may be gone forever by the middle of the next century.

Plantu. Copyright © 1991 Cartoonists and Writers Syndicate.

.... Did you know?

In the minute it takes to read this, a section of tropical rain forests the size of ten city blocks will be burned or cut down.

Many of the lesser developed nations are struggling with huge debt, high inflation, and weak economies. Their people cut down trees in order to survive. The industrialized nations must realize that in order to prevent a catastrophe, the problem must be confronted at its source by helping to raise the standards of living of these countries rather than forcing them to pursue environmental policies that may hurt their economies.

Henry Breck, a trustee of the Natural Resources Defense Council, discusses in the December 5, 1988 issue of *Newsweek* the challenge of solving deforestation: "If the world really needs the remaining forests, a crash effort must be made to raise the living standards of people in and around them. . . . This puts questions like foreign aid and Third World debt into a new perspective."

A WORLDWIDE PROBLEM

Although much of the world's deforestation is occurring in Third World nations, the problem is not confined to these areas. As mentioned earlier, rain forests play an invaluable role for the earth's ecosystems. For instance, destruction in Brazil may eventually affect U.S. weather.

☆ ☆ THE STARS ARE SHINING! ☆ ☆

ROCKIN' FOR THE RAIN FORESTS

Sting, Madonna, and other rock stars are crusading to save the world's rain forests from destruction.

Sting's Foundation Mata Virgem (Virgen Forest) has raised more than $1 million for the cause.

Madonna, Sandra Bernhard, The B-52's, and Bob Weir of the Grateful Dead rocked for the rain forests during their charitable ''Don't Bungle the Jungle'' concert in New York.

Moreover, America actually has a deforestation problem of its own. Much of the country's forests are being destroyed by governmental and corporate policies that allow the clear-cutting of countless acres of priceless trees.

Therefore, the demise of our valuable rain forests represents a monumental challenge for the entire world. The United States cannot afford to look the other way while a major eco-tragedy takes place. The problems and the solutions lie with every person on the planet.

Although deforestation may seem to occur so far away, its tragic impact will surely be felt if we do not act quickly.

WHAT IS BEING DONE?

. . . .

Public Sector

▶ In 1989, Brazil made several policy changes to help slow the burning. These include suspending tax incentives that make it profitable for landowners to clear large expanses of jungle for cattle ranches, and no longer penalizing owners of unproductive land.

▶ The World Bank has embarked on a $90 million environmental action plan aimed at protecting the rain forests in Madagascar. Madagascar has 25 million acres of tropical trees and a higher variety of plants and animals than any place else in the world.

▶ The government of Thailand passed laws virtually ending all logging in Thailand. Though less than 20 percent of its natural forests remain, Thailand still houses the most important wildlife area in all of mainland Southeast Asia.

Private Sector

▶ In September 1986, the Environmental Defense Fund and an international consortium of conservation organizations protested a World Bank-financed project in Indonesia. Their report stated that the project would destroy millions of acres of rain forest and would replace the natives in an environment that would be detrimental for long-term development. The World Bank also delayed hundreds of millions of dollars of loans to build dams in Brazil because of pressure from environmentalists.

▶ Due to pressure from groups such as the Rainforest Action Network, corporations are changing policies that endanger the rain forests:

    ▶ Burger King canceled $35 million in beef purchases from rain-forest regions.

    ▶ Coca-Cola, which owns Minute Maid orange juice, scrapped plans to turn rain forest into orange groves and cattle pasture.

    ▶ Scott Paper Company terminated its participation in a $653 million eucalyptus plantation and pulp mill in Indonesia. According to RAN, the project would have destroyed up to 2 million acres of savanna and rain forest and ruined the lives of at least 25,000 indigenous tribespeople.

MacNelly. Reprinted by permission of Tribune Media Services, Inc.

WHAT CAN I DO?

• •

ORDINARY PEOPLE—EXTRAORDINARY ACTIONS

CHICO MENDES, 1944–1988

Chico Mendes, a Brazilian rubber tapper, worked tirelessly to end the destruction of Brazil's rain forests. A proud and peaceful man, Mendes led an impassioned crusade against short-sighted developers to preserve what has been called ''the lungs of the world''—vast tracts of invaluable forest land, home to millions of species and one of the largest producers of the world's oxygen supply.

Tragedy struck in December 1988 when Mendes was viciously gunned down at his home in the rain forests he fought so courageously to protect.

Called by *Time* magazine ''the world's most celebrated environmental martyr,'' and recipient of The Better World Society's Environmental Award, Mendes' legacy continues. His inspiring life, and his brutal death, serve as powerful reminders to a struggle that, for the sake of the planet, cannot be forgotten.

There are as many solutions to the problem of deforestation as there are causes. Here are some ideas:

▶ **Support agencies and organizations that help curb population growth in Third World countries.** Seventy-six nations, with a population of 2 billion people, lie near or within the tropical latitudes. Controlling excessive population rates will help preserve the environment. Refer to "Population Overload" in the Human Welfare section for a list of organizations that work for better population policies.

▶ **Eat less meat.** Raising cattle and other livestock for meat puts an enormous strain on the environment. No where is this more evident than in the rain-forest regions. Ranchers in these areas employ "slash and burn" clearing techniques to create pastureland. Unfortunately, rain-forest soil is not fertile enough to sustain herds of cattle for long periods of time. Rainforest Action Network finds that each year meat production in rain-forest regions yields only 50 pounds per acre, versus more than 500 pounds per acre in northern Europe. So every few years ranchers must move on into the rain forest in search of new soil. This inefficient method of meat production is exemplified by one report which estimates that 55 acres of Central American rain forests are destroyed to make one quarter-pound hamburger!

Most of the beef raised in rain-forest regions is consumed in nearby countries. However, RAN reports that in the past the United States has bought some 90 percent of Central American beef exports—more than 132 million pounds annually. Due to the "hamburgerization" of Central America, two-thirds of their rain forests have already been cut for ranching.

Some of the aforementioned beef came to the United States to be made into hamburgers, canned meat, and pet foods. At the end of the 1980s RAN led a successful campaign against fast-food chains that bought Central American beef. Those companies subsequently claimed that they would no longer purchase their meat from this region. Nonetheless, it is virtually impossible to track rain-forest beef. RAN is encouraging people to write to the Secretary of Agriculture to create a bill which would regulate tracking of beef imports. Contact RAN for more information; their telephone number is on page 99.

So, although it is difficult to determine if your hamburger comes from rain-forest cattle, a general policy of consuming less meat will help alleviate the stress on the environment—both here and abroad.

▶ **Contact a rain-forest advocacy group and ask about companies that endanger rain forests.** Then write to these corporations, protest their policies, and threaten to boycott their products if they do not change their actions.

Chico Mendes 1944-1988

Father of three, Union Organizer and founder of the Alliance of the People of the Forest.

Working with rubber tappers and the Union of Indigenous Nations, he pioneered the creation of extractive reserves (areas set aside for collecting sustainable forest products such as rubber and Brazil nuts). He opposed the cattle barons and plantation owners who were turning the fertile rainforest into barren desert, and who eventually ordered his murder.

To help carry on Chico's work and to join in the international demand that his killers be brought to justice and cease attacks on union organizers and rubber tappers, please contact:
Rainforest Action Network, 301 Broadway, San Francisco, CA 94133

RAN director Randy Hayes believes that Scott Paper's withdrawal from their Indonesian project was a direct reaction to the thousands of letters Scott received from RAN members, and to the national attention focused on Scott by the full-page ad RAN published in the *New York Times*.

▶ **Contribute directly to local rain forest region organizations.** There are many highly effective rain-forest advocacy groups that are indigenous to the region. For instance, Project for Ecological Recovery is one of the leading grass-roots groups working in Thailand to stop the construction of hydroelectric dams in wetland areas. In Amazonia, Por la Vida is a coalition of 15 environmental and human rights organizations from Ecuador formed to oppose oil development in the Huaorani territory and in the Yasuni National Park. And COICA (Coordinating Body for the Indigenous People's Organizations of the Amazon Basin), seeks to defend the rights, territory, and self-determination of indigenous people.

If you would like to contribute to an organization from a rain-forest region you can donate money to RAN and they will pass it on directly to any group you choose. To learn more about these groups and others like them and to find out how to donate, contact RAN.

▶ **Publicize the tragedy of deforestation to others.** Ask rain-forest advocacy groups to send you brochures, fliers, and information packets that you can share with your friends, business associates, and classmates.

▶ **Contribute money to plant endangered tropical trees.** Arbofilia, a conservation organization in Costa Rica, plants endangered tropical trees along deforested rivers and in other parts of the country. A $5.00 donation will plant a single tree—$250.00 will plant a hectare (1,000 trees). Contact the Basic Foundation for more information; their number is on page 99.

▶ **Avoid tropical timber such as teak, rosewood, liana, and mahogany.** Entire forests are cut down to export these types of wood. According to RAN, commercial logging of tropical timber is responsible for the loss of at least 19,500 square miles of rain forest each year. At this rate, virtually all the accessible forests of West Africa, Southeast Asia, and Central America will be destroyed in the next 20 years. Your refusal to buy furniture and other items made of these types of wood will make a major impact!

Endangered species

Reprinted with permission of Corky Trinidad, *Honolulu Star-Bulletin.*

▶ Protest the rampant deforestation of U.S. forests as well. According to The Forest Voice, less than 5 percent of America's native virgin forests, including the last temperate rain forests on earth, remain.

DEFORESTATION IN OUR OWN BACKYARD

Although the destruction of rain forests is a matter of worldwide concern, the United States also faces its own particular dilemma of forest destruction. According to the Sierra Club Legal Defense Fund, "many of America's rain forests are themselves on the chopping block."

▶ Puerto Rico's "El Yunque" rain forest is threatened by the Forest Service's proposed commercial logging program, which would cut up to 21 percent of the forest.

▶ The Forest Service is seeking to allow timber companies to clear-cut more than 1 million acres of Alaska's Tongass Forest—the largest temperate rain forest in the world and home to grizzly bears, black bears, and bald eagles.

▶ Washington State's old-growth rain forests, with trees reaching 27-story heights, face almost complete destruction from commercial logging.

▶ 95 percent of the redwood trees in California's old-growth forests have been cut down. Each day an average of 150 trees are cut. According to Forests Forever, "it took thousands of years to create these virgin forests. It could take less than five years to wipe them out."

▶ A geothermal project on the Big Island of Hawaii threatens the destruction of the Puma rain forest, the last tropical lowland rain forest in the United States.

For more information on how you can help stop the destruction of America's forests contact: EarthTrust, Forests Forever, Sierra Club Legal Defense Fund, and the Rainforest Action Network.

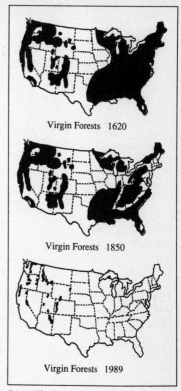

Virgin Forests 1620

Virgin Forests 1850

Virgin Forests 1989

From The Forest Voice, March 1990, Native Forest Council, Eugene Oregon.

▶ Write letters to government officials, expressing your concern about policies causing deforestation.
    ▶ The Environmental Defense Fund suggests that you write letters to the U.S. Treasury Department. Protest any U.S. support and financial backing of development projects that are destroying tropical rain forests and other precious natural resources.

In 1988, the World Bank responded to more than 20,000 petitions from EDF members by creating an environmental department to consider the environmental impact of proposed development projects.

▶ **Rainforest Action Network** suggests that you send a letter to the president of the World Bank. Urge him to stop financing rain-forest dams and fund small-scale projects that benefit rain forests and their inhabitants instead.

The World Bank, the International Monetary Fund, and the InterAmerican Development Bank finance large-scale economic programs, such as huge hydroelectric dams and colonization projects. These projects threaten the fragile rain-forest ecosystems in countries like Brazil. They must increase their pressure on these countries to impose strict environmental safeguards in the rain-forest regions. The U.S. government, as a major provider to these development banks, must use its clout to see that these measures are imposed and followed. Write to: Mr. Lewis T. Preston, President, The World Bank, 1818 H. St., NW, Washington, DC 20433.

▶ **Support organizations that arrange for "debt for nature" swaps and that buy land in rain-forest regions.** For example, Conservation International bought $650,000 of Bolivia's debt for $100,000 in return for Bolivia's promise to protect 3.7 million acres of Amazon rain forest. The Nature Conservancy actually purchases land in order to ensure its protection.

Send $1 for Save Tropical Forests bumper sticker to:
Conservation International, 1015 18th St., N.W., Washington, DC 20036

CONSERVATION INTERNATIONAL

SAVE TROPICAL FORESTS
30 Million Insects Can't All Be Wrong

Organizations and Resources

The Basic Foundation
813-526-9562
The Foundation advocates the balance of natural resources with population levels by committing its resources to promoting public awareness about rain-forest destruction.

Better World Society
202-331-3770
Their Chico Mendes Campaign and their documentary, *Voice of the Amazon,* has done much to further the cause of rain-forest protection.

Conservation International
202-429-5660
Tropical rain forests provide a home to more than 60 percent of all life on earth! Conservation International is a nonprofit organization dedicated to protecting tropical forest ecosystems through a careful balance of conservation and economic development. Ask about their quarterly newsletter, *Tropicus,* which keeps members informed about Conservation International's efforts toward rain-forest conservation.

Cultural Survival Inc.
617-495-2562
An organization of anthropologists and researchers whose goal is to help indigenous peoples like those who live in tropical forests around the world develop at their own pace and with their own valuable cultures intact.

The Environmental Defense Fund
212-505-2100/800-CALL-EDF
Their action against deforestation includes protesting U.S. support and financial backing of development projects that are destroying tropical rain forests and other precious natural resources.

Forests Forever
707-462-2370
Strives to protect the forests in America from clear-cutting.

The Nature Conservancy
703-841-5300
Acquires land through either outright purchases, gifts, or exchanges. To make sure the land is properly protected, the Conservancy either manages them or turns them over to responsible public or private conservation groups or educational institutions.

Rainforest Action Network (RAN)
415-398-4404
A nonprofit organization working both nationally and internationally to protect the world's tropical rain forests. One of RAN's chief goals is to inform the public on how they can take action to preserve rain-forest habitats. They offer two publications, the monthly *Action Alert* and the quarterly *World Rainforest Report,* and produce numerous fact sheets and brochures targeting specific rain-forest issues.

Wildlife Conservation International
212-220-5155
Their Tropical Forest Campaign supports field researchers and conservation action plans at work in 37 tropical forests around the globe.

World Wildlife Fund
202-293-4800
Ask them about their Rainforest Rescue Campaign

OTHER COMMITTED ORGANIZATIONS

Earth First!
818-906-6833

Earth Island Institute
415-788-3666

Earth Trust
808-595-6927

Friends of the Earth
202-544-2600

Greenpeace
202-462-1177

Natural Resources Defense Council
212-727-2700

Rainforest Alliance
212-941-1900

Sierra Club Legal Defense Fund
415-567-6100

The World Resources Institute
202-638-6300

OUR POLLUTED WATER

■ ■ ■

.... Did you know?

▶ Medical wastes, including used syringes, have washed up on New Jersey beaches.

▶ In Louisiana and the Everglades, water pollution restricts oxygen levels, causing "dead zones" of killed fish.

▶ California and New Jersey companies have been charged with dumping toxic chemicals into the ocean, threatening marine life.

CAUSES OF WATER POLLUTION

Water pollution occurs for a variety of reasons. The most common sources include industrial waste disposal, nonpoint runoff, the dumping of wastes, and oil spills.

INDUSTRIAL DUMPING

Of the 250 million tons of industrial waste produced each year, much is dumped in landfills, rivers, and oceans in an unregulated and unsafe manner. Major companies discharge deadly chemicals such as DDT and PCBs directly into lakes, rivers, and oceans, or into sewage systems that drain into these sources.

These toxins do not disappear just because they are underwater. They pollute the soil, making it difficult for plants to grow. They also accumulate in the fatty tissues of organisms and work their way up the food chain, eventually reaching consumers in extremely high concentrations.

The contaminated food we ingest causes many types of health hazards. PCBs, which come from many chemicals, and heavy metals such as mercury, lead, and chromium, damage the vital organs and cause cancer. DDT, dieldrin, and other pesticides cause cancer and birth defects. Many new chemicals are even more dangerous, and their effects will not be discovered for some time.

NONPOINT POLLUTION

Another cause of water pollution is nonpoint pollution—pollution that comes from various sources and runs off into water supplies. Fertilizers applied to farmlands and suburban yards wash from the soil into streams, sewers, rivers, and oceans. These nutrients create "dead zones" where no marine life can survive.

Pesticides seep into the soil and contaminate underground wells. According to a study, nearly 50 million Americans are exposed to pesticide-contaminated groundwater.*

To aggravate the problem, coastal development projects

*Sandra Postel, "Defusing the Toxic Threat," Worldwatch Institute, September 1987, 18.

fill in wetlands, which normally serve as a filter to pollution runoff, buffering pollutants before they have a chance to enter the main water sources.

THE DUMPING OF WASTE

Our water systems act as a huge trash can for the disposal of sewage and litter.

▶ **Sewage dumping.** Sewage systems contribute heavily to water pollution when waste is dumped directly into the ocean.

Solid matter from sewage treatment is deposited in landfills where it contaminates the surrounding land, and in the ocean where it is absorbed by the marine life. Sewage is not comprised only of human wastes; much of it contains industrial chemicals and household products, such as detergents and oil-based solvents that are flushed into sewer systems.

▶ **Litter.** We treat our rivers and oceans as giant garbage cans, disposing of waste from many sources into the water. Few will forget the scenes of New Jersey beaches littered with medical waste that had regularly been dumped in the sea. Recreational and commercial boats deposit much of their refuse into the water rather than hauling it back to shore.

Plastic debris from bags, can yokes, and fishing nets entangle and kill hundreds of thousands of marine animals, including birds, sea lions, seals, and turtles.

OIL SPILLS

Oil spills pollute oceans and shorelines in a devastating fashion. More than 10,000 oil spills occur each year, although many are relatively insubstantial in size and damage. In 1989, five spills involving leakage of more than 10,000 gallons occurred, with the Exxon *Valdez* spill in Alaska topping the list in its enormity and destruction. Eleven million gallons of oil spilled into the Prince William Sound, killing thousands of animals, including birds and otters and fouling miles of coastline. The cost of clean-up and fines will cost billions of dollars.

> **THE BEACHES WILL BE CLOSED TODAY DUE TO THE DEMAND OF THE DEPARTMENT OF HEALTH.**

Did you know? ▪▪▪▪▪▪▪▪▪▪

▶ In Alaska's Prince William Sound and in Huntington Beach, California, major oil spills polluted and poisoned the ocean, beaches, and wildlife.

▶ In some U.S. farmlands, pesticides seep into the soil and pollute the rivers and underground water supplies.

Sign on New Jersey beach, 1987.

·········· Did you know?

▶ According to a report from the Natural Resources Defense Council, 5 trillion gallons of industrial waste water and 2.3 trillion gallons of untreated sewage end up in coastal waterways each year.

▶ Approximately 6 million metric tons of litter are thrown overboard from boats and ships each year.

CONSEQUENCES

The contamination of our water has led to the destruction of many plants and animals and endangers human welfare, as well.

Health problems. Ultimately, humans pay the price. More than a decade ago, oceanographer and environmentalist Jacques-Yves Cousteau warned that "Poisoning the sea will inevitably poison us." Health problems, ranging from birth defects to cancer, result from toxins in the water and fish. In the New River in California, health officials have identified 28 viruses, including typhoid, salmonella, and polio in the fetid waters.

Environmental destruction. Vital links in the food chain in many different environments are destroyed by water pollution. Nutrients from fertilizers feed algae blooms, causing them to grow to abnormal levels. The blooms take over, sucking the oxygen supply from the waters, and choking off both plant and animal life.

Polluted waters also harm other wildlife. Birds eat tainted fish and drink fouled water, and dolphins and seals are slowly poisoned to death. The Environmental Defense Fund estimates that more than 5,000 waterfowl are killed each day due to lead poisoning alone.

Costs. Polluted waters have jeopardized the fishing industry throughout the country. Although the ocean seems like a vast source of seafood, most of our supply comes from only 2 to 3 percent of the ocean's waters, mostly along the coastline—directly in the path of deadly waste. If the effects of the pollution do not kill the fish, it will eventually make them inedible.

Cases of hepatitis and food poisoning from contaminated fish have closed down entire fishing locations. In 1987, 33 percent of U.S. shellfish beds were closed. Health officials warn people not to eat fish caught in the Hudson River in New

---

ORDINARY PEOPLE—EXTRAORDINARY ACTIONS

"Disaster in the oceans means disaster for man."
Jacques-Yves Cousteau

No one is more impassioned about our planet's waterways than Jacques-Yves Cousteau, oceanographer and environmentalist. Because he has devoted his life to the protection and study of oceans and rivers, he is most aware of man's apparent uncaring attitude for this life-giving natural resource.

Cousteau warns in a Cousteau Society brochure, "Our wastes cannot be 'thrown away.' We dump pollutants seemingly out of sight in the rivers and sea, but they eventually come back to us and our children with devastating impact—through the food we eat, the water we drink, and the air we breathe."

Water is the source of life and the way we treat it symbolizes, and ultimately affects, the way we treat ourselves.

York. And the costs to clean up this mess will be enormous. The United States and Canada have spent more than $9 billion to clean up the Great Lakes, and the job is far from over. New Jersey's 1988 medical waste scare cost the tourist industry approximately $780 million in lost business.

REACHING SATURATION

Our nation's waterways, and especially its coastlines, are reaching a saturation-point much like that of the landfills in this country. The summers of 1987 and 1988 serve as grim reminders of an ecosystem forced to vomit back the poisons and other wastes so carelessly dumped and dismissed. Senator Bill Bradley of New Jersey, notes, "I think that the summer of 1988 at the Jersey shore and around the world called attention to the fact of how much further we have to go." Fortunately, many heard the call. In the few years since the summers of 1987 and 1988, stricter enforcement and greater public awareness have led to cleaner oceans and shorelines in this country. Hopefully, in the future we will not need such blatant ecological signals to make us protect our precious waterways.

WHAT IS BEING DONE?

The Public Sector

▶ The EPA sued 11 communities for allowing untreated, toxic industrial waste water into the sewage plants. Communities violate clean water laws if they do not treat toxic waste before it is combined with regular sewage.

▶ In 1987, Maryland, Virginia, Pennsylvania, and the District of Columbia decided to curb pollution runoff into the Chesapeake Bay by upgrading sewage plants and enacting better management of development and agricultural runoff. The actions will reduce by 40 percent the amount of nitrogen and phosphorus flow into the bay.

The Private Sector

▶ The Natural Resource Defense Council's Citizen Enforcement Project has successfully forced hundreds of companies to abide by state and federal clean water laws.

Did you know? ....

▶ U.S. industry emits more than 250 million tons of noxious waste each year.
▶ Total spillage in 1989 amounted to 11.7 million gallons—the highest in 12 years, according to a report by Golob's *Oil Pollution Bulletin.*

▶ In 1989, Clean Water Action organized three summer events to celebrate America's coasts and to call attention to the pollution problems and solutions.

▶ After the *Valdez* oil spill, the petroleum industry created a $250 million fund, the Petroleum Industry Response Organization, to combat major spills.

▶ Due to pressure from Greenpeace and other organizations, in 1988 the EPA shelved plans to allow incineration of hazardous wastes at sea.

▶ More than 100,000 volunteers from the Texas "adopt-a-beach" program picked up 2 million pounds of beach garbage.

☆ ☆ THE STARS ARE SHINING! ☆ ☆

LET'S ALL "HEAL THE BAY"

A star-studded cast joined Santa Monica's environmental group Heal the Bay in a consciousness-raising event about the dangers of pollution.

Featured participants were *thirtysomething*'s Ken Olin and Patricia Wettig, Justin Bateman, Moon and Dweezil Zappa and John Ritter, as "Toxic Man."

WHAT CAN I DO?

● ●

▶ **Remember, water pollution begins at home!** Everyday household products can pollute the environment when they are poured down the drain or flushed down the toilet. You can help right now by taking a few simple steps to ensure that your house is not contributing to the water pollution problem.

▶ **Buy low-phosphate products or use less detergent.** Household detergents contain phosphates, which cause water eutrophication, an overabundance of chemical food in the water that causes plants to grow rapidly using all the oxygen.

▶ **Try using natural garden products and cut down on your use of toxic chemicals.** Americans spread about 30 million pounds of chemicals on their lawns each year. Herbicides and fertilizers can run off your property and feed into nearby water sources or sewers.

WATCH OUT FOR THE UNDERTOW, DEAR!

Copyright 1990, *USA Today*. Reprinted with permission.

▶ **Watch where you dispose of your household toxins.** Paints, oil, solvents, and other chemicals should never be poured down the drain because they will go directly into the water cycle. Three-quarters of all oil contaminations in the water come from the land sources, including household products. Many communities have a toxic chemical cleanup site where people can get rid of toxic home chemicals.

Reprinted with permission of Joe Heller, *Green Bay Press-Gazette.*

> ▶ **Recycle your motor oil.** Do not pour it into the ground or down the sink. One gallon of oil will contaminate 65,000 gallons of water. More than 257 million gallons of oil are poured into our water supply each year.
>
> ▶ For more information about household wastes refer to the sections entitled "Pesticide Poisoning" and "Toxic Pollution."

▶ **Boycott the products of toxic industrial polluters and write them voicing your concern.** The EPA Toxic Release Inventory (800-535-0202) lists the offenders of toxic pollution. You can also contact any of the organizations listed here for more information.

▶ **If boycotting is not enough, sue polluters!** Call the Natural Resources Defense Council about their Citizen Enforcement Project, which organizes citizen lawsuits against the nation's largest and worst polluters.

▶ **Ask your local authorities how they dispose of treated and untreated waste.** Let them know your feelings, especially if they pollute local rivers and beaches.

Do not assume that your municipality abides by the letter of the law. According to Clean Ocean Action, 90 percent of the 1,500 pipelines in New Jersey violate regulatory codes when they discharge effluent into the sea.

▶ **Contact Clean Water Action and other environmental groups.** Ask how you can join the fight to make sure the Clean Water Act is properly funded and enforced.

Organizations and Resources

Clean Water Action
202-457-1286
A national citizen's organization that works for clean and safe water at an affordable cost, control of toxic chemicals, and the protection of our nation's natural resources. Has more than 400,000 members and 18 offices in 10 states and the District of Columbia. Publishes *Clean Water Action News.*

Environmental Action, Inc./Environmental Action Foundation
202-745-4870
Helps citizens threatened or harmed by toxic pollutants and works to protect the safety of our drinking water.

Citizen's Clearinghouse for Hazardous Waste, Inc.
703-276-7070
A nonprofit environmental crisis center that focuses primarily on grass-roots environmental organizations across the nation. Its Grassroots Movement Campaign works for waste reduction and recycling and protests toxic waste.

Cousteau Society
804-627-1144
A worldwide organization that serves to protect the oceans, marine animals, and ultimately humans from pollution.

Friends of the Earth Oceanic Society
202-544-2600
Protects the oceans from toxic waste dumping.

Greenpeace
202-462-1177
Their Toxics Campaign seeks to solve the toxic pollution problem through waste prevention. The *Rainbow Warrior,* an oceangoing vessel of protest, has been effective in publicizing, protesting, and stopping toxic dumping in the seas.

International Rivers Network
415-788-7324
Publishes *World Rivers Review,* a newsletter that addresses the protection of rivers and other waterways from pollution and development, such as dams that are environmentally or socially destructive.

National Audubon Society
212-832-3200
Ask for a copy of *Controlling Non-point-source Water Pollution—A Citizen's Handbook.* $7.50.

Natural Resources Defense Council
212-727-2700
Their Citizen Enforcement Project successfully initiates citizen lawsuits against the nation's largest and worst polluters, forcing them to stop polluting our nation's waterways.

OTHER COMMITTED ORGANIZATIONS

American Oceans Campaign
213-576-6162

American Rivers, Inc.
202-547-6900

Environmental Defense Fund
800-CALL-EDF

Friends of the Earth
202-544-2600

Heal the Bay
213-394-4552

Scripps Institution of Oceanography
619-534-6945

Survival of the Sea Foundation
202-994-3885

Worldwatch Institute
202-452-1999

The Pollution Solution– Conservation and Recycling

■■■

ENERGY AND WATER CONSERVATION

■■■

Even though the United States has a stronger economy than much of the world, we could operate just as well by using about half the energy.

Furthermore, although we have become more efficient than we were during the decade of the 1970s, we still lag behind many of our industrialized peers in the areas of energy-saving policies. For example:

▶ Sweden and West Germany consume one-third less energy per capita than Americans.

▶ A person living in North America uses the energy equivalent of 22 barrels of oil a year just in the home. His Japanese counterpart uses only 8.5 barrels.

The United States also uses much more water than is necessary:

▶ We use two and one-half times as much water per person as a Japanese citizen, nine times that of someone from Great Britain.

▶ The average southern Californian uses 120 gallons of water a day. Southern California industrial, residential, and

CAPTAIN PLANET
AND THE PLANETEERS℠

▶ According to the U.S. Department of Energy, an average American household consumes energy equal to 1,253 gallons of oil per year.

▶ Refrigerators alone use the output of 25 large power plants, comprising about 7 percent of the nation's total electricity consumption and more than half of the power generated by all nuclear power plants.

commercial sources combined utilize 900 billion gallons of water a year.

This is not to say that the United States has ignored conservation measures. In fact, as a nation we have become 20 percent more energy efficient than we were two decades ago. Airlines and automobiles have become more efficient and general conservation policies have made us much less dependent on oil. Nevertheless, we can do more.

In many other countries, energy-saving policies are a way of life:

▶ Swedish homes are twice as well insulated as homes in northern Minnesota, and as a result use much less energy.

▶ Japan and Europe utilize more energy-efficient appliances and light bulbs than the United States, making their homes and businesses more efficient.

Approximately one-third of our total energy production

ORDINARY PEOPLE—EXTRAORDINARY ACTIONS
USA TODAY'S ECOFAMILY

The Wiggs family of Sioux Falls, SD, was chosen by *USA Today* to serve as eco-examples for the nation by living ecologically pure for a one month period. Chosen from a field of 700 across the nation, the Wiggs agreed to follow earth saving measures in their household and received advice from the environmental groups EarthWorks Group and the Environmental Defense Fund.

The Wiggs' embarked on a month long journey of education and action. Their experiences include recycling, cutting down on the use of paper and plastic, conserving water and electricity, and choosing environmentally "safe" products.

Each family member participated and had their own special assignment. Barbara Wigg, the mother, took charge of household cleaners and food-related items. Kent Wigg, the father, handled energy and water conservation and toxic chemicals. Gavin, 14, and Kyle, 11, were designed as the "Waterboy" and the "Crusher." Gavin installed water saving devices and Kyle crushed cans and plastic bottles for future recycling. Dana, 9, and the youngest ecofamily member, earned the nickname "Newspaper Ninja" by collecting and bundling the newspapers.

The Wiggs summed up their experiences knowing "it's made a difference. . . . We'll do the best we can, taking the steps we need to take as a family."

USA Today highlighted the "grand experiment" in their special Earth Day supplement.

goes toward heating and cooling our homes. We can cut that number in half through more efficient insulation and weatherproofing.

WHAT CAN I DO?

You can make a difference right now by understanding this simple fact: We can all live more efficiently *without* sacrificing our standard of living.

There are many things you can do both inside and outside the home to conserve, without changing your lifestyle. Osage, a town of some 3,600 people in Iowa, saved an estimated $1.2 million in energy costs in 1988 in a model conservation program. They not only saved money but they also contributed to saving the environment!

There is no reason why other communities cannot follow the example of Osage. The important thing to remember is that you can make a significant difference now!

Getting Started First, you need to know two things: How much energy and water are you using and how much money does this usage cost you?

▶ **Amount of usage.** Your current bill will show you the amount of usage for the past month and will provide a daily average for the current year compared to last year. Water is recorded in increments of 100 cubic feet (there are 748 gallons per 100 cubic feet). For example, last month you may have used 1,000 cubic feet, or 7,480 gallons of water, which averages about 250 gallons per day.

Energy is based on kilowatt-hour usage; 500 kwh last month equates to almost 17 kwh per day.

▶ **Cost of usage.** How much does this usage cost you? Utility prices vary from time to time, so each bill may differ in price although usage may be similar. Nonetheless, it is important to track your utility bill because you will

Did you know? ----------

▶ If every gas-heated home were properly caulked and weatherstripped, the Department of Energy claims that we would save enough natural gas each year to heat about 4 million homes.

▶ The average American home uses approximately 300 gallons of water each day. Almost a quarter of it is flushed down the toilet!

Reprinted with permission from the White House Office of National Service.

❂ PAMELA CALHOUN ❂

Sparks, NV
DAILY POINT OF LIGHT RECIPIENT: FEBRUARY 10, 1990

Pamela Calhoun created the "Energy Awareness in the Northern Nevada Community" initiative to inform the public about energy and its conservation.

In 1986, after taking a class on energy resources, Ms. Calhoun asked her fifth graders to think of ways to educate the community on energy sources and the need to conserve. They created an assignment book, which was used by 650 students the next year. For the last four years, Ms. Calhoun has implemented various projects to create public awareness about energy conservation issues. She also uses energy issues to teach reading, writing, science, and math.

·········· Did you know?

▶ Due to inefficient energy policies Americans consume more than twice as much fuel as is needed to maintain their present standard of living.

▶ Less than 5 percent of the world lives in the United States, yet as a country we consume more than 16 percent of the world's energy production.

notice a gradual difference in savings as you conserve. You can also look back in your records and take an average of the past year to get a better picture. Keep track of water and energy separately.

Now you have a point of reference to see how much money you can save through simple conservation measures. If you spend money on energy and water-saving devices, you will have to factor in that amount. Over time, any extra money spent to conserve will produce results.

HOW TO SAVE

It is easy to begin conserving energy and water when you understand that the bulk of home energy usage goes toward three uses: heating and cooling, lighting, and appliances. Most of your water is consumed through outdoor use, the toilet and bath, and the laundry and kitchen.

Each of these categories is highlighted in a later section. You can obtain detailed information concerning all types of home energy and water conservation from your local utility or from a number of publications. Observe how you operate your home in each of these areas and then decide how you can become more efficient in your energy and water usage.

HOME ENERGY CONSERVATION

■ ■ ■

HEATING AND COOLING

About one-half of our home energy costs goes toward the heating and cooling of our houses (this depends obviously on where you live). Two ways to cut back in this area are better home insulation and more efficient thermostat settings.

▶ **Heat and cool your house, not your neighborhood.** Each year the amount of energy that leaks through American windows equals the amount of oil that flows through the Alaskan pipeline. Although American houses are being built more efficiently, extra insulation, caulking, and weatherstripping may be necessary.

▶ **Proper thermostat settings.** Proper control of your home furnace and air-conditioner temperature settings is very important to conserving energy. Most energy authorities suggest setting your daytime heating at 68°F and reducing it to between 60 and 65°F at night.

When your air-conditioner is on, set the thermostat at 78°F or higher, and turn it off when you leave the house. Each 1 degree higher setting on your air-conditioner thermostat will save 3 percent on your energy bill.

These simple actions not only save you money, they also help conserve our natural resources.

LIGHTING

Lighting accounts for more than 16 percent of the average electric bill. Using lights only when necessary and buying energy-efficient bulbs will help a lot.

▶ **Turn off the lights!** One of the easiest ways to conserve energy is to make sure you turn off lights in any room that is not being used, and use outdoor lights only when necessary. Dimmers and fluorescent lighting can also help conserve.

▶ **Energy-efficient bulbs.** Energy-efficient light bulbs, such as compact fluorescent bulbs, do the same job as regular light bulbs with a lot less energy.

Compact fluorescent bulbs are available at many stores, including supermarkets, building supply stores, and retailers. Consult the Yellow Pages under "Lighting" and look for those manufactured by GE, Phillips, Sylvania, and Osram. Contact the Alliance to Save Energy for fluorescent light bulb information.

APPLIANCES

A large percentage of most energy bills is devoted to appliances. These costs add up during the course of a year. According to The American Council for an Energy-Efficient Economy (ACEEE), "Using appliances and heating and cooling equipment costs an average household more than $1000 per year." Correct use of appliances and use of energy-efficient appliances will reduce that bill *and* help the environment.

▶ **Refrigerator temperature.** Proper setting of the thermostat will help conserve energy. Recommended temperature is 38°F

Did you know? ....

▶ If every U.S. home that uses oil heat decreased its average heating temperatures by 6 degrees, we would save the equivalent of 570,000 barrels of oil per day.

▶ Raising the air conditioning temperature by 6 degrees would save 190,000 barrels of oil every day.

▶ Compact fluorescent bulbs are four times more energy efficient as incandescent bulbs, and cut electrical consumption by as much as 6 percent.

▶ If 100 million households converted to compact fluorescent lighting, carbon dioxide emissions would be reduced by 30 million tons each year.

·········· Did you know?

▶ 10 pounds of carbon dioxide are produced by the energy needed to run one load of clothes in the dryer.

▶ Just one day's energy usage of the refrigerator emits more than 12 pounds of carbon dioxide into the air.

to 40°F, and 5°F for the freezer. A 5°F colder setting will increase electrical consumption by 30 percent.

▶ **Turn them off!** Remember to turn off appliances and other electrical gadgets when not in use. In Los Angeles, TV sets account for 11 percent of the residential electrical energy use.

▶ **Energy-efficient appliances.** When you buy appliances, consider their energy efficiency. You might be surprised to know how much energy your dryer or refrigerator uses each day and how that consumption affects the environment.

You can help conserve this energy by purchasing an energy-efficient appliance. An energy-saving model will do the same job or better than others while using less energy.

CONSIDER ENERGY-EFFICIENT HOME APPLIANCES*

·····································

Furnace
Freezer
Refrigerator
Dishwasher
Water heater
Washer and Dryer
Heat & Air-Conditioning System

ACEEE publishes a guide, *The Most Energy-Efficient Appliances,* which lists the most energy-efficient residential appliances in the United States. Write to them for a copy and remember to consider energy efficiency when you buy home appliances. (Address and phone number are listed at the end of this section.)

HOME WATER CONSERVATION

■ ■ ■

EXTERIOR USE

More than half of the average water bill is devoted to exterior use—landscape irrigation, car wash, pool, and such. Care and common sense can help reduce wasted water. Here are some tips:

▶ **Minimize hosing.** Your garden hose can pour out 600 gallons or more in only a few hours. Don't let the sprinkler run all day or leave the hose unattended. Use a broom instead of a hose to clean up debris, dirt, and leaves. Ten minutes with a hose uses 150 gallons of water.

*Manufacturers must include labels that show the estimated annual operating costs of these models.

▶ **Lawn care.** Don't overwater your lawn. If you water every day, do it every other day instead. To determine your lawn-watering needs, step on the grass. If it rebounds, wait another day.

▶ **Creative landscaping.** Another way to conserve outdoor water is to landscape creatively. Xeriscaping is an approach to landscaping that can save as much as 80 percent of your exterior water usage; this method utilizes plants that need less water and creates an efficient watering system.

Call your local water company for more information about water-saving landscaping ideas.

INTERIOR USE

Toilet and bath More than three-quarters of our indoor water consumption is used in the bathroom, mostly for flushing toilets and for showers and baths.

▶ **Don't flush water away.** As much as 25 percent of all domestic water use goes down the toilet, most of it unnecessarily.

Normal toilets in the United States flush between 3.5 and 7 gallons of water. New low-flush toilets do the same job using only 1.5 gallons. Low-flush toilets will save about 5,000 gallons of water a year for a family of two adults.

A cheaper alternative would be to install water-saving devices into your existing toilet. These devices are easy to install and can save between 2.5 and 5 gallons per flush. If you place a plastic jug filled with a gallon of water into your toilet storage tank, you can save as much as 5,000 gallons a year!

▶ **Shower with a friend!** Ten minutes in the shower uses about 40 gallons of water, whereas each bath takes about 20 gallons. Try to take fewer baths and shorter showers. Low-flush shower heads reduce water flow by as much as 7 gallons per minute. They are easy to install and cost about $10.00.

Did you know? ··········

▶ Refrigerators are one of the greatest energy users in your house. In Los Angeles, refrigerators and freezers account for about 30 percent of the average residential energy bill.

▶ If all the households in the United States had energy-efficient refrigerators, the electricity savings would eliminate the need for about 12 large power plants.

Metropolitan District of Southern California.

WATER USED FOR COMMON ACTIVITIES
···

Brushing teeth	3 gallons/day
Shower	40 gallons/10 minutes
Bath	20 gallons
Toilet	28 gallons/day/person
Clothes washer	45 gallons/load
Cooking	5 gallons/day
Dishwasher	15 gallons/load
Landscape	350 gallons/day
Hosing driveway	150 gallons
Car Washing	150 gallons

▶ **Three gallons to brush your teeth?** You do not need to keep the faucet open while you shave and brush your teeth. Turn it on only when necessary. This practice can save 5 to 10 gallons a day.

Laundry and kitchen Approximately 12 percent of your water is used in the laundry and kitchen.

▶ **Laundry.** You can save water in the laundry by setting water levels to match your load and by washing full loads of clothing whenever possible.

▶ **Kitchen.** Scrape your plates first before rinsing, and try not to let the water run while you rinse dishes.

Organizations and Resources

The Alliance to SaveEnergy
202-857-0666
A nonprofit coalition of business, government, and consumer leaders dedicated to increasing the efficiency of energy use. The Alliance conducts research, pilot projects, and educational programs and offers many publications available to the public. Ask about their energy conservation brochure.

American Council for an Energy-Efficient Economy (ACEEE)
202-429-8873
A nonprofit organization that publishes information on the use of energy-conserving technologies and practices. Ask for two guides that discuss the purchase and use of energy-efficient home appliances: "Saving Energy and Money with Home Appliances" ($2.00) and "The Most Energy Efficient Appliances" ($2.00).

Conservation and Renewable Energy Inquiry and Referral Service (CAREIRS)
800-523-2929/800-233-3071 (AL & HA)
Operated by Advanced Sciences, Inc., through the U.S. Department of Energy CAREIRS provides basic information on energy conservation and the full spectrum of renewable energy technologies—solar, wind, hydroelectric, photovoltaics, geothermal, and bioconversion.

National Wildlife Foundation
202-797-6800
Ask for "A Citizen's Guide to Community Water Conservation."

Renew America
202-232-2252
An education and networking forum dedicated to the efficient use of all natural resources. Publishes an annual *State of the States* report, which provides an overview of developments in environmental protection in each state.

Rocky Mountain Institute
303-927-3128
A research organization dedicated to developing conservation programs, ranging from agricultural policy to economic renewal. Offers information on super-insulated homes, water conservation, and resource-efficient living. For a booklet on home energy conservation order Practical Home Energy Savings ($5.00).

OTHER COMMITTED ORGANIZATIONS

American Solar Energy Society
303-443-3130

National Center for Appropriate Technology (NATAS)
800-428-2525

National Energy Information Center/ Energy Information Administration
202-586-8800

Safe Energy Communication Council
202-483-8491

RUNNING OUT OF ROOM

■ ■ ■

Our cities are confronted with a garbage crisis. In essence, we are running out of space in which to put our refuse, and many current disposal methods have endangered the environment.

This problem is coming to a head very quickly. In the summer of 1987, a barge containing garbage from the town of Islip, New York, was refused entry by six states and three nations. Philadelphia, a city of 6 million, has run out of landfill space and is shipping its refuse as far away as Virginia and Ohio.

Did you know? ··········

The U.S. Conference of Mayors reports that more than half of the nation's cities have less than a decade of capacity remaining in existing landfills.

WHY ARE WE RUNNING OUT OF ROOM?

We live in a disposable society—out of sight, out of mind. The problem is that we consume and discard more and more each year, from 2.5 pounds a day per person in 1960 to more than 3.5 pounds today. With more than 250 million people in this country, these numbers add up.

Reprinted with special permission of North American Syndicate, Inc.

·········· Did you know?

▶ The Beverage marketing Association reports that in 1989 approximately 65.9 billion soft drink bottles and cans were sold in the United States.

▶ According to *Omni* magazine, Americans use an average 2.5 million plastic beverage bottles each hour and throw away enough glass every two weeks to fill the World Trade Center's 1,377-foot-tall twin towers.

▶ Citizens for a Better Environment reports that Los Angeles residents haul 14 million tons of trash each year to area landfills; enough to fill Dodger Stadium every 9 days!

Reprinted with permission from the White House Office of National Service.

Americans dump 90 percent of their garbage in landfills. Excessive dumping creates more than a problem of space. Hazardous household items, such as mercury from batteries and pesticides, leak into the soil and pollute our groundwater. Seattle had to close two landfills after methane gas seeped into surrounding homes.

We can no longer expect this problem to just disappear. A 1988 EPA study found that the United States produces more than 150 million tons of municipal solid waste each year—or 1,277 pounds per year for every citizen. By the year 2000, the amount of waste is expected to grow by 30 percent! Strong action must be taken to solve this serious refuse disposal dilemma.

ONE SOLUTION: RECYCLE!

Recycling is one of the best solutions to the growing problem of solid-waste management. According to the California Waste Management Board, "recycling is the process of collecting and remanufacturing used products into new products instead of throwing them away as garbage."

And recycling works! Japan recycles 95 percent of its bottles, 75 percent of its aluminum cans, and 50 percent of many other products. As a result of its efforts, Japan is one-eighth as dependent on landfills as the United States.

The recycling process involves three phases: recovery, reprocess, and resale.

RECOVERY PROGRAMS

Recovery programs deal with collecting recyclable materials. The California Waste Management Board reports that the three most common types of recycling recovery programs are curbside pickup, drop-off, and buy-back.

▶ **Curbside pickup.** Residents sort recyclable items and place them in bins at their curb. A private or municipal group will collect them on a specific day of the week.

✪ PAGE ATTACKS TRASH ✪

Page, AZ
DAILY POINT OF LIGHT RECIPIENT: MARCH 8, 1990

The residents of Page take exceptional pride in their community, which hosts 2 to 3 million tourists each year.

Page Attacks Trash helps keep the community litter-free. Since its founding in 1983, this effort has grown to include the entire city of Page, Navajo lands, and the Glen Canyon National Recreation area. On the third Saturday of each May, organizations, scouts, local and state officials, and community members lend a helping hand. Degradable plastic garbage bags are used to collect the waste, of which more than 140 tons was discarded in 1989.

▶ **Drop-off.** Consumers bring their recyclable items to a central drop-off area. A municipal or private group will then take care of them.

▶ **Buy-back.** Similar to the Drop-Off program, except the consumer is paid for recyclable materials.

Your community may have all three types of recovery programs—or they may have none. Check with your local or state governments to find out about your options.

THE RECYCLING PROCESS

Once products are collected and sorted they are taken to a recycling plant, where they are converted into a product that can be utilized again. Glass is cleaned and either remolded or marketed in its original form. Plastic is melted and formed into another product. Paper is reprocessed into new sheets.

The recycling process begins with every individual. You must separate your trash and in order to start the recycling process. Some of the materials that can be recycled include:

▶ Paper (newsprint, computer cards, white office paper, etc.)
▶ Plastics
▶ Tires

▶ Motor oil
▶ Scrap metal (e.g., aluminum, copper, and tin)
▶ Glass
▶ Corrugated cardboard

USING IT AGAIN

Recycled materials are fashioned into a myriad of products, the most innovative being plastic resins. The Council for Solid Waste Solutions, which is a coalition of oil, chemical, plastic, and paper companies, initiates joint research designed to find long-term solutions to the nation's solid waste problem as it pertains to plastic. For example, plastic beverage containers and liquid detergent bottles become fence posts, carpet backing, and drainage pipes. Other products made from recycled plastic include fiberfill stuffing for coats and sleeping bags, bathtubs, and boat hulls.

HOW RECYCLING HELPS

Since more than 30 percent of our "garbage" is recyclable, successful programs will help alleviate the landfill problem

Did you know? ▪▪▪▪▪▪▪▪▪▪▪▪

Californians discard 202 million pounds of garbage every day, yet nearly 13 million tons, or 34 percent of the garbage generated in California, is recyclable.

In the time it takes to read this, more than a million pounds of materials that could have been recycled will be thrown away all over California.

—Californians Against Waste (CAW) newsletter

.... **Did you know?**

► For each ton of paper recycled, 3,700 pounds of lumber and 24,000 gallons of water are saved. Recycling a single press run of a Sunday *New York Times* could save 75,000 trees.

► If the United States recycled half of the newspapers it discards every year, 6 million tons of waste would never reach landfills, alleviating the need for 3,200 garbage trucks that normally haul trash to the dump each day.

► Each aluminum can recycled saves the energy equivalent of a half can of gasoline.

and ease the strain on the environment. Recycling a product requires less energy and utilizes fewer natural resources than making it from scratch. Therefore, the recycling process conserves energy and water, reduces water and air pollution, and saves valuable trees and minerals.

As Cynthia Pollock-Shea, of the World Resources Institute, explains in a July 1988 *USA Today Magazine,* "Lower taxes, energy savings, and a cleaner environment are the real bottom lines. As landfill costs continue to rise due to space constraints and stricter environmental regulations, and as the high capital costs of incinerators and their pollution control technologies sap city budgets, the appeal of recycling will inevitably grow."

Indeed, evidence supports an increasing demand to recycle across the country. Consumers, business leaders, and politicians all realize the important role recycling can play in protecting and cleaning up the environment.

WHAT IS BEING DONE?
....

Public Sector

► In 1989, more than 800 pieces of recycling legislation were introduced creating 134 new laws in 38 states. For example:
> ► In July 1989, New York City began a mandatory program aimed at recycling 25 percent of the city's waste during the next five years.
> ► A California recycling law requires communities to reduce their trash volume by 25% by 1995 and 50% by the year 2000.
> ► More than 1,500 communities have implemented curbside recycling.

► The Environmental Protection Agency reports a 30 percent increase in the amount of trash being recycled from 1986 to 1990.

► Los Angeles is considering a plan which limits the amount of trash a household can discard. Households disposing of more than the allotted amount will be charged. (A similar plan in Seattle helped reduce trash volume by 22% in the first year.)

118

▶ Seattle has one of the most aggressive and successful recycling programs in the country. Sixteen different recycling systems collect and recycle 34 percent of the city's trash.

Private Sector

▶ Between 1991 and 1996 more than $2 billion will be spent in the United States for recycling equipment to meet the demand for recycled products.

▶ McDonald's McRecycle USA plans to buy $100 million worth of recycled products to build and/or remodel its restaurants. They also spend $60 million on recycled paper and have implemented trash separation programs in many of their restaurants. McDonald's now saves 68 million pounds of packaging a year by shipping and storing soft-drink syrups in tanks rather than in cardboard containers. And by phasing out polystyrene foam containers they are dramatically reducing their trash volume.

▶ In the first half of 1989, Americans recycled 56 percent of all aluminum beverage cans produced in the United States. That equates to 45 billion cans weighing 1.6 billion pounds. Alcoa estimates that Americans earned more than $900 million by recycling aluminum cans.

WHAT CAN I DO?

Helping to solve the garbage glut by recycling is something every person can do each day without expending a lot of money or effort. Recycling offers the opportunity to decrease waste-disposal needs and costs while helping to combat global environmental problems. As the Environmental Defense Fund cleverly points out, "If you're not recycling you're throwing it all away."

▶ Recycle everything you can at home. Encourage your friends and neighbors to do so as well. The average family generates 2000 pounds of trash a year. Recycling could keep at least 400 pounds of this trash out of the landfills.

Did you know?

▶ Curbside recycling in California alone would save 20,000 barrels of oil daily. If all garbage in America were recycled, we could save as much as 1 million or more barrels of imported oil a day, cutting the trade deficit by at least $7 billion a year.

▶ Recycling paper causes 50 percent less water pollution than making new paper. Air emissions are slashed 95 percent when aluminum is recycled; 80 percent when steel is recycled.

▶ If 50 percent of the trash in New York City (25,000 tons each day) were recycled, taxpayers would save $456 million annually.

★ ☆ **THE STARS ARE SHINING** ☆ ★

THE ENVIRONMENT'S TOP GUN

Actor Tom Cruise sat in the pilot's seat as a key speaker for the twentieth Earth Day celebration.

Addressing a crowd of 125,000, Cruise explained that "If we make the environment sick, it's going to make us sick." The actor asked the crowd "Do you recycle? If not, start. Have you planted a tree? Do it. You can change things. We must change things."

·········· Did you know?

▶ **75,000** trees are used to make the one Sunday's *New York Times* newspaper. In *Hints for a Healthy Planet,* (New York: *Perigee Books,* 1990), Heloise explains that recycling a four-foot stack of newspapers will save a 35- to 40-foot tree.

▶ According to the Environmental Defense Fund we could rebuild our entire commercial air fleet with the aluminum cans we throw away every three months.

▶ **Learn about home composting.** Twenty percent of our trash is made up of yard wastes, yet 100 percent of these lawn clippings, soil, and leaves can be composted. Why send it to a landfill in a plastic bag when it can be put to use? Composting can turn your kitchen and yard "garbage" into nutrient-rich soil for your lawn and garden.

▶ **Encourage recycling in your community and your workplace.** Participate in or start groups that recycle in your community and office.

▶ **Contact your local officials and ask what they are doing about recycling.** Your state or municipality has an agency that deals with recycling, waste reduction, and other resource recovery activities. Your state and local representatives can direct you to the proper sources.

▶ **Start or invest in a private recycling center.** This can be a very profitable and rewarding business. To learn more, consult:

> ▶ "How to Start a Recycling Center" by the California Solid Waste Management Board.
> ▶ *How to Start a Neighborhood Recycling Center,* c/o the Ecology Center Bookstore, 2701 College Ave., Berkeley, CA 94705.

▶ **Show your support by voting for recycling bills.**
Support the Environmental Defense Fund's proposals to:

> ▶ Require a federal government ban on the use of certain toxic substances under terms of the Toxic Substances Control Act.
> ▶ A sales or user tax based on the amount of packaging, or a national sales tax on such disposable products as razors, plates, and diapers.

▶ **Give it away—don't throw it away.** Donate unwanted clothes, furniture, dishes and other items to a thrift organization instead of the dump. You will be helping others as well as the environment.

▶ **Buy recycled items.** One example of an educational effort directed at consumers is the Environment Shopping Campaign initiated in 1987 by the Pennsylvania Resources Council (PRC). PRC compiled a list of some 400 items packaged in recycled material and asked that stores mark these products with a recycling logo. The group then urged shoppers to take certain steps when shopping, including:

▶ Make a list of what is recyclable before going to the market.

▶ Buy products packaged in easily recyclable materials, such as glass, paper, and aluminum.

▶ Avoid disposable and nonrecyclable products, such as lighters, razors, and Styrofoam cups.

▶ Reuse nonrecyclable containers.

▶ Write to manufacturers. PRC reports that shoppers were very interested in "voting their dollars" for better packaging.

For more information contact the Pennsylvania Resources Council and ask for a copy of "Become an Environmental Shopper."

Did you know? ....

▶ American workplaces discard enough paper each year to build a 12-foot-high wall stretching from Los Angeles to New York.

RECYCLED AND RECYCLABLE PRODUCTS—HOW TO TELL

The Paper Recycling Committee of the American Paper Institute designed two symbols to identify recycled and recyclable paper and paperboard products.

Recycled Use the recycled symbol to identify:

▶ packages and other products made entirely or predominantly from recycled paper fibers

▶ newspapers or other publications printed on recycled paper

▶ the concept of recycling in publications, advertisements, or promotional material

▶ organizations engaged in paper recycling

Recyclable Use the recyclable symbol to identify:

▶ paper and paperboard products made from fibers which, after use, are suitable for recycling

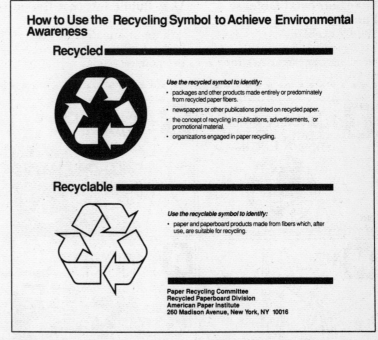

How to Use the Recycling Symbol to Achieve Environmental Awareness

Recycled

Use the recycled symbol to identify:
• packages and other products made entirely or predominately from recycled paper fibers.
• newspapers or other publications printed on recycled paper.
• the concept of recycling in publications, advertisements, or promotional material.
• organizations engaged in paper recycling.

Recyclable

Use the recyclable symbol to identify:
• paper and paperboard products made from fibers which, after use, are suitable for recycling.

Paper Recycling Committee
Recycled Paperboard Division
American Paper Institute
260 Madison Avenue, New York, NY 10016

Printed with permission from the American Paper Institute.

Organizations and Resources

American Paper Institute
212-340-0600
Provides general information about recycling in your office and community.

Citizen's Clearinghouse for Hazardous Wastes
703-276-7070
Offers recycling research and ideas for individuals and groups interested in working with local legislators.

Environmental Action Foundation
202-745-4870
Provides alternatives to harmful, less-efficient waste management by promoting source reduction, reuse, recycling, and composting.

Environmental Defense Fund
800-CALL-EDF
EDF sponsors a national recycling campaign. Ask for their special brochure on recycling.

The Institute for Local Self Reliance (ILSR)
202-232-4108
Helps municipalities and community groups develop more efficient waste management.

National Recycling Coalition
202-625-6406
A coalition of recycling companies and organizations.

Pennsylvania Resources Council (PRC)
215-565-9131/800-GO TO PRC
Ask for "Become an Environmental Shopper."

U.S. Public Interest Group
202-546-9707
Ask for information on the garbage crisis and ways to promote recycling.

Worldwatch Institute
202-452-1999
Ask for a copy of "Materials Recycling: The Virtue of Necessity," Worldwatch Paper #56.

OTHER COMMITTED ORGANIZATIONS

Center for Marine Conservation
202-429-5609

INFORM
212-689-4040

National Soft Drink Association
202-463-6771

U.S. Conference of Mayors—National Resource Recovery Association
202-293-7330

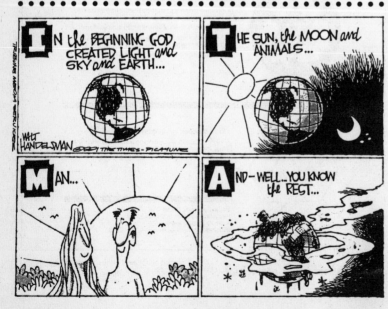

IN the BEGINNING GOD CREATED LIGHT and SKY and EARTH...

THE SUN, the MOON and ANIMALS...

MAN...

AND—WELL...YOU KNOW the REST...

WALT HANDELSMAN ©1991 THE TIMES-PICAYUNE

Matt Handlesman. Reprinted with special permission of Tribune Media Services, Inc.

THE PROBLEM WITH PLASTIC
■ ■ ■

PLASTICS, PLASTICS, EVERYWHERE . . .

Today, plastics are found virtually everywhere, from nylon stockings and diapers to car bumpers and telephones. If you look around your home and office, it would be difficult to find many products that do not contain some element of plastic. Your toaster oven, microwave, television, and computer all have plastic parts and fittings. Your hamburger may not taste like plastic, but it might have been handed to you in a Styrofoam container. Your groceries may not be plastic, but it is likely that they are bagged in it.

EXCESS PACKAGING

Trying to avoid plastic is more difficult than you might imagine. Even if you find a nonplastic product, chances are that it was packaged in plastic.

Ironically, although plastic is designed to last for many years, a third of the plastics produced in the United States are used in items with a lifespan of less than one year. Our "throwaway" society does just that, and the repercussions will be felt for decades to come.

PLASTICS FOREVER

Why should we worry about the amount of plastic we use and discard? Well, for one thing, plastic products will be around for a long time, and the production and disposal of plastics are harmful to the environment.

Plastics and plastic packaging are nondegradable and therefore remain in the environment for centuries, whether in landfills as solid waste or on the land and in the ocean as litter. Plastics packaging is also less recyclable than many other standard packaging materials, including paper, glass, and metals. Finally, the production of plastic packaging releases significant levels of toxic pollutants into the atmo-

Did you know? ■■■■■■■■■■■

According to the Environmental Action Foundation:

▶ In 1985, 48 billion pounds of plastic resins were used to produce plastic products in America. The plastics industry estimates that by the year 2000, that number will increase by 36 percent to an incredible 76 billion pounds.

▶ Plastic packaging represents one of the major uses of the plastic resin.

▶ More than 12 billion pounds are now used for packaging in the United States.

▶ By the year 2000 the volume of plastics packaging will almost double.

sphere and adds to the nation's growing hazardous waste burden.

The United States is rapidly running out of landfill space. And the landfills themselves pollute the surrounding environments, including underground water aquifers. Therefore, it is imperative to find solutions to control the tremendous supply of plastic produced each year.

"DEGRADABLE" PLASTICS

Much attention has been focused on degradable plastics. Many corporations market plastic products that are degradable, including diapers and plastic bags. Certain processes accelerate the decomposition of plastics, the most common being photodegration and biodegration. Photodegration occurs from exposure to ultraviolet light and biodegration results when microorganisms break down the plastics. Some processes work better than others; however all require special conditions in order for the decomposition process to occur. For instance, certain processes require sunlight, air, soil, and/ or water. However, if an item is buried 30 feet down in a landfill, does it really matter how degradable it is? Researchers have found undecomposed foodstuffs (hot dogs, corn on the cob), clothing, and uncoated paper products in landfills that are years old. If these items do not break down, then plastic items probably have even less chance.

This does not mean that we should avoid degradable plastic products or curtail research into that area. Rather, it means that we should not assume that degradability is the answer to our plastic garbage problem. The primary solutions to the challenge of plastics in our trash still must be source reduction and recycling.

▶ For more information about degradable plastics consult *Wrapped in Plastics* by the Environmental Action Foundation; read the *"Degradable" Plastics Report* published by the Environmental Defense Fund and the Environmental Action Foundation; contact Greenpeace for their research on degradable plastics.

PLASTICS IN THE OCEAN

Plastic litter in the oceans has become a very serious problem. Not only does this litter make the ocean and shorelines unsightly, plastic dumped in the water endangers sea life as well. According to David Laist of the Marine Mammal Commission in Washington, DC, "Plastics may be as great a source of mortality among marine mammals as oil spill, heavy metals, or other toxic materials."[*]

Birds, turtles, sea lions, and seals mistake floating plastic as food. They often choke or become entangled in the debris.

WHAT IS BEING DONE?

Public Sector

▶ Minneapolis and St. Paul have banned all plastic food packaging that cannot degrade or be recycled. Six states and 31 municipalities restrict polystyrene packaging. Nebraska is planning to ban most disposable diapers by 1993. As of 1990, over 3.5 million households in more than 400 communities across the country recycled plastic items.

▶ Effective December 31, 1988, a worldwide ban was placed on the disposal of plastic debris by ships of all types. The marine Plastic Pollution Research and Control Act of 1987 (MPPRCA) and Annex V of MARPOL prohibit dumping of plastics and restrict the dumping of other garbage at sea.

Private Sector

▶ Kodak plans to offer recycling programs for empty plastic

Did you know? ⬤⬤⬤⬤⬤⬤⬤⬤⬤⬤

EACH YEAR AMERICANS THROW AWAY

2 billion razors
220 million tires
30 billion tin cans
2.5 billion batteries
50 million tons of paper
80 million auto batteries
25 billion Styrofoam cups
18 billion disposable diapers
35 billion tons of yard waste

The Green Consumer, J. Elkington, J. Hailes, & J. Makower (New York: Penguin Books, 1990).

BIG MACS TO USE PAPER INSTEAD OF FOAM

In a major move, McDonald's announced that they will no longer wrap their food in polystyrene foam. The "clamshell" packaging will now be replaced by paper instead.

The world leader in fast-food restaurants teamed up with the Environmental Defense Fund to come up with the more environmentally sound solution. McDonald's serves 22 million meals a day in more than 11,000 locations throughout the world. Each restaurant uses an average of 22 pounds of the polystyrene each day!

Polystyrene is believed to emit dangerous chemicals during production and in landfills. The move may reduce McDonald's trash volume by as much as 90 percent.

[*]Jeanne Wirka, "Wrapped in Plastics," Environmental Action Foundation.

·········· Did you know?

▶ On average, each American uses and discards 60 pounds of plastic packaging a year. As plastic continues to replace glass and metals, this number will only increase. In fact, packaging is the fastest-growing segment of the plastics industry.

▶ Americans currently throw away 18 billion disposable diapers per year—equivalent to filling a garbage barge every 6 hours, accounting for up to 2 percent of garbage in landfills and taking hundreds of years to decompose. Disposables account for about 80 percent to 85 percent of the $3 billion annual diaper market.

film containers. Kodak produces 600 million containers a year, enough to generate 7.5 million pounds of recycled plastic.

▶ Procter and Gamble is working to recycle disposable diapers into other products. In one program, they recycled diapers collected from 1,000 Seattle families into plastic for flowerpots and park benches. They also plan to use recycled plastic for their liquid detergent and cleaner containers.

▶ In the New York Metropolitan area, a group of fast-food restaurants sends their garbage to recycling centers where it is separated and processed. The recycled polystyrene (plastic) is then delivered to facilities where it is made into such materials as building insulation and foundation protection board.

▶ Massachusetts school students recycle their polystyrene trays by sending them to a recycling facility.

▶ Eight major plastic manufacturers have formed the National Polystyrene Recycling Company (NPRC) with a goal to recycle 25 percent of all disposable polystyrene products by 1995.

▶ In 1988, 9,000 pounds of plastic "lumber" made from used polystyrene foam coffee cups, food containers, and other plastics were used to construct park benches, wildlife signs, wetland walkways, and other items at the John Innskeep Environmental Learning Center in Portland, Oregon.

▶ Du Pont Canada's recyclable plastic milk containers are used by over 1 million schoolchildren in the United States, in place of the standard paperboard milk cartons.

WHAT CAN I DO?
·····································

▶ **Become an environmental shopper.** You can easily reduce your plastic consumption and recycle the plastics you do use. A simple exercise is to keep track of the plastic, disposable and nondisposable, that you use in one week. You will be astounded at the amount, and you will realize the extent of your contribution to a growing problem.

The cloth diaper can be laundered and reused an average of 150 times as opposed to being discarded after one use. (On the other hand, critics argue that cloth diapers use 3 times as much energy to produce and add 10 times as much pollutants to the water system. The debate continues.)

▶ **Ask for paper instead of plastic.** Tell your grocery store managers that you prefer paper to plastic. And ask them to recycle their bags. In southern California, Thrifty's, Vons, and Lucky Supermarkets offer programs to recycle plastic shopping bags, and Mrs. Gooch's grocers recycle their paper bags. Shoppers simply bring their plastic and paper shopping bags back to the stores and the grocers will recycle them into new bags. Some supermarkets encourage shoppers to bring in their own bags and give a refund of several cents for each bag used. Better yet, buy a canvas shopping bag and bring it with you to the grocery store.

Some companies that make canvas shopping bags include The Coalition for Recycled Waste, Treesavers of Solanda Beach, CA, Save a Tree Co. of Berkeley, CA, and CO-OP America.

▶ **Use environmentally conscious plastic products.** Many degradable products are now available on the market. These include six-pack loop carriers, trash bags, film, shopping bags, food wraps, bottles, and diapers. The Environmental Action Foundation lists some of these manufacturers in its report entitled *Wrapped in Plastics*.

▶ **Participate in plastics education campaigns.** The goal of educational campaigns is to raise awareness of the connection between products we use and the waste they create. Ultimately, consumers and producers are encouraged to change their shopping and production habits in order to reduce waste.

Some educational programs are directed toward consumers. Posters and signs on supermarkets shelves urging shoppers to avoid excessive or nonrecyclable packaging, labels indicating recyclability, pro–paper bag rallies, and local media campaigns have all been tried at the local level.

Contact the Pennsylvania Resources Council for more information.

▶ **Support plastics recycling legislation.** The energy of committed individuals and groups brings about changes in legislations. For example, the Californians Against Waste Foundation (CAW), a nonprofit, research and education group, led the way for major legislative victories for recycling in California, including the California Solid Waste Recycling Act. CAW's "Throwaway Packaging Reduction and Recy-

Did you know? ▪▪▪▪▪▪▪▪▪▪

As many as 100,000 marine mammals die each year after ingesting or becoming entangled in plastic plastics debris.

DON'T TEACH YOUR TRASH TO SWIM!

Center for Marine Conservation. Marine Refuse Disposal Project, Newport, OR.

########## **Did you know?**

▶ Only 1 percent of the 9.7 million tons of plastics discarded in 1984 was recovered for recycling.

▶ Every hour, Americans use 2.5 million plastic beverage bottles.

▶ According to The Society of Plastics Industry (SPI), 125 million pounds (or about 20 percent) of PET beverage bottles are collected each year for recycling.

▶ More than 2 billion pounds of HDPE bottles were sold in 1987. Less than 2 percent is being recycled.

cling Campaign" seeks to eliminate the overuse of materials, like plastic, used in packaging and products, and requires that these materials be recyclable.

Write your own legislators and let them know what you think about recycling and support the campaigns of groups such as CAW.

▶ **Recycle your plastics!** The technology for recycling plastics is improving on a daily basis. Now many plastic products can be recycled into other items, but much more recycling needs to be done.

PET and HDPE bottles, which are used for carbonated beverages, dairy products, liquid detergents, bleach, and oil, can be reprocessed into many other products including fiber-fill stuffing, industrial strapping, fence posts, carpet backing, drainage pipes and even golf-bag liners.

For more information about recycling consult the "Running Out of Room" section.

To learn more about plastic recycling, contact one of the organizations listed below or call the EPA and ask for their free fact sheet on plastic recycling (800-424-9346; in D.C. 382-3000).

▶ **Write to the Center for Marine Conservation for information about the marine debris problem.** Here are some of their suggestions, and some from the National Marine Fisheries Service:

▶ Get involved in a coastal cleanup campaign. In 1984, Judie Nielson led a grass-roots cleanup of Oregon beaches. The idea has spread:

TRASH COLLECTED BY VOLUNTEERS DURING A 3 HOUR CLEANUP ALONG 157 MILES OF TEXAS BEACHES IN 1987

31,773	Plastic bags
30,295	Plastic bottles
15,631	Plastic six-pack rings
28,540	Plastic lids
1,914	Disposable diapers
1,040	Tampon applicators
7,460	Milk jugs

From "Plastic Reaps a Grim Harvest in the Oceans of the World," *The Smithsonian*, March 1988.

▶ Write to the Center for Marine Conservation for their "Nuts and Bolts Guide to Organizing a Beach Cleanup Campaign the Easy Way."

▶ Keep trash in the boat. Not in the water. Much of the trash collected in these beach cleanups comes from boats!

▶ Use alternative, biodegradable, or readily recyclable materials. This applies to everyone, not just boat owners.

▶ Loops from six packs can choke fish. They can also become locked around the bills of geese and other water fowl. Cut them apart and dispose of them properly.

Did you know? ·········

In 1989 more than 65,000 volunteers picked up almost 900 tons of debris along the coasts of 25 states and territories, as well as in parts of Canada and Mexico. Volunteers found more than 3 million discarded items in just 3 hours!

Center for Marine Conservation

Organizations and Resources

Citizen's Clearinghouse for Hazardous Waste, Inc.
703-276-7070
A nonprofit environmental crisis center that works mostly with grass-roots environmental organizations across the nation. Its Grassroots Movement Campaign works for waste reduction and recycling and protests toxic waste.

The Council for Solid Waste Solutions
800-2-HELP-90
A program of the The Society

of the Plastics Industry, Inc., the Council represents the 1.1 million employees of the plastics industry working to meet the solid-waste challenge.

The Environmental Action Foundation
202-745-4870
Send $10.00 for *Wrapped in Plastics,* a comprehensive report on all facets of plastic, including many ideas and sources to help reduce the plastic waste problem.

Greenpeace
202-462-1177

Ask them for information on recycling.

New York Public Interest Group
Ask for *Plagued by Packaging: A Consumer Guide to Excess Packaging and Disposable Waste Problems.* NYPIRG Publications, 9 Murray St., NY, NY 10007. $3.00

Pennsylvania Resources Council (PRC)
215-565-9131/800-GO TO PRC
Ask about their plastics education and recycling campaigns.

**Plastics Recycling
Foundation (PRF)**
202-371-5200
Started with funds from SPI,
they sponsor research into
plastics recycling.

**The Society of the Plastics
Industry Inc. (SPI)**
202-371-5200
Lobbies for the plastic industry
and provides information
about recycling.

ORGANIZATIONS TO CONTACT ABOUT THE MARINE DEBRIS

EarthTrust
808-595-6927
Concerned with the protection
of marine mammals.

**The Entanglement
Network**
202-659-9510
(c/o Defenders of Wildlife);
ask about their *Entanglement
Network Newsletter*

**The Environmental
Defense Fund (EDF)**
800-CALL-EDF
Their emergency campaign,
Save Our Marine Animals, is
helping to reverse the tide of
lethal plastics and related
threats at sea.

**Center for Marine
Conservation**
202-429-5609
Conducts research and
promotes change concerning
the entanglement of marine
animals in plastic debris. Ask
for a copy of *A Citizen's Guide
to Plastics in the Ocean*.

Clean Water Action
202-457-1286
Ask for their status report,
which monitors the deaths of
marine mammals along the
Atlantic shores.

**The Society for the
Plastics Industry**
202-371-5200
Lobbies for the plastic industry
and provides information
about recycling, degradability,
and other packaging issues.

Other Environmental Action Ideas

Environmental Job Opportunities

L.L.Bean
800-341-4341

**Western Environmental
Jobletter**
P.O. Box 269,
Westcliffe, CO 81252

Job Scan
(c/o Student Conservation
Association)
P.O. Box 550,
Charlestown, NH 03603

Protecting Our Farmers and Farmland

**American Farm Bureau
Federation**
312-399-5700

American Farmland Trust
202-659-5170

Religion and the Environment

**North American
Conference on Religion
and Ecology**
202-462-2591

**The National Council of
Eco-Justice Working
Group**
Ask for their *101 Ways to
Save the Earth: With 52
Weeks of Congregational
Activities to Save the Earth*.
$3.00

Protecting Our Wilderness

**The American Camping
Association**
317-342-8456

Boy Scouts of America
214-580-2000

Camp Fire, Inc.
816-756-1950

Girl Scouts of the USA
212-940-7500

**The Izaak Walton League
of America**
703-528-1818

National Parks Service
202-208-3100

**National Parks and
Conservation Association**
800-448-NPCA

Sierra Club
415-776-2211

Wilderness Society
202-833-2300

The U.S. Forest Service
202-447-3957

ENVIRONMENTAL ORGANIZATIONS

● ●

For a comprehensive listing of environmental organizations, refer to The National Wildlife Federation's *Conservation Directory* or *The Encyclopedia of Associations* by Gale Research.

Air Resources Information Clearinghouse (ARIC)
46 Prince St.
Rochester, NY 14607
716-271-3550

The Alliance to Save Energy
1925 K St., NW, Suite 206
Washington, DC 20006
202-857-0666

Alliance for Responsible CFC Policy
2011 Eye St., NW, Ste 500
Washington, DC 20006
202-429-1614

The American Camping Association
5000 State Rd., 67 North
Martinsville, IN
46151-7902
317-342-8456

American Conservation Association
30 Rockefeller Plaza,
Room 5510
New York, NY 10112
212-247-3700

American Council for an Energy-Efficient Economy (ACEEE)
1001 Connecticut Ave., NW
Suite 535
Washington, DC 20036
202-429-8873

American Farm Bureau Federation
225 Touhy Ave.
Park Ridge, IL 60068
312-399-5700

American Farmland Trust
1920 N St., NW, Suite 400
Washington, DC 20036
202-659-5170

American Forestry Association (AFA)
1516 P. St., NW
Washington, DC 20005
202-667-3300

American Oceans Campaign
1427 7th St., Suite 3
Santa Monica, CA 90401
213-576-6162

American Rivers, Inc.
801 Pennsylvania Ave.,
Suite 303
Washington, DC 20003
202-547-6900

Americans for the Environment
1400 16th St., NW, 2d floor
Washington, DC 20036
202-707-6665

American Solar Energy Society
2400 Central Ave., #B1
Boulder, CO 80301
303-443-3130

Americans for Safe Food
1501 16th St., NW
Washington, DC 20036
202-332-9110

The Basic Foundation
P.O. Box 47012
St. Petersburg, FL 33743
813-526-9562

The Better World Society
1100 Seventeenth St., NW,
Suite 502
Washington, DC 20036
202-331-3770

Boys Scouts of America
1325 Walnut Hill Lane
P.O. Box 152079
Irving, TX 75015
214-580-2000

Bureau of Land Management (BLM)
Washington, DC 20240
202-343-5717

Rachel Carson Council, Inc.
8940 Jones Mill Rd.
Chevy Chase, MD 20815
301-652-1877

Center for Environmental Education (CEE)
1725 DeSales St., NW, #500
Washington, DC 20036
202-429-5609

Center for Hazardous Material Research
320 William Pitt Way
Univ. of Pittsburgh Applied
    Research Center
Pittsburgh, PA 15238
412-826-5320
800-334-CHMR

Center for Marine Conservation
1725 DeSales St., NW,
Suite 500
Washington, DC 20036

Center for Plastics Recycling Research (CPRR)
Bldg. 3529, Busch Campus
Piscataway, NJ 08855
201-932-4402

Citizens for a Better Environment
942 Market St., #505
San Francisco, CA 94102
415-788-0690

Citizen's Clearinghouse for Hazardous Waste
P.O. Box 926
Arlington, VA 22216
703-276-7070

Clamshell Alliance
P.O. Box 734
Concord, NH 03301
603-224-4163

Clean Water Action
1320 18th St., NW
Washington, DC 20036
202-457-1286

Clean Water Fund
1320 18th St., NW
Washington, DC 20036
202-457-0336

Climate Change Activist Program
c/o Robert Lester, National
Audubon Society
950 Third Ave.
New York, NY 10022

Coalition for Recyclable Waste
P.O. Box 1091
Absecon, NJ 08201

Concerned Educators Allied for a Safe Environment (CEASE)
17 Gerry St.
Cambridge, MA 02138
617-864-0999

Conservation and Renewable Energy Inquiry and Referral Service (CARIERS)
Box 8900
Silver Spring, MD 20907
800-523-2929

Conservation International
1015 18th St., NW, 10th floor
Washington, DC 20036
202-429-5660

Consumer Pesticide Project of the National Toxics Campaign
37 Temple Pl., 4th floor
Boston, MA 02111
617-482-1477/
202-291-0863

Council for Solid Waste Solutions
1275 K St., NW, Suite 400
Washington, DC 20005

The Cousteau Society
930 W. 21st St.
Norfolk, VA 23517
804-627-1144

Critical Mass
215 Pennsylvania Ave., SE
Washington, DC 20003
202-546-4996

Cultural Survival Inc.
11 Divinity Ave.
Cambridge, MA 02138
617-495-2562

Defenders of Wildlife
1244 19th St., NW
Washington, DC 20036
202-659-9510

Ducks Unlimited
One Waterfall Way
Long Grove, IL 60047
708-438-4300

Earth Day 1990 Headquarters
Box AA

Stanford, CA 94305
415-321-1990

EarthTrust
2500 Pali Highway
Honolulu, HI 96817
808-595-6927

Earth First!
P.O. Box 5871
Tuscon, AZ 85703
602-622-1371

Earth Island Institute
300 Broadway, Suite 28
San Francisco, CA 94133
415-788-3666

EarthSave Foundation
P.O. Box 949
Felton, CA 95018-0949
408-423-4069

The Entanglement Network
c/o Defenders of Wildlife
1244 19th St., NW
Washington, DC 20036
202-659-9510

Environmental Protection Agency
401 M St., NW
Washington, DC 20460
202-382-2080

Environmental Action Inc./Environmental Action Foundation
1525 New Hampshire Ave., NW
Washington, DC 20036
202-745-4870

Environmental Defense Fund
257 Park Ave. South
New York, NY 10010
212-505-2100/
800-CALL EDF

Environmental Hazards Management Institute
10 Newmarket Road
P.O. Box 932
Durham, NH 03824

Environmental Opportunities
Box 969
Stowe, VT 05672
802-253-9336

Friends of the Earth
218 D St., SE
Washington, DC 20003
202-544-2600

Environmental Research Foundation
P.O. Box 3461
Princeton, NJ 08543

Fossil Fuels Policy Action Institute
Federal Square-E
P.O. Box 8558
Fredericksburg, VA 22404
703-371-0222

Forests Forever
106 W. Standley
Ukiah, CA 95482
707-462-2370

Friends of Trees
P.O. Box 40851
Portland, OR 97240
503-233-8172

Friends of the U.N.–Transmissions Project
730 Arizona Ave., Suite 329
Santa Monica, CA 90401
213-451-1810

Fund for the Environment
c/o The Environmental Federation of America
3007 Tilden St., NW, Suite 4L
Washington, DC 20008
800-673-8111

Girl Scouts of the USA
830 3rd Ave. & 51st St.
New York, NY 10022
212-940-7500

Global Tomorrow Coalition
1325 G St., NW, Suite 915
Washington, DC 20005
202-628-4016

Goddard Space Center, NASA
Office of Public Affairs
Greenbelt, MD 20771
301-286-8955

Greenhouse Crisis Foundation
1130 17th St., NW, R630
Washington, DC 20036
202-466-2823

Greenpeace
1611 Connecticut Ave., NW
Washington, DC 20009
202-462-1177

Greenpeace Action
1436 U St., NW
Washington, DC 20009
202-462-8817

Heal the Bay
1640 5th St., Suite 112
Santa Monica, CA 90404
213-394-4552

Home Hazardous Waste Project
901 S. National Ave., Box 108
Springfield, MO 65804
417-836-5777

INFORM
381 Park Ave. South
New York, NY 10016
212-689-4040

The Institute for Local Self Reliance (ILSR)
2425 18th St., NW
Washington, DC 20009
202-232-4108

Institute for Gaean Economics
64 Main St.
Montpelier, VT 05602
802-223-7943

Institute for Transportation & Development Policy (ITDP)
1787 Columbia Rd. NW 3d fl
Washington, DC 20009
202-387-1434

International Rivers Network
300 Broadway, Suite 28
San Francisco, CA 94133
415-788-7324

Keep America Beautiful, Inc.
9 W. Broad St.
Stamford, CT 06902

Izaak Walton League
1401 Wilson Blvd., Level B
Arlington, VA 22209
703-528-1818

League of Conservation Voters
2000 L St., NW, Suite 804
Washington, DC 20036
202-785-VOTE

Mothers and Others for a Livable Planet
c/o Natural Resources Defense Council
40 W. 20th St.
New York, NY 10011
212-727-4474

NASA Goddard Institute for Space Studies
2880 Broadway
New York, NY 10025

National Arbor Day Foundation
100 Arbor Ave.
Nebraska City, NE 68410
402-474-5655

National Association for Plastic Container Recovery (NAPCOR)
P.O. Box 7784
Charlotte, NC 28241
704-523-8543

National Audubon Society
950 Third Ave.
New York, NY 10022
212-832-3200

National Center for Appropriate Technology (NATAS)
P.O. Box 2525
Butte, MT 59702
800-428-2525

National Clean Air Coalition
801 Pennsylvania Ave., SE
3d floor
Washington, DC 20003
202-624-9393

National Coalition Against the Misuse of Pesticides (NCAMP)
530 7th St., SE
Washington, DC 20003
202-543-5450
202-638-5828

National Council of Churches ECO Justice Working Group
c/o United Methodist General Board of Church and Society
100 Maryland Ave., NE
Washington, DC 20002

National Energy Information Center/ Energy Information Administration
Room 1F-480, Forrestal Bldg.
1000 Independence Ave., SW
Washington, DC 20585
202-586-8800

National Fish and Wildlife Foundation
18th and C Sts., NW
Room 2626
Washington, DC 20240
202-343-1040

National Geographic Society
17th and M Sts, NW
Washington, DC 20036

National Parks and Conservation Association
1015 31st St., NW
Washington, DC 20007
800-448-NPCA

National Pesticide Telecommunications Network
Texas Tech University Health Sciences Center
Lubbock, TX 79430
800-858-PEST

National Recreation and Parks Association
3101 Park Center Drive
Alexandria, VA 22302
703-820-4940

National Recycling Coalition
110 30th St., Suite 305
Washington, DC 20007
202-625-6406

National Rifle Association
1600 Rhode Island Ave., NW
Washington, DC 20036

National Soft Drink Association
1101 16th St., NW
Washington, DC 20036
202-463-6771

National Solid Wastes Management Association
1730 Rhode Island Ave., Suite 1000
Washington, DC 20036
202-659-4613

The National Toxics Campaign
1168 Commonwealth Ave.
Boston, MA 02134
617-232-0327/
202-291-0863

National Water Center
P.O. Box 264
Eureka Springs, AR 72632
501-253-9755

National Wildlife Federation
1400 16th St., NW
Washington, DC 20036
202-797-6800

Native Forest Council
P.O. Box 2171
Eugene, OR 97402

Natural Resources Defense Council
40 W. 20th St.
New York, NY 10011
212-727-2700

The Nature Conservancy
1815 N. Lynn St.

Arlington, VA 22209
703-841-5300

North American Conference on Religion and Ecology (NACRE)
5 Thomas Circle, NW
Washington, DC 20005
202-462-2591

Pennsylvania Resources Council (PRC)
44 E. Front St.
Media, PA 19063
215-565-9131

Pesticide Action Network
965 Mission St.
San Francisco, CA 94103
415-541-9140

Philadelphia Green
c/o The Pennsylvania Horticultural Society
325 Walnut St.
Philadelphia, PA 19106
215-625-8250

Plastics Recycling Foundation (PRF)
1275 K St., NW, Suite 400
Washington, DC 20005
202-371-5200

Rails to Trails Conservancy
1701 K St., NW, Suite 304
Washington, DC 20006
202-659-8520

Rainforest Action Network
301 Broadway, Suite A
San Francisco, CA 94133
415-398-4404

Rainforest Alliance
295 Madison Ave., Suite 1804
New York, NY 10017

Renew America
1001 Connecticut Ave., NW
Room 638
Washington, DC 20036
202-232-2252

Resource Recycling Magazine
P.O. Box 10540

Portland, OR 97210
503-227-1319

Rocky Mountain Institute
1739 Snowmass Creek Rd.
Old Snowmass, CO 81654-
9199
303-927-3128

**Safe Energy
Communication Council**
1717 Massachusetts Ave.,
NW, #LL215
Washington, DC 20036
202-483-8491

Save the Earth Campaign
attn. Dick Russel
Route 2, Box 34
Frankfort, KS 66427

Save the World
P.O. Box 84366
Los Angeles, CA 90073

**Scripps Institute of
Oceanography, UCSD**
9500 Gilman Dr.
La Jolla, CA 92093-0210
619-534-6945

**Sea Shepherd
Conservation Society**
Box 7000-S
Redondo Beach, CA 90277
213-373-6979

The Sierra Club
730 Polk St.
San Francisco, CA 94109
415-776-2211

**Sierra Club Legal Defense
Fund**
2044 Filmore St.
San Francisco, CA 94115
415-567-6100

**Society for an Extended
Ethic, Inc.**
1139 Woodside Trail
Troy, MI 48098

**The Society of the Plastics
Industry, Inc. (SPI)**
1275 K St., NW
Washington, DC 20005
202-371-5200

**Survival of the Sea
Foundation**
3299 K St., NW
Washington, DC 20007
202-994-3885

TRAFFIC-USA
1601 Connecticut Ave., NW
Washington, DC 20009
202-797-7901

Trees Atlanta
96 Poplar St., NW
Atlanta, GA 30303
404-522-4097

Trees for Houston
P.O. Box 13096
Houston, TX 77219-3096
713-523-8733

Tree People
12601 Mulholland Dr.
Beverly Hills, CA 90201
818-769-2663

Trust for Public Land
82 Second St.
San Francisco, CA 94105
415-495-4014

**Union of Concerned
Scientists**
24 Church St.
Cambridge, MA 02238
617-547-5552

**United Nations
Environmental
Programme (UNEP)**
DC2-0803 United Nations
New York, NY 10017
212-963-8093

**U.S. Conference of
Mayors—National
Resource Recovery Assoc.**
16201 I St., NW
Washington, DC 20006
202-293-7330

**U.S. Department of
Energy**
Washington, DC 20585
202-586-5000

**U.S. Environmental
Protection Agency (EPA)**

(Office of Public Affairs)
Room 311 West Tower
401 M St., SW
Washington, DC 20460
202-382-4335/
202-382-4361

U.S. Forest Service
P.O. Box 96090
Washington, DC 20090-6090

U.S. Public Interest Group
215 Pennsylvania Ave., SE
Washington, DC 20003
202-546-9707

**Washington Sea Grant,
Marine Advisory Services**
3716 Brooklyn Ave., NE
Seattle, WA 98105
206-543-6600

**Water Information
Network**
P.O. Box 909
Ashland, OR 97520
800-533-6174

**Wildlife Conservation
International**
c/o New York Zoological
Society
Bronx, NY 10460
212-220-5155

The Wilderness Society
900 17th St. NW
Washington, DC 20006
202-833-2300

Windstar Foundation
2317 Snowmass Creek Rd.
Snowmass, CO 81654-9168
303-927-4777

World Wildlife Fund
1250 24th St., NW
Washington, DC 20037
202-293-4800

Worldwatch Institute
1776 Massachusetts Ave., NW
Washington, DC 20036
202-452-1999

World Resources Institute
1735 New York Ave., NW
Washington, DC 20006
202-638-6300

Zero Population Growth
1400 16th St., NW, Suite 320
Washington, DC 20036
202-332-2200

● ●

ANIMAL RIGHTS

• • •

**The greatness of a nation can be judged by
the way its animals are treated.**

• • •

—MOHANDAS GANDHI

Increasing Awareness

In 1988, the plight of three whales trapped in an Alaskan ice flow attracted worldwide attention. Everyone reached out to help—oil company officials, Eskimo whalers, concerned citizens, environmentalists, and even the Russians. The heart and soul of the world went out to these magnificent mammals.

The efforts to rescue Putu, Siku, and Kanik symbolize the concern for all animals on this planet. However, it seems that society often forgets about our creature companions. We often treat them cruelly and threaten their lives and the very existence of their species.

Fortunately, many concerned individuals and animal welfare organizations remind us of the tragedy of endangered species, the horrors of factory farming, the brutality of vivisection, and other types of animal abuse.

And many people are now listening—and acting. Some refuse to eat tuna to protest slaughter of the dolphin. Others boycott fur coats to protest the cruel treatment of fur-raised animals. Mass protests of animal experimentation and cries of "save the whales" are commonplace. High-school student Maggie McCool risked a failing grade in her biology class because she refused to dissect a frog. The story made national news.

As the great Indian Chief Seattle so eloquently wrote when he was forced to surrender his tribe to the U.S. government in 1852:

> We are part of the earth and it is part of us. The perfumed flowers are our sisters. The bear, the deer, the great eagle—these are our brothers. The rocky crests, the juices in the meadow—the body heat of the pony and man, all belong to the same family.

Mankind is not the only inhabitant of this planet. Learn about the plight of our animal friends and contact an animal rights organization to find out how you can get involved.

Declaration of The Rights of Animals

Whereas It Is Self-Evident

That we share the earth with other creatures, great and small;
That many of these animals experience pleasure and pain;
That these animals deserve our just treatment; and
That these animals are unable to speak for themselves;

We Do Therefore Declare That These Animals

HAVE THE RIGHT to live free from human exploitation, whether in the name of science or sport, exhibition or service, food or fashion;

HAVE THE RIGHT to live in harmony with their nature rather than according to human desires; and

HAVE THE RIGHT to live on a healthy planet.

THIS DECLARATION OF THE RIGHTS OF ANIMALS,
ADOPTED AND PROCLAIMED
ON THIS, THE TENTH DAY OF JUNE 1990,
IN WASHINGTON, D.C.

Declaration of the Rights of Animals Endorsing Organizations

American Fund for Alternatives to Animal Research • Albert Schweitzer Council for Animals and the Environment • American Anti-Vivisection Society • The American Society for the Prevention of Cruelty to Animals • Animal Legal Defense Fund • Animal Protection Institute • Animal Rights International • Animal Rights Mobilization • The Animals' Agenda • The Animals' Voice Magazine • Association of Veterinarians for Animal Rights • Beauty Without Cruelty, USA • CHAI • Compassion for Animals Foundation • Culture and Animals Foundation • Disabled and Incurably Ill for Alternatives to Animal Research • Doris Day Animal League • EcoVision • Farm Animal Reform Movement • Farm Sanctuary • Feminists for Animal Rights • Focus on Animals • Friends of Animals • The Fund for Animals • Gaia Institute • In Defense of Animals • International Network for Religion and Animals • International Primate Protection League • International Society for Animal Rights • Jews for Animal Rights • National Alliance for Animal Legislation • National Anti-Vivisection Society • National Humane Education Society • New England Anti-Vivisection Society • North Carolina Network for Animals • People for the Ethical Treatment of Animals • Performing Animals Welfare Society • Physicians Committee for Responsible Medicine • Primarily Primates • Psychologists for the Ethical Treatment of Animals • United Action for Animals • United Animal Nations—USA

Declaration for Rights of Animals/Summit for Animals

THE ANIMAL-
EXPERIMENTATION DEBATE

■ ■ ■

THE DEBATE

True abuse results from neglect or malicious mistreatment of animals and is rare. Most scientists do not mistreat animals and would prefer not to use animals if at all possible.

—THE AMERICAN MEDICAL ASSOCIATION

It is routine for the animals' vocal cords to be cut so that their cries of pain and terror will not disturb the experimenters at their work.

When they are not being worked on, the animals are simply ignored, left alone and untended in the cramped and dirty cages.

The reason for this callous treatment is found in the vivisector's own words: they regard animals as merely "tools for research," not sentient beings.

—STEVEN TIGER, former clinical practitioner and editor of two medical journals

*"Use of Animals in Biomedical Research," American Medical Association, pamphlet, 1989.

Vivisection is defined as medical research that involves surgery performed on living animals, although it is commonly expanded to include all types of testing. Many animal rights advocates estimate that 60 to 70 million live animals are used in research, education, and product testing each year. (Federal agencies estimate that number at a lower 17 to 22 million.) Animal rights groups argue that:

▶ Animals are often subjected to cruel living conditions in labs and suffer greatly when tested.

▶ Effective research can be made on tissue samples, computer models, and other nonanimal-based alternatives.

▶ Many tests are duplicated, thus submitting animals to unnecessary pain and suffering.

▶ It is unethical to assume that securing practical benefits for humans automatically justifies experimentation on animals.

Medical researchers and others contend that animal research is necessary to advance the study of many diseases, including cancer, diabetes, and AIDS, and is needed to develop surgical techniques, drugs, and vaccines. They point out that such research is responsible for most notable scientific and medical advances. The American Medical Association explains that "virtually every advance in the 20th century, from antibiotics and vaccines to antidepressant drugs and organ transplants, has been achieved either directly or indirectly through the use of animals in laboratory experiments."*

THE DEBATE IN THE SPOTLIGHT

Public criticism is not new, but increased support and exposure have begun to focus national attention on such issues as consumer product testing and medical research. Boycotts of cosmetic manufacturers, lobbying for stronger legislation, and protests against the use of animals for medical experimentation have garnered significant attention and positive results.

Dr. Frank Loew, dean of the School of Veterinary Medicine at Tufts University, observes that "A lot of people branded [animal activists] as little old ladies in tennis shoes and as mindless anti-technology Luddites. Now people in Congress are starting to listen to them. Consumers are starting to think: 'I want a safe product, but wouldn't it be nice to assure safety without inflicting pain and suffering on animals.' "*

TYPES OF ANIMAL TESTING

Two types of animal testing—product and medical testing—currently receive widespread attention from animal rights groups and the press. Medical research accounts for approximately 30 percent of all research, with the remaining 70 percent divided in toxicity testing; experimental psychology; education, product, and drug development; Department of Defense warfare testing; and Department of Energy research.

Product Testing. An estimated 14 million animals suffer and are killed each year by cosmetics and household products companies. A PETA newsletter vividly describes this dilemma:

> Particularly cruel are the tests to which over five million animals are subjected each year to test new products. For example:
> ▶ The household product industry determines the toxicity (poison level) of floor wax and detergents by injecting gallons of these substances into the stomachs, or under the skins, of beagles, rabbits, and calves . . . producing vomiting, diarrhea, respiratory distress, convulsions and paralysis. The so-called Lethal Dose 50 test ends only when half the animals have died. And no anesthesia or

pain killers are given.
▶ The cosmetics industry routinely subjects rows of rabbits, immobilized in wooden stocks, to the infamous Draize test. The rabbits' eyes are smeared with drugs, nail polish remover, hair spray or shampoo . . . and since rabbits cannot make tears (they have no tear ducts), they cannot wash their eyes clean. The predictable results are cor-

Because I have a deep concern for the welfare of other species, before I contribute to your organization I must be assured that the research you conduct or finance does not involve the mutilation and abuse of animals.

STAMP OF CONCERN
In Defense of Animals

*George White, "Confronting Animal Rights Activism," *Los Angeles Times,* 3 December 1989.

The American Society for the Prevention of Cruelty to Animals

---

THE ASPCA'S TEN MOST "UNWANTED" LIST

1. The Draize and LD50 tests
2. Pound seizure
3. Pet overpopulation
4. Animals in entertainment
5. Animal fighting
6. Dolphin slaughter
7. Fur
8. Poaching of wildlife
9. Factory farming
10. Commercial horse carriage rides

.... Did you know?

Some "important" findings from medical research on live animals have shown:

▶ Spine-severed rats twitch their legs more after amphetamine dosing. (Addiction Research Center)

▶ Morphine and forced ice-water swimming produce analgesia in rats burned on hotplates. (Edgewood Arsenal, MD, 1983)

neal ulcers, hemorrhaging, and blindness.

These tests become even more nightmarish when you realize that they are unnecessary. New technologies offer us proven alternatives that are far cheaper, more exact, and more humane. Like sophisticated computer essays, simulated tissues and body fluids, live cell cultures, mass spectrometry, and gas chromatography—not to mention the use of cadavers—which the American Ophthalmology Association calls our "most ignored and valuable research tool."

Proponents of animal research, such as the AMA, "recognize that no animal research program can be considered human unless it includes a commitment to employ alternative methods whenever possible."* However, they point out that such alternatives are not perfected and cannot be used in all cases and that "popular expectations for the use of alternatives outdistance actual performance."**

Medical Testing. Many animal advocates contend that countless experiments in the name of medicine isolate, starve, shock, blind, maim, and kill animals to achieve dubious and often duplicated results. The Physicians Committee for Responsible Medicine argues that money spent on needless laboratory research should be diverted to preventive medicine instead. They state, "We spend billions of dollars every year on animal experimentation in futile efforts to discover cures for ailments, many of which need never happen in the first place."

The United Action for Animals claims that duplication of experiments causes not only suffering and death of millions of laboratory animals but also wastes billions of taxpayer dollars each year.

The AMA argues that "improved public health and nutrition have played only a minor role" in curing infectious diseases. Scientists argue that proper scientific method calls for duplication in order to achieve the best possible results and to prove validity. They note that peer and public pressure, along with better regulation, have improved communication and has led to a decrease in unnecessary experimentation.

ANTI-VIVISECTIONISTS' MANDATES

Most animal advocates do not argue against the necessity of medical research. However they would like to see the animals

*"Use of Animals in Biomedical Research," American Medical Association, 1989.
**Ibid.

utilized in such research treated with more compassion, and they would like assurance that these programs are necessary. Some of their demands include:

▶ Better treatment in labs

▶ Lowering the numbers of animals used for research

▶ Eliminating suffering during experimentation

▶ Using cell simulations or cell cultures in place of animals

Peter Singer, author of *Animal Liberation* (Avon Books, 1977), puts their protests in perspective: "But to be opposed to what is going on now it is not necessary to insist that all experiments stop immediately. All that we need to say is that experiments serving no direct and urgent purpose should stop immediately, and in the remaining areas or research, methods involving animals should be replaced as soon as possible by alternative methods not involving animals."

Did you know? ▪▪▪▪▪▪▪▪▪▪

Other "important" findings:

▶ Pregnant beagles dosed with alcohol via stomach tube throughout their entire pregnancies give birth to deformed puppies or have spontaneous abortions of dead fetuses. (U.N.C., 1980)

▶ Cats drink more alcohol with a companion than when alone. (UCLA, 1983)

▶ Monkeys will self-inflict cocaine until they mutilate themselves and die in excruciating agony. (Downstate Med. Ctr., Brooklyn, 1980)

Animal Agony in Addiction Research, United Action for Animals, Inc.

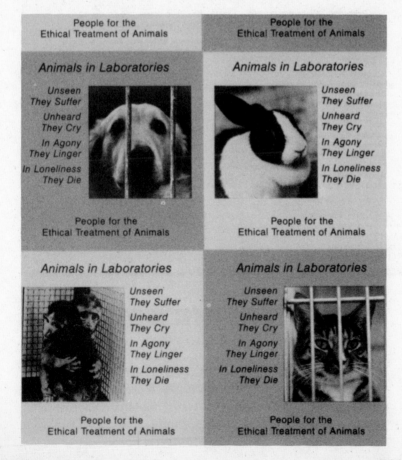

People for the Ethical Treatment of Animals

Animals in Laboratories

Unseen They Suffer
Unheard They Cry
In Agony They Linger
In Loneliness They Die

People for the Ethical Treatment of Animals

PETA, People for the Ethical Treatment of Animals

Here is an example of how some concerned people voiced their support for compassionate treatment of laboratory animals.

Declaration of Concern and Support

We, the undersigned, do hereby express our support for the efforts of the Physicians Committee for Responsible Medicine.†

We oppose: the shameful conditions under which laboratory animals are caged, transported and treated in laboratories.

We support: the right of medical students to choose not to participate in laboratory experiments involving live animals.

We support: the promotion of effective, alternative educational methods that do not use animals.

We support: effective, humane research methods which reduce or replace the use of animals in research, including epidemiological research, clinical studies, cellular research, and computer models.

We support: improved legal protection for all animals in laboratories.

Doris Day, Actress
Mike Farrell, Actor
Loretta Swit, Actress
Howard Jones, Singer/Musician
Libra Max
Michael Franks, Singer/Musician
Nina Hagen, Singer/Musician
Lene Lovich, Singer/Musician
Jane Goodall, Primatologist
Alex Pacheco, People for the Ethical Treatment of Animals (PETA)*
Ingrid Newkirk, PETA*
Cleveland Amory, The Fund for Animals*
Aaron Medlock, New England Anti-Vivisection Society*
Tom Regan, Professor of Philosophy, North Carolina State University*
Shirley McGreal, International Primate Protection League*

Jean Goldenberg, Washington Humane Society*
Bob and Loretta Hirsh, Washington Humane Society*
Kim Sturla, Peninsula (CA) Humane Society*
Patrice Green, R.N., National Association of Nurses Against Vivisection (NANAV)*
Ann Smart, R.N., NANAV*
Neal D. Barnard, M.D., Psychiatrist
Carlo Buonomo, M.D., Radiologist
Michael Klaper, M.D., General Practitioner
Richard M. Carlton, M.D., Psychiatrist
Murry J. Cohen, M.D., Psychiatrist
Donald E. Doyle, M.D., Surgeon
Stephen R. Kaufman, M.D., Ophthalmologist
Tom Giduz, M.D., Psychiatrist
Jay Brody Lavine, M.D., Ophthalmologist
James F. Grillo, M.D., Surgeon
Dallas Pratt, M.D., Psychiatrist

Kenneth P. Stoller, M.D., Pediatrician
Ulrich Fritzsche, M.D., Obstetrician/Gynecologist
Daniel H. Silver, M.D., Internal Medicine
Herbert N. Gundersheimer, M.D., Internal Medicine
J. Herbert Fill, M.D., General Practitioner
Larry F. Kron, M.D., Psychiatrist
Richard S. Blinstrub, M.D., Dermatologist
Russell J. Bunai, M.D., Pediatrician
Donald C. Doll, M.D., Oncologist
Walter Nowak, M.D., Hematologist
Herbert M. Simonson, M.D., Orthopedic Surgeon
Steven Tiger, Physician's Assistant
Nedim Buyukmihci, D.V.M.
Ron Allison, M.D., Radiation Oncology
Roger C. Breslau, M.D., General, Thoracic and Vascular Surgery
Roy Selby, M.D., Neurosurgery

†Due to space limitation we are unable to list all 2000 participating physicians.

*Organizations listed for identification purposes only.

Physicians Committee for Responsible Medicine
P.O. Box 6322, Washington, D.C. 20015

Recycled Paper

WHAT IS BEING DONE?

● ●

Public Sector

▶ The Federal Animal Welfare Act and certain amendments govern animal care in labs and other nonfarm facilities. Due to pressure from animal rights groups, reforms have been made in many labs across the country.

▶ Legislation to ensure the protection of animals has been introduced as a result of the pressure from many animal welfare organizations.

▶ The Research Accountability Act-HR 560 has been reintroduced. If passed it would create a National Center for Research Accountability, which would conduct full text literature searches of all research proposals involving live animals before funding, thus providing easy and economical access to the information necessary to end the wasteful duplication of many experiments.

▶ The Consumer Products Safe Testing Act (S.891, HR 1676) seeks to protect animals from unnecessary and cruel testing in product research.

Private Sector

▶ Due to pressure from PETA's Compassion Campaign as well as demands from many other animal rights groups, at least 11 of the nation's major cosmetics firms stopped live animal testing in 1989. These include such industry giants as Avon, Revlon, Christian Dior, Mary Kay, and Faberge.

▶ Berke Breathed's "Bloom County" comic strip targeted the issue of product tests on animals. The series focused on cosmetic and soap tests and portrayed the cruel lethal dose, Draize eye irritancy, and dermal skin irritancy tests. Corporations mentioned in the comic series hastened to inform the public that products must be tested on animals for "moral and legal" reasons.

Did you know? ▪▪▪▪▪▪▪▪▪▪▪▪

According to PETA 26 animals die every minute in the U.S. alone to test shampoos, hairsprays, laxatives and oven cleaners.

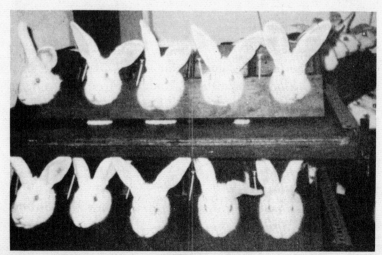

Rabbits are routinely used in product testing. American Anti-Vivisection Society.

WHAT CAN I DO?

The debate over animal experimentation touches upon very philosophical and pragmatic questions. To learn more about both sides of the debate contact the American Medical Association (a supporter of animal testing), and ask for its paper, "Use of Animals in Biomedical Research" (312-464-5000). To learn more from opponents of animal testing, contact one of the many groups listed below.

▶ **Urge your legislators to support and enforce laws that will reduce the amount of needless product and medical testing.** Such acts include the Consumer Products Safe Testing Act (S.891, HR 1676), the Federal Animal Welfare Act, and the Research Accountability Act (HR 560).

Contact PETA, NEAVS, In Defense of Animals, or another animal welfare group for additional information regarding current legislative matters.

Here is a sample petition from *In Defense of Animals*:

PETITION TO THE UNITED STATES CONGRESS

Whereas: millions of Americans desire to see an end to the harming and killing of animals in laboratories; And whereas thousands of scientists are testifying to the advantages of alternate technologies; and whereas certain individuals and research institutions are fighting efforts to end animal suffering out of financial self interest; we, the undersigned, urge Congress to use its power in a national effort to end the current reliance on biomedical and teaching technologies that harm and kill animals.

Your Name _____   Name of Friend or Relative _____

Address _____   Address _____

City _____ State _____ Zip _____   City _____ State _____ Zip _____

Please return this petition as soon as possible to *In Defense of Animals*.

▶ **Support the Joint Resolutions for the 1990s by American Animal Protection Organizations.** Endorsed by over one hundred animal-rights groups, the Joint Resolutions for the 1990s call for the protection of laboratory animals, farm animals, wild animals, companion animals, and exhibition/work animals. For more information, copies of the Joint Resolutions, or to express your support, please contact any of the following humane societies:

The ASPCA, c/o Joint Resolutions, 441 East 92nd Street, New York, NY 10128

The HSUS, c/o Joint Resolutions, 2100 L Street NW, Washington, DC 20037

The MSPCA, c/o Joint Resolutions, 350 South Huntington Avenue, Boston, MA 02130

▶ **Write a letter to The Cosmetic, Toiletry, and Fragrance Association.** Express your opposition to product testing on laboratory animals. Write to:

The Cosmetic, Toiletry and Fragrance Association
1110 Vermont Ave., NW, Suite 800
Washington, DC 20005

▶ **Boycott companies that use animals in the testing of their products.** The ASPCA, HSUS, PETA or another animal rights group will send you with a list of such companies. Contact them and voice your opinion.

Note: As a direct result of PETA's efforts and pressures from thousands of individuals, Avon and Tonka Toys have agreed to stop testing their products on animals. Benetton, the cosmetics and clothing company, stopped testing when PETA organized an international boycott against Benetton's products.

▶ **Buy cruelty-free products.** Many companies manufacture and sell products that are not tested on animals. These products include common household items such as detergents, soaps and dishwashing liquids, and cosmetics, shampoos, and toiletry articles.

WARNING CRUELLY TESTED ON ANIMALS

PETA, People for the Ethical Treatment of Animals

ORDINARY PEOPLE—EXTRAORDINARY ACTIONS

Few people will admit that they enjoyed the part of biology class that involved the dissection of an animal, usually a frog. Some feel sick—others cry—many feel uneasy. Nonetheless, most take part in the experiment.

However, two young girls in opposite parts of the country refused to partake in classroom dissection. Jennifer Graham, a California high schooler, and Maggie McCool, from New Jersey, stood up for their beliefs even though they risked lower grades or other more punitive actions.

And their protests worked!

Jennifer Graham's refusal to dissect on a frog in her high-school biology class led to a California law permitting students to choose alternatives to dissection. Maggie McCool's similar decision led to a lawsuit, and brought much attention nationwide. Maggie ultimately settled out of court and subsequently had her grade raised.

▶ Call 1-800-922-FROG if you need information on how to deal with teachers, school administrators, and others who oversee the rights of students in the debate of the killing of animals for research.

NOT TESTED ON ANIMALS

PETA, People for the Ethical Treatment of Animals

PETA Kid Mindy Dawniff

For more information about cruelty-free shopping refer to that section in "You Can Make a Difference."

▶ **Take a stand!** If you have strong feelings about animal experimentation, let it be known. Countless actions of individuals and small groups throughout the world are helping change society's views concerning animal experimentation.

Organizations and Resources

American Anti-Vivisection Society
215-887-0816
AA-VS is "totally opposed to experiments on living animals, whether performed under anesthesia or not; or whether the conditions under which the animals are kept prior to experimentation are better in some laboratories that others. Nor does this Society favor legislation attempting to 'regulate' the practice of vivisection, while accepting the legality of the basic practice itself."

In Defense of Animals
415-453-9984
A multi-issue group helping to "end the tragic mutilation and suffering of defenseless animals."

International Society for Animal Rights (ISAR)
717-586-2200
A leading animal rights group that uses "the law,

publications and education to work for their ultimate goal— abolishing vivisection, hunting and other 'animal abuses.' "

National Anti-Vivisection Society
312-427-6065

New England Anti-Vivisection Society
617-523-6020
Their goal is to "eventually end the use of live animals for research, experimentation, or testing in the belief that it is morally wrong and in most cases, scientifically unsound, to subject animals to vivisection." NEAVS publishes *Reverence for Life,* a magazine that discusses animal experimentation issues and pursues lobbying efforts, boycotts, and other means to protest vivisection as well as offering research alternatives to live animal experimentation.

People for the Ethical Treatment of Animals (PETA)
301-770-7444
PETA's Compassion Campaign is well known for its effective boycotts of corporations that test their products on live animals and its "cruelty-free" solutions to shopping. Ask for their Cosmetics/Product Testing Action Pac. This kit includes the fact sheet "Cosmetics Testing: Toxic and Tragic," together with a *Cruelty-Free Shopping Guide.* Also ask for their *Guide to Compassionate Living.* For more detailed information about Cruelty-Free Shopping, read the section entitled "Socially Responsible Shopping."

Physicians Committee for Responsible Medicine (PCRM)
With more than 1,900 participating physicians, PCRM intends to change the

public and the medical association's attitude toward animal protection: "We're working to achieve better health for people through humane treatment of animals."

United Action for Animals
212-983-5315
This organization was originally founded to work for the replacement of laboratory animals in research and testing. One of the best informed on this subject.

OTHER COMMITTED ORGANIZATIONS

American Fund for Alternatives to Animal

Research (AFAAR)
212-989-8073

A.S.P.C.A.
212-876-7700

Animal Rights Mobilization (formerly Trans-Species Unlimited)
717-322-3252

Animal Welfare Institute
202-337-2332

Association of Veterinarians for Animal Rights
707-451-1391

Beauty Without Cruelty USA
212-989-8073

Cambridge Committee for Responsible Research
617-547-9255

Doris Day Animal League
202-842-3325

Humane Society of the United States
202-452-1100

Last Chance for Animals
213-271-6096/213-271-1409 (hotline)

Progressive Animal Welfare Society (PAWS)
206-743-3845

Psychologists for the Ethical Treatment of Animals
207-926-4817

DOLPHIN SLAUGHTER

∎∎∎

Dolphins are highly intelligent, graceful mammals that are dying painful, unnecessary deaths by the thousands at the hands of tuna fishers across the world. According to Earth Island Institute, more than 6 million dolphins have been killed by the tuna industry in the past 30 years. So many dolphins have been killed by the tuna industry that the entire population is at risk.

This is a tragic death sentence for a mammal that in many instances has befriended humans, saved people from drowning and from shark attacks, and has even guided boats to safer waters.

INNOCENT VICTIMS

Each year, dolphins die by the thousands as a result of two fishing methods, drift netting and purse-seining. Fisherman use these techniques to catch tuna and other fish. Unfortunately, dolphins get in the way.

I was just amazed. I was a fisherman, a biologist. I thought I was informed about environmental things. . . . But I had thought whales and dolphins were sacrosanct species, above abuse. Nobody had told me they were being captured in nets, with speed boats and explosives and helicopters.

—SAM LABUDDE, whose shocking videotape of dolphin slaughter aboard a fishing boat received national attention (*The Atlantic Monthly,* July 1989).

···········Did you know?

▶ A dolphin is killed on average every five minutes by the international tuna industry, the largest killing of marine mammals in the world.

▶ According to the Earth Island Institute, more 100,000 dolphins have been killed per year by the tuna industry during the past two decades, a rate the institute calls unsustainable.

Drift nets. Also known as gill nets, drift nets are long nets that hang like huge invisible curtains under water. The nets float at a 45-degree angle and in a straight line from the fishing boat. The length of these nets ranges from one and a half miles to more than 50 miles long! The nets are made of nylon mesh and are put out at night so that ocean animals cannot see them. As fish and other marine creatures swim into the nets they become entangled. The fishing boats then reel the nets in, pull out the targeted species, and throw out the "incidentals."

The real crime is against these "incidental" animals. Because these nets catch anything unlucky enough to get in the way, sea lions, dolphins, whales, sea turtles, seals, and seabirds are often the unintended victims. Since many of these "incidental" animals are mammals they need air to breathe, but the nets hold them under the surface of the water causing them to drown.

Most drift-net boats do not have observers so no one really knows how many "incidental" animals are thrown back dead into the water. For this reason it is virtually impossible to accurately count the number of "incidental" animals killed by drift nets, but the numbers are estimated to be at least 50,000 each year. Due to the inherently destructive nature of this fishing method, Earth Island Institute and other marine animal advocacy groups call for a complete ban on all drift nets throughout the world.

Purse-seine nets. Like huge draw-string purses, purse-seine nets encircle targeted animals and are drawn closed at the top. These nets can be 1 mile in length. They are used to catch tuna and other fish.

For reasons not completely known, yellowfin tuna and dolphins swim together. Since dolphins swim on the surface of the water they are easy to locate. Fishing boats in search of tuna spot the dolphins and send helicopters and speedboats in quick pursuit. The dolphins and tuna are chased for hours until they become exhausted and confused. The boats then corral the tuna—and the dolphins—into the huge nets by igniting underwater explosives. Earth Island Institute explains that nursing and pregnant dolphins are the most likely victims. So the current population, as well as future generations, are needlessly killed by this cruel technique.

Ironically, 95 percent of all tuna is caught without harming dolphins, according to Earth Island Institute. However, greedy companies can make more money by catching yellowfin tuna, which is larger and commands a higher price. So, although yellowfin tuna accounts for only 5 percent of all tuna caught, the purse-seine method of catching yellowfin endangers the very existence of dolphins! For instance, the coastal spotted dolphin population has been depleted by at least 40 percent and the eastern spinner dolphin population is down by an astounding 80 percent.

Unlike drift nets, the technique of purse seining is not in itself destructive. However, the use of these nets to encircle nontargeted species such as dolphins is! Therefore, Earth Island Institute calls for an end to any use of purse-seine nets that endangers or kills dolphins or any other nontargeted species.

WHAT IS BEING DONE?

Public Sector

▶ The Dolphin Protection Consumer Information Act of 1990 was passed and signed into law by the 101st Congress. The legislation, prompted by a coalition of 20 advocacy groups, including Earth Island Institute and the Humane Society of the United States, regulates the use of "dolphin-safe" claims on any labels. It also prohibits false and misleading labels and sets up a system to monitor and enforcement the labelling requirements.

Other significants points in the law include bans on all drift-net-caught tuna beginning in July 1991 and on the importation of all drift-net-caught fish products beginning in July 1992. Also, in order to be labelled "dolphin safe," tuna coming from the Eastern Tropical Pacific region must have a certificate signed by the National Marine Fisheries Service or the InterAmerican Tropical Tuna Commission stating that no dolphins were harmed in the process.

Private Sector

▶ The three largest U.S. tuna companies, StarKist Seafood Co., Bumble Bee Seafoods, and Van Kamp Seafood Company, have adopted worldwide dolphin-safe policies. They will only buy tuna that has been deemed dolphin safe.

▶ EarthTrust's "Flipper Seal of Approval" endorses environmentally safe seafood products.

▶ The Hard Rock Cafes in the United States and Australia will serve only dolphin-safe tuna.

·········· Did you know?

▶ Earth Island Institute estimates that the total number of dolphins killed in 1990 by the United States and foreign fleets fell by approximately 50,000.

This success was due to a number of factors, including dolphin-safe legislation, a consumer campaign against tuna companies, and a subsequent decision by the these companies to buy only dolphin-safe tuna.

▶ Earth Island Institute, EarthTrust, Dolphin Connection, and the Marine Mammal Fund initiated the "Save the Dolphins Campaign," a national multifaceted effort to eliminate the unnecessary slaughter of dolphins as a result of the practices of the U.S. and foreign fishing industries. Their programs include prompting special legislative policies to protect dolphins, demanding greater enforcement of the Marine Mammal Protection Act, creating a labeling campaign of "safe tuna," and catalyzing actions such as boycotts and protests.

WHAT CAN I DO?

··

When asked what is the greatest threat immediate to dolphins, Ric O'Barry, the official trainer of Flipper and president of The Dolphin Project, replied: "I think apathy is. The tuna fishing industry has really killed between 7 and 10 million dolphins. People are aware of this and they don't do anything about it." (*Whole Life Times,* June 1989).

Fortunately, however, many people and organizations are now abandoning this pattern of apathy; however, they need much support. Here are a few easy and effective actions you can take to help stop the slaughter of dolphins.

▶ **Speak out for the dolphins.** Let the tragedy of dolphin slaughter be heard! If you don't say anything, who will?

One idea to publicize the dolphin issue is to make your neighborhood, school, club, business, or city a dolphin-safe zone. Contact Earth Island Institute for teaching kits, posters, brochures, videos, and bumperstickers.

☆ ☆ THE STARS ARE SHINING! ☆ ☆

"I'm genuinely concerned about the kind of world our children will inherit from us.

"The death of so many of these animals in so many places is a message—a tragic message that we are abusing the very system which makes life on earth possible.

"For now, if dolphins are to talk, we must be their voices."
—Actor and producer Michael Douglas as host of a dolphin documentary.

▶ **Let the media know that you care!** Write or call your local television and radio stations and your newspapers. Educate them about the dolphin issue and express your concern for the welfare of these beautiful animals. Television stations can get special footage from Earth Island Institute on 3/4-inch tape.

▶ **Write letters to your political leaders.** The Marine

Mammal Protection Act (MMPA) was changed in 1981 to exempt the U.S. commercial tuna fleet, resulting in the continued use of purse-seine nets. The Act also set dolphin kill quotas of 20,500 per year. Earth Island Institute believes that since U.S. tuna companies have ceased purchasing dolphin-caught tuna, the quota should be reduced to zero. Show your support in a letter!

▶ House Subcommittee on Fisheries and Wildlife Conservation, Gerry Studds, Chairman, House Office Bldg., Washington, DC 20515

▶ U.S. Secretary of Commerce, Robert Mosbacher, Commerce Building, 14th St. NW, Washington, DC 20230

▶ Your Representative, House Office Building, Washington, DC 20515.

▶ Your Senator, Senate Office Building, Washington, DC 20510

Here is an example of a brief but effective letter provided by the Earth Island Institute's Save the Dolphins Project.

Earthtrust

Sec. Mosbacher:

We can't allow the massacre of dolphins to go on. It's time to enforce the Marine Mammal Protection Act and bring the dolphin kill down to zero. Future generations won't forgive inaction. Keep me informed.

Sincerely,
Your Name and Address

Printed with permission of Earth Island Institute's Save the Dolphins Project 300 Broadway, Suite 28, San Francisco, CA 94133 (415)788-3666/ 1-800-DOLPHIN

Earth Island Institute urges you to also write to foreign leaders to protest their country's participation in fishing methods which endanger or kill dolphins. Contact Earth Island Institute and ask for the current names and addresses of all parties still involved with dolphin slaughter.

▶ **Buy only dolphin-safe tuna.** Earth Island Institute explains that although some of the major tuna companies are complying with dolphin-safe guidelines, many private companies, supermarkets, and house-brand tuna labels are still buying and selling tuna caught at the expense of dolphins.

So, the best way to determine if a certain brand of tuna is dolphin-safe is to contact an organization such as the Earth Island Institute. They have rigid guidelines and consistent

Earthtrust

monitoring systems to ensure the credibility of dolphin-safe claims. Call their office or dial 800-DOLPHIN to find out which tuna brands are dolphin-safe.

▶ **Put pressure on your local supermarkets to stock only dolphin-safe tuna.** You are the client of the supermarket. They care about what you think, especially if they believe that your opinion, as well as the opinions of others, will affect their sales. If supermarkets choose to stock only dolphin-safe tuna, the companies that buy unsafe-dolphin tuna will no longer have a market for their product.

Write or talk to local supermarket managers or call Earth Island Institute and ask about their 900 number for dolphins. By calling the Earth Island Institute's Dolphin Campaign's 900 number, three mailgrams will be sent in your name to the largest supermarket chains in your area urging them to sell only dolphin-safe tuna products. Earth Island Institute explains that this is a quick way to make a huge impact, and the cost is only $5.95.

▶ **You can make a difference!** Your actions will influence others and add energy to the movement. When dolphin advocacy groups called for a boycott of tuna, students from across the country rose to the occasion.

ORDINARY PEOPLE—EXTRAORDINARY ACTIONS
STUDENTS STAND UP FOR DOLPHINS

Students across the country are doing something to help the dolphins—they're convincing their school cafeterias to stop serving tuna. The school systems in Aurora, Colorado, and Milford, Connecticut, have agreed to take tuna off the menu until it can be certified as dolphin-safe.

Other schools are considering similar actions.

The actions of these concerned students have helped to raise the awareness of the plight of the dolphins. As mentioned earlier, if you are wondering whether or not your cafeteria serves certified dolphin-safe tuna, contact Earth Island Institute.

Organizations and Resources

• •

Dolphin Hotline
800-DOLPHIN
A toll free number from the Save the Dolphins Project. You will receive a free Dolphin Action Kit when you call.

Dolphin Coalition
c/o Defenders of Wildlife
202-659-9510
A coalition of animal welfare groups including HSUS, Defenders of Wildlife, Earth

Island Institute, Marine Mammal Fund, ASPCA, Friends of Animals, and the National Audubon Society.

OTHER COMMITTED ORGANIZATIONS

ASPCA
212-876-7700

Center for Marine Conservation
202-429-5609

Dolphin Connection
213-471-7953

HSUS
202-452-1100

The Earth Island Institute
415-788-3666

EarthTrust
808-595-6927

Greenpeace Marine Division
202-462-1177

The Marine Mammal Fund
415-775-4636

The Sea Shepherd Society
213-373-6979

Whale and Dolphin Conservation Society
617-259-0423

• •

ENDANGERED SPECIES

▪ ▪ ▪

Many species are now disappearing at an alarming rate—one type of plant or animal each day according to some experts. That rate could increase to one species an hour by the year 2000. During the next 20 years, one-fifth of all species may become extinct. James Gustave Speth, president of World Resources Institute, says in an October 1989 *USA Today* article, that the impact of such losses on human welfare is potentially devastating.

According to the National Audubon Society, a species is considered endangered when its numbers drop so quickly that it is in danger of becoming extinct. A species is considered threatened when it is in trouble, but is not in immediate danger of becoming extinct. A species may also be called endangered or threatened if it is rare in most of the areas in which it used to live.

It is difficult to estimate the exact number of species on this planet. Although it is believed that between 5 and 30 million species exist on this planet, only 1.5 million have actually been named and categorized.

CAUSES OF ENDANGERMENT

Many factors contribute to the tragedy of endangered species. Habitat encroachment and/or destruction, pesticides and other pollutions, and greed all play roles.

Habitat destruction. Many animals are simply forced

Q. What do elephants, gray wolves, gorillas, condors, and the rosy periwinkle have in common?

A. They all are species that are threatened with extinction.

·········· Did you know?

These are just a few endangered or threatened species:

Gray Wolf
Ivory-Billed Woodpecker
Whooping Crane
Brown Pelican
Bald Eagle
Gorilla
California Condor
Grizzly Bear
American Crocodile
Desert Tortoise
African and Asian Elephant
Chimpanzee

out of their environment by necessary and unnecessary human expansion. Plants are also affected when marshes and forests are cleared. Rain forests provide a home for more than half of all the earth's species. Yet, according to biologist Edward O. Wilson of Harvard University, as many as 6,000 species are becoming extinct each year due to deforestation alone, at a rate 10,000 times greater than before the appearance of humans on the planet.

Potential threats. Some animals have been viewed as threats to humans and their pets when their habitats overlap, and therefore have been killed out of fear. Gray wolves, grizzly bears, alligators and Florida panthers are such examples.

Chemical poisoning. Manmade chemicals such as pesticides enter the water and the soil, poisoning fish and birds. If these compounds fail to kill animals directly, they make healthy reproduction impossible.

Greed and trade. Some animals are killed for "valuable" products such as clothing and jewelry. Elephants, alligators, lizards, turtles, seals and whales are just a few examples of endangered animals that are slaughtered, often illegally, for the sake of fashion.

WHY SAVE AN ENDANGERED SPECIES?

There are many good reasons for saving species. Plants and animals help maintain the levels of oxygen and carbon dioxide in the atmosphere. Worms, insects, fungi, and bacteria recycle nutrients in the soils in which we plant our crops. Plants also help to regulate the flow of water and prevent floods.

All of our food and most of our medicines are developed from plants and animals. Aspirin first came from willow bark; quinine, used to treat malaria, came from cinchona bark. If we lose these plants, we may suffer much greater losses. For example, Madagascar's rosy periwinkle, which is used in the medication used to treat childhood leukemia and Hodgkin's disease, and a plant extract that may serve as an AIDS drug from the Australian rain forests, are now threatened.

If species continue to disappear at the present rate, many will be gone before scientists have a chance to discover their possible benefits to humanity.

WHAT IS BEING DONE?

Public Sector

▶ Prevention of loss of habitat is one of the most important ways to save plants and animals from extinction. Habitat conservation measures such as America's Endangered Species Act are now included in many laws. Other actions have been instituted:

> ▶ Australia has proposed legislature regulating development that endangers species.
>
> ▶ Costa Rica sets aside 10 percent of its land for national parks and animal reserves.
>
> ▶ Mexican and U.S. shrimpers must use a new net that will not drown endangered turtles.
>
> ▶ Southern California land developers and state and federal agencies estimate they will pay more than $100 million for the land to protect the endangered Stephen's Kangaroo rat.

Private Sector

▶ Ecological conservation groups such as the Nature Conservancy, Conservation International, and the World Wildlife Fund buy or trade for land to protect threatened species. This may take the form of an actual purchase, such as the Nature Conservancy's purchase of land for a 15,000–60,000 acre preserve in Nevada for the endangered desert tortoise. Or it may entail a "debt-for-nature" swap, in which land is set aside and a portion of national debt is forgiven.

▶ The sanctuary system of the National Audubon Society protects a quarter-million acres of rare habitats protecting such animals as the wood stork in Florida and the California clapper rail—a marsh bird.

▶ The American Association of Zoological Parks and

✪ DALE SHIELDS ✪

Sarasota, FL
DAILY POINT OF LIGHT RECIPIENT: JULY 2, 1990

"I believe that everybody in the world can do something to help the environment."

While fishing in 1980, Mr. Shields found a pelican with a damaged wing and nursed it back to health. After returning the pelican to its natural environment, Mr. Shields was inspired to seek out and care for other injured birds.

In 1985, Mr. Shields, now known as the Pelican Man, founded the Pelican Man's Bird Sanctuary. Located on City Island, the sanctuary provides birds and other wildlife a safe place in which to live, and a learning environment for visitors. Mr. Shields and more than 200 volunteers rescue injured birds on the shores of Florida and transport them to the sanctuary, where they obtain medical treatment, food, and nurturing. The volunteers also guide visitors through the sanctuary, describing the various birds and explaining the importance of caring for wildlife.

Aquariums (AAZPA) saves species from extinction through captive breeding programs. Animals such as the black rhino and the Bornean orangutan participate in a program that includes zoos from 39 states and the District of Columbia.

▶ When Exxon's *Valdez* oil spill endangered Alaskan wildlife, many people from around the country volunteered to help clean up the landscape and save birds and other animals. Their efforts helped to make this disaster much more manageable.

THE AFRICAN ELEPHANT

■ ■ ■

ORGANIZATIONAL EFFORTS, CITIZEN CONCERN AND LEGISLATIVE ACTION—A RECIPE FOR SUCCESS!

During the 1980s, the African elephant faced dire circumstances: Populations were cut in half, from approximately 1.2 million to about 600,000, according to the World Wildlife Fund. Greedy poachers, motivated by an enormous international demand for ivory products, threatened this majestic animal's very existence.

The assault on Africa's elephant population was widespread and brutal. The African Wildlife Foundation estimated that in a single year at the end of the 1980s 90,000 elephants and 10,000 orphan calves were killed—equaling more than 270 per day, 11 an hour, or an astounding one elephant every five and a half minutes! Friends of Animals reports that so many elephants were killed during this period that during aerial inspections in Somalia dead elephants outnumbered live ones. Poachers would track and shoot groups of elephants, quickly cut off the tusks, and leave the carcasses to rot. An African Wildlife Foundation photographer explains that in order to get the tusk the poachers had to "carve off most of its face." Often, orphaned calves were left to fend for themselves in the wild. However, when herds noticeably declined and a large number of tusks on the market weighed as little as three and a half ounces Friends of Animals pointed

Friends of Animals

out that infant elephants were being slaughtered for ivory.

It became clear that the demand for ivory products was one of the major factors contributing to the rapid decline in the African elephant populations. Ivory is found in everything from billiard balls and knife handles to necklaces and figurines. During this period, annual worldwide consumption of ivory averaged about 1,000 tons—which translates to more than 100,000 elephants! Poachers illegally entered special game reserves and savagely killed elephants by the thousands for their tusks. They then smuggled the ivory out of the country and sold it on the international market for a hefty profit.

Recognizing that saving the elephants required an end to the worldwide ivory market, the World Wildlife Fund, Friends of Animals, African Wildlife Foundation and other elephant advocacy groups began a two-fold strategy. First, they educated the public about the staggering rate of destruction of the African elephant population. Along with this heightened awareness, these groups pointed out that consumer demand for ivory goods was causing the problem. As Mark Stanley Price, a director of the African Wildlife Foundation remarked, "people in the United States just [didn't] connect ivory with elephants, but every bracelet represents a dead elephant." Elephant advocacy organizations then urged consumers to refuse to buy ivory goods. Bill Clark, International Program Director for the Friends of Animals, explains that even though the elephant may long be dead, the wearing of ivory "creates a fashion and a demand and a black market."

Heeding the call to save the elephant, consumers and retailers began to boycott ivory products. Major retailers, such as Macy's, Dayton Hudson, and Bloomingdale's, and designers, including Liz Claiborne, Bill Blass, and Oscar de la Renta, showed their support by refusing to buy ivory products and urging their customers to do the same.

The second strategy to save the elephants was to lobby for an international ban on ivory. Most of the world's ivory was supplied by poachers and the large demand for ivory products kept prices high. It was felt, therefore, that a reduction in the demand would drastically lower the prices for ivory, thus making poaching less financially attractive. This idea was heard loud and clear. In the fall of 1989, a regulation making the sale of ivory illegal was passed under CITES, the international endangered species treaty. Soon after, the ban began to make a tremendous impact. The price of black-market ivory dropped dramatically, and the retail price of

SAVE THE ELEPHANTS

WILDLIFE CONSERVATION INTERNATIONAL
NYZS, Bronx, NY 10460

ivory products has declined by more than 75 percent. Moreover, since the CITES regulation, poaching has dramatically declined.

So the combined efforts of elephant advocacy groups, retailers and consumers, and legislative authorities paid off. People began equating ivory with elephants and this enlightenment led to effective action. But the African elephant is not completely in the clear. Michael O'Connell of the World Wildlife Fund notes that "the moratorium on ivory trading has been a good first step in slowing the rate of decline." However, he explains that this is just the first step. The African elephant still must face another threat—habitat encroachment. Like many other threatened or endangered animal species, long-term solutions to protecting the elephant depend on the way man ultimately decides to coexist with this grand creature.

WHAT CAN I DO?

▶ **Learn more about endangered species.** The State Fish and Game Department or a conservation group should be helpful. You can also write for a list of federally protected endangered and threatened species and for a free copy of "Why Save an Endangered Species?" the U.S. Fish and Wildlife Service, Publications Department, Washington, DC 20240.

▶ For a free booklet on how you can help save an endangered species write: Endangered Species, Consumer Information Center, Department 561-X, Pueblo, CO 81009.

▶ **Join a conservation or animal rights group.** Conservation and animal-rights organizations and concerned individuals help the U.S. Fish and Wildlife Service and the National Marine Fisheries Service implement and monitor the Endangered Species Act. They pressure these agencies to put more names on the list of endangered species and aid in programs to protect the species protected by the law.

Most success stories, such as the whooping crane and the American alligator, are due to the concerted effort of all parties. For example, the efforts of the Florida Audubon Society and its members helped save the American alligator.

ALLIGATORS MAKE A COMEBACK!

Everyone, from retailers to consumers, enjoyed the high demand for alligator skin purses, wallets and shoes. Everyone, that is, except the alligator.

When the valuable American alligator hide became fashionable the population of the large reptiles declined so rapidly that it was placed on the endangered species list.

The Florida Audubon Society responded with a holiday season campaign to "Save an Alligator's Hide for Christmas." Shoppers quickly got the message and quit buying alligator hide products. And the government followed, banning the sale of alligator products throughout the country.

As a result of these concerted efforts the American alligator population is again thriving and has been taken off the endangered species list.

Reprinted with permission from the National Audubon Society.

▶ **Visit a National Wildlife Refuge.** Trained specialists will teach you all about endangered species and how to protect them. Take your whole family there on an outing, and to educate them as well.

▶ **Send letters to your newspaper.** The more attention you can bring to the importance of saving endangered species the better chance of their survival.

▶ **Adopt an animal!** Contact one of the many animal Adoption Agencies listed under "Other Important Animal Rights Issues," p. 183, if you are interested in animal adoption. Your contribution helps these organizations protect threatened or endangered animals.

▶ **Be careful what you buy.** Many products and souvenirs are made from the hides, shells, teeth, or feathers of endangered species. According to PETA, almost one-third of all "exotic" leather goods come from endangered, poached animals. For more information contact:

   ▶ Division of Law Enforcement, U.S. Fish and Wildlife Service, P.O. Box 28006, Washington, DC 20005.

   ▶ For a copy of "Facts about Federal Wildlife Laws," which explains what items cannot be imported, contact the U.S. Fish and Wildlife Service Publications Unit, Washington, DC 20240.

   ▶ TRAFFIC (USA), c/o World Wildlife Fund (ask for *Buyer Beware* a booklet on how to recognize products from endangered species).

Endangered Species

DEPARTMENT OF THE INTERIOR
U.S. FISH AND WILDLIFE SERVICE

Organizations and Resources

African Wildlife Foundation
202-265-8393
Concerned with all African wildlife, including elephants, black rhinos, and mountain gorillas. Publishes *Wildlife News,* a quarterly report that discusses important conservation issues in Africa and provides information about trips to African wildlife sanctuaries.

Friends of Animals
203-866-5223
In addition to efforts to rescue the elephant, Friends of Animals is active in Africa and other parts of the world in protecting animals of all species.

Defenders of Wildlife
202-659-9510
Their mission is to "preserve and enhance the natural abundance and diversity of wildlife through education, advocacy, and litigation." They have more than 80,000 members, including an activist network of 8,000 individuals, and they publish the *Annual Endangered Species Report.*

National Audubon Society
212-832-3200
For more than three quarters of a century the National Audubon Society has provided leadership in scientific research, wildlife protection, conservation education, and environmental action. They publish *Audubon* magazine and have approximately 500,000 members.

National Wildlife Federation
202-797-6800
Publishes *National Wildlife* magazine. Editorial Creed: "To create and encourage an awareness among the people of the world of the need for wise use and proper management of those resources of the Earth upon which our lives and welfare depend: the soil, the air, the water, the forests, the minerals, the plant life and the wildlife."

The Nature Conservancy
800-628-6860
The Conservancy saves natural areas for their ecological significance and their distinct wildlife through actual land purchases. Since 1951, they have been involved in the preservation of nearly 3$^1/_2$ million acres in all 50 states, the Virgin Islands, Canada, the Caribbean, and Latin America.

Wildlife Conservation International (WCI)
212-220-5155
A division of the New York Zoological Society. For almost 100 years, WCI has been in the forefront of critical work providing the impetus and the information to save endangered species and threatened ecosystems.

World Wildlife Fund
202-293-4800
Since its founding in 1961, World Wildlife Fund has been a leader in the international struggle to protect the world's threatened wildlife and the habitats necessary for their survival.

OTHER COMMITTED ORGANIZATIONS

American Association of Zoological Parks and Aquariums
304-242-2160

ASPCA
212-876-7700

Conservation International
202-429-5660

Earth Island Institute
415-788-3666

EarthTrust
808-595-6927

Friends of Conservation
708-954-3388

Greenpeace
202-462-1177

Humane Society of the United States
202-452-1100

The gray wolves were eliminated from most of the lower forty-eight states in the early part of this century. Department of Interior U.S. Fish and Wildlife Service.

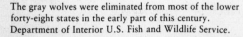

FACTORY FARMING AND HOW IT AFFECTS OUR WORLD

. . .

Every year millions of farm animals, including cows, sheep, goats, and pigs, are slaughtered in large "modern" farms for their flesh and skin. They suffer the horrors of factory farming, including crowding and confinement, deprivation, unanesthetized castration, branding, tail-docking and de-horning, and brutal treatment during transportation and slaughter.

The abuse these animals must endure represents only part of the problem. The process of raising our meat supply also affects our environment and health. Excessive pesticide and fertilizer use poisons topsoil, ultimately ending up in our food and water supply. Antibiotics, administered to animals to keep them alive in unhealthy surroundings, finds its way into our food. Salmonella and other dangerous diseases fester in unhealthy factory farm conditions, sometimes infecting the milk and eggs we eat.

Ironically, the end result—a veal chop, a hamburger, or an omelet—is not beneficial to our diet. Excessive dietary protein can cause osteoporosis, and diets high in saturated fat and cholesterol are linked to atherosclerosis, and lead directly to heart disease and strokes.

FARM ANIMAL ABUSE

Many of today's farm animals are raised on "factory-type" farms, consisting of large buildings with small stalls. Pigs, cows, and chickens rarely see the outside and are subjected to cruel conditions in their living quarters.

This environment can be very abusive to the animal. The Humane Farming Association states that the "overcrowding and intensive confinement of animals on factory farms, coupled with the inhumane handling and transportation of livestock, constitute the most widespread abuses animals have ever faced. The most fundamental concepts of animal husbandry, such as proper veterinary care, adequate nutrition, even the freedom for animals to assume natural postures . . .

This year, a million baby calves will be tortured every day of their lives in veal factories.

They'll grow up chained in wooden boxes, unable to move. In darkness. Barely breathing—choking on the ammonia from their own accumulating waste.

So weak and sick that many will die taking the first steps of their lives—the steps from their "veal crates" to their slaughter.

And this year, millions of Americans will eat veal, unknowingly consuming the pale tainted meat from the carcasses of these sick, tortured animals.

—THE HUMANE FARMING ASSOCIATION

163

are vanishing along with America's family farms."

Chicken farms. Large-scale chicken farms are dismal shelters for the millions of chickens raised for eggs and food. For example, in one chicken egg facility, more than 2 million eggs are laid daily by 3 millions hens, which are housed five to each 16- by 18-inch cage. John Robbins, president of EarthSave, puts it in perspective in his *Diet for a New America* (Stillpoint Publishing, 1987).

> To get a chicken's eye view of these conditions, picture yourself standing in a crowded elevator. The elevator is so crowded, in fact, that your body is in contact on all sides with other bodies. Even to turn around in place would be difficult. And one more thing to keep in your mind—this is your life. It is not just a temporary bother, until you get to your floor. This is permanent. Your only release will be at the hands of the executioner.

According to the The Humane Farming Association this is a "House of Horrors." In their brochure "Anything Goes With Eggs," they describe the plight of chickens in factory farms:

> The hen is pressed against the side of the wire cage. Her feathers fall out. Her skin becomes raw, often bloody. Her feet are injured by the sloping wire floor. Propped up beside her is another hen, one which could no longer reach the food when her feet entangle in the wire. So she slowly starved to death. . . . Barely able to move, the hens incessantly strike out in frustration—pecking at the only thing available; each other. . . .
>
> To reduce cannibalism, laying hens are "debeaked." Debeaking is a painful procedure whereby the hen's sensitive upper beak is sliced off with a hot blade. Many die from shock during the process. . . .
>
> Male chicks are of no value to the egg industry. They are thrown into plastic garbage bags to suffocate slowly under the weight of chicks dumped on top. Others are ground into animal feed—while still alive.

John Robbins aptly evaluates this process by telling us that "these are the conditions which the industry tells us is a

·········· Did you know?

50,000 farm animals will be slaughtered in the time it takes to read this page.

'chicken heaven.' This is the actual living situation of the chickens whose flesh and eggs Americans eat."

"Milk-fed" veal. Chickens are not the only animals that suffer abuse. In veal factories, newborn male calves are taken from their mothers and chained alone in crates 22 feet wide and 58 feet long for their entire lives.

The Humane Farming Association is one organization that leads the fight against factory farming of calves raised for veal. Some of their "veal facts" are listed here.

► To prevent muscle development and speed weight gain, the calves are allowed absolutely no exercise.

► Chained in tiny crates, veal calves cannot turn around, groom, stretch their legs, or lie down in a natural position. They are kept in total darkness to reduce restlessness.

► To obtain the light colored meat sold as "premium" or "milk-fed" veal, calves are kept anemic by withholding sufficient irons.

► Veal calves are denied all solid food and are deprived of drinking water. In a futile attempt to quench their thirst, the calves gain weight quickly by drinking more of their milky liquid feed.

► Veal calves suffer from chronic diarrhea from being exclusively fed a liquid diet of growth stimulators, antibiotics, powdered skim milk, and mold inhibitors. Respiratory and intestinal diseases run rampant.

► This is the terrible fate of 1 million calves every year in the United States.*

Chickens and veal calves serve as just two horrific examples of factory farm animal abuse. Cows, pigs, goats, and other animals suffer similar and sometimes worse fates.

*Humane Farming Association.

Q: Why can't this veal calf walk?

A: He has only two feet.

Copyright © Humane Farming Association, 415-485-1495.

·········· Did you know?

OVERUSE OF WATER

▶ Producing a single pound of meat takes an average of 2,500 gallons of water—as much as a typical family uses for all its combined household purposes in a month. The amount of water needed to produce 1 pound of wheat is only 25 gallons.

▶ More than half the water used in the United States for all purposes goes to livestock production.

▶ According to *Newsweek* magazine, "the water that goes into a 1,000 pound steer would float a destroyer."

▶ According to Greenpeace, a city of 22 million people could be supplied with the water it takes to grow grass for California's cows.

AN INEFFICIENT USE OF RESOURCES

Livestock feeding requires an inordinate amount of energy and raw materials, resources that could be utilized more efficiently and equitably to supply a more vegetarian diet.

For instance, the amount of energy and resources it takes to feed farm animals is mind-boggling. And what little we receive in return is equally amazing.

The Society for an Extended Ethic, Inc., finds that:

▶ For every 16 pounds of grain and soy fed to beef cattle in the United States, only 1 pound of meat is returned. And we lose more than 90 percent of the protein we invest as feed in our livestock.

▶ One acre of land produces 2,500 pounds of wheat or 20,000 pounds of potatoes. Yet, this much grain fed to cattle would only yield 169 pounds of beef.

Not only does it cost a lot to get little, but the amount of food and land utilized to raise a meat-based diet could be spent feeding the many hungry people on this planet. As John Robbins explains, "In a world in which a child dies of starvation every two seconds, an agricultural system designed to feed our meat habit is blasphemy." The facts listed here put it into perspective:

▶ The world's cattle alone, not to mention pigs and chickens, consume a quantity of food equal to the caloric needs of 8.7 billion people—nearly double the entire human population of the planet.

▶ The livestock population of the United States today consumes enough grain and soybeans to feed over five times the entire human population of the country. We feed these animals more than 80 percent of the corn we grow, and more than 95 percent of the oats.*

FACTORY FARMING AND THE ABUSE OF THE ENVIRONMENT

The effects on our environment are equally disturbing and threatening. The nation's topsoil is becoming rapidly depleted from overuse and misuse, fossil fuel costs are enormous, and the forests are being lost to animal grazing grounds. Farmers

*John Robbins, *Diet for a New America,* (Walpole, N.H.: Stillpoint Publishing/ EarthSave 1987) 350, 353.

utilize tremendous amounts of water to grow feed for farm animals, and then return it to the soil and rivers polluted with chemicals and animal waste.

Some hard-hitting statistics from *Diet for a New America*, to the right and on the previous and following pages, explain the detrimental impact large-scale farm animal production has on our planet.

HEALTH EFFECTS OF FACTORY FARMING AND A MEAT-BASED DIET

The adverse health impacts of a meat-based diet are becoming increasingly apparent. Excess protein intake may lead to mineral loss, which can create osteoporosis and liver and kidney diseases. Too much fat and cholesterol can cause heart disease, strokes, and diabetes. Foreign substances in meat, such as carcinogens, viruses, antibiotics, hormones, and pesticides, have been linked to colon and breast cancer, as well as to salmonella poisoning. Perhaps there should be a warning label on meat packaging like the one found on cigarette boxes.

> WARNING:
> This Product Can Cause
> Cancer, Heart Disease
> & Stroke!

PETA, People for the Ethical Treatment of Animals

Did you know? •••••••••

TOPSOIL DESTRUCTION FROM CHEMICAL APPLICATION

▶ 75 percent of our precious topsoil has been lost from poor agricultural methods such as chemical fertilizer and pesticide use; 85 percent of this loss is directly associated with livestock raising.

▶ American farmers now apply more than 20 million tons of chemical fertilizers to our farmlands each year, more than the combined weight of the entire human population of the country.

Did you know? •••••••••

DEFORESTATION

▶ 260 million acres of America's forests have been cleared to create cropland to produce a meat-centered diet. Many of the tropical forests in Central America have been cleared to graze the cattle used for our hamburgers.

PETA, People for the Ethical Treatment of Animals

.... Did you know?

POLLUTION FROM ANIMAL EXCREMENT

▶ Every 24 hours, the animals destined for America's dinner tables produce 20 billion pounds of waste. That amounts to 250,000 pounds of excrement a second.

▶ U.S. livestock produces 20 times as much excrement as the entire human population of the country. More than half of this staggering production—over a billion tons a year—comes from confinement operations from which it cannot be recycled. Much of it goes into our water supply.

▶ Animal wastes account for more than 10 times as much water pollution as the total amount attributable to the entire human population.*

HOW SIMPLE DIETARY CHANGES CAN HELP THE PLANET

Using an extreme example, if the entire U.S. population changed its eating habits from a meat-based to a vegetarian diet, the amount of resources saved and the decrease in environmental stress would be startling.

Obviously, a complete shift to vegetarianism in this country is unrealistic, but consider these few points. First, the current methods of meat production in this country enact a devastating toll on the environment. And second, because everyone consumes food, the efforts and actions of each individual are tantamount either to compounding or alleviating the problem.

THINKING BEFORE WE EAT

....

At the present time, when most of us sit down to eat, we aren't very aware of how our food choices affect the world. We don't realize that in every Big Mac there is a piece of the tropical rainforests, and with every billion burgers sold another hundred species become extinct. We don't realize that in the sizzle of our steaks there is the suffering of animals, the mining of our topsoil, the slashing of our forests, the harming of our economy, and the eroding of our health. We don't hear in the sizzle the cry of the hungry millions who might otherwise be fed. We don't see the toxic poisons accumulating in the food chains, poisoning our children and our earth for generations to come.

But once we become aware of the impact of our food choices, we can never really forget. Of course we can push it all to the back of our minds, and we may need to do this, at times, to endure the enormity of what is involved.

But the earth itself will remind us, as will our children, and the animals and the forests and the sky and the rivers, that we are part of this earth, and it is part of us.

–John Robbins, President, The Earth Save Foundation, 408-423-4069

WHAT IS BEING DONE?

● ●

▶ People across the country are cutting down on their meat consumption to protest farm animal suffering and the negative environmental effects of a meat-based diet. The Great American Meatout is one great way to show your support:

*John Robbins, *Diet for a New America*.

THE GREAT AMERICAN MEATOUT

Every year on the first day of Spring (March 20th) people all across the nation put down their steak knives and lift their awareness for a meatless diet. Since 1985, Farm Animal Reform Movement (FARM) has sponsored "The Great American Meatout"—a national campaign to educate the public about the destructive impact of a meat-based diet.

Last year an estimated 20 million people heard the Meatout message promoted by 100 events and over 250 newspapers and radio and television stations.

Celebrity Supporters of the Great American Meatout Doris Day • Casey Kasem • Ally Sheedy • River Phoenix • Cesar Chavez • Cleveland Amory • Berke Breathed • Harvey and Marilyn Diamond • David Goldbeck • Tony LaRussa • and Jeremy Rifkin

For more information contact Farm Animal Reform Movement (FARM) at 301-530-1737.

GREAT AMERICAN MEATOUT
CHOOSE LIFE - KICK THE MEAT HABIT!
MARCH 20th

Did you know? ▪▪▪▪▪▪▪▪▪▪▪

▶ In "Realities 1989," EarthSave reports that 20 pure vegetarians can be fed on the amount of land needed to feed one meat eater.

▶ A meat-based diet uses 33 percent of all raw materials consumed in the United States for all purposes. A fully vegetarian diet uses only 2 percent.

▶ 60 million people could be adequately fed by the grain saved if Americans reduced their intake of meat by 10 percent.

▶ An acre of trees disappears every 8 seconds in the United States, yet 1 acre could be spared per year by each individual who switches to a pure vegetarian diet.

Reprinted with permission from EarthSave.

WHAT CAN I DO?

▶ **Cut down on meat and consider vegetarian diets.** Meat, dairy products, and eggs are the leading sources of saturated fat and cholesterol in American diets. Almost half of all deaths in America are due to heart disease, whereas a pure vegetarian has only a 4 percent chance of dying from a heart attack. A meat-based diet also contains a greater concentration of pesticides and antibiotics. According to pesticide expert Lewis Regenstein in "Realities 1989," meat contains approximately

Many Americans have switched to a vegetarian diet. And they are in good company:

Famous Vegetarians Today

Candice Bergen
Carol Burnett
Belinda Carlisle
Michael Jackson
Carole King
Casey Kasem
Madonna
William Shatner
Susan St. James
Dennis Weaver

Famous Vegetarians Past

Buddha
Henry David Thoreau
Charles Darwin
Ralph Waldo Emerson
Albert Einstein
Thomas Edison
Mohandas Gandhi
Sir Isaac Newton
Leonardo da Vinci
Plato

14 times more pesticides than plant foods; dairy products 5$^{1}/_{2}$ times more.

One immediate way to benefit yourself and your society is to change your diet. A well-balanced vegetarian diet will fulfill all your nutritional needs without these detrimental effects. You should consider cutting down on the amount of meats and eggs you consume and replacing them with more fruit and vegetables.

Some other ideas:

▶ **Buy a good vegan cookbook.** Try a few recipes at home, then invite friends to share vegetarian dinners.

▶ **Organize a vegetarian Thanksgiving dinner.** Promote a meatless diet to your friends and family.

CELEBRITIES FOR VEGETARIANISM

Dennis Weaver:
"There are many reasons . . . everything from spiritual reasons to saving the environment. But the reason that should appeal to everyone is health. Without it there is little chance of happiness."

Natalie Merchant of 10,000 Maniacs:
"If you can't conceive of beating an animal, you shouldn't conceive of eating an animal."

Paul and Linda McCartney:
"We won't eat anything that has to be killed for us. We've been through a lot and we've reached a stage where we really value life."

▶ **Show your support at the grocery store!**

▶ Boycott meat and eggs that come from factory farms. If you are unsure, ask your grocer. Also ask him or her to stock free-range meats and eggs.

▶ Refuse to buy "milk-fed" veal. Tell your grocer that you will only buy free-range items.

▶ Be careful that meat and eggs advertised as free range actually come from such sources. Ask your grocer to verify this.

▶ **Protest farm-animal suffering.**

▶ On October 2, 1989, at least 50 dramatic events were held across the United States in observance of the seventh annual World Farm Animals Day, which is promoted and coordinated each year by the Farm Animal Reform Movement (FARM). These events included a rally at the U.S. Department of Agriculture, protests in Chicago, and a symposium at Stanford University.

▶ As a result of the Humane Farming Association's National Veal Boycott and other such pressures, Congressman Charles Bennett (D-Fla.) introduced "The Veal Calf Protection Act" (HR 2859).

▶ On March 1, 1990, thousands of concerned individuals celebrated the Great American Meatout by voicing their cause of kicking the meat habit and exploring a less violent, healthier diet.

▶ Activist pressure caused a number of hotel, restaurant, and supermarket chains to discontinue the sale of milk-fed veal.

▶ **Educate yourself and your friends.** Buy copies of *Diet for a New America,* by John Robbins (Stillpoint Publishing, 1987) and send them to your friends and relatives. For a condensed, less expensive version contact EarthSave and ask for "Realities 1989."

Another interesting brochure, "The Realities of Animal-Based Agriculture," is produced and distributed by Society for an Extended Ethic, Inc. (their address in on page 192).

▶ **Write to your state and federal legislators and to the editors of your local papers.** Farm-animal legislation covers topics such as Veal Calf protection, meatless options in federally funded school lunch programs, and measures to safeguard animals in transport. Contact FARM for a farm animal Legislative Action Kit.

FARM suggests that you write to the Secretary of the Department of Agriculture, requesting the appointment of a

> **I**f radio stops playing all vocal vegetarians, we'd have no Madonna, Paul McCartney, Michael Jackson, B-52's, or Belinda Carlisle.
>
> —PETA's Dan Matthews

How to Prepare Veal Cordon Bleu

- First, take a baby calf from his mother.
- Place him in a stall 5′ × 2′, making sure he cannot move. (Even stretching his legs could ruin the flavor.)
- Feed him milky gruel 2–3 times a day.
- Season with antibiotics and hormones to taste.
- After 15 weeks, remove calf from stall, kill him, and eat him.

PETA, People for the Ethical Treatment of Animals

HERMAN®

"It's time we heard from the silent majority."

"Herman" copyright © 1990 Jim Unger. Reprinted with permission of Universal Press Syndicate. All rights reserved.

commission to investigate and correct the abuses of factory farming. Write to:

Hon. Edward Madigan, Secretary, Department of Agriculture
Administration Building
14th St. and Independence Ave. SW
Washington, D.C. 20250

▶ **Adopt a farm animal.** Farm Sanctuary offers animal adoption projects, where your donation helps feed animals rescued from abusive factory farms. For example, more than 27 million turkeys are raised for Thanksgiving alone—many in conditions of gross abuse and neglect.

Farm Sanctuary encourages you to "feed a turkey rather than eat one."

▶ **Become informed!** Contact the farm animal welfare organizations listed here and ask for more information.

ORDINARY PEOPLE—EXTRAORDINARY ACTIONS

"A dog or cat has the same feelings that we do. They feel pain just like us. They're animals . . . just like we are."

Sarah Hoeb was so upset when she found out how veal calves are raised that she asked her father, who owns the Clarion Hotel in Cincinnati, Ohio, to take veal off the hotel's menu.

He agreed—veal is a cruel meal!

Newspapers around the country carried the story of Sarah, her father, and her victory for the calves.

Congratulations, Sarah!—PETA Kids

Organizations and Resources

• •

ASPCA
212-876-7700
Send for study on human health consequences from factory farming as well as the video, "The Other Side of the Fence." ($69.95)

EarthSave Foundation
408-423-4069
An organization that provides education and leadership for

transition to more healthful and environmentally sound food choices, non-polluting energy supplies, and a wiser use of natural resources. John Robbins, author of *Diet for a New America,* is president of EarthSave.

Farm Animal Reform Movement (FARM)
301-530-1737

"To moderate and eliminate animal suffering and other adverse impacts of animal agriculture."

The Humane Farming Association
415-485-1495
Their goal is to protect human health and animal welfare. The Humane Farming Association (HFA) is a

nonprofit organization of public health specialists, veterinarians, consumer advocates, family farmers, humane societies, and others. HFA members are united in a campaign to protect consumers from the dangerous misuse of chemicals in food production and to eliminate the severe and senseless suffering to which farm animals are subjected.

The Humane Society (HSUS)
202-452-1100
Ask for a copy of their *Recommended Humane Guidelines for Raising Livestock, Poultry, and Dairy Animals* (c/o The Farm Animals/Bioethics Department).

OTHER COMMITTED ORGANIZATIONS

Adopt-a-Cow
717-527-2476

American Vegan Society
609-694-2887

Animal Legal Defense Fund
415-459-0885

Animal Protection Institute of America
916-731-5521

Compassion in World Farming
The Culture and Animals Foundation
919-782-3739

Food Animals Concern Trust
312-525-4952

Friends of Animals
203-866-5223

Fund for Animals
212-246-2096

Humane Society of the United States
202-452-1100

In Defense of Animals
415-453-9984

International Fund for Animal Welfare
508-362-4944

International Society for Animal Rights
717-586-2200

People for the Ethical Treatment of Animals (PETA)
301-770-7444

Progressive Animal Welfare Society (PAWS)
206-743-3845

Society for an Extended Ethic, Inc.
Vegetarian Awareness Network
800-872-8343/615-558-VEGE

• •

THE GREAT FUR DEBATE

▪ ▪ ▪

THE FIGHT OVER FUR

A battle rages on Madison Avenue in New York City, in department stores in Toronto, and outside retail specialty stores in Bethesda, Maryland. This is a "fight over fur" and its battlefield stretches from Western Europe to Aspen and Beverly Hills.

The two opposing forces are the animal rights activists and the fur producers and retailers. Trapped in the middle stands the consumer.

ANTI-FUR MESSAGE

In the past few years, animal rights activists have launched

Fashion shouldn't cost an arm and a leg.

—In Defense of Animals

**Fur: A Dying Fashion
A Dead Investment**

In Defense of Animals.

more confrontational, and sometimes controversial, tactics to voice their opposition against the fur industry.

Their argument: That animals utilized for fur coats and other fur products suffer undue pain and discomfort in their trapping, captivity, and death, all for the sake of fashion.

According to anti-fur advocates, 5.2 million animals were raised and killed on fur ranches in 1986. They live trapped in small cages, crazed with claustrophobia and stress, and are killed in convenient yet often brutal ways such as carbon monoxide asphyxiation, poisons, electrocution, or by having their neck snapped. Often the animals undergo great pain and suffering and sometimes are still alive when the skinning begins. Unlike factory farms, there are no federal regulations regarding compassionate treatment and inspection of facilities.

Seventeen million animals were trapped in 1986, accounting for 72 percent of all pelts produced in the United States that year, according to the Humane Society. Death by trapping can be equally brutal. Animals are often caught by leghold traps or whole body traps. They can be left for days, often dying slowly from exhaustion, dehydration, starvation, freezing, and/or predation. Some actually chew their own leg off in order to escape. Incredibly, state trapping authorities promote trapping to gain license revenue.

THE FUR INDUSTRY FIGHTS BACK

The fur industry has embarked on an aggressive campaign to promote its own message: that owning fur is a freedom of choice. Members of the industry and owners of coats argue that they have a right to do what they choose, a right the Fur Information Council calls "the cornerstone of our country." Perhaps in a show of support for the freedom of choice, a 1990 *USA Today* poll revealed that 74 percent of those questioned did not think that fur sales should be banned.

Fur advocates also believe that it is a violation of their rights to be abused by anti-fur demonstrators. (There have been cases of verbal and even physical abuse used against fur coats wearers and fur retailers.) Furthermore, they dispute the amount of abuse that the animals allegedly endure. According to Robert Buckler of the Fur Farm Animal Welfare Coalition, "I've never heard of a mink being electrocuted. The vast majority of animals are killed without stress, using carbon monoxide or dioxide gas, a technique recognized by the American Veterinary Medical Association."*

I f they succeed [anti-fur activists] . . . say goodbye to freedom—freedom to live life as you choose and to eat and wear what you like.

—MARSHA KELLY, Fur Farm Animal Welfare Coalition

*USA Today, 24 November 1989.

174

THE DECISION IS UP TO YOU!

The fur battle is a public debate that requires individual choices. Only you can decide whether or not to wear fur. Anti-fur activists feel that fur is not a necessity and the wearing of it blatantly advertises cruelty. Opponents believe that people have a right to make their own choices and that it is hypocritical to condemn fur and still eat meat and use leather products.

The mistreatment of animals for fur symbolizes the larger issue of the abuse of all animals, whether they are used for our food, our companionship, or our dress. Perhaps by exploring this debate we will become more aware of the many other animal welfare issues.

Friends of Animals

TO MAKE JUST ONE FUR COAT YOU MUST KILL AT LEAST:

55 Wild minks	30 Muscrats
35 Ranch minks	15 Bobcats
40 Sables	25 Skunks
11 Lynx	14 Otters
18 Red foxes	125 Ermines
100 Chinchillas	30 Possums
30 Rex rabbits	100 Squirrels
9 Beavers	27 Raccoons

In Defense of Animals 415-453-9984

WHAT IS BEING DONE?

▶ Due to pressure from animal activists, during the past few years, 75 percent of the fur retailers in Germany, England, and Holland have closed down. In 1988, three of the largest fur retailers in the United States reported record losses, and in early 1991 Nordstroms, a large department store chain, announced that it would close its fur departments.

▶ PETA's Fur Is Dead campaign, Trans-Species Unlimited's nationwide Fur-Free Friday, and the Humane Society's Shame of Fur messages, together with pressure from many other organizations, have focused national attention on this issue.

▶ In 1987, Bob Barker resigned as host of the Miss Universe

Animal Rights Mobilization (formerly Trans-Species Unlimited).

and Miss U.S.A. pageants when contest officials refused to stop awarding fur coats as prizes. Pageant officials later agreed to ban the use of furs.

WHAT CAN I DO?

If you are against the sale of fur, here are some actions you can take:

▶ Boycott fur products and get others to do the same. Your actions will give strength to a growing movement against fur.

▶ **Boycott stores that sell fur items.**
    ▶ Write to the store owners and managers to let them know your feelings.
    ▶ Tell them that you refuse to shop in their store until they stop selling fur, and turn in your store credit cards to make the point. Trans-Species Unlimited calls this strategy creating a "Fur-Free Zone." The HSUS strategy: "When consumers stop buying, the animals stop dying."

▶ **Be aware of the agony every animal went through to make a fur coat.** According to PETA, "up to 120 animals are barbarically killed to make just one fur coat."

—120 ANIMAL LIVES!

That's right, up to 120 animals are barbarically killed to make just one fur coat.

Animals killed for fur are electrocuted, poisoned, gassed, and suffocated. Or caught in the wild in cruel steel-jaw leghold traps—which also kill and maim deer, birds, domestic dogs and cats and other helpless animals.

When you wear fur, you promote cruelty. When you stop wearing fur, you help stop the suffering.

For the facts about fur, write

PEOPLE FOR THE ETHICAL TREATMENT OF ANIMALS

P.O. Box 42516, Washington, D.C. 20015

THE COST OF ONE FUR COAT IS...

▶ **Contact the media about this issue.** Let them know that you refuse to wear fur and that you protest the treatment of animals raised for fur.

▶ **Write the sellers of fur and let them know your feelings.** Write to local or national department stores that sell fur, or write to specialty retailers of fur. Tell them that you will not buy fur products and ask them to stop selling fur.

▶ **Educate others.** PETA suggests that you should let fur wearers know of your feelings by saying "Shame" when you see them wearing a fur coat. They believe that if people hear the message often enough, they'll stop buying and wearing fur.

PETA, People for the Ethical Treatment of Animals

▶ **Donate your fur to an animal welfare organization.** They will be more than happy to dispose of it for you. Deduct it on your income tax, if possible. Contact In Defense of Animals or another animal welfare group for more information.

▶ **Help distribute anti-fur materials and use bumper stickers.**

ANTI-FUR SLOGANS FOUND ON BUMPER STICKERS, PINS, PRINT ADS, AND T-SHIRTS:

Fur Hurts.

Fur Is Dead.

Stop the Agony. Don't Buy Fur.

You Should be Ashamed to Wear Fur.

This Year Millions Will Be Killed Because of What They're Wearing—Don't Wear Fur (PETA)

FUR COATS are worn by BEAUTIFUL ANIMALS and UGLY PEOPLE.

Get a Feel for Fur. Slam Your Fingers in a Car Door (Friends of Animals)

▶ **Support anti-fur legislative initiatives.** Measures include banning the leghold trap, curtailing or eliminating trapping, and monitoring ranch-raised fur production. Contact one of the groups listed here for information about current legislation.

☆ ☆ THE STARS ARE SHINING! ☆ ☆
FASHION AGAINST FUR

''I think fur is wonderful. . . . As long as it's on the animals!''
—Supermodel Paulina Porizkova at PETA's 1990 Rock Against Fur Concert

Other Anti-Fur Celebrities
Candice Bergen • Rosanna Arquette • Daryl Hannah • Kirstie Alley • The ''Golden Girls''—Betty White, Bea Arthur, and Rue McClanahan • Ally Sheedy • Ali MacGraw • Kim Basinger • Brooke Shields • Caroline Herrera • Georgio Armani • Bill Blass •

Organizations and Resources

ASPCA
212-876-7700
Ask for their video, "The Price They Pay."

The Humane Society of the United States (HSUS)
202-452-1100
Representing more than 500,000 people, HSUS has fought for animals since 1954 through educational, legislative, investigative, and legal means. Responsible for the Shame of Fur campaign seen on billboards and in magazines across the country.

In Defense of Animals
415-453-9984
Ask for extra copies of their anti-fur leaflets.

Animal Rights Mobilization (formerly Trans-Species Unlimited)
717-322-3252

A national animal rights organization based in Pennsylvania, which is dedicated to the total elimination of animal abuse and exploitation. Sponsor of the Fur-Free America campaign.

People for the Ethical Treatment of Animals (PETA)
301-770-7444
"Incorporated to educate policy-makers and the public to the issues involving the intense, prolonged, and unjustifiable abuse of animals, and to promote an understanding of the inherent rights of sentient animals to be treated with respect and decency." PETA's Fur Is Dead campaign has been one of the most vocal and effective protests against fur.

OTHER COMMITTED ORGANIZATIONS

Refer to the end of this section for phone numbers and addresses.

Alliance for Animals

Animal Rights Information Service

Beauty without Cruelty

Culture and Animals Foundation

Friends of Animals

Fur-Bearer Defenders

LYNX

World Society for the Protection of Animals (WSPA)

PET ABUSE

HOMELESS PETS

Why are so many animals abandoned? One reason is that many owners do not realize the responsibilities involved in owning a pet. They abandon a pet that is "just too much to handle," leaving it homeless and helpless.

Other pet owners do not realize the costs involved in owning an animal. For some reason, some pet owners feel that their animals will have a better chance on the streets than in a shelter where they may eventually be destroyed if no home is found.

Thanks to PETA's Animal Rescue Fund, Rogan (*left*) now shares a loving home with Druzhok and Koro—safe from the danger of the animal dealer. Courtesy of People for the Ethical Treatment of Animals.

▪▪▪▪▪▪▪▪▪▪ Did you know?

Cat Fancy, a leading animal publication, reports that of the 25 million pets left homeless each year, 14 to 18 million are killed as surplus animals in shelters, or donated to research where they may face even more gruesome fates. The remaining 7 to 11 million are abandoned to hunger, traps, disease, highway slaughter, and starvation.

Pound Seizure

The Compassion for Animals organization claims that every year an estimated 300,000 dogs and cats, most of which are lost, stolen or abandoned pets, are sold by animal "shelters" to laboratories for use in animal research. This practice is known as "pound seizure."

Once an animal is sold to a research laboratory, its fate is grim. The International Society for Animal Rights claims that once an animal goes into a shelter or pound it could be sent to a research laboratory, where it faces the possibility of long, agonizing torture and slow, painful deaths. Dogs and cats are especially vulnerable, because they possess so many "human" qualities.

If your pet is lost or stolen, it could end up in a lab—a fate worse than death.

"Puppy Mills"

Pets suffer abuse even if they are not abandoned. "Puppy mills" breed animals for the many pet stores across the nation. Often, these dog-breeding establishments expose the animals to abominable conditions, including starvation, outright abuse, and lack of veterinary care.

According to the American Humane Association, USDA licensed "puppy mills" continue to mass breed dogs in deplorable conditions. Some of these breeders keep puppies in outdoor cages with no protection from freezing temperatures, rain, or intense sun. Many have even been caught feeding puppies contaminated water and food, and leaving dead puppies in the cages with living ones.

Puppies become sick with parasites, upper respiratory infections, and genetic disorders due to inbreeding. They often become ill or die soon after they are taken home, subjecting the owners to much heartbreak and expense.

I FOUND THE LOVE OF MY LIFE AT THE ANIMAL SHELTER

"Cathy" Copyright © 1989 Cathy Guisewite. Reprinted with permission of Universal Press Syndicate. All rights reserved.

WHAT CAN I DO?
•••••••••••••••••••••••••••••••••••••••

Although pets give unconditional love to their owners, sometimes it is not returned. Many pet owners are irresponsible, and unfortunately it is the animal who suffers. Numerous cases of abandonment, cruel treatment, inadequate nutrition, and poor health go unreported each day.

The challenge of pet abuse begins with animal owners; you have an opportunity to help solve this problem.

▶ **Report all cases of animal abuse.** In Los Angeles a toll-free number (800-540-SPCA) to report animal abuse has been started by the Los Angeles SPCA. The hot line is intended to bring help to abused pets. Sgt. Cori Whetstone explains, "We want to bring public awareness to the community about the horrendous acts of violence against animals and let the people know that we are here to assist, to rescue these creatures and give them better homes."*

If you know of an animal abuse case, contact your local SPCA or an animal welfare organization in your area.

PETA'S ANIMAL RESCUE FUND

There is an important part of PETA's work you may not have heard about. I'm talking about the survivors of animal abuse and cruelty—the lucky animals whose stories of suffering have a happy ending.

▶ Dogs like Angel, Rogan, Blackie, and Bruin, who PETA rescued moments before they were to be thrown into the back of an animal dealer's truck on the way to a laboratory and certain death. All were malnourished, suffering from severe mange, terrified and homeless.

▶ Or the three young, intelligent pigs in North Carolina who had been abandoned by a heartless "owner" and left to starve, but had managed to survive until PETA found out about them and brought them to a loving home.

▶ Or Chester, a young bull we found in a Washington, DC, basement with his legs tightly bound, awaiting a terrifying, slow and painful death in a cult sacrifice.

With patience, understanding, and hard work, PETA is providing the resources, funds, and in many cases, the facilities, to nurture these and thousands of other survivors back to health. We also find them safe and permanent homes.

All this is made possible by PETA's ANIMAL RESCUE FUND, 301-770-7444

PETA, People for the Ethical Treatment of Animals

▶ **Spay/neuter your own pet and fight for low-cost spay/neuter clinics in your community.** Many animals that are not spayed or neutered contribute to pet overpopulation. Get your next pet from the local pound or shelter.

▶ **Report abandoned animals to the proper authorities.** Your

*Michael Quintanilla, "Toll-Free Line Seeks to Curb Animal Abuse," *Los Angeles Times*, 2 October 1989.

Animal Protection Institute

prompt call may save a lost pet. And the faster the authorities get abandoned animals off the street, the sooner they will be placed in a home.

EMERGENCY ANIMAL RESCUE SERVICE (EARS)

Operated by the United Animal Nations, EARS—a "911" for Animals, responds quickly to animal emergencies. Through its international network of 30 member agencies and 1.5 million supporters, the United Animal Nations has helped rescue and rehabilitate suffering animals across the world.

EARS has been there to help during disasters such as Hurricane Hugo, the Alaskan oil spill, and the Australian wild horse slaughter.

For information contact United Animal Nations-U.S.A. at 916-429-2457.

Printed with permission of the International Society for Animal Rights 717-586-2200

IT COULD HAPPEN TO YOUR PET NOW.

All the institutions below, plus thousands more across the nation, conduct their experiments with taxpayer funds appropriated by Congress—over $6 billion each year.

At Princeton University, a researcher "puts screws in a cat's skull and wires its neck muscles. . . . Then the cat is put on a brick placed in water. If the cat begins to relax, it falls into the water. When the cat has been sufficiently deprived of sleep . . . its brain is removed."

At Case Western University, pregnant dogs were deprived of food for up to five days to study the effects of starvation on their puppies. Newborn pups were guillotined.

At New York University, hundreds of cats have had their spinal cords crushed by dropping weights on them. Having been rendered paraplegic, the cats are observed for up to one year before they are killed.

Scientists from Cincinnati Shriners' Burn Institute and the University of Cincinnati Medical Center burned over one-third the skin on the bodies of live beagles with kerosene-soaked gauze.

At the University of Pennsylvania, tourniquets were put around cats' necks to keep blood from reaching their head for 30 minutes, and cats' arteries were severed to induce massive hemorrhaging.

▶ Support the introduction and passage of legislation designed to protect pets. One pressing concern among animal rights advocates is the use of pets for scientific research. In many cases, stray animals such as dogs and cats are auctioned off to research laboratories for testing purposes. In 1989, the Pet Protection Act was introduced in Congress. The Act was designed to prohibit funding from the National Institutes of Health from going to any researcher using lost, stolen, or shelter animals, thus abolishing 80 percent of the pound seizure in the United States. Although the Act did not pass, many anti-vivisection organizations and animal rights groups support such legislation.

Contact Compassion for Animals, PAWS, I.S.A.R., PETA or another animal rights group for more information.

Organizations

ASPCA
212-876-7700.
Provides care and shelter for homeless, mistreated, and injured animals. Helps find suitable homes for animals and educates the public about animal care and animal rights. Ask for their video, "Throwaways" ($15.00).

Animal Protection Institute of America
916-731-5521
An organization dedicated to solving the problem of animal mistreatment and abandonment.

Compassion for Animals Foundation
800-82-VOICE
Ask for their "Outreach Brochure," which will help you spread the word against pound seizure.

International Society for Animal Rights
717-586-2200

Humane Society (HSUS)
202-452-1100
Call your local chapter or the national headquarters.

Progressive Animal Welfare Society (PAWS)
206-743-3845

PETA's Animal Rescue Fund
301-770-7444

United Animal Nations– U.S.A.
916-429-2457

OTHER IMPORTANT ANIMAL RIGHTS ISSUES

■ ■ ■

Only a few of the many pressing animal welfare concerns are discussed in this book. Listed here are a few other important issues and their corresponding advocacy groups. Refer to the end of this part for their addresses and phone numbers.

For a more extensive list of animal rights topics and organizations, as well as a bimonthly update on all major animal welfare issues, order a subscription to *The Animal's Voice Magazine* (P.O. Box 341347, Los Angeles, CA 90034/1-800-82-VOICE).

ANIMAL "ADOPTION" AGENCIES

You can help endangered species by adoption! Many environmental groups give you the chance to contribute through actual adoption of an animal or a piece of the environment.

When you adopt a whale, for example, your money will go toward preservation of the species, and in return you will receive a photo of your tagged whale. Other "orphans" in-

Traditional Lessons For Boys

Raaodeo

Rodeos teach us that cruelty to animals is manly and that domination is more important than compassion.

Reprinted with permission from Doug Minkler.

clude birds, wild horses, deer, streams, beaches, and forests.

In some cases all you have to do is contribute, whereas in others you can get personally involved. For instance, if you "adopt" a beach, you can help keep it clean by picking up litter.

Organizations

Adopt-a-hawk, eagle, or owl:	Delaware Valley Raptor Center
Adopt-a-deer:	Whitetails Unlimited
Adopt-a-bird:	Project "Wind Seine"
Adopt-a-whale:	International Wildlife Coalition/EarthTrust
Adopt-a-horse or burro:	U.S. Dept. of the Interior
Adopt-a-national forest:	Operation COC
Adopt-a-greyhound:	(See listing under greyhounds)

Animals in Entertainment

Traveling shows and circuses have been known to subject animals to severe abuses, including cruel training practices; rough handling during transportation; and unnatural acts such as mule water diving, boxing kangaroos, and bear wrestling.

Other animals such as pit bulls and chickens participate in ruthless sport fighting where crowds of bettors cheer them on—to their death.

It is most important to remember that an animal owner or exhibitor is not necessarily an animal lover. Keep an eye out for mistreated animals and report cruel treatment to an animal rights organization.

Organizations

PETA
HSUS
ASPCA

BATS

Bats control vast numbers of insect nests and pollinate many of the world's plant life. Moreover, they are responsible for as much as 95 percent of the seed dispersal essential to the regeneration of tropical rain forests. They, like many other animals, are being threatened with extinction due to habitat encroachment and other causes.

Organizations

Bat Conservation International

BEARS

Habitat encroachment and hunting have vastly reduced the bear population in North America. Bear welfare groups help preserve the "king" of American forests.

Organizations

The Great Bear Foundation
National Society for Animal Protection (NSAP)

HORSES

Horse advocacy groups seek to protect the population and treatment of wild horses in America.

Organizations

American Horse Protection Association
American Mustang & Burro Association
U.S. Wild Horse Foundation
Wild Horse Coalition
Wild Horse Sanctuary

GORILLAS

The current world price for a lowland baby gorilla is more than $100,000. Baby gorillas are captured in the wild by poachers and sold to zoos throughout the world. Many of the baby gorillas die in captivity before they reach their final destination. Because the gorilla's parents are so fiercely protective of their young, they are slaughtered during the initial capture.

These senseless deaths and illegal kidnappings threaten the very existence of lowland gorillas.

Organizations

International Primate Protection League (IPPL)
American Wildlife Foundation

GREYHOUNDS

The idea of a dog chasing another animal, such as a cat or a rabbit, is nothing new. However, greyhound racetracks have been known to use live rabbit lures to entice the dogs to run. The rabbits, terrified from whirling around a track at 35 mph, are then killed by the dogs. Equally as tragic, the greyhounds themselves are destroyed at very young ages when they become no longer "fit" to race.

Organizations

In Defense of Animals
Greyhound Friends
Retired Greyhounds as Pets

Legislation

The following organizations monitor and promote federal legislation on behalf of animals and the environment. This includes coordination of lobbying efforts among animal welfare organizations across the country, helping members of groups become effective lobbyists, and updating individuals and groups on legislative issues.

Organizations

Animal Legal Defense Fund
Animal Political Action Committee
California Political Action Committee for Animals
Citizens to Save Our Pets
Committee for Humane Legislation
Legal Action for Animals
Legislation in Support of Animals
National Alliance for Animal Legislation
Political Action Committee
Sierra Club Legal Defense Fund
Society for Animal Protective Legislation

SPORT HUNTING

Each year an estimated 27 million hunters invade the U.S. countryside, killing approximately 200 million animals. These estimates include 24,000 bears, 102,000 elk, 3 million deer, 27 million rabbits, and 94 million upland birds.

The Endangered Species Act of 1973 states "The two major factors in the endangerment of wildlife species is habitat destruction and hunting." Although hunting as a factor has since been omitted from this act, the U.S. Department of Interior estimates that recreational hunters are killing 200 endangered bald eagles a year, 78 percent during hunting season. At least a half a million animals are killed or wounded each year on sanctuaries that were originally conceived as ecological reserves where wildlife would be left in its natural state and sport hunting would be prohibited.

Animal welfare groups argue that hunting is not economically necessary, that it endangers the environment, and that it promotes needless suffering and killing of wildlife.

Organizations

Committee to Abolish Sport
   Hunting, Inc.
League Against Cruel Sports
Fund for Animals
Hunt Saboteurs

Humane Society of the
   United States (HSUS)
Wildlife Refuge Reform
   Coalition (WRRC)

WHALES AND OTHER MARINE LIFE

Although the world rallied to help save three whales trapped in an ice flow in Alaska, many of their species were hunted close to extinction. A 1986 international moratorium on whaling has helped, although the law has loopholes, allowing countries such as Japan, Norway, and Iceland to kill some 400 in 1988.

Organizations

American Cetacean Society
Center for Marine
   Conservation
Cetacean Society
   International
Cousteau Society
Earth Island Institute
EarthTrust
Friends of the Sea Otter
Greenpeace
Oceanic Society

Porpoise Rescue Foundation
Save the Whales
International Sea Shepherd
   Conservation Society
The Whale Info Line
International Wildlife
   Coalition
Whale Adoption Project
Whale Center
World Wildlife Fund

WOLVES

Wolves have all but disappeared from North America, except in parts of Canada, Alaska, and Minnesota. They have been killed out of hate and fear, and from their exaggerated reputation as killers of livestock and other animals.

Wolves actually help regulate herds of deer, elk, moose, and caribou at desirable population levels. However, they are often killed so these herds can grow unchecked, all for the

187

sake of adding to the bounty of sport hunters.

Animal's Voice magazine reports that "the trapping, poisoning and gunning of wolves in North America has reduced the species' range to less than one percent of its original size, and seven of the 23 races of wolf are now considered extinct."*

Organizations

Alaska Wildlife Alliance	*Project Wolf USA*
Clem & Jethro Lecture	*Voice of the Wolf*
Service	*Wolf Haven*
Earth First! Wolf Action	*Wolf Park*
Network	*Wolf Sanctuary*
Friends of the Wolf—USA	*Wolves and Related Canids*

*Robert Hunter and Paul Watson, "There's Never Been a Killing Like It . . ." *Animal's Voice*, September/October 1988.

ANIMAL RIGHTS ORGANIZATIONS

● ●

Adopt-A-Cow
RD. 1, Box 839
Port Royal, PA 17082

African Elephant and Rhino Specialist Group (AERSG)
c/o IUCN
Avenue du Mont-Blanc
CH-1196
Gland, Switzerland

African Elephant Conservation Coordinating Group
c/o Dr. David Weston
Wildlife Conservation Intl.
P.O. Box 62844
Nairobi, Kenya

African Wildlife Foundation
1717 Massachusetts Ave., NW
Washington, DC 20036
202-265-8393

Alaska Wildlife Alliance
P.O. Box 202022
Anchorage, AK 99519
907-277-0897

Alliance for Animals
P.O. Box 909
Boston, MA 02103
617-265-7577

American Anti-Vivisection Society
Suite 204, Noble Plaza

801 Old York Road
Jenkintown, PA 19046-1685
215-887-0816

American Association of Zoological Parks and Aquariums
Rt. 88, Ogelbay Park
Wheeling, WV 26003
304-242-2160

American Fund for Alternatives to Animal Research (AFAAR)
175 West 12th St., Suite 16G
New York, NY 10011
212-989-8073

American Cetacean Society
P.O. Box 2639
San Pedro, CA 90731
213-548-6279

American Fund for Alternatives to Animal Research (AFAAR)
175 W. 12th St., Suite 16-G
New York, NY 10011
212-989-8073

American Fur Industry Committee for Wildlife Conservation and Legislation
363 7th Ave.
New York, NY 10001

American Horse Protection Assoc.
1000 29th St., Suite T-100
Washington, DC 20007
202-965-0500

American Humane Association
9725 E. Hampden Ave.
Denver, CO 80231
303-695-0811

American Mustang and Burro Association
P.O. Box 216
Liberty Hill, TX 78642-0216

American Society for the Prevention of Cruelty to Animals (ASPCA)
441 East 92nd St.
New York, NY 10128
212-876-7700

American Vegan Society
501 Old Harding Highway
Malaga, NJ 08328
609-694-2887

Animalines
814 Castro St.
San Francisco, CA 94114
415-826-7658

Animals' Agenda Magazine
c/o Humane Alternative
   Products

8 Hutchins St.
Concord, NH 03301

Animals Magazine
350 South Huntington Ave.
Boston, MA 02130

The Animal's Voice Magazine
(c/o Compassion for Animals Foundation)
Subscription Dept.
P.O. Box 1649
Martinez, CA 94553-9868
800-82-VOICE

Animal Legal Defense Fund
1363 Lincoln Ave.
San Rafael, CA 94901
415-459-0885

Animal Political Action Committee
P.O. Box 2706
Washington, DC 20013
703-527-1539

Animal Protection Institute of America (API)
P.O. Box 22505
Sacramento, CA 95822
916-731-5521

Animal Rights Information & Education Service (ARIES)
P.O. Box 332
Rowayton, CT 06853
203-866-0523

Animal Rights Information Service (ARIS)
P.O. Box 20672
Columbus Circle Station
New York, NY 10023

Animal Rights Mobilization
(formerly Trans-Species Unlimited)
P.O. Box 1533
Williamsport, PA 17703
717-322-3252

Animal Welfare Institute
P.O. Box 3650
Washington, DC 20007
202-337-2332

Animals Lobby
1025 9th St. #219
Sacramento, CA 95814
916-441-1562

Association of Veterinarians for Animal Rights (AVAR)
707-451-1391

Bat Conservation International
P.O. Box 162603
Austin, TX 78716
512-327-9721

Beauty Without Cruelty— U.S.A.
175 West 12th St. #16-G
New York, NY 10011
212-989-8073

Between the Species
P.O. Box 254
Berkeley, CA 94701
415-526-5346

California Political Action Committee for Animals
P.O. Box 2354
San Francisco, CA 94126
415-885-2679

Cambridge Committee for Responsible Research
P.O. Box 1626
Cambridge, MA 02238
617-547-9255

Center for Marine Conservation
1725 DeSales St., NW
Washington, DC 20036
202-429-5609

Cetacean Society International
P.O. Box 9145
Wethersfield, CT 06109
203-563-6444

Citizens to End Animal Suffering and Legislation
P.O. Box 27
Cambridge, MA 02238

Citizens to Save our Pets
5629 Carlton
Los Angeles, CA 90028

Clem & Jethro Lecture Service
Box 5817
Santa Fe, NM 87502

Committee for Humane Legislation
1506 19th St, NW, Suite 3
Washington, DC 20036
202-393-3647

Committee to Abolish Sport Hunting (CASH)
P.O. Box 43
White Plains, NY 10605
914-428-7523

Compassion for Animals Foundation, Inc.
P.O. Box 5312
Beverly Hills, CA 90209
800-82-VOICE

Compassion in World Farming
20 Lavant St.
Petersfield, Hants
ENGLAND

Concern for Helping Animals in Israel (CHAI)
P.O. Box 3341
Alexandria, VA 22302
703-698-0825

Convention on International Trade in Endangered Species (CITES)
c/o UNEP
DC2-0803 United Nations
New York, NY 10017
212-963-8093

Conservation International
1015 18th St. NW, Suite 1000
Washington, DC 20036
202-429-5660

Cosmetic, Toiletry and Fragrance Association
1110 Vermont Ave., NW,
Suite 800
Washington, DC 20005

Cousteau Society
930 West 21st St.

Norfolk, VA 23517
804-627-1144

The Culture and Animals Foundation
3509 Eden Croft Drive
Raleigh, NC 27612
919-782-3739

Defenders of Wildlife
1244 19th St., NW
Washington, DC 20036
202-659-9510

Delaware Valley Raptor Center
RD 2, Box 9335
Milford, PA 18337
717-296-6025

Dolphinarium
2407 Wilshire Blvd., Suite 507
Los Angeles, CA 90403

Dolphin Connection
1416 N. La Brea Ave.
Hollywood, CA 90028
213-471-7953

Dolphin Project
Box 224
Coconut Grove, FL 33233

Doris Day Animal League
111 Massachusetts Ave., NW
#200
Washington, DC 20001
202-842-3325

Ducks Unlimited
One Waterfowl Way
Long Grove, IL 60047
708-438-4300

Earth First Wolf Action Network
HCR 79 P.O. Box 1046
Crowley Reservation, CA 93456
619-935-4720

Earth Island Institute
300 Broadway, Suite 28
San Francisco, CA 94133
415-788-3666

EarthSave Foundation
P.O. Box 949
Felton, CA 95018-0949
408-423-4069

EarthTrust
900 Fort St, Suite 1270
Honolulu, HI 96813
808-595-6927

East-West Journal
17 Station St.
Box 1200
Brookline, MA 02147

Farm Animal Reform Movement (FARM)
Box 30654
Bethesda, MD 20897
301-530-1737

Farm Sanctuary
P.O. Box 37
Rockland, DE 19732
302-654-9026

Feminists for Animal Rights
P.O. Box 10017
N. Berkeley Station
Berkeley, CA 94709
415-547-7251

Focus on Animals
P.O. Box 150
Trumbull, CT 06611
203-377-1116

Food Animals Concern Trust
P.O. Box 14599
Chicago, IL
312-525-4952

Friends of Africa
P.O. Box 6388
Aspen/Snowmass Village, CO 81615
303-923-2349
P.O. Box 24499
Nairobi, Kenya
254-2-882260

Friends of Animals
P.O. Box 1244
Norwalk, CT 06856
203-866-5223

Friends of Conservation
1420 Kensington
Oak Brook, IL 60521
708-954-3388

Friends of the Sea Otter
P.O. Box 221220
Carmel, CA 93922

Friends of the Wolf-USA
P.O. Box 16
Davis, CA 95617-0016

Fund for Animals
200 West 57th St.
New York, NY 10019
212-246-2096

Fur-Bearer Defenders
P.O. Box 188950
Sacramento, CA
916-391-4617

GAIA Institute
P.O. Box 852
South Lynfield, MA 01940
508-535-4203

**The Great Bear
Foundation**
P.O. Box 2699
Missoula, MT 59806

Greenpeace
1611 Connecticut Ave., NW
Washington, DC 20009
202-462-1177

**Greenpeace Marine
Division**
1436 U St., NW
P.O. Box 3720
Washington, DC 20007

Greyhound Friends
2 Sacramento Place
Cambridge, MA 02138

**Humane Farming
Association**
1550 California St., #6
San Francisco, CA 94109
415-485-1495

Hunt Saboteurs
P.O. Box 2102
Anaheim, CA 92814
714-995-4889

**The Humane Society of
the United States (HSUS)**
2100 L St., NW
Washington, DC 20037
202-452-1100

HSUS Wildlife Division
2100 L St., NW
Washington, DC 20037

In Defense of Animals
21 Tamal Vista Blvd.
Corta Madera, CA 94925
415-453-9984

**International Fund for
Ethical Research**
53 W. Jackson Blvd.
Chicago, IL 60604

**International Fund for
Animal Welfare**
411 Main St.
Yarmouth Port, MA 02675
508-362-4944

**International Fund for
Ethical Research (IFER)**
53 West Jackson Blvd.
Chicago, IL 60604
312-427-6025

**International Network for
Religion and Animals**
2913 Woodstock Ave.
Silver Spring, MD 20910
301-565-9132

**International Primate
Protection League (IPPL)**
P.O. Drawer 766
Summerville, SC 29484
803-871-2280

**International Society for
Animal Rights (ISAR)**
421 South State St.
Clarks Summit, PA 18411
717-586-2200

**International Union for
Conservation of Nature &
Natural Resources (IUCN)**
Avenue du Mont-Blanc
CH-1196
Gland, Switzerland

**International Wildlife
Coalition Whale Adoption
Project**
634 North Falmouth Highway
P.O. Box 388
North Falmouth, MA 02556
508-564-9980

Jews for Animal Rights
255 Humphrey St.
Marblehead, MA 01945
617-631-7601

**Last Chance for Animals
(LCA)**
18653 Ventura Blvd.
Tarzana, CA 91356
213-271-1409

Legal Action for Animals
205 E. 42nd St.
New York, NY 10017
212-818-0130

LYNX
P.O. Box 509
Dunmow, Essex CM6 1UH

March for the Animals
P.O. Box 2978
Washington, DC 20013
703-684-0688

**Massachusetts Society for
the Prevention of Cruelty
to Animals (MSPCA)**
350 South Huntington Ave.
Boston, MA 02130

**National Alliance for
Animal's Educational Fund**
P.O. Box 2978
Washington, DC 20013-2978
703-684-0654

**National Alliance for
Animal Legislation**
P.O. Box 75116
Washington, DC 20013
703-684-0654

**National Anti-Vivisection
Society**
53 West Jackson, #1550
Chicago, IL 60604
312-427-6065

National Audubon Society
950 Third Ave.
New York, NY 10022
212-832-3200

**National Board of Fur
Farm Organizers**
13965 Burleigh Rd.
Suite 109
Brookfield, WI 53005

National Humane Education Society
211 Gibson Ste. 104, NW
Leesburg, VA 22075
703-777-8319

National Society for Animal Protection (NSAP)
100 North Crooks Rd.
Suite 102
Clawson, MI 48107

National Society of Musicians for Animals (NSMA)
61 Hedgely Road
Springfield, OH 44506
513-322-1624

National Wildlife Federation
1400 16th St., NW
Washington, DC 20036-2266
202-797-6800

Nature Conservancy
1815 N. Lynn St.
Arlington, VA 22209
703-841-5300

New England Anti-Vivisection Society (NEAVS)/American Assoc. for Animals
333 Washington St., Suite 850
Boston, MA 02108
617-523-6020

North Carolina Network for Animals
P.O. Box 33565
Raleigh, NC 27636
919-787-7435

Oceanic Society
Fort Mason Center E
San Francisco, CA 94123

Operation COC Adopt-a-National Forest
Crown Chapter #3
3623 Rendale Dr.
Jacksonville, FL 32210

People for the Ethical Treatment of Animals (PETA)
Box 42516

Washington, DC 20015
301-770-7444

Physicians Committee for Responsible Medicine
P.O. Box 6322
Washington, DC 20015
202-686-2210

Political Action Committee
149 South Villa 15
Bridgeville, CA 95526

Porpoise Rescue Foundation
405 N. Washington St.,
Box 162
San Diego, CA 92103
619-295-5682

Primarily Primates
P.O. Box 15306
San Antonio, TX 78212
512-755-8868

Progressive Animal Welfare Society (PAWS)
P.O. Box 1037
Lynwood, WA 98046
206-743-3845

Project "Wind Seine"
Cape May Bird Observatory
P.O. Box 3
Cape May Point, NJ 08212
609-884-2736

Project Wolf USA
6529 32d Ave., NE
Seattle, WA 98115

Psychologists for the Ethical Treatment of Animals (PsyETA)
P.O. Box 87
New Gloucester, ME 04260
207-926-4817

Retired Greyhounds as Pets
P.O. Box 41307
St. Petersburg, FL 33743

Save the Whales International, "Humpback Adoption Project"
P.O. Box 1358
Lahaina, HI 96767
808-661-8755

Sea Shepherd Conversation Society
Box 7000-S
Redondo Beach, CA 90277
213-373-6979

Sierra Club Legal Defense Fund
2044 Fillmore St.
San Francisco, CA 94115
415-567-6100

Society for Animal Protective Legislation
P.O. Box 3719
Washington, DC 20007

Society for an Extended Ethic, Inc.
1139 Woodside Trail
Troy, MI 48098

Society for Animal Rights
900 First Ave.
New York, NY 10022

Trade Records Analysis of Flora and Fauna Commerce (TRAFFIC)
c/o World Wildlife Fund

Trans-Species Unlimited
P.O. Box 1553
Williamsport, PA 17703
717-322-3252

U.S. Department of the Interior
Adopt-a-horse or burro/BLM
350 S. Pickett St.
Alexandria, VA 22304
202-343-9435

U.S. Fish and Wildlife Service Dept. of the Interior
Washington, DC 20240
202-208-5634

U.S. Wild Horse Foundation
P.O. Box 82038
Las Vegas, NV 89180-2038

United Action for Animals
205 East 42nd St.,
Room 1923
New York, NY 10017
212-983-5315

United Animal Nations
5892A South Land Park Drive
P.O. Box 188890
Sacramento, CA 95818
916-429-2457

Vegetarian Awareness Network
P.O. Box 50515
Washington, DC 20004

Vegetarian Resource Group
P.O. Box 1463
Baltimore, MD 21203

Vegetarian Times
141 S. Oak Park St.
P.O. Box 570
Oak Park, IL 60603

Voice of the Wolf
1988 Damascus Rd., Route 4
Golden, CO 80403

The Whale Center
3929 Piedmont Ave.
Oakland, CA 94611
415-654-6621

Whitetails Unlimited
P.O. Box 422
Sturgeon Bay, WI 54235

Wild Horse Coalition
P.O. Box 362
Onyx, CA 93255

Wild Horse Sanctuary
P.O. Drawer B
Shingletown, CA 96088

Wildlife Conservation Fund of America
50 W. Broad St., Suite 1025
Columbus, OH 43215
614-221-2684

Wildlife Conservation International (WCI)
New York Zoological Society
Bronx, NY 10460
212-220-5155

Wildlife Foundation
1717 Massachusetts Ave., NW
Washington, DC 20036

Wildlife Refuge Reform Coalition (WRRC)
P.O. Box 18414
Washington, DC 20036-8414
202-778-6415

Wolf Haven
3111 Offut Lake Rd.
Tenino, WA 98589

Wolf Park
North American Wildlife
Foundation
Battle Ground, IN 47920

Wolf Sanctuary
P.O. Box 760
Eureka, MO 63025

Wolves and Other Related Canids
P.O. Box 1026
Agoura, CA 91301

The World Society for the Protection of Animals (WSPA)
29 Perkins St.
Boston, MA 02130

The World Wildlife Fund
1250 24th St., NW
Washington, DC 20037
202-293-4800
800-634-4444

Worldwide Fund for Nature
World Conservation Centre
CH-1196
Gland, Switzerland

HUMAN WELFARE

• • •

Only with opportunity—full, free, open opportunity—will poverty be relieved and hunger eliminated.

• • •

—BRADFORD MORSE, former administrator, United Nations Development Program

A Call for Action

• • •

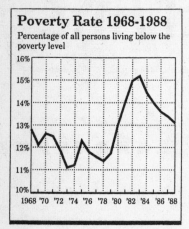

Poverty Rate 1968-1988
Percentage of all persons living below the poverty level

Reprinted by permission of the *Wall Street Journal*, Copyright 1989 Dow Jones & Company, Inc. All rights reserved worldwide.

THE TWENTIETH CENTURY—A PERIOD OF SUCCESS

The twentieth century has been a period of great achievement and success. A technological explosion brought about advances ranging from the assembly line to the computer. Modern health care eradicated such diseases as polio and has helped people live longer, more healthy lives. Agricultural methods multiplied the world's grain harvest by more than $2^{1}/_{2}$ times since mid-century. Industrialization and economic progress raised the standard of living in many parts of the world. In 1989, more than 150 billionaires and 2 million millionaires occupied the planet. Never in history have so many enjoyed such riches.

ALSO A TIME OF DESPAIR

This century, however, also marks a period of immense poverty. The World Bank and the United Nations Food and Agriculture Organization estimate that in the early 1980s between 700 million and 1 billion people lived inpoverty. The Worldwatch Institute believes that these numbers are too conservative. They estimate that 1.2 billion people, or almost one-quarter of the world's population, live in poverty.

The world's poor live mostly in Asia, sub-Saharan Africa, Latin America, North Africa, and the Middle East. But even industrialized nations have their share of poverty. One-fifth of the Soviets live below their official poverty level. And the U.S. Census Bureau reports that in 1989 12.1 percent of the U.S. population, or 31.5 million people, lived in poverty.

THE POVERTY GAP

The gap between the "haves" and "have nots" has increased throughout the century. As the twentieth century closes, the disparity between rich and poor is at its widest. Population Reference Bureau reports that in 1988 world per capita GNP stood at about $3,000. Per capita income in more developed countries averaged over three times that number at $10,000. On the other hand, people in less developed countries made on average $640, or less than 10 percent of their wealthier counterparts. The disparity of wealth becomes even more shocking when you look at the sheer number of people living in poor countries. According to Population Reference Bureau, in 1988 approximately 1.2 billion people lived in more developed nations, yet more than three times that number, or 3.9 billion people, lived in less developed regions.

In the last 40 years developing countries as a whole have gotten poorer, whereas the industrialized nations on average have grown richer. This trend has increased during the last decade. According to the Worldwatch Institute more than 40 Third World nations will be poorer in terms of per capita income in 1990 than they were in 1980. And by the end of the 1980s the average incomes of the wealthiest fifth of the world stood 15 times higher than the fifth living in the poorest. Moreover, as the rich get richer and the poor get poorer the lifestyle differences between the two will become even more pronounced. In *State of the World 1990* (New York: W. W. Norton), Alan B. Durning of the Worldwatch Institute points out a tragic irony: "Americans spend $5 billion each year on special diets to lower their calorie consumption, while 400 million people around the world are so undernourished their bodies and minds are deteriorating."

CLOSING THE GAP

The millions of people throughout the world living in poverty have not gone unnoticed. Numerous organizations, legislators, and concerned individuals realize that many of the world's inhabitants lack the basic necessities of life. They understand that unless a concerted effort is made to help the world's poor and reverse the trend of poverty, the planet is headed for dire consequences.

The signs of poverty include ill health, hunger and starvation, homelessness, and insufficient education. These problems lead to many other challenges facing the world today, such as crime, alcohol and drug abuse, and child abuse.

Now each citizen has the ability to do something positive toward eliminating world poverty. Joining human welfare organizations, lobbying for more funding for the poor, helping relief organizations, recognizing the needs of our children, and teaching people to read are among some of the actions one can take to redirect the path of deprivation for so many.

24.5% no longer in poverty

The Census Bureau found 11.5 percent of U.S. citizens living in poverty in 1984. In 1985, one in four of the poor had escaped poverty. Who got out, by selected characteristics:

On welfare all year	9.6%
No job either year	14.5%
Divorced, separated women	15.7%
65 and up	15.9%
Under 18	20.8%
Married both years	32.6%
Divorced, separated men	35.3%
18 to 24	35.8%
Worked full time both years	40.7%

Source: U.S. Census Bureau

Human Needs

■■■■■■■■■■■■■■■■■■■■■■■■■■■■■■■■■■■■■■

• • •

The only thing that's going to save this world is not going to be political agreements. It's going to be love, pure and simple, just love.

• • •

—ROBERT C. MACAULEY, President of AmeriCares

POPULATION OVERLOAD

■ ■ ■

No matter how distracted we may be by the number of problems now facing us, one issue remains fundamental: overpopulation. The crowding of our cities, our nations, underlies all other problems.

—DR. PAUL EHRLICH, Honorary President, Zero Population Growth

*"1 Billion People on the Way in '90s," *Los Angeles Times*, 22 February 1990.

IT'S GETTING CROWDED

Approximately 5.2 billion people live on the planet Earth. Long-term projections of world population estimate that number will more than double by the year 2100 to anywhere from 10 to 14 billion people.

That is a sizable increase from the 2.5 billion that lived on the planet in 1950. During the 1980s, the world population increased by more than 840 million, averaging 84 million each year. The decade of the 1990s alone will add 1 billion people—1990 has brought almost 100 million.

Although birthrates appeared to slow in the mid-1980s (except in Africa and parts of Southeast Asia), the progress has not been as great as expected. According to Nafis Sadik of the U.N. Population Fund the "1990s will see faster increases in human numbers than any decade in history. All that Asian countries have struggled to achieve could be swept away."*

POPULATION GROWTH AREAS

A little less than half of the world's inhabitants live in areas that have stable or rising standards of living. These areas include North America, Eastern Europe and the Soviet Union, Western Europe, Australia, New Zealand, and East Asia. The collective growth rate of these countries is relatively slow—.8 percent a year. However, a greater number of people—almost 3 billion—live in regions in which living standards are low and population rates continue to climb.

The rate of population increase in lesser developed countries (LDCs) will continue to surpass the rate increase in more developed countries (MDCs). For example, Africa's share of the world population will increase from 12 percent in 1991 to nearly 20 percent by 2020. If Nigeria's 100 + million population continues to increase at present rates, in 60 years it will have more people than the entire continent of Africa today.

In contrast, the more developed countries' share of the world population will fall from 25 percent to about 17 percent. The United States is estimated to add another 40 million people by the year 2000 and level off at about 295 million by 2020.

PLANETARY STRESS

Even at current population levels, the stress on our planet is immense. Food, water, and other necessities are in short supply in many parts of the world. Cities are overflowing with people, and the environment is wrought with pollution and decay.

Shortages of necessities. Although the world currently produces enough grain to feed 7 billion people, that food is not being properly distributed. Much of the world already lives in hunger and poverty.

Moreover, as the population increases so will the demand for a diminishing world water supply. Groundwater levels are falling faster than they are being replenished in the United States, India, and China—three major food producers for the world. In Africa, a continent of exceedingly fast population growth, water scarcity is also a problem. According to the Worldwatch Institute, "In much of northern and eastern Africa, increasing human numbers are on a collision course with scarce water resources."

Did you know? ....

▶ Three people are born every second—250,000 each day.

Did you know? ....

According to Zero Population Growth, globally more than 800 million people suffer from starvation, with 12 million children under the age of 5 dying each year.

▶ In the 6 seconds it takes you to read this sentence, 24 people will be added to the Earth's population.

▶ Before you've finished reading this, that number will reach 1000. Within an hour . . . 11,000. By day's end . . . 260,000.

▶ Before you go to bed two nights from now, the net growth in human numbers will be enough to fill a city the size of San Francisco.

▶ It took 4 million years for humanity to reach the 2 billion mark. Only 30 years to add a third billion. And now we're increasing by 95 million every single year.

▶ No wonder they call it the human race.

Zero Population Growth 202-332-2200

·········· Did you know?

▶ China cut its birth rate in half through its "one-family, one-child" policy.

▶ Thailand experienced a similar reduction through its Population and Community Development Association, which combines family planning with birth control.

Anastasia Toufexia, "Too Many Months," *Time*, 2 January 1989.

Urban overpopulation. Our cities are becoming vastly overcrowded as well, contributing to urban pollution, poverty, and unemployment. Zero Population Growth claims that in Mexico City (the world's most populous city) almost one-third of its 16 million inhabitants are forced to live in slums, and both Mexico and Central America face unemployment rates as high as 50 percent.

Environmental stress. This population overload also places stress on the environment by polluting our land, water, and air; depleting our natural resources such as tropical rain forests; and threatening wildlife.

To deal with these immense problems we must learn not only how to slow growth, we must also learn how to coexist at our present level.

The Cure for Population Stress

ZERO POPULATION GROWTH

Zero Population Growth.

CONTROLLING EXCESSIVE GROWTH

What can be done to slow the world population growth? Governments, private organizations, and other advocates have recommended and/or implemented a number of policies to stem the rate of growth. These measures include: policies limiting the number of children per family, family planning consultation, birth control, and sterilization. In some cases these programs have proved successful.

Nevertheless, the success in these programs is overshadowed by limited progress in many high-population, rapidly-growing areas of the world. The amount of money allocated for population control programs is not sufficient, and is not distributed in lower-priority areas.

Cultural barriers, a lack of government consensus, minimal funding, and religious group objections block greater progress in reversing or slowing the world's population rate by use of these methods.

INCREASING LIVING STANDARDS

Another effective way to control population growth, besides special programs specifically designed for birth control and counseling, is to enact programs designed to build long-term economic stability. People have children for reasons other than lack of knowledge about birth control. In countries with high infant mortality rates, many parents fear for their children's survival; they want to have large families because they need all the help they can get with farming and other work. Thus population rates increase in these areas due to economic necessity.

Interestingly enough, most countries with higher standards of living and lower rates of infant deaths (Infant Mortality Rates = IMR), have smaller population growth rates.

COUNTRY	IMR	BIRTH RATE	POPULATION
		(per 1,000 pop.)	Growth Rate
Gambia	143	47	2.6
India	95	32	2.1
Thailand	39	22	1.5
United States	9.7	16	0.8
Japan	4.8	10	0.4

1990 World Population Data Sheet Source: The Hunger Project

Arthur Simon, Executive Director of Bread for the World, explains that those countries "that have substantially lowered high population growth rates are countries in which the poor have noticeably improved their living conditions." He notes that China and parts of India cut back on their population growth rate significantly by "reducing hunger, making health care available, and increasing the rate of literacy."*

Instead of "downgrading the importance of family planning," Simon states that "If we are serious about dealing with the population problem, our sensible course, as a nation, would be to take a whole network of actions designed to let people work their way out of hunger and poverty."

Therefore, programs that raise a country's standard of living, coupled with family planning and birth-control efforts, offer the best chance of reducing population growth rates.

Did you know? ■■■■■■■■■

▶ Although 60 million people across the world use contraceptive devices such as diaphragms, condoms, and sponges, two-thirds of them live in industrialized countries where the population growth rate is less of a problem.

▶ Although $3 billion is spent annually on family planning services, including birth control, the World Bank estimates that another $5 billion needs to be spent to reverse the population boom.

Anastasia Toufexia, "Too Many Months," *Time*, 2 January 1989.

*Arthur Simon, *Bread for the World*, (New York: Paulist Press, 1984), 39.

From *Planned Parenthood 1989 Annual Report*.

AMERICAN ATTITUDES ABOUT INTERNATIONAL FAMILY PLANNING AND POPULATION ISSUES

▶ Nearly 90 percent recognize that population growth will exacerbate worldwide environmental problems.

▶ Nearly 90 percent think population growth will prevent poor countries from achieving economic stability.

▶ More than 90 percent think food shortages and famines will worsen, increasing poor countries' dependence on U.S. aid.

▶ Nearly 70 percent think more U.S. jobs will go overseas because millions of people in Asia and Africa are willing to work for low wages.

Organizations

• •

International Planned Parenthood Federation (IPPF)
212-995-8800

Negative Population Growth (NPG)
201-837-3555

Population Council
212-644-1300

Population Crisis Committee
202-659-1833

Population Institute
202-544-3300

Population-Environment Balance
202-879-3000

Population Reference Bureau, Inc. (PRB)
202-483-1100

Zero Population Growth (ZPG)
202-332-2200

• •

THE WORLD'S HUNGRY

■ ■ ■

.... Did you know?

▶ As many as 1 billion people on this planet are undernourished. Each year, an estimated 13 to 18 million die as a result of hunger-related diseases and starvation—35,000 each day!

WHO ARE THE WORLD'S HUNGRY?

The hungry in the world live everywhere—from affluent nations such as the United States, to poor countries like India.

Hunger abroad. According to The Hunger Project, three-quarters of the world's 1 billion hungry live and work in rural areas. The remainder live mostly in sprawling urban slums, ghettos, and shantytowns. One-half of the world's hungry live on the Indian subcontinent. Approximately 40 percent live in Africa and the rest of Asia. The Hunger Project claims that if hunger could be eliminated in India, Indonesia, Bangladesh, Pakistan, and Nigeria, nearly half of the world's hunger would be eradicated.

Hunger in the United States. As stated earlier, hunger is not confined only to developing nations; people in the United States are hungry as well.

HUNGER DEFINED

The five general types of hunger are classified as chronic undernutrition, malnutrition, malabsorptive hunger, seasonal undernutrition, and famine. Although famine is most often associated with the worldwide hunger problem, it accounts for only 10 percent of hunger-related deaths.

The following excerpt from The Hunger Project's *Ending Hunger Briefing Workbook* defines the five types of hunger:

"**Chronic undernutrition** is the consumption, over a long period of time, of fewer calories and less protein than are needed by the body. It is the most basic and widespread manifestation of hunger today, and the least recognized. The effects are particularly severe in children and infants. They often die of diseases that would be thrown off quickly by a healthy, well-nourished body. For example, in Latin America, undernutrition is the primary cause or a major contributing factor in some 60 percent of the deaths of children aged one to four. In some countries, this proportion may rise to 75 percent or more.

Malnutrition is the lack of specific vitamins or minerals that are vital to health. Between 450 million and one billion people in the world suffer from chronic malnutrition. More than three-quarters of these people live in Africa, Asia and Latin America. More than half are children, and significantly more women than men are malnourished. The lack of vitamin A causes blindness in 200,000 children each year. Vitamin A tablets costing only a few cents could prevent this.

Malabsorptive hunger occurs when a person actually takes in enough food, but parasites take up much of the nutritional value of the food or cause it to be passed out of the system, instead of being used by the body. As much as 20 percent of a person's food may be malabsorbed due to parasites. The level of parasites can only occur where water is contaminated and medical care is almost completely absent.

Seasonal undernutrition occurs annually before each harvest, when food from the last harvest runs out. Until the new crop comes in, people may be hungry for weeks or even months at a time.

Famine is a widespread lack of access to food, caused when drought, war or flood disrupts the availability of food in a society of chronically undernourished people. Famine has received greater attention from the news media than the other types of hunger, but it is only the tip of the iceberg."*

Did you know? ∙∙∙∙∙∙∙∙∙∙

▶ In 1985, the Physician Task Force on Hunger concluded that hunger was a "growing epidemic," and estimated that 20 million people in the United States were chronically hungry at least at some point each month.

▶ In a survey of 25 major U.S. cities there has been a steady increase in the number of families and individuals seeking emergency food assistance—a 71 percent increase since 1983.

▶ In 1987, two-thirds of the surveyed cities reported having to turn people away from soup kitchens and food pantries without the food they had been seeking. And although the U.S. economy is stronger than most other nations, the number of hungry and homeless continues to climb.

U.S. Hunger: The Problem Grows, a Bread for the World Publication, 1989.

*"Ending Hunger Briefing Workbook," *The Hunger Project*, 1984.

CAN THE HUNGER PROBLEM BE SOLVED?

One of the important things to understand about hunger is that people do not go hungry simply because there is not enough food. In fact, there is more than enough food to go around. The Hunger Project notes that worldwide food production could feed approximately 7 billion people: "Even with the projected population in the year 2000 of 6.1 billion, our planet can certainly provide enough food for us all. Just 40 million tons of grain, less than 3 percent of the world's grain production, if made available to those most in need, would end the most severe hunger everywhere."

If lack of food is not the problem, then what is? Is it too costly? But what would it cost to end hunger? James P. Grant, Executive Director of UNICEF, explains that "an extra $10, $15 billion a year addressed to this problem, combined with the political will—with this combination one can very readily see success in sight before the end of the century." The $10 to $15 billion a year is a minuscule amount compared with other expenditures, such as defense. The world could easily afford this amount. So lack of money is not the problem either.

What is really missing is what James Grant calls "political will," which means a consistent and sustained worldwide commitment to ending hunger. Many experts believe that until we embrace this idea fully, we will always have worldwide hunger. The Presidential Commission on World Hunger explains that "the persistence of hunger reflects a lack of sufficient political will to eliminate its causes."

Yet, if we make a firm decision to end hunger—and follow it with unified, appropriate action—we will not only solve the problem, we will solve it quickly. If the leaders of the world got together today and decided to end hunger, the National Academy of Sciences believes that it should be possible to solve the most serious incidences of widespread hunger and malnutrition within one generation.

·········· Did you know?

▶ If a jumbo jetliner crashed killing all its passengers, the news would receive national attention. Yet, the number of people it would take to fill 300 such fateful planes die each day from hunger-related causes—with almost half the passengers being children.

▶ In actuality, chronic, persistent hunger kills more people in one year than the total number of people who died from the world's major famines of the last 20 years.

The Hunger Project

Reprinted with permission by Food for the Hungry/800-2HUNGER.

HUNGER'S DEVASTATION

···

Imagine what it would be like if, over the course of the next year, twelve major cities were completely wiped out. What if all the residents of Cincinnati, Milwaukee, Kansas City, Vancouver, San Jose, Buffalo, New Orleans, Indianapolis, San Antonio, Fort Lauderdale, Memphis, and Louisville died an agonizing death:

If in your mind's eye you can imagine those cities—in just one year—as empty shells, you can begin to grasp the enormous scale of world hunger.

Every month, more than one million people die of hunger-related causes.

This decision to end hunger must be made, and it must entail an honest and concerted effort by everyone.

WHO ARE HUNGRY PEOPLE? —ONE PROFILE

....

Ari—Lusaka, Zambia

Ari is almost eighteen, and her closest friend is her twenty-year-old brother, Bruce. They live with fifteen relatives in a small house near the airport just outside of Lusaka, the capital of Zambia. Several aunts and uncles recently moved in because the factory where they worked had to be shut down. The company could not afford to buy parts to repair some broken machinery, and everyone who worked at the factory was sent home.

Although they have a small garden, Ari must sell the vegetables she grows because they are worth more that way than if the family ate them. Instead, they subsist on corn mush that provides enough calories but lacks nutrients. Three of their brothers and sisters have died during Bruce and Ari's short lifetimes. They died from illnesses such as a common cold and diarrhea—ailments that healthy people easily shake off.

To win their battle against hunger, Ari and her family need access to jobs, a larger plot of land to grow enough vegetables to feed themselves, health care and health care training. They need the opportunity to generate the resources to become self-sufficient.

Did you know? ....

According to The Hunger Project

▶ More people have died of hunger since 1985 than have been killed in all the wars, revolutions, and murders in the past 150 years.

▶ The human devastation caused by hunger is equivalent to a Hiroshima bomb being dropped on our planet every three and a half days.

▶ The worst earthquake in modern history killed 242,000 people in China in 1976. Hunger kills that many every seven days.

From "Famine and Chronic, Persistent Hunger: A Life and Death Distinction," The Hunger Project

---

WHAT IS BEING DONE?

•••••••••••••••••••••••••••••••••••••••

International Efforts

▶ In the fall of 1984 drought and famine swept through 27 African nations, threatening the welfare of 150 million people—35 million of them faced dire circumstances. Within one year, an unprecedented worldwide effort averted further catastrophe by saving 3 million lives and assisting tens of millions of others.

▶ On July 13, 1985, an estimated 1.6 billion people throughout the world participated in the global telecast of the *Live Aid Concert.*

▶ On May 25, 1986, 20 million people around the world joined in Sport Aid's Race Against Time, while on the same day, 5 million participated in Hands Across America for the hungry and homeless in the United States.

▶ As of March 1, 1991, more than 6.2 million individuals in 152 countries—1 out of every 1,000 people on the planet—had declared their commitment to end hunger by enrolling in the Hunger Project.

National Efforts

▶ Due to the efforts of Bread for the World and other hunger organizations, in 1989 the House and Senate increased funding for the Women, Infants, and Children nutrition program by $118 million, the largest increase in five years.

▶ In November 1989, millions of Boy Scouts collected cans of food from door to door, from coast to coast and gave it to local agencies for distribution. They asked Americans to Help the Boy Scouts Help the Hungry in their Scouting for Food drive.

Creator's Syndicate

DEAR ANN LANDERS:

I hope you will see fit to include this in your column:

Speaker #1: "Sometimes I would like to ask God why He allows poverty, famine and injustice when He could do something about it."

Speaker #2: "Well, why don't you ask Him?"

Speaker #1: "Because I'm afraid God might ask me the same question."

A Bread for the World/BFW Educational Fund Quarterly Newsletter

Helping Others Find Bread

Tim Achor-Hoch. Bread for the World/ Bread for the World Institute on Hunger and Development.

WHAT CAN I DO?

▶ **Donate time or money to a hunger organization.** Your efforts will help the hungry in your community, across the nation, and throughout the world. And it does not take much. For instance, at the U.S. Mission in Los Angeles, $50.00 will provide daily hot lunches for five people a week; $100 will serve lunch for a dozen people for a week.

▶ **Volunteer in a soup kitchen.** Hunger groups rely on the generosity of others. Call a local group and ask if they need help.

▶ **Collect food in your neighborhood, business, school, church, or club.** Spearhead a food drive for a local hunger organization. Get your friends and family involved! Carol

DeMayo received a Daily Point of Light award for her efforts to help the hungry:

ORDINARY PEOPLE—EXTRAORDINARY ACTIONS

CAROL DEMAYO,
Williamstown, MA
DAILY POINT OF LIGHT RECIPIENT: JULY 6, 1990

"[I] don't think of it [helping others] as anything other than the way life should be."

Mrs. DeMayo, 50, began delivering food to low-income individuals in 1984. Because of the growing need for this service in her community, she recruited young people to help her with deliveries, offering them an opportunity to serve the community.

Mrs. DeMayo's effort, now called the "Food Pantry," is located in St. Patrick's Catholic Church. Members of the community donate food, clothing, and toys to the pantry, which Mrs. DeMayo and others volunteers then distribute to those who are homeless, unemployed, or financially burdened.

Reprinted with permission from the White House Office of National Service.

▶ **Donate food and clothing to a hunger drive.** If you have extra food and clothing, do not throw them away! Call a local hunger group and donate these items to people in need.

▶ **Raise money for a hunger group.** Call a hunger organization in your area and ask how you can start a program to raise money for them. One easy and creative way is to become a WorldVision CounterTop Volunteer.

... and learn how you, too can become a CounterTop Volunteer

World Vision, Inc.

WORLD VISION COUNTERTOP VOLUNTEERS

As a CounterTop Partner, you simply ask your neighborhood stores or restaurants (usually people you do business with anyway) to place a CounterTop display near their cash register. Then, once or twice a month, just stop by and collect the money and send it to World Vision along with your monthly report. You'll also be responsible for changing the inserts every two or three months and for keeping your displays clean.

But that's all there is to it!

And you can place as many or as few displays as you like . . . anywhere from one to a hundred. It's up to you. . . . And you'll know that for every 50 cents you collect, somewhere a hungry child will be able to eat for two days.

Reprinted with permission from World Vision/800-444-2522.

·········· Did you know?

▶ Kentucky Harvest, an all-volunteer hunger organization, collects more than 1,200 million pounds of food from area hotels, restaurants, caterers, and bakeries. The organization currently feeds more than 2,700 people a day, serving 25 mission homes and soup kitchens in Kentucky and southern Indiana.

▶ Love Is Feeding Everyone (L.I.F.E.) feeds more than 102,000 people weekly in the L.A. area.

▶ The Perishable Foods Program in Chicago, under the guidance of the Greater Chicago Food Depository, distributes food to the city's hungry.

▶ **Participate in rallies, marches, and other events that publicize the issue of hunger.** Many local and national events help the hunger cause. For instance, your church may hold a hunger walk. If they do not, then organize one! Or get your school or friends to join a hunger rally.

Contact a hunger organization for a list of their activities.

WORLD FOOD DAY

···

World Food Day (WFD) is a worldwide event designed to increase awareness, understanding and informed, year-round, long-term action on the complex issues of food security for all.

The eleventh World Food Day will be held on October 16, 1991. WFD is observed each October 16 in recognition of the founding of the U.N. Food and Agriculture Organization (FAO). World Food Day is observed in 150 nations and in the United States it has the support of over 400 sponsoring organizations.

WFD is observed in hundreds of ways across the world, including media events, educational seminars, and added help to existing hunger service organizations.

For more information, contact: U.S. National Committee for World Food Day at 202-653-2404.

▶ **Contact a food distribution center in your area.** Food distributors collect unsalable but usable food and give it to hunger organizations to feed the hungry and homeless. Food distribution centers are feeding people across the nation. Volunteer your services or start a center to distribute food in your area.

▶ **Write letters to your representatives about the issues of hunger.** According to Senator Paul Simon, "Someone who sits down and writes a letter about hunger . . . almost literally has to be saving a life."

▶ **Ask for a reduction in military spending so some of that money can help feed the world's hungry.** Arthur Simon, president of BFW and the 1988–89 World Hunger Award Winner states, "Worldwide, we spend $1 trillion on arms. It far exceeds the total income of the poorest half of the world. Meanwhile, estimates show from half a billion to a billion people in severe need of food." BFW's "Share the Harvest of Peace" resolution asks for a one-half reduction of the $1 trillion spent worldwide on the military.

LIFESAVER STORY

Some years ago Great Western dedicated the John Wayne statue after his death. Dennis [Weaver] was, of course, attending the dinner along with the other Great Western folks. Dennis was lamenting that he had this very small organization started with the goal of ending hunger here in the Los Angeles area. He had determined through research that there was an abundance of food to be had, but there was no conduit or group that was getting the food to the people that were in need of it. He and a small group of dedicated people were operating out of the executive director's house and the trunk of Dennis' car to feed a couple of hundred people each week. It was at this dinner that interest brewed and a fund raising event was planned and executed not six weeks later netting some $15,000 to help continue the work.

When we gave Dennis the check, he said "Oh, you girls are just lifesavers," and sure enough, that is what we are today. We are a group of concerned and dedicated neighbors intent on ending the plight of hunger in our own community and making a significant impact on this crucial issue.

L.I.F.E. currently helps to feed more than 102,000 people every week in Los Angeles County through a network of more than 100 social service agencies.

Co-Founders—Gerry Weaver and Suzanne Erikson

▶ **Your letters will make a difference!** According to Bread for the World only 1 out of every 10 U.S. citizens ever writes a letter to his or her congressional representative, senator, or to the president. Yet, an estimated 250,000 letters were generated in support of the Right-to-Food bill. As a result, this resolution was voted out of the committee where it had been held up and was passed by both the Senate and the House.

▶ **Refer to the section entitled "Writing Letters," or contact BFW and ask for a copy of** *A Guide to Effective Letter Writing on Hunger Issues.*

Organizations and Resources

Bread for the World (BFW)
202-269-0200/800-82-BREAD
A Christian membership organization headed by Arthur

Simon, which educates citizens to direct action and lobbies for hunger issues. The BFW Education Fund publishes books and documents on

hunger and hunger-related issues.

Center on Budget and Policy Priorities
202-408-1080

A research and education organization that publishes information on poverty, housing, and other hunger-related issues.

The End Hunger Network
213-273-3179
Uses a network of organizations, mass media, and celebrity talent to battle hunger.

Food First—The Institute for Food and Development Policy
415-864-8555
Founded in 1975 by Frances Moore Lappe and Joseph Collins, Food First is a research and education center that provides information on topics ranging from hunger and population control to pesticides.

Food Research and Action Center (FRAC)
202-986-2200
Provides materials, training, and other efforts in fighting hunger. Deals especially with federal food programs.

Handsnet
408-427-0808
A computer communications network that provides human-services organizations nationwide with data on the availability of housing and emergency food, as well as news on state and federal legislation and updates on special programs.

Heifer Project International
501-376-6836
Provides livestock and training to poor families in rural areas of the world. Has provided livestock to 110 countries and 33 American states since 1944.

The Hunger Project
U.S.: 415-928-8700/ Global: 212-532-4255

Works to inform people about world hunger in a way that supports them in participating effectively in its solution. Ask for *The Ending Hunger Briefing Workbook,* a comprehensive source on the facts of hunger and what you can do to help.

Interfaith Hunger Appeal (IHA)
212-870-2035
An educational and awareness agency sponsored by Catholic Relief Services, Church World Service, Lutheran World Relief, and The American Jewish Joint Distribution Committee. Through IHA these agencies join to promote global awareness of hunger and hunger-related issues in the United States. They conduct relief and development programs in more than 110 countries around the world. Ask for their *Education and Development Report,* which addresses important issues concerning the poorer countries of the world.

Kentucky Harvest
502-589-FOOD
Collects and distributes food in Kentucky and Indiana.

Love Is Feeding Everyone (LIFE)
213-936-0895
By collecting mostly edible but unsalable food that would otherwise be wasted, the LIFE organization helps feed 100,000 people every week in the Los Angeles area.

Oxfam America
617-482-1211
International agency that funds self-help development and disaster relief projects in Africa, Asia, Latin America, and the Caribbean. It also produces and distributes educational materials in the

United States on issues of hunger and development.

Results
202-543-9340
International organization that uses grass-roots efforts to lobby effectively for hunger-related issues.

Seeds Magazine
404-371-1000
Ask for a copy of *The Hunger Action Handbook: What You Can Do and How to Do It;* $7.95 + $1.50 for shipping.

Share Our Strength (SOS)
800-222-1767
In 1989, SOS provided an estimated $1 million in supplies and assistance to shelters and food banks in more than 90 cities nationwide and supported development projects throughout the world. SOS and Bon Appetit organized "Taste of the Nation" a coast-to-coast benefit for the hungry and homeless. Every dollar of ticket proceeds goes to hunger and homeless organizations.

The World Hunger Education Service
202-298-9503
Send $5.00 for *Who's Involved with Hunger?,* an organizational guide for education and advocacy, which lists more than 400 hunger-related organizations with names and addresses of the major U.S.-based hunger organizations.

World Hunger Year
212-629-8850
Informs the general public, the media, and policymakers on extent and causes of hunger in the United States and abroad. Publishes *WHY* magazine, which contains up-to-date information on hunger and poverty.

STUDENT ORGANIZATIONS

Campus Outreach Opportunity League (COOL)

612-624-3018

Promotes student involvement in community needs, including hunger, homelessness, and illiteracy. Ask for publications such as *Building a Movement: A Resource Book for Students in Community Service* and *Hunger/Homelessness Action: A Resource Book for Colleges and Universities.*

National Student Campaign Against Hunger and Homelessness (NSCAHH)

617-292-4823

A national nonprofit network of colleges and universities helping the hungry and homeless. Its quarterly newsletter, *Students Making a Difference*, reaches thousands of students across the nation.

OTHER COMMITTED ORGANIZATIONS

CARE

212-686-3110

Catholic Relief Services

301-625-2220

Christian Children's Fund

804-644-4654

Compassion International

719-594-9900

Coordination in Development (CODEL)

212-870-3000

Food for the Hungry

602-998-3100

Freedom from Hunger Foundation

916-758-6200

Interfaith Action for Economic Justice

202-543-2800

Peace Corps

800-424-8580

Second Harvest

312-263-2303

U.S. National Committee for World Food Day

202-653-2404

UNICEF

212-326-7000

RELIEF AND DEVELOPMENT PROGRAMS

■■■

Many of the world's hungry and poor are refugees from countries at war. Nearly all of them languish in desolate camps, suffering from persecution, hunger, and disease. The vast majority of refugees are women and children. They come from countries such as Afghanistan, Ethiopia, Cambodia, the Soviet Union, Iran, Iraq, Nicaragua, and Vietnam. Turmoil in the Persian Gulf caused thousands of people to flee from Kuwait and Iraq. These people flee their countries to escape death and tyranny.

For example, 5½ million Afghans left their country to escape the Soviet invasion. After years of hardship as refugees, those who are now coming back find their country devastated from the war—their villages and cities are in shambles and their compatriots face disease and starvation.

International relief programs seek to help people like the Afghans, whether they live in refugee camps or have returned to their native country.

Feed a man a fish and he will eat for a day. Teach him to fish and he will eat for a lifetime.

—Chinese proverb

211

▶ According to the International Rescue Committee the world's refugee population exceeded 14 million in 1989.

The American Red Cross

A History of Helping Others

American Red Cross

Courtesy of The American Red Cross.

Relief and development programs are funded by public and private sources. They give immediate aid and long-term training to the needy.

Relief programs. These programs aid millions of people who suffer from the devastation caused by natural disasters, such as floods, hurricanes, and droughts; and who suffer as a result of war and tyranny.

When a natural disaster such as an earthquake or monsoon strikes, relief programs provide immediate help to those who may have lost their homes or who require medical care. Drought and famine sometimes last for years, making the hardships in these areas last much longer. Many of those who live in these areas are homeless, hungry, and eventually perish from diseases that are easily treatable in other parts of the world.

Relief programs are prepared to provide emergency supplies, such as food, medicine, and shelter, and offer educational programs in forestry and farming techniques, and other useful trades.

Development programs. These programs assist a country by making its people self-sufficient. They teach farming and irrigation techniques; assist with family planning, health care, and education, and offer advice on economic and financial strategies.

Development programs are paramount to long-term relief. William Chandler of the Worldwatch Institute (in "Investing in Children") explains the importance of such long-term programs, "When development relief does more than stave off famine, when it is invested to provide benefits for years to come, then savings—in lives and money—will be made." It is hoped that such education will help overcome a struggling nation's poverty, illiteracy, and hunger.

WHO ADMINISTERS RELIEF EFFORTS?

Relief comes from many sources and in numerous fashions. In 1989, Americans donated more than $1.5 billion to fight hunger and poverty across the world. The United States as a country gave $9.5 billion. Although the United States gives the most in absolute terms, it donates less in terms of percent of GNP than all but 2 of the 17 nations of the Organization for Economic Cooperation and Development (OECD).

Besides governmental aid, private organizations also contribute to relief efforts. Many such groups establish special programs to handle natural disasters or other particular problems. Money and other donated items are then allocated specifically to that area of concern. For instance, the American Red Cross and Save the Children set up specific funds to help the victims of the 1989 San Francisco earthquake. AmeriCares solicits millions of dollars of medical supplies and other necessities and administers them to disaster victims throughout the world.

Some relief programs aid countries ravaged by war. The Quixote Center has donated more than $200 million worth of supplies to Nicaragua. Their citizen appropriations matched the Congressional aid to the Contras dollar for dollar. The International Rescue Committee and the Afghanistan Relief Committee provide care to refugees of war-torn countries.

Other groups such as CARE and the Peace Corps deal with all types of problems—from those caused by man-made and natural disasters, to helping poor people throughout the world raise their standard of living.

Jeff Greenwald, Direct Relief International.

WHAT IS BEING DONE?

● ●

▶ Organizations like the Afghanistan Relief Committee are now helping Afghanistan rebuild after a 10-year war with the Soviet Union.

▶ The International Rescue Committee has helped refugees since 1933 in war-torn Europe, and now aids refugees across the world, from such countries as Afghanistan, Ethiopia, and Vietnam.

▶ Since its inception in 1961, more than 120,000 Americans have been Peace Corps volunteers, serving in 94 countries.

▶ The Salvation Army operates service centers around the world, including more than 3,000 centers across Africa, providing services such as schools for the blind and rehabilitation centers for crippled children.

▶ The Freedom from Hunger Foundation helps people help themselves in many parts of the world. In the Korat Province

I intend to join the Peace Corps again after I retire. I fell in love, I fell sick, I fell off my mule (twice) and most of all, I fell for my town. Peace Corps gives you a healthy dose of how the majority of people in the world live.

—Peace Corps volunteer

☆ ☆ THE STARS ARE SHINING! ☆ ☆

"GO AHEAD. MAKE MY DAY"

A benefit that raised $300,000 "made the day" for victims of the 1989 San Francisco earthquake.

Clint Eastwood hosted a benefit for the Monterey County community of Pajaro, which was devastated by the quake. Among the other celebrities who lent a hand for the cause were Paul Anka, Chevy Chase, Doris Day, Norm Crosby, and Joan Fontaine.

More than 1,000 people paid $60 each for the benefit performance. Clint also persuaded Major League Baseball to contribute $75,000—and he didn't even use his 44 Magnum!

of Thailand, the relief and development group gave revolving loans to build 331 latrines (repayment rate was 95 percent) and partially funded the construction of reservoirs in seven villages.

▶ In the fall of 1989, flooding covered 75 percent of Bangladesh—affecting at least two-thirds of the total population of 110 million. According to Direct Relief International, "twenty-eight million people were left homeless and spent weeks living on roofs, treetops, and in camps without safe drinking water, cooked food, or medical care." DRI responded to the disaster by sending a relief shipment of 3,000 pounds of desperately needed medical goods.

WHAT CAN I DO?

● ●

▶ **Donate to relief and development groups.** If you would like to help those victimized by a disaster, contact you local TV or radio station or check your newspaper for information about volunteering.

After Hurricane Hugo and the San Francisco earthquake, for example, the media provided ample information as to where to give and what items were most needed to donate.

Besides money, disaster relief groups often need food, blood, blankets, clothes, and medical supplies. Groups that concentrate on long-term development programs need continued support for their efforts.

Your contributions will enable groups like CARE and UNICEF to carry out these vital programs.

WHAT WILL MY DONATION PAY FOR?

Your generosity:

▶ Helps provide complete immunization for a child against the major childhood diseases.

▶ Will sponsor a child for a month—helping meet his or her basic needs.

▶ Will help organizations provide oral rehydration treatment to help prevent life-threatening dehydration in malnourished children.

▶ Will go toward programs to build medical facilities in areas that need them.

▶ Will help relief groups ship food and other supplies to victims of disasters.

▶ **Volunteer Overseas!** Many relief and development organizations need the help of committed volunteers. These volunteers can join efforts throughout the world by assisting in agriculture, health training, setting up small businesses, and other important programs.

Activities range from teaching people to read to helping construct irrigation ditches. Whatever the type of work, you are sure to find your experience very rewarding. And most important, someone else benefits!

PROVING IT'S WORTH IT

"In past years, we exhausted our food stores before the harvest. This is the first year we haven't had to pay the 'hungry season' prices just to feed our children!"
—Kolani Damguilaye, mother and community leader, Tabiele, Togo

"I wish I could listen to you all the time. You've taught me how to improve the nutrition and health of my son."
—Khem Gurung, mother, Tipeni, Nepal

▶ Contact one of the organizations listed here for more information about volunteering overseas. Also, *Seeds Magazine's Hunger Action Handbook* contains a chapter on international volunteer opportunities with more than 20 programs detailed.

Did you know? ▪▪▪▪▪▪▪▪▪▪

▶ CARE programs across the world provide emergency food and supplies to victims of natural disasters, as well as help people to develop long-term strategies toward health, education, farming, and industry.

▶ UNICEF immunization programs seek to protect children in many areas of the world from deadly, yet preventable diseases.

From Freedom from Hunger Foundation *1988 Annual Report.*

Organizations and Resources

● ●

Afghanistan Relief Committee
212-355-2931
Since 1980, ARC has distributed more than $900,000 for direct relief projects and has persuaded Congress to authorize extra money for governmental relief aid for the Afghans.

American Red Cross Disaster Relief
800-453-9000 (to make a donation only)

Each year, Red Cross paid and volunteer staff respond to more than 50,000 disasters, ranging from single-family house fires to major hurricanes, floods, tornadoes, and earthquakes. They help hundreds of thousands of their neighbors by providing food, clothing, shelter, and other emergency needs—free of charge.

AmeriCares
800-486-4357/203-966-5195

AmeriCares efforts involve long-term medical programs and emergency disaster relief. Many of its donations of medicines, medical supplies, and other relief materials are contributed by American companies. Since 1982, they have provided more than $300 million worth of donated products to the needy throughout the world.

CARE
212-686-3110

CARE supplies or makes available goods and services abroad for the purpose of relief, rehabilitation, and reconstruction.

Direct Relief International (DRI)
805-687-3694
DRI provides medical goods to disaster victims; these goods are donated and collected by manufacturers, health-care professionals, and service groups.

El Rescate
213-387-3284
Concerned with Central American refugees in the United States and with the protection of the human rights of people in Central America.

Interfaith Hunger Appeal (IHA)
212-870-2035
An educational and awareness agency sponsored by Catholic Relief Services, Church World Service, Lutheran World Relief, and The American Jewish Joint Distribution Committee. Through IHA these agencies join to promote global awareness of hunger and hunger-related issues in the United States. They conduct relief and development programs in more than 110 countries around the world. Ask for their *Education and Development Report,* which addresses important issues concerning the poorer countries of the world.

International Red Cross and Red Crescent Movement
202-737-8300
In accordance with the Geneva Convention the International Committee of the Red Cross (ICRC) has been mandated to serve as a neutral intermediary in times of conflict. The ICRC offers emergency relief by providing food and medical supplies and visits and inspects prisoner-of-war camps. The League of Red Cross and Red Crescent Societies coordinate relief efforts following natural disasters, as well as assisting war refugees. Contact the American Red Cross for more information.

International Rescue Committee (IRC)
212-679-0010
IRC is a nonsectarian voluntary agency devoted to helping refugees who escape from political, religious, and racial persecution, as well as uprooted victims of war, aggression, and famine.

Office of the United Nations High Commissioner for Refugees (UNHCR)
Provides legal and political aid to refugees. Its primary responsibility is to return refugees to their homelands or resettle them abroad, ensuring legal rights regarding employment and social benefits and providing identity and trade documents. The UNHCR office was awarded the Nobel Peace Prize in 1954 and again in 1981.

Oxfam America
617-482-1211
International agency that funds self-help development and disaster relief projects in Africa, Asia, Latin America, and the Caribbean. It also produces and distributes educational materials in the United States on issues of hunger and development.

Peace Corps
800-424-8580
Peace Corps helps people in developing countries learn new ways to fight hunger, disease, poverty, and lack of opportunity.

Project HOPE (Health Opportunity for People Everywhere)
703-837-2100
The primary goal of Project HOPE is the improvement of health care through education. HOPE teaching spans the entire spectrum of the health sciences from medicine, nursing, and dentistry to health administration, all kinds of allied health sciences, and vital auxiliary support.

Salvation Army
(call your local chapter)/201-239-0606
Whenever disaster strikes, the Salvation Army provides food, clothing, blankets, and medical supplies. Their workers comfort victims, help reunite families, and find emergency shelter. They also provide extended services in major disasters involving massive cleanup or reconstruction.

The United Nations International Children's Emergency Fund (UNICEF)
212-326-7000
Established in 1946 to meet the urgent need for food, medicine, and clothing among children in post-World War II Europe and China. Soon after, UNICEF's mandate was broadened beyond emergency relief to include assistance to the least developed nations in establishing essential services to prevent child deaths occurring from disease, malnutrition, and disasters.

U.S. Committee for Refugees
202-347-3507

Ask for a copy of *The World Refugee Survey—1990 in Review,* an authoritative source of information on refugee situations around the world ($8.00).

OTHER COMMITTED ORGANIZATIONS

American Refugee Committee (ARC)
612-872-7060

Committee on Migration and Refugee Affairs c/o InterAction
212-777-8210

Compassion International
719-594-9900

Feed the Children
800-367-2400/405-942-0228

Freedom from Hunger Foundation
916-758-6200

Interaction/American Council for Voluntary International Action
212-777-8210

Medical Aid for El Salvador
213-937-3596

Migration and Refugee Service
202-659-6630/202-541-3000

National Council of Returned Peace Corps Volunteers (NCRPCV)
202-462-5938

Overseas Development Network (ODN)
415-431-4204

Plenty
916-753-0731

Seva
313-475-1351

United Way
703-836-7100

World Vision
800-444-2522

World Relief
708-665-0235

RELIGIOUS RELIEF ORGANIZATIONS

American Friends Service Committee (AFSC)
215-241-7000

American Jewish Joint Distribution Committee (JDC)
212-687-6200

American Jewish World Service
212-468-7380

Catholic Charities
703-549-1390

Catholic Relief Services (CRS)
301-625-2220

Church World Service
212-870-2061

Global Missions
312-380-2650

Interchurch Medical Assistance
301-635-6474

Lutheran World Relief
212-532-6350

MAP International
912-265-6010

Mennonite Central Committee
717-859-1151

National Catholic Disaster Relief Committee
202-639-8400/703-549-1390

Presiding Bishop's Fund for World Relief (PBFWR)
212-867-8400

Quixote Center
301-699-0042

OUR NATION'S HOMELESS

...

WHO ARE THE HOMELESS?

The National Coalition for the Homeless defines the homeless as "anyone whose primary nighttime residence is a public or private shelter, an emergency lodging house, a commercial hotel or motel, or any other public space. Public parks, transportation terminals, cars, abandoned buildings and aque-

Q. Which group constitutes the fastest and largest growing segment of America's homeless population?

A. If you answered middle-aged male "derelicts" or the mentally ill you are wrong.

.... Did you know?

According to the National Coalition for the Homeless:

▶ There are approximately 3 million homeless people in America (in 1989), 25 percent higher than in 1988.

▶ A recent congressionally funded study predicts nearly 19 million homeless people by the year 2000.

▶ 25 percent of homeless adults are employed full time and are still unable to find affordable housing.

▶ 30 percent of the male population are veterans.

▶ 10 to 15 percent are mentally ill.

▶ 15 to 25 percent have drug and/or alcohol problems.

▶ About 14 percent are single women and about half are single men.

*Bruce Frankel and Michele Coleman, "No Home for the Holidays," *USA Today,* 30 November 1989.

ducts are among the likely places for homeless people to live."

According to the Greater Los Angeles Partnership for the Homeless "today's homeless are likely to be families, senior citizens, young adults, veterans and the chronically mentally ill . . . not the stereotypical middle-aged, white male alcoholic."

CAUSES OF HOMELESSNESS

According to the National Coalition for the Homeless, the leading causes of homelessness are the lack of affordable housing, economic factors, insufficient care for the mentally ill, and federal cutbacks of social services to the poor.

The drug epidemic and alcoholism are also important factors. Substance abuse creates problems in the home, school, and workplace. An alcoholic man or woman may be unable to hold a job. A mother addicted to crack may be incapable of caring for her family. A child on drugs may run away from home and end up on the streets. And many homeless people resort to drug or alcohol use, compounding an already difficult predicament.

A PROBLEM THAT REQUIRES ATTENTION . . .

The homeless problem in our country is no longer limited to sections of a few large cities, nor does it involve a few poor individuals. The American Institute of Affordable Housing Institute estimates that there are approximately 14 million "hidden homeless"—people who are now doubled and tripled-up in housing.* According to the National Coalition for the Homeless Tough economic times could cause the homeless population to swell. In fact, many individuals and families are only a few paychecks away from losing their home. A loss of job, illness, or any other unforeseen circumstance could easily force a family into the streets.

The National Coalition for the Homeless explains that the homeless can not be ignored. In fact, the situation is likely to get worse before it gets better. The advocacy group believes that until homelessness is recognized as a national crisis and dramatic changes are made, the problem will only get worse. They call for better federal housing and welfare programs, and a higher minimum wage. They also suggest that emergency measures, as well as long-term commitments, be made by the government and enforced by the McKinney Act and other legislation designed to help the homeless.

... AND A CONCERTED EFFORT

Because homelessness results from a variety of factors and because it affects a diverse group of people, no one cure can eliminate the problem. In fact, the struggle to remain above the poverty level may threaten even more families.

The challenge to provide a job, a home, and a future for each homeless person requires a concerted national effort. These efforts must come from all sources—ranging from grass-roots activism to federal legislation. As the National Coalition for the Homeless clearly explains, "But for most of America's homeless people, it is not too late. And progress is being made—the public is stirring and government is beginning to respond to this public pressure. Yet the need is immense, and the need to advocate for responsible, humane and efficient solutions has never been greater."

WHAT IS BEING DONE?

Public Sector

▶ In the spring of 1987, Congress passed the Stewart B. McKinney Homeless Assistance Act, which authorizes more than $1 billion for 1987 and 1988 to support emergency and temporary programs ranging from housing and shelters to job training, health, and mental health care.

▶ In 1989, New York City expects to spend $577.4 million on shelters and to support services for the homeless. San Francisco spends a total of $57 million a year on homeless services, about $26 per homeless person each day.

Did you know? ....

▶ More than 30 percent of the U.S. homeless population are families. According to the National Law Center on Homelessness and Poverty, families with children are the fastest-growing segment among the homeless population.

Reprinted with permission from the White House Office of National Service.

✪ BARBARA TOMBLINSON ✪

Kansas City, MO
DAILY POINT OF LIGHT RECIPIENT: MARCH 26, 1990

"Everything begins with a dream or an idea. Our dream is for no person to be homeless ..."

Barbara Tomblinson is dedicated to giving homeless families a new start in life.

Ms. Tomblinson, once homeless herself, founded "New Start-New Life Ministries," a nonprofit corporation that provides transitional housing assistance for homeless families. Families are given rent-free apartments for 90 days. In return, they are required to find a job within two weeks and save half their earnings. They also receive counseling in home economics and budgeting. Eventually these families become productive, self-supporting members of society.

Private Sector

▶ The National Coalition and 10 other organizations drafted an omnibus legislative package entitled Homeless Persons' Survival Act, which goes beyond the Stewart B. McKinney Act by addressing emergency relief, preventative measures, and long-term solutions.

▶ An organization called Hotels/Motels in Partnership Inc. provides temporary shelter space to the homeless. More than 700 hotels participate, and in 1989 the group housed approximately 5,000 people.

▶ Homeless families get help through a United Way rental-assistance program in California. The services include monetary assistance for lump-sum payments of rental deposits, financial counseling, and transitional shelters.

☆ ☆ THE STARS ARE SHINING! ☆ ☆
SOME RELIEF TO THE HOMELESS

HBO's fourth *Comic Relief* raised millions for America's homeless. The all-star telecast featuring Whoopi Goldberg, Billy Crystal, Robin Williams, Susan Sarandon, and about 40 other entertainers put a nationwide audience in such a good mood that they reached into their wallets and contributed a record $7.5 million for the homeless.

WHAT CAN I DO?

▶ **Donate money and food.** These donations go a long way to feed the homeless. For example, at the Los Angeles Mission each Easter dinner served costs only $1.57 because so much of the food is donated. That means you can help feed 10 hungry people for just $15.70 . . . 100 people for $157 . . . or 650 people for $1,020.

▶ **Volunteer at a local shelter, soup kitchen, food bank, or other facility that serves the homeless.** Many nonprofit and religious organizations operate soup kitchens and shelters. They are often staffed by volunteers, and would appreciate your time, money, or other donations such as food and clothing.

If you do not have enough services to help the homeless

▶ Since 1981, the federal housing budget has been reduced more than 75 percent, from $32 billion to $7.5 billion. These federal cuts have led to a critical shortage of affordable housing. There is a shortfall of nearly 4 million units of low-cost housing in the U.S.

▶ Low wages and high unemployment among the nation's poor contribute to homelessness. The numbers of poor are increasing, and the availability and affordability of housing are decreasing.

▶ Between 1963 and 1980, the population of psychiatric institutions decreased by 367,000 people; many of these mentally disabled people ended up on the streets.

▶ Cutbacks in Federal Entitlement programs such as AID to Families with Dependent Children (AFDC), the Food Stamp Program, and Social Security also contributed to the rising homeless problem.

in your community, consider starting one. Joan Stairs and Juanita Suggs received a Daily Point of Light award for their efforts to fill the need for homeless services in their community.

Andrea Justin. National Coalition for the Homeless Safety Network.

❂ JOAN STAIRS AND JUANITA SUGGS ❂

New Castle, IN
DAILY POINT OF LIGHT RECIPIENTS: MARCH 23, 1990

Recognizing the needs of the growing number of homeless individuals in their community, Joan Stairs and Juanita Suggs now dedicate their time and energy to bettering the plight of the homeless.

Ms. Stairs, as chairperson of the New Castle/Henry County Homeless Task Force, and Ms. Suggs, as director of Christian Love Center, have combined their resources to create the Christian Love Help Center/Shelter. The center provides housing, food, clothing, counseling, and literacy programs for 20 people at a time, encouraging them to better their lives and obtain employment.

Reprinted with permission from the White House Office of National Service.

▶ **Organize an event or a service to benefit the homeless.** You might be interested in recruiting your business, school, church, or club to donate time, money, or resources to helping the homeless. For instance:

▶ A Chili cook-off sponsored by 20 L.A. businesses netted about $15,000 for homeless groups.

▶ Downtown Los Angeles law firms offer free legal advice to homeless people.

▶ Project Northstar, Washington, DC, provides educational and emotional support for homeless and formerly homeless children through one-to-one tutoring. Project Northstar is sponsored by local civic groups, law firms, and concerned citizens.

Reprinted with permission from the White House Office of National Service.

▶ **Teach your skills to homeless people.** Contact or start an organization that educates homeless people. In San Diego, for example, the Alpha Project helps homeless people gain the necessary skills to secure a job.

▶ **Contribute to worthy organizations.** Organizations that help the homeless on a day-to-day basis require money and human resources

❂ THE ALPHA PROJECT ❂

San Diego, CA
DAILY POINT OF LIGHT RECIPIENT: JULY 3, 1990

Founded in 1986 by Robert McElroy, the Alpha Project hires homeless people at $6 per hour or more to work on construction projects. The employees receive on-the-job training, enabling them to learn a marketable trade so they may seek employment in the future.

Many concerned citizens, ranging from retired carpenters to college students, teach homeless individuals carpentry skills, administrative skills, and financial budgeting. In addition, the Alpha Project provides the employees with food, shelter, and clothing free of charge until they save enough money to become independent.

Thanksgiving won't come to Skid Row unless people care enough to help. We're just praying that Americans who have been blessed will share with those who have so little.

—GEORGE CAYWOOD, Executive Director, Union Rescue Mission, Los Angeles

to survive. They are on the "front line" of the battle against homelessness so any help you can give would be received immediately by those most in need. Contact such an organization and ask what you can do.

▶ **Participate in activities that publicize homeless issues.** Homeless advocacy groups organize local and national events to raise money and awareness. As an example, more than 10,000 students volunteered in the National Student Campaign Against Hunger and Homelessness Hunger Cleanup, raising $150,000 to aid the hungry and homeless. And 250,000 people marched in Washington, focusing national attention to the homeless problem.

HOUSING NOW!

On October 7, 1989, more than 250,000 people attended the Housing Now! demonstration in Washington, DC. Described by the *Los Angeles Times* as a "sea of humanity" and compared to the civil rights marches of the 1960s, the demonstrators marched to the U.S. Capitol to demand an end to the homelessness problem.

Many homeless people marched from as far as New York City to attend the event. They were joined by concerned people from every state of the union, including such celebrities as Jon Voight, Valerie Harper, and Linda Evans.

The leadership of Housing Now! and numerous homeless marchers met with the House of Representatives to voice their opinions and offer solutions.

In response to Housing Now!, HUD Secretary Jack Kemp delivered a letter in which he committed to make 10 percent of HUD's single-family home inventory available for homeless people. The Democratic leadership of the House promised to introduce legislation that would restore budget cuts in housing made during the Reagan administration.

▶ **Support legislation to help the homeless.**

 ▶ Urge your elected officials to support state and federal legislation designed to provide services for the poor and homeless.

 ▶ Ask your local representatives to to enact legislation that would secure funding for emergency services, transitional housing programs, low-income housing, and adequate entitlements for the poor.

 ▶ The National Coalition for the Homeless has a Legislative Alert System, which is a telephone tree and letter

MacNelly. Reprinted with permission of Tribune Media Services, Inc.

chain that pressures representatives to support pending legislation. Contact the Coalition to join.

▶ **Try to give when you see someone in need.** There are many ways to help a homeless person. If you have some spare change, give it to a needy person. If you feel uncomfortable giving money to a homeless person on the street, then donate to a homeless organization. If you would rather give clothing or other items, organize a clothing drive and donate the goods to a shelter.

The National Coalition for the Homeless suggests ways to help individuals who live on the streets by offering anything from a meal, a cup of coffee, a blanket, or a pair of gloves. This can be done individually, or as part of an organized effort, in which a group of people gather essential items and distribute them to people on the streets.

Your small contributions can make the day better for someone who is tired, hungry, cold, and depressed.

Diane Dering. National Coalition for the Homeless Safety Network.

Organizations and Resources

Coalition for the Homeless
212-695-8700
A New York–based coalition that addresses homelessness issues primarily in that region.

Habitat for Humanity
912-924-6935
A national group that organizes volunteer efforts to build and rehabilitate housing projects.

HANDSNET
408-427-0808
A computer communications network that provides data to human-services organizations in the United States on the

availability of housing and emergency food, as well as news on state and federal legislation and updates on special programs.

Homelessness Information Exchange
202-462-7551
A national service that provides information and assistance on programs for the homeless.

The National Coalition for the Homeless
202-265-2371
A federation of individuals, agencies, and organizations committed to the principle that decent shelter and housing and adequate food are fundamental rights of society. Acts as a clearinghouse to share information and resources.

National Law Center on Homelessness and Poverty
202-638-2535
Committed not only to responding to the immediate needs of the homeless, but also to addressing the broader issue of poverty in America through legal advocacy in Congress and the courts.

National Resource Center on Homelessness and Mental Illness
800-444-7415
The successor to the Clearinghouse on Homelessness Among Mentally Ill People (CHAMP), and under contract to the National

Institute of Mental Health (NIMH), the Center provides technical assistance and information on the homeless, especially the mentally-ill homeless population. Along with many other services, they offer a comprehensive database of information on the mentally-ill homeless and publish materials including a list entitled "Organizations Concerned with Homelessness and Mental Illness."

National Volunteer Clearinghouse for the Homeless
800-HELP-664
Links potential volunteers with organizations in their area that provide service to the homeless.

STUDENT ORGANIZATIONS

Campus Outreach Opportunity League (COOL)
612-624-3018
Promotes student involvement in community needs, including hunger, homelessness, and illiteracy. Ask for publications such as *Building a Movement: A Resource Book for Students in Community Service*, and *Hunger/Homelessness Action: A Resource Book for Colleges and Universities*.

National Student Campaign Against Hunger and Homelessness (NSCAHH)
617-292-4823
A national nonprofit network of colleges and universities geared to helping the hungry and the homeless. Its quarterly newsletter, *Students Making a Difference*, reaches thousands of students across the nation.

OTHER COMMITTED ORGANIZATIONS

Community for Creative Non-Violence (CCNV)
202-393-4409

Housing Assistance Council
202-842-8600

National Alliance to End Homelessness
202-638-1526

National Low Income Housing Coalition
202-662-1530

Salvation Army
201-239-0606
(or call your local chapter)

▶ Contact the National Coalition for the Homeless for a list of organizations in your state or local area and the National Resource Center on Homelessness and Mental Illness for a comprehensive list of national organizations concerned with homelessness and mental illness.

David Adams. National Coalition for the Homeless Safety Network.

Helping Our Children

▪▪

● ● ●

When one out of four American children is raised in poverty, and at least one-half million children go hungry, it's time for us to ask, "Is this what we mean by democracy?"

● ● ●

—FRANCES MOORE LAPPE, co-founder of Food First

BASIC NEEDS

■ ■ ■

Children throughout the world suffer and die on a daily basis due to a lack of basic needs. Millions of infants and youths in the United States and the rest of the world live in hunger, without proper shelter and medical attention, and with little or no chance of receiving a decent education. The statistics of child suffering estimated by UNICEF and other child-care organizations are heartbreaking.

There is a crisis in being able to feed all the world's children adequately.

—CARDISS COLLINS, D-House, member of Congressional Black Caucus

INTERNATIONAL CHILD-CARE CONCERNS

During the decade of the 1980s, Third World countries faced severe circumstances. Average incomes fell by 10 to 25 percent in most of Africa and Latin America, and in the 37 poorest nations health and educational spending dropped 50 percent and 25 percent respectively.

Children suffer the most as a result of a developing country's impoverishment. The UNICEF 1987 Annual Report states that "Throughout 1987, the death toll among the world's under-fives was about 38,000 a day from frequent infection and undernutrition. . . . Some 200,000 children were permanently disabled by polio, and about 4.6 million

Did you know? ▪▪▪▪▪▪▪▪▪▪

▶ Each hour of every day, five babies take their last breath.

225

·········· Did you know?

INTERNATIONALLY

► Approximately 160 million children under the age of 5 live in absolute poverty in Third World countries.

► 16,000 children die each day in developing nations from drinking contaminated water.

► Nearly 40,000 infants die before their first birthday.

·········· Did you know?

IN THE UNITED STATES

► Approximately 13 million children live in poverty.

► If the current trend continues, by the year 2000, one in four of all American children—16 million children—will be poor.

died of causes related to undernutrition." In fact, according to Oxfam America, children make up two-thirds of the 60,000 people who die of hunger each day!

CAUSES OF CHILD DEATHS

In *Investing in Children,* published by Worldwatch Institute, William Chandler discusses the causes of infant-child deaths in the developing world. Rather than placing the blame on famine and other natural disasters, he cites a lack of education and insufficient resources to raise a family properly.

> More children die because they are improperly weaned than because of famine. More children die because their parents do not know how to manage diarrhea than because of epidemics. More children die because their mothers have no wells, hoes, or purchasing power than because of war. They die because their mothers are exhausted from excessive child birth, work, and infection. And when children are stunted and retarded from disease and malnutrition, when overburdened parents cannot generate wealth for education and development, then burgeoning populations inadequately prepared for life add to the degradation of natural systems. These stresses perpetuate drought, disease, and famine.

Chandler argues that to solve the problems of Third World poverty and the resulting burdens it places on children, development strategies must include not only fostering economic growth, but should also focus on improving education and health.

A PROBLEM THAT CAN BE SOLVED

Most of the 41,000 children under age 5 who die each day throughout the world do so as a result of malnutrition, infections, and repeated bouts of diarrhea. According to James Grant, UNICEF Executive Director, half of these children could be saved if four simple, inexpensive methods were available:

Oral rehydration therapy— to replace body fluids

Growth monitoring—to detect early signs of malnutrition

Immunizations—against childhood diseases

Breast-feeding—to provide natural immunities.

Due to the influence of organizations such as UNICEF, the U.S. Agency for International Development, and the World Health Organization, many child health-care agencies, and world political and religious leaders are promoting these four life-saving methods.

And their efforts are showing results. Significant progress has been made in UNICEF's global campaign to address the prevalent killers of children through vaccination, maternal education, and distribution of oral rehydration therapy kits that can save the lives of the millions affected by diarrheal infection.

The costs of these programs are low compared with their results. According to Hiroshi Nakajima, Director General of WHO, "about 46 million infants every year are not fully immunized against childhood diseases—polio, diphtheria, pertussis and tuberculosis. It costs about $10 per child to vaccinate against these diseases. For less than $1 billion, the cost of 20 modern military planes, the world could control these illnesses."*

Instead, every year 3 million children die from diseases such as measles, tetanus, TB, whooping cough, polio, and diphtheria, which can easily be prevented through immunization. Ordinary measles killed more than 1 million children in 1987 alone!

U. S. CHILD-CARE CONCERNS

Although the United States is one of the most affluent countries in the world, many American children live in poverty. Many youths have insufficient housing and medical attention and inadequate educational opportunities.

Each night thousands of children go to bed hungry. Hungry children get sick easily. They have trouble concentrating and have difficulties at school. According to the Food Research and Action Center in 1991 an estimated 5.5 million children under the age of 12 are hungry.

A QUESTIONABLE FUTURE

A Congressional report on the welfare of our nation's children states that the "persistent problems of poverty and poor health are compounded by alarming rises in homelessness, youth violence and the emergence of drug addiction and AIDS among babies." Representative George Miller (D-Calif.) and former Chairman of the House Select Committee on Children, Youth, and Families states that "we're launching mil-

Did you know? ■■■■■■■■■■■

▶ A UNICEF report states that 97 percent of the children in the developing world now live in countries with operational programs to control diarrheal diseases (CDD).

▶ The use of either homemade solutions or Oral Rehydration Salts (ORS) have averted at least 500,000 child deaths from dehydration.

Did you know? ■■■■■■■■■■

According to Save the Children, every week, 250,000 children in the world's developing nations lose their lives to diarrheal dehydration and disease. That's 13 million needless— and preventable—deaths each year!

*USA Today, 26 September 1989.

227

·········· Did you know?

POVERTY

▶ One in five American children is poor.

▶ Poor children die at a rate three times greater than the nonpoor.

▶ In 1987, 21 percent of youths under age 18 lived below the poverty line. Among blacks it was 48 percent, among Hispanics, 42 percent.

HOUSING

▶ 200,000 children are homeless on any given night of the year.

HEALTH AND INFANT MORTALITY

▶ Every year 40,000 infants in the United States die before their first birthday.

▶ According to Bread for the World, the United States ranks first among 142 nations in military expenditures, military foreign assistance, nuclear reactors and nuclear testing and nineteenth in the developed world in infant mortality.

lions of children on courses of failure."

Because our children represent the future of our country this nation is obligated to provide a decent chance for them to live and succeed.

WHAT IS BEING DONE?

···

International Efforts

▶ UNICEF formed the "Grand Alliance," a partnership of international agencies, voluntary organizations, grass-roots movements, and professional groups to create a child survival and development "revolution" around the world.

▶ In October 1990, world leaders met at the United Nations for the World Summit for Children. The leaders discussed the plight of hungry, poor, and sick children throughout the world and formulated a 10-year plan to address these and other problems.

National Efforts

▶ Women, Infants, and Children (WIC), established and funded by Congress, is one of the nation's most effective social programs. WIC reduces the incidence of later fetal deaths, low birth weight and premature births, and anemia.

▶ As a result of the efforts of Children Defense Fund and other child welfare groups, more than 10,000 articles and editorials, together with extensive radio and TV attention, have covered children and their problems. Coverage has included cover story features in *Time, Ebony, U.S. News & World Report, Fortune, Business Week, Newsweek,* and *Forbes.*

▶ In October 1987, the Child Welfare League of America (CWLA) initiated a nonpartisan public education campaign, the Children's Presidential Campaign. The goal was to place children's issues high on presidential candidates' agendas.

WHAT CAN I DO?

···

▶ **Contribute to a Child-Welfare Organization.** Although these problems seem so immense in nature and require global efforts to solve your individual actions can also help.

▶ **Contact your political representative and show your sup-**

port for child welfare legislation. Many organizations lobby for more governmental programs for children, such as Head Start, Women, Infants and Children (WIC), and the Job Corps. Letters and calls to your elected representatives will help insure adequate funding for these and other programs.

Contact Bread for the World (800-82-BREAD) or another concerned group and ask about current drives to support child-welfare legislation.

▶ **Sponsor a needy child!** Child sponsorship organizations like Plan International and Save the Children link interested people with needy children throughout the world. Donations go directly toward helping a child and his or her family.

For more information about child sponsorship refer to "Sponsoring Needy Children."

▶ **Look for ways to help needy children in your community.** Regardless of where you live in this country there are children who need extra care. Contact a local organization and ask about programs in your area that provide necessities to economically disadvantaged children. Or consider starting a program yourself. Lou and Lola Stouffer of Terra Alta, WV, figured out a fun way to help children in their town.

❂ LOU AND LOLA STOUFFER ❂

Terra Alta, WV
DAILY POINT OF LIGHT RECIPIENT: FEBRUARY 17, 1990

The Stouffers, endearingly known as "Santa and Mrs. Claus," bring the joy of the holiday season to needy children in their community.

For the past 17 years, the Stouffers have delivered gifts during the holiday season. Throughout the year, the Stouffers collect clothing and toys and refurbish them during the summer months. The gifts are then boxed according to the needs of the economically disadvantaged families. During the holiday season, "Santa and Mrs. Claus" dress in their red suits and deliver the gifts to delighted children. Without the Stouffers, many economically disadvantaged families would not have a merry holiday season.

Reprinted with permission from the White House Office of National Service.

▶ **Write letters to the media to express your support for more events like the World Summit for Children and National Children's Day.** These events bring worldwide attention to the plight of children. Your interest in these causes will further the drive for better child-welfare programs.

Did you know? ·········

EDUCATION

▶ The percentage of black and Hispanic youths attending college is continuing to decline.

▶ 1 of 4 high school students drops out before graduation.

Did you know? ·········

ON AN AVERAGE DAY IN THE UNITED STATES

▶ 689 babies are born to women who had inadequate prenatal care.

▶ 719 babies are born with low birth weights (less than 5 lb., 8 oz.)

▶ 129 babies are born at birth weights less than 3 lb., 5 oz.

▶ 67 babies die during their first month.

▶ 105 babies die before their first birthday.

▶ 27 children die from poverty.

From *Children 1990*, by Children's Defense Fund.

·········· Did you know?

▶ A contribution of just 50 cents helps UNICEF provide enough medicine to treat one child with TB for two weeks—$372 pays for 320 blankets for a day-care center—$1,000 buys 1 ton of paper for production of elementary school textbooks.

▶ Oral rehydration therapy provided by UNICEF and WHO costs less than 10 cents a packet—that 10 cents could save the life of a child suffering from diarrheal dehydration.

☆ ☆ THE STARS ARE SHINING! ☆ ☆

HARDLY A "HONEYMOON" FOR AMERASIAN CHILDREN

Audrey Meadows Six, Alice of *The Honeymooners*, is trying to make the lives of Amerasian children a little better. As a spokeswoman for the Pearl S. Buck Foundation, Audrey describes the plight of Amerasians and explains,

"You have the power to help these children. You can put food in their mouths. You can see that they receive an education. You can clothe them. And you can provide them with basic health care.

NATIONAL CHILDREN'S DAY

··

The first National Children's Day was held on October 8, 1989, in Washington, DC. Forty youth ambassadors representing 18 states traveled to the nation's capital to meet with members of Congress, express their views at a congressional hearing, and have lunch with Representative Joseph Kennedy II, the original sponsor of the Children's Day resolution.

The congressional hearing discussed economic, social, educational, and health issues affecting children today. A joint effort of the Select Committee on Children, Youth, and Families, and the Task Force on Human Resources of the Committee on the Budget, the hearing investigated the budgetary impact of policies directed toward our country's youth.

Show your support by contacting a child-welfare organization and asking what you can do to participate in the next National Children's Day celebration.

For more information call the Child Welfare League of America (202-638-2952).

Organizations

Children's Defense Fund
202-628-8787
Provides a strong and effective voice for the children of America, paying particular attention to the needs of poor, minority, and handicapped children. Ask for a copy of *Children, 1990* ($2.95).

Child Welfare League of America (CWLA)
202-638-2952
A national association for 550 leading public and voluntary child welfare agencies, which help more than 2 million abused, neglected, and troubled children in their own

homes and in out-of-home care—shelter care, foster homes and residential programs—annually.

The United Nations International Children's Emergency Fund (UNICEF)
212-326-7000

Established in 1946 to meet the urgent need for food, medicine, and clothing among children in post-World War II Europe and China. Soon after, UNICEF's mandate was broadened beyond emergency relief to include assistance to the least developed nations in establishing essential services to prevent child deaths occurring from disease, malnutrition, and disasters.

OTHER COMMITTED ORGANIZATIONS

American Academy of Pediatrics
708-228-5005

American Humane Association
303-792-9900

Bread for the World
800-82-BREAD

Children's Aid Society
212-949-4800

Family Research Council
202-393-2100

United Way
703-836-7100

SPONSORING NEEDY CHILDREN

∎∎∎

For just a few dollars a month you can sponsor a needy child in the United States or in many other parts of the world. The money you donate will provide a child with necessities such as emergency food and vitamins, clothing and shelter, dental and medical care, education, and counseling on housing, agricultural, and nutrition. A dollar goes much farther in most overseas countries.

Sponsoring a needy child is a rewarding experience for all parties involved. The child will receive extra care, which may be critical to his or her welfare. And, along with the satisfaction of helping others, the sponsor will be able to learn more about his sponsored child through letters and other forms of communication.

▶ **Sponsoring a child is easy!** Just contact one of the organizations listed here and tell them that you are interested in sponsoring a needy child.

▶ **Groups can sponsor children also.** Many schools, clubs, and organizations sponsor needy children. For instance, the 293 members of the Comsewogue High School Junior class sponsor Joelinson Guillermo Sosa, a three-year-old boy from the Dominican Republic. By sponsoring Joelinson and his family through Plan International USA, the students help Joelinson go to school and they also help the family to receive better and more affordable medical care, which allows them

Did you know? ∙∙∙∙∙∙∙∙∙∙

According to Plan International USA (formerly Foster Parents Plan):

▶ Just 73 cents a day (or $22.00 a month) will help vaccinate a child, teach a child to read, or replace a thatch roof with a tin roof.

▶ A vaccination costs less than $5.

▶ A rehydration solution to save a child dying of diarrhea (the biggest child-killer) costs only pennies.

to retain income. When the Junior class graduates, they will hand the sponsorship down to the incoming freshman class.

Approximately 750 school groups (classes, clubs, student councils, etc.) are Childreach Sponsors for Plan International USA alone. The students write letters to the child, conduct fund-raising activities, and in some cases even visit their sponsored child.

For more information, contact Plan International USA or another similar organization.

▶ **Looking for the perfect present?** How about the gift of a child sponsorship? Michelle Morse was looking for just the right present for her niece, Christine. She noticed an advertisement for Plan International USA in a magazine and decided that this would be the perfect gift for her first Christmas. In a letter to Christine, Michelle tells why she chose to give her a child sponsorship:

> I realized how lucky you are to have been born here, and how easily you or me or anyone else could have been born in a poor country, with little or no opportunity for an "advantaged" life. And I decided this would be the perfect "gift" for your first Christmas. The only thing disturbing about this was that I didn't want you ever to feel that I was "giving" you a person. No one person is more deserving of a fair chance in life than anyone else. Instead, I've given you the gift of sharing. This is one of the most important things you will ever learn, and if you grow up practicing it, it will also be one of the most rewarding.

Contact Plan International USA or another child sponsorship organization and ask how you can give this thoughtful, rewarding and beneficial gift.

✰ ✰ THE STARS ARE SHINING! ✰ ✰

PLAN INTERNATIONAL USA SPONSORS:

I'm delighted to be a part of such a marvelous organization. You make the world a happier place for "our" children.
Frank Sinatra

I can think of no more gratifying or rewarding endeavor than to be a Childreach Sponsor. I look forward to being one for many, many years to come.
Neil Simon

At first I called PLAN because I wanted to give Childreach sponsorships as holiday gifts to my family and friends. When I found out the organization was about to assign its 100,000th child, Karl and I immediately decided to sponsor that special child ourselves. I can't think of anything more rewarding or more important than helping a child in need during the season of giving, or anytime for that matter.
Sally Jessy Raphael

Organizations

- -

Children, Inc.
804-359-4562

Children International
816-942-2000

Christian Children's Fund
804-644-4654

Christian Foundation for Children and Aging
816-941-9100

Feed the Children
800-367-2400/405-942-0228

Food for the Hungry
800-2HUNGER

Holy Land Christian Mission
816-942-9150

Pearl S. Buck Foundation
215-249-0100

Plan International USA (formerly Foster Parents Plan)
800-556-7918/In RI 738-5600

Save the Children
203-226-7272/800-243-5075

World Vision
818-357-7979/800-444-2522

- -

AMERICA'S YOUTH AT RISK

...

Being young isn't what it used to be. Our nation's youth face some very difficult problems today. A typical adolescent may be involved with alcohol or drugs; he or she may come from a broken home or may have suffered parental abuse; she might become pregnant; or he or she could get a sexual disease. Many teenagers resort to crime and gangs, and some drop out of school. Other young people face unemployment or financial barriers to further education.

Adolescents across the nation confront these problems on a daily basis regardless of race or economic status. It's not surprising that many teens get involved with gangs and crime, abuse drugs and alcohol, or even commit suicide. A sad statistic is that teen suicide has increased more than 300 percent since 1950. And more than a million youths run away annually, placing an extra burden on our foster care system and adding to the problems of crime, prostitution, and substance abuse.

ALCOHOL AND DRUG ABUSE

Alcohol and drug abuse weighs heavily on the teen crowd as young adults attempt to try new things or resort to dangerous substances to escape intolerable circumstances. According to

Did you know?..........

ON AN AVERAGE DAY IN THE UNITED STATES:

▶ 2,795 women under 20 get pregnant

▶ 1,106 teenagers have abortions

▶ 6 teenagers commit suicide

▶ 7,742 teenagers become sexually active

▶ 623 teenagers contract syphilis or gonorrhea

▶ 1,512 teenagers drop out of school

▶ 211 youths are arrested for drug abuse

▶ 437 youths are arrested for drinking or drunk driving

From *Children 1990*, by Children's Defense Fund.

·········· Did you know?

► According to a 1987 National Institute on Drug Abuse report, 57 percent of all high school seniors have used an illegal drug and 92 percent have used alcohol at least once while in high school.

► A 1989 National Institute of Drug Abuse survey of high-school seniors discovered that almost 20 percent of students questioned had used an illicit drug once the previous month. (This is a decline from 21.3 percent in 1988.)

► According to a 1989 Gallup poll, 60 percent of teens surveyed put drugs at the top of their list of problems.

► That same 1989 Gallup poll found that one out of four youths ages 13 to 17, or 4.25 million, had been offered illegal drugs in the previous 30 days.

the National Institute of Drug Abuse, although the illicit drug use among American high-school seniors, college students, and young adults is declining, it is still the highest in the industrialized world.

The abuse of alcohol and drugs among young adults can lead to many other problems, including addiction, crime, and death. Although drug use among teenagers is on the decline, those who use drugs and alcohol are becoming more addicted. A 1989 PRIDE survey found that almost 75 percent of admitted high-school cocaine users and approximately 51 percent of high-school liquor drinkers say that they get "very high." These addictive traits may lead to criminal acts. For instance, the FBI reports that in 1989, 42 percent of all juvenile drug arrests involved cocaine or heroin and 47 percent were associated with marijuana. And misuse of drugs and alcohol can cause death. According to Roseann Bentley, president of the National Association of State Boards of Education, 77 percent of teen deaths in the United States are the result of high-risk behavior, such as drinking and taking drugs. There are many different causes of death from substance abuse, including overdose, automobile accidents, and AIDS, which is spread through the sharing of IV-drug needles or syringes.

SEXUAL BEHAVIOR

The United States Department of Health and Human Services reports that the average age for a girl to have sexual intercourse for the first time is 16. The average age for a boy is 15.5. Along with experiencing sex at young ages, America's youth also faces the problems associated with sex, such as unplanned pregnancy and sexually transmitted diseases, including AIDS.

These and other problems take a heavy toll on our nation's young adults, especially as they struggle with the expected adolescent problems.

WHAT IS BEING DONE?

·······································

Public Sector

► The government's Job Corps program provides many young people with better opportunity and pay than a job

234

found by other means. And every $1.00 of taxpayer money invested in Job Corps returns $1.45.

▶ A national commission to help solve teenage health problems has been formed and will be funded and assisted by the Federal Centers for Disease Control. Established with the help of the National Association of State Boards of Education and the American Medical Association, the commission will tackle such problems as alcohol and drug abuse, smoking, AIDS, and pregnancy.

Private Sector

▶ Private organizations lead the way in reshaping public policy designed to help teens. The Children's Defense Fund and the Child Welfare League have been instrumental in strengthening governmental programs in adolescent pregnancy and parenting, AIDS education, and alcohol and drug abuse treatment.

▶ More than 200,000 Americans call the National Parents' Resource Institute for Drug Education (PRIDE) 800 hotline each year. In 1989, the Drug Abuse Resistance Education program (DARE) reached 3 million children in 50,000 classrooms in all 50 states.

WHAT CAN I DO?

▶ **Become educated and involved.** Contact one of the many groups listed here or seek professional help in your area to learn more about substance abuse, teen pregnancy, and other problems that affect our nation's youth.

For more information about substance abuse consult the section on alcohol and drug abuse (page 329). To learn more about runaways refer to the missing children section (page 237).

▶ **Volunteer your services with a youth program in your area.** Groups such as the Boy Scouts, Girls Incorporated, and Big Brothers/Big Sisters need interested volunteers. This kind of work is highly gratifying and extremely beneficial. If you like to relate one-on-one to kids, this type of work may be just right for you. For more information refer to the youth programs section (page 250).

Did you know?

▶ According to the Children's Defense Fund, in 1988 approximately 500,000 teenagers gave birth. On average, each year 1 out of every 10 teenage women age 15 to 19 will get pregnant. Four out of every 10 teenage women will become pregnant by the age of 19.

▶ The Centers for Disease Control estimates that 2.5 million teens are infected with sexually transmitted diseases (venereal diseases [VD]) each year.

▶ The Children's Defense Fund reports that on any given day over 1,000 teenage girls have an abortion and about 600 get gonorrhea or syphilis.

··········· Did you know?

▶ Today a teen in the United States gets pregnant every 30 seconds.

▶ Every 13 seconds a teen in the United States gets a sexually transmitted disease (STD), such as gonorrhea or chlamydia.

▶ The same sexual activities that cause pregnancy and give you STD's can infect you with the virus that causes AIDS.

America Responds to AIDS, 1989 report, Department of Health and Human Services, Public Health Service, Centers for Disease Control, 800-458-5231.

Reprinted with permission from the White House Office of National Service.

▶ **Contact an organization that works to improve the lives of young people.** There are many national and local groups that try to help adolescents. Call one of the many listed below and ask what you can do.

❂ EDITH LEWIS ❂

Garland, TX
DAILY POINT OF LIGHT RECIPIENT: MARCH 5, 1990

Edith Lewis, known as "Grandma," has selflessly dedicated her life to helping troubled youth become productive citizens.

Ms. Lewis, 63, converted her home into a shelter for abandoned young adults. She takes in those whom most of society has written off as hopeless. Their stories vary, from ones of broken families, abused childhoods, alcoholic or drug-addicted parents to depression. Most have run away or been kicked out of their homes and are dangerous. Ms. Lewis serves as a 24-hour counselor, psychiatrist, cook, and surrogate mother, while individuals and church groups donate food, clothing, and medical care. While many of these young people are accustomed to expressing themselves through violence, she handles outbursts calmly but firmly. Ms. Lewis' rehabilitation method of love and affection has encouraged many distressed youth to finish school and lead a successful adult life.

Organizations and Resources

Children's Defense Fund (CDF)
202-628-8787
Programs such as the Adolescent Pregnancy Prevention Child Watch and publications such as *Adolescent Pregnancy Prevention Clearinghouse* have done much to help prevent teen pregnancy and AIDS. Ask for publications such as *Preventing Children Having Children: What You Can Do,* and *Adolescent Pregnancy: Whose Problem Is It?*

Child Welfare League of America (CWLA)
202-638-2952
A national association of 550 leading public and voluntary child-welfare agencies, which help more than 2 million abused and troubled children in their own homes and in out-of-home care. Their Children's Campaign has been highly effective in giving a voice to the youth of America. They offer publications on many different topics pertaining to children and young adults.

Drug Abuse Resistance Education (DARE)
800-223-DARE (to get information about starting or joining a local DARE chapter or to donate money).
800-TALK-KFC (a recorded message about DARE and how to get involved). Their in-school drug education program provides information about drug abuse for parents and children and offers ways to get involved in fighting drug abuse.

Mothers Against Drunk Driving (MADD)
800-438-MADD
MADD mobilizes victims and their allies to establish the public conviction that impaired driving is unacceptable and criminal, in order to promote corresponding public policies, programs, and personal accountability.

National Parents' Resource Institute for Drug Education (PRIDE)
800-241-7946
A private, nonprofit organization whose goal is to stem the epidemic of drug use, especially among adolescents and young adults, by the dissemination of accurate health information, as well as the information of parent and youth networks. Ask for publications such as *Drugs of Abuse Digest: A Prevention Guide for the Family, School, and Workplace.*

Salvation Army
201-239-0606 (or call your local chapter)
The Army provides emergency shelter for troubled, abused, or neglected youngsters. They also provide counseling, medical care, and child-care instruction for pregnant teenagers.

MISSING CHILDREN

■ ■ ■

MISSING CHILDREN

The National Center for Missing and Exploited Children explains that "as a society, our efforts to prevent crimes against children have not kept pace with the increasing vulnerability of our youngest citizens. After hearing the tragic stories about abducted or exploited children, most Americans are surprised to learn that many crimes against children CAN BE PREVENTED."* To learn more about what you can do to protect your children contact the National Center or another child protective organization.

RUNAWAYS

Some groups estimate that as many as 1 million children run away from their homes each year. The reasons vary from unstable home environments due to divorce or other family problems, to unhappy school and peer experiences. In some instances the child leaves voluntarily whereas in others the youth is thrown out of the house by one or both parents.

Most runaways flee from intolerable situations. According to the National Network of Runaway and Youth Services, more than one-third of the young people who leave home do so out of fear of abuse. The streets do not provide a solution, however. Teens often encounter drugs, alcohol, and squalid living conditions—resulting in disease, crime, and unwanted pregnancies. Jim Kennedy, medical director for New York's Covenant House, notes that "Today more than ever, living the lifestyle of the streets means sex, drugs and crime. Half

*"Child Protection," a brochure by the National Center for Missing and Exploited Children.

237

COVENANT HOUSE

NINELINE

1-800-999-9999

Covenant House photo by George Wirt.

*"AIDS, drugs threaten runaways," Marco R. della Cara, *USA Today*, 18 October, 1989.

**Data from the Juvenile Justice Clearinghouse (800-638-8736 or 301-251-5500).

of the kids I see are involved in prostitution, many to get money for drugs. But I'd say 100 percent are involved in survival sex—sex for drugs, shelter or companionship."* And with "survival sex" comes not only unwanted pregnancies but another very serious problem—AIDS. *USA Today* reported that 6.1 percent of 1,840 New York runaways tested positive for the AIDS virus (the national average is .002 percent).

The National Incidence Studies of Missing, Abducted, Runaway, and Thrownaway Children (NISMART) estimates the incidence of missing children for 1988 in the following five categories:

Abducted by family members (354,100 children). Often called "child snatching," these incidents usually involve a custody dispute.

Abducted by nonfamily members (attempted: 114,600 children; stereotypical kidnappings: 200 to 300 children). Abductions and/or kidnappings usually involve force.

Runaways (450,700 children). Children who left home or a juvenile facility voluntarily.

Thrownaways (127,100 children). Youths who were "thrown out" or if they ran away, they were asked not to return by one or both parents or guardians.

Lost, injured, or otherwise missing (438,200 children). Children who were missing for a number of reasons, such as being lost or injured, for varying periods of time (usually a few minutes to overnight).**

WHAT IS BEING DONE?

Public Sector

▶ Federally funded youth centers share approximately $27 million. In 1987, the U.S. Department of Health and Human Services estimated that approximately 395,000 children were served by these centers, up from 15,000 in 1976.

▶ The Missing Children's Assistance Act of 1984 created the National Center for Missing and Exploited Children and instituted other programs to help missing and exploited children.

Private Sector

▶ Since 1984 the nonprofit National Center for Missing and Exploited Children (NCMEC) has been instrumental in helping families searching for their missing children.

► According to the National Network of Runaway and Youth services, approximately 1,000 client calls are received each day by the three national runaway hot lines.

WHAT CAN I DO?

•••

► **Become informed.** Greater education for yourself and your children may help prevent potential problems. Contact the National Center for Missing and Exploited Children or one of the Adam Walsh Child Resource Centers to learn more.

Ask the National Center for their brochures "Just in Case . . . Parental Guidelines in Case Your Child Might Someday Be Missing" and "Child Protection."

► **Stop the problem before it starts.** If you are a youth, parent, or guardian experiencing a serious domestic problem, contact a counseling service immediately; try to solve the problem before it gets out of hand.

► **Volunteer.** Runaway and youth service centers need all types of volunteers. You could help handle calls and offer counsel to those in need or you might help care for the youths during their stay at a center. (Note: Certain volunteer activities require special skills. In some instances, the center or service can provide the necessary training.)

Contact the National Network of Runaway and Youth Services for "Helping Them Do Best," a study of how volunteers are used in runaway and youth services programs.

► **Contact the authorities and child protection groups if you have information about a missing child or a runaway youth.** The sooner a child receives professional, caring help, the better. Some of these groups are listed below or call your local police or child protective services. For a comprehensive list of child protection organizations contact the National Center for Missing and Exploited Children.

Organizations and Resources

•••

Adam Walsh Child Resource Center (AWCRC)
714-898-4802 (CA)
407-820-9000 (FL)

716-461-1000 (NY)
803-254-2326 (SC)
AWCRC merged with the National Center for Missing and Exploited Children in

1990. The AWCRC branch offices allow the National Center to expand its reach to families at the community level.

Covenant House
212-727-4000/800-999-9999
Offers shelter and sanctuary for 25,000 youths every year. Their NINELINE (800-999-9999) is a 24-hour national toll-free hotline, which provides advice, referrals, and support for troubled parents and teens.

National Center for Missing and Exploited Children (NCMEC)
703-235-3900
Serves as a clearinghouse of information on missing and exploited children; provides technical assistance to citizens and law-enforcement agencies; offers training programs to law-enforcement and social

service professionals; distributes photos and descriptions of missing children nationwide; coordinates child protection efforts with the private sector; networks with nonprofit organizations and state clearinghouses; and provides information on effective state legislation to ensure the protection of children.

National Network of Runaway and Youth Services
202-682-4114
A membership organization of more than 900 youth-serving agencies, individuals, and associations that provides and facilitates services for

runaway, homeless, and economically displaced youth.

TELEPHONE HOTLINES
Child Find
800-426-5678
Covenant House 9-Line
800-999-9999
Missing Children Help Center
800-872-5437
National Center for Missing and Exploited Children
800-843-5678/800-826-7653 (TTD Hotline)
The National Runaway Switchboard
800-621-4000/312-880-9860
Runaway Hotline
800-231-6946/800-392-3352 (in Texas)

CHILD ABUSE

∎ ∎ ∎

·········· Did you know?

In 1989, 2.4 million children were reported abused and/or neglected, according to the National Committee for the Prevention of Child Abuse.

WHAT IS CHILD ABUSE?

Childhelp USA explains that child abuse "consists of any act of commission or omission that endangers or impairs a child's physical or emotional health and development. Child abuse

❂ **SHELLEY JOYCE SPELL** ❂

Houston, TX
DAILY POINT OF LIGHT RECIPIENT: APRIL 27, 1990

"In a way, it [TACA] is a therapy for me because I know that somebody is getting helped."

Once a victim of child abuse herself, Shelley Spell, 19, has devoted her life to helping other victims. After learning that a large number of her peers had experienced child abuse also, Shelley Spell founded Teens Against Child Abuse (TACA), a support group and public awareness organization.

For more than three years, Ms. Spell has coordinated TACA's after-school meetings where TACA members share their experiences, offer information on child abuse, listen to professionals speak on the subject, and coordinate special fund-raising events. Ms. Spell encourages parents, teachers, law enforcement officials, and counselors to participate in the support meetings and activities.

240

includes any damage done to a child which cannot be reasonably explained by an injury or series of injuries appearing to be non-accidental in nature."

Neglect is the largest percentage of reported types of abuse. An American Humane Society study finds that in 1989 neglect represented 55 percent of all reported child-abuse cases. Physical abuse accounted for 21 percent; sexual abuse, 16 percent; and emotional abuse, 8 percent.

A PROBLEM GETTING BIGGER AND BIGGER

The incidence of child abuse and neglect in this country is reaching epidemic proportions. The 2.4 million reported cases of child abuse in 1989 represents a 10 percent increase from 1988 and is the largest year-for-year increase since 1985. According to government statistics, in the last decade there has been a 200 percent increase in the number of reported child-abuse cases, and from 1985 to 1990 child-abuse cases were up 55 percent. An alarming percentage of America's youth are victims of some type of abuse.

Child abuse creates extreme physical and emotional stress, which often leads to many problems as the child grows up. Many abused children become runaways and turn to drugs, alcohol, and crime. And some do not get the chance to grow up at all.

The consequences of physical abuse are far greater for young children. The National Committee for Child Abuse reports that children between the ages of 0 to 5 represent 28 percent of the general abused child population and an astounding 78 percent of the fatalities. Younger children obviously have more difficulty protecting themselves. The average age of an abused child is 7.2 years, but the average age of a child dying from abuse is 2.6 years.

The problem of child abuse is too great to be ignored. How can we better our society if we destroy the lives of our children?

WHAT CAN I DO?

▶ **Learn the signs of child abuse.** Because child abuse can be physical, emotional, and/or sexual in nature, there are numerous signs to look for. Just a *few* symptoms are listed to the right.

Did you know? ----------

According to Childhelp USA, the major forms of child abuse are:

▶ Physical abuse, including neglect or lack of adequate supervision

▶ Emotional abuse or deprivation

▶ Sexual abuse

Did you know? ----------

▶ Physical abuse signs include unexplained injuries, bruises, welts, and burns.

▶ Emotional abuse entails symptoms ranging from apathy to anti-social behavior.

▶ Sexual abuse can be identified if a child complains of pain, itching, or bleeding in the genital area or if a young child is overly interested in adult sexual behavior.

Childhelp USA

·········· Did you know?

According to the National Committee for Child Abuse:

▶ In 1989, 1,277 children died as a result of abuse and neglect. That averages to more than 3 children who lose their lives each day!

▶ Child-abuse fatalities increased 38 percent from 1985 to 1989.

▶ Over half of all child-abuse fatalities are children under the age of 1!

▶ One in 3 girls and 1 in 5 boys are sexually abused before the age of 18.

▶ In 80 percent of the cases either a parent or someone the child knows is the abuser.

Reprinted with permission from the White House Office of National Service.

To obtain a more extensive list, call Childhelp USA or the National Child Abuse Hotline (800-4A-CHILD), or another child welfare group and ask for additional information.

▶ **Volunteer your services.** Contact a child advocacy group and let them know of your interest. Activities might entail fund raising, lobbying, or answering help-line calls. Or get involved at a community service center, such as a crisis center, emergency day-care facility, or a counseling service. Eva Filice of Salinas, CA, received a Daily Point of Light award for her commitment to helping victims of child abuse.

✪ EVA DOLORES FILICE ✪

Salinas, CA
DAILY POINT OF LIGHT RECIPIENT: MAY 17, 1990

Ms. Filice, 75, has dedicated her life to brightening the lives of abused children. For over four years, Ms. Filice has volunteered for the Family Resource Center, an organization which serves abused children. Every morning she arrives at the center at 8:00. She reads to the children, plays with them, prepares their meals, and provides them with love and care. Ms. Filice's consistent presence provides the children with stability in their otherwise unstable lives. She has gone beyond her duties by effectively becoming their foster grandmother.

▶ **If you suspect child abuse, contact a local agency as soon as possible.** Your prompt call may save the life of an abused child. Call one of the agencies listed here, such as the National Child Abuse Hotline (800-4A-CHILD), or contact a local agency such as the Department of Child Protective Services or the Department of Social Services, or the police.

▶ **Lobby to get adequate child protective laws and services in your area.** Contact your local Department of Social Services or Department of Child Protective Services or a local child-welfare agency and ask about the laws that protect children from abuse. If they are not adequate, contact your local legislators and politicians and voice your concern.

▶ **Raise awareness about child abuse in your community.** Work with your community and school leaders to create educative programs about child abuse. For instance, your community could sponsor a child abuse awareness campaign, your schools could offer educational courses that train teachers how to recognize and deal with cases of child abuse, or your school curriculum could provide classes to teach students about child abuse.

Organizations and Resources

Childhelp USA
818-347-7280
Sponsor of the Childhelp USA National Campaign for the Prevention of Child Abuse and Neglect and sponsor of the National Child Abuse Hotline (1-800-4A-CHILD).

The Covenant House 9-LINE
800-999-9999
Connects you directly to local help.

The National Child Abuse Hot Line
800-4-A-CHILD/800-422-4453
Has telephone numbers of state agencies, information, or counseling 24 hours a day, seven days a week.

National Center for Missing and Exploited Children
800-843-5678

National Committee for the Prevention of Child Abuse
312-663-3520
A national citizen-based organization that seeks to prevent child abuse through public awareness and education programs. Ask for a copy of *How to Teach Your Children Discipline* and for their comic book that shows kids how they can avoid abuse.

National Court Appointed Special Advocates Association (NCASAA)
206-328-8588
Court appointed special advocates (CASAs) are trained community volunteers who speak in court for abused and neglected children. NCASAA supports and maintains CASA programs.

OTHER COMMITTED ORGANIZATIONS

American Humane Association
303-792-9900

American Professional Society on the Abuse of Children
312-554-0166

Center for Child Protection and Family Support, Inc.
202-544-3144

Child Welfare League of America
202-638-2952

Clearinghouse on Child Abuse and Neglect/Family Violence
703-821-2086

C. Henry Kempe National Center for the Prevention and Treatment of Child Abuse and Neglect
303-321-3963

National Center on Child Abuse and Neglect (NCCAN)
703-821-2086

National Children's Advocacy Centers
205-533-5437

National Coalition Against Domestic Violence
202-638-6388

National Council on Child Abuse and Family Violence
800-222-2000/202-429-6695

The National Resource Center on Child Sexual Abuse
800-KIDS-006

Parent's Anonymous Hotline
800-421-0353

DAY CARE

###

In 1989, 10 million children under the age of 6 needed some type of child care because both their parents or a single parent were working.

According to the U.S. Census Bureau, while Mother is at work:

▶ 2.5 million children under the age of five stay at home (usually under the supervision of a relative or friend)

▶ 3.8 million are cared for in another home (usually under the supervision of a relative or friend)

▶ Almost 2 million are cared for in some type of day-care facility.

A GROWING PROBLEM

The shift in the makeup of America's work force has led to the need for child day care. The number of households in which both parents work has increased dramatically in the last two decades. More than 3 out of 5 school children have mothers in the labor force. And with divorces becoming more and more commonplace, a large percentage of households with children are led by just one parent. According to the Bureau of Labor Statistics, about 4.5 million women, or one quarter of today's working mothers, are the primary wage earners for their household. And the problem is only getting worse. The Labor Department estimates that the number of children requiring day care increased by 2 million in 1990 alone.

THE HIGH COST OF DAY CARE

If parents are not fortunate enough to have a relative or friend take care of their children while they are at work, they must find an adequate and safe place to keep their children, and they must also be able to pay for it. The types of day-care centers range from churches and private businesses to facilities funded by corporations for their employees. Currently, there are approximately 1.5 million family day-care providers caring for 5.5 million children.

However, the costs of many of these facilities is prohibitive. A nationwide survey of child-care costs in 1989 found that the average cost of full-time day care for one child was $3,432.* For a poor family, this cost is almost impossible to afford. A 1986 Bureau of the Census report found that poor working women with children under the age of 15 spent 22 percent of their family monthly income on day care. In 1987,

CROCK By Bill Rechin and Don Wilder

Reprinted with special permission of North American Syndicate, Inc.

*Runzheimer International news release, 17 April 1989.

the Bureau of the Census found that half of all female-headed families with children had incomes less than $10,500. In that same year, approximately two-thirds of all women in the work force were single or had husbands who earned less than $15,000 a year, according to the Bureau of Labor Statistics.

VIRTUALLY EVERYONE IS AFFECTED

The Children's Defense Fund explains that "America is in the midst of a child-care crisis—working parents too often cannot find or afford safe, adequate child care. Low-income parents in particular face the painful choice of placing their children in potentially harmful situations or forgoing work and training opportunities because they cannot afford quality child care. Even employers suffer when their employees are absent or distracted because of child care problems." Parents, employers, and legislators struggle to determine the best ways to help.

▶ Politicians are trying to determine what role state and federal governments will play, and how much they'll spend. The question of who should pay for child care is still unresolved.

▶ Parents want a safe place for their children to spend the day and are unable to forgo extra income to stay at home. Many low-income families cannot afford child-care costs.

▶ Businesses realize they will lose productivity and money if they don't help, yet they don't want to shoulder all the cost.

▶ State and federal day-care funding competes with many other programs for a limited pool of money.

Tackling the issue of day care requires a concerted effort from all parties. It is likely that many plans will be implemented, involving joint contributions from everyone.

WHAT CAN I DO?

● ●

▶ **Contact a child welfare organization.** You can donate time, money, and energy. Volunteer possibilities include supervising children at a center and raising money for a facility.

▶ **Volunteer your time at a child-care facility.** We not only need more child-care programs, we also need more people to run them. Volunteer activities include actual care of children

Did you know? ▪▪▪▪▪▪▪▪▪▪▪

In Los Angeles, companies such as Paramount Pictures and Arthur Anderson offer on-site day care for employees' children.

▶ Washington law firm, Arnold & Porter, offers onsite child care for $20.00 per day for its employees.

▶ In Arcadia, CA, the Methodist Hospital provides nursery and preschool service for all 1,200 of its employees on a wait-list basis.

✪ TONI ALLEE ✪

Norfolk, VA
DAILY POINT OF LIGHT RECIPIENT: MARCH 17, 1990

Toni Allee, a military wife for 21 years, has served others in every community in which she and her husband have been stationed.

Ms. Allee has volunteered in many family-related efforts concerning military personnel. When stationed in Charleston, she worked to alleviate the shortage of adequate child care. Currently, she is a board member and volunteer with the Bertha Snyder Children's Care fund. She spends 18–20 hours a week, in addition to her work schedule, developing promotional strategies for the fund. In addition, she volunteers on the Child Care Answer Line, which serves as a child care resource and referral system. She counsels adults about child care options, offering advice and support.

Reprinted with permission from the
White House Office of National Service.

and administrational tasks. Toni Allee received a Daily Point of Light Award for her child-care efforts in her community.

▶ **Write to your political representatives.** Ask their stance on this issue and tell them how you feel. Child day-care legislation will affect everyone. Letters and calls will ensure that leaders institute the best day-care system possible.

▶ **Talk to your employer about setting up a child-care program.** The Child Care Action Campaign, a national advocacy group, estimates that absenteeism due to child-care emergencies costs companies $3 billion a year. Yet only 3,000 of the nation's 44,000 major employers offer any help with child care, and only 1 in 10 American workers receives some type of child-care benefits. Some programs that are being set up now by corporations are proving highly successful.

Organizations and Resources

● ●

Child Care Action Campaign
212-239-0138

Child Care, Inc.
212-929-7604
The nation's largest nonprofit child-care resource and referral agency.

The Children's Defense Fund
202-628-8787
CDF has launched a major national public education campaign to focus attention our nation's child-care system. Ask for a copy of *Child Care: The Time Is Now* and *State Child Care Fact Book*.

Children's Foundation
202-347-3300
Provides a voice for children and their families on issues of critical concern, at both national and local levels. Current programs include: The National Family Day Care Project and the National Child Support Enforcement Project.

Family Research Council
202-393-2100

Families and Work Institute
212-465-2044
A New York based nonprofit clearinghouse for information and policy research.

Jewish Child Care
212-371-1313

National Center for Missing and Exploited Children
703-235-3900 / 800-843-5678 / 800-826-7653 (hearing impaired)
Ask for a copy of "Just in case . . . Parental guidelines in case you are considering day care."

National Child Day Care Association
202-397-3800

United Planning Organization
202-546-7300

● ●

ADOPTION

. . .

Adoption can be one of the most rewarding experiences of your life. The adoption process, however, requires much time and patience. And even after the adoption takes place most adoptive families need counseling in order to insure a healthy and successful adoption experience.

There are many children who need permanent adoption. More than 35,000 children in the United States are currently awaiting adoption. The kinds of children available for adoption range from American white and minority infants to children from other countries such as Korea, Central and South America, India, and the Philippines.

Children with "special needs" comprise a significant percentage of adoptable children. These children may be older (grade school through teens), have physical, emotional, or mental handicaps, or siblings who should be adopted together.

WHAT CAN I DO?

▶ **Adoption is a lifetime commitment and requires the utmost consideration.** Contact one of the organizations listed here. They will give you information and counseling to help you make such a decision.

▶ **Donate your time and resources to an adoption agency.** Many adoption agencies and resource centers are partially or completely self-funded. Your contribution will be greatly appreciated.

There are no unwanted children . . . just unfound parents.

—Adoption Center of Delaware Valley

Did you know? . . . .

According to the National Committee for Adoption, in 1986 there were 51,000 U.S. adoptions, including:

▶ 24,600 infants under the age of 2

▶ 13,600 children with special needs

▶ 10,109 foreign-born children

Organizations and Resources

National Adoption Information Clearinghouse (NAIC)
202-842-7600
Provides professionals and the general public with information on all aspects of infant, intercountry adoption, or the adoption of special needs children. Authorized by Congress, the Clearinghouse is funded by the U.S. Department of Health and Human Services and the Administration for Children,

Youth and Families; it is operated by CSR, Inc., in conjunction with the National Adoption Center.

Child Welfare League of America (CWLA)

202-638-2952

Led the way to secure funding for post-legal adoption services and recruitment of permanent families for minority children in foster care. Publishes information about adoption and lobbies for adoption legislation.

National Adoption Center

215-925-0200

Provides information and a referral service for families to agencies in their communities, registers approved families and waiting children with special needs, and suggests matches of families and children to appropriate agencies.

The Adoption Center of Delaware Valley

An affiliate of the National Adoption Center, this is a private nonprofit organization that promotes adoption opportunities, particularly for children with special needs.

National Committee for Adoption

202-328-1200

An organization of private adoption agencies and individuals interested in adoption. Accredits private agencies, monitors legal development in the adoption field, and provides information about adoption. Also serves as a counseling service to individuals and agencies about pregnancy, infertility, and adoption.

National Resource Center for Special Needs Adoption

313-475-8693

Offer publications, training, and technical assistance to individuals and organizations concerning the adoption of special needs children.

OURS, Inc.

An adoptive parents' support organization.

OTHER RESOURCES

▶ The NAIC American Adoption Directory lists other national organizations and publications. Contact the NAIC for a copy of their directory and for the fact sheet "Adoption—Where Do I Start?"

▶ *The Penguin Adoption Handbook,* Edmund Blair Bolles, Penguin USA, NY, 1984.

▶ *The Adoption Resource Book,* Lois Gilman, Harper & Row, NY, 1987.

▶ *Adoption: Parenthood Without Pregnancy,* Charlene Canape, Henry Holt, NY, 1986.

▶ *Successful Adoption: A Guide to Finding a Child and Raising a Family,* Jacqueline H. Plumez, Harmony Books, NY, 1987.

▶ *CWLA's Guide to Adoption Agencies: A National Directory of Adoption Agencies and Adoption Resources,* Julia L. Posner, Child Welfare League of America, 1989.

▶ *The Adoption Directory,* Ellen Paul, editor, Gale Research Inc., 1989. 800-877-GALE. $55.00.

FOSTER CARE

■ ■ ■

.... Did you know?

Approximately 500,000 children participate in the foster care system each year.

Foster care and group care provide temporary support to children who are unable to live with their biological families. According to the Child Welfare League of America, each day, about 276,000 children stay in "out of home" placements, ranging from state institutions to group homes to foster families.

There are many reasons why a child may not be able to live with his or her family. Physical, emotional, and/or sexual abuse often plays a major role. If a child has been abused and is in danger of further abuse, he or she may be assigned to foster care for protection. Alcohol and drug abuse in the home often contributes to child abuse. If a child is neglected, the foster care system may seek to place the child in a better environment.

The Child Welfare League of America (CWLA) attributes the rise in the number of children in "out of home" care to:

▶ An increase in abuse and neglect.

▶ An increased number of families with substance abuse problems.

▶ An increased number of families losing their homes due to unemployment and poverty.

▶ A rising number of infants born to drug-addicted mothers.

The CWLA also states that children who require out-of-home care today are "more likely to have had difficulties in school, to have run away from home, and to have been physically abused and sexually molested. They are more likely to be involved in prostitution, drugs, or alcohol, or to be homeless. Most of them have emotional scars and require evaluation and counseling. Many come from poor families."*

The hardships imposed on these children create problems that require immediate and constant attention. Foster care programs seek to provide a safe and positive atmosphere for children in need.

WHAT CAN I DO?

▶ **Become a foster parent.** Caring for an out-of-home child is a big commitment. The child will live in your house and in essence become a member of your family. The amount of time a child will remain with you varies with the type of program, the child's needs, and your wishes. Foster parents receive an average allotment of $212 a month to feed, clothe, and house a child.

Becoming a foster parent requires a license. Most potential foster parents contact either a local, state, or private agency in their area. Once connected with one of these groups, the interested party will undergo training, home inspections, and some type of testing to become certified.

Taking on the challenge of a new child will prove very re-

Did you know? ....

In New York City in 1988, more than 300 infants a month were born already addicted to cocaine. In that same year, more than 5,000 families volunteered to be foster families for these infants.

*Child Welfare League of America, *The First 100 Days: A Child's Initiative,"* 1988.

FOSTER CARE YOUTH INDEPENDENCE PROJECT

Syracuse, NY
DAILY POINT OF LIGHT RECIPIENT: DECEMBER 27, 1989

Foster Care Youth Independence Project, a non-profit organization, helps foster youth make a successful transition from foster care to independence.

The project's volunteers serve as mentors to foster youth aged 14-21, offering them training and guidance. Through different programs, young people participate in lessons on independent living. They gain valuable knowledge and skills in money management, communication, and teamwork. Through their one-on-one relationships with mentors, the young people gain self-confidence which gives them an opportunity to lead a successful life.

Reprinted with permission from the White House Office of National Service.

warding for you and highly beneficial for the child. If you would like to learn more:

▶ Contact a local child welfare organization or child abuse advocacy group and ask about foster parent programs in your area.

▶ Contact your local Department of Social Services.

▶ Check the Yellow Pages under Social Service Organizations or Foster Care.

▶ Watch for local Foster Care drives in your community. You may see a PSA on television, hear about a program on the radio, or read about one in the newspaper.

▶ **Contribute to a foster care organization.** There are many specific federal, state, and private programs that aid and/or administer foster care. Contact a child welfare group and ask how you can contribute.

YOUTH PROGRAMS

■ ■ ■

SHOWING THAT WE CARE

Many children and adolescents need a place to go where they can participate in a positive, enriching atmosphere. Youth organizations give attention and provide direction to such children and young adults, and getting involved one-on-one with a young person in an educational and fun-filled environment is highly beneficial for the youth and extremely rewarding for the volunteer. Counselors and volunteers serve as positive role models for our nation's young people. And once you start, you may never stop being involved. Norman Asselstine received a Daily Point of Light award for his efforts with youth groups.

There are countless ways to get involved with youth organizations. Youth programs offer educational and career training, together with sports and other recreational activities. Here are just a few ways to help:

▶ Youth programs involve special events, such as athletic contests—and ongoing programs, such as child care, educational courses, and career development.

▶ You can help build the confidence of handicapped or underprivileged youngsters and offer direction and insight to youth of all ages.

▶ Youth organizations need all types of volunteers, from camp counselors, coaches, and troop leaders to fund-raisers, organizers, and special consultants.

Many children thrive when they realize that someone cares for them, and excel when they become involved in a interesting and fulfilling program.

One of the best things you can give to a young person is your time and attention. Call a local youth organization and ask how you can get involved.

✵ NORMAN ASSELSTINE ✵

Flint, MI
DAILY POINT OF LIGHT RECIPIENT: MAY 2, 1990

Mr. Asselstine, 87, has dedicated his life to serving others.

After becoming a Scout master over 50 years ago, he became aware of a troubled young man who needed help and volunteered to serve as his Big Brother. After 45 years as a Big Brother, he has recently been assigned to his sixteenth Little Brother. He has mentored his Little Brothers throughout their childhood and beyond. In addition, he has served over 50 years with the Boy Scouts.

Reprinted with permission from the White House Office of National Service.

Youth Organizations

• •

Amateur Athletic Union (AAU)
317-872-2900

Athletes and Entertainers for Kids
213-768-8493

Best Buddies
202-347-7265

Big Brother/Big Sister
215-567-7000

Boys and Girls Club of

America
212-351-5900

Boy Scouts of America
214-580-2000

Camp Fire, Inc.
816-756-1950

Direction Sports
213-627-9861

Girls Incorporated
212-689-3700

Girl Scouts of the USA
212-940-7500

4-H
301-961-2806

Junior Achievement
719-540-8000

Special Olympics
202-628-3630

YMCA-USA
312-977-0031

YWCA-USA
212-614-2700

• •

Social Needs

■■

• • •

All, regardless of race or class or economic status, are entitled to a fair chance and to the tools for developing their individual powers of mind and spirit to the utmost.

• • •

—"A Nation at Risk: The Imperative for Education Reform"

EDUCATING AMERICA

■ ■ ■

If you are thinking a year ahead, sow seed. If you are thinking ten years ahead, plant a tree. If you are thinking one hundred years ahead, educate the people.

—Chinese poet, 500 B.C.

*U.S. Department of Education, Washington, D.C., April 1, 1983.

**From M. Cutright, *The National PTA Talks to Parents*, (New York: Doubleday, 1989).

AN EDUCATIONAL SYSTEM REPORT CARD

In 1983 the report "A Nation at Risk: The Imperative for Education Reform," shocked many people with its findings on the state of the U.S. educational system. According to this report:

▶ Average SAT scores had declined over the previous two decades.

▶ Tests revealed that 40 percent of America's high-school students were behind in skills required for complex math problems, writing and reading comprehension.

▶ During that same period the proficiency of students in other countries increased.

Secretary of Education Terrel Bell, commissioner of the report, wrote that "The educational foundations of our society are presently being eroded by a rising tide of mediocrity that threatens our very future as a Nation and a people."* The National Commission concluded that "the average graduate of our schools and colleges today is not as well-educated as the average graduate 25 or 35 years ago."**

The report recommended a number of measures designed to improve our failing school system, including tougher high-school graduation requirements, more core academic courses, higher teacher salaries, and higher standards for entering teachers.

THE NATION RESPONDS

"A Nation at Risk" focused attention on the nation's schools and spurred further research and, more important, reform. In 1984, a report entitled "The Nation Responds" outlined progress that had been made as a result of new policies administered by school systems across the country.

Progress and study continued throughout the decade capped by President Bush's Education Summit at the University of Virginia in September 1989. During the meetings the president summarized a national commitment to education: "No modern nation can long afford to allow so many of its sons and daughters to emerge into adulthood ignorant and unskilled. The status quo is a guarantee of mediocrity, social decay and national decline."

The summit established national education goals to address areas of concern, including dropout rates, illiteracy, the quality of our teachers, and drugs. It called for annual report cards to measure the success of educational efforts, on all levels.

STILL ROOM FOR IMPROVEMENT

Although reports and meetings such as "A Nation at Risk" and the Education Summit do much to advance the cause of educational reform there is still much to be accomplished. In an Allstate Insurance Co. and the American Association of School Administrators survey of 385 school administrators, 68 percent gave the U.S. public education system a B grade and only 7 percent gave an A. A majority of those questioned cited problems such as lack of parental involvement, poor student motivation, cuts in state or local budgets, and under-motivated teachers.

DROPOUTS

Approximately 1 million youths, or more than one-fourth of all students, drop out of school each year. Without a degree

Did you know? ▪▪▪▪▪▪▪▪▪▪▪

▶ A Carnegie Foundation for the Advancement of Teaching college-faculty survey found that in the area of student abilities 75 percent of the 5,450 college faculty members say students are seriously underprepared in basic skills.

Dennis Kelly, "College Faculty Says Students Underprepared," *USA Today,* 6 November, 1989.

Did you know? ▪▪▪▪▪▪▪▪▪▪

▶ Local businesses formed 145,000 partnerships with public schools during the decade of the 1980s.

▶ Coca-Cola is donating $50 million to education programs over the next 10 years.

▶ Executives from more than 150 companies, including IBM, General Electric, and General Motors, meet with teachers in the Philadelphia High School Academies, a joint group of the school district and businesses.

▶ Local businesses in the Cleveland Scholarship Program help high-school graduates learn about financial aid for college. The program has helped more than 60,000 students attend college.

Nancy Petry, "How to Help America's Schools," *Fortune,* 4 December 1989.

.... Did you know?

▶ In 1988, just over a quarter of black high-school graduates went on to college, a rate that has declined from 34 percent in 1976.

▶ The percentage of Latino graduates attending college dropped from 50 percent to 35 percent during that same period.

*M. Cutright, *The National PTA Talks to Parents.*

Reprinted with permission from the White House Office of National Service.

and a proper education these students find it difficult to enter into the workplace. In fact, about 25 percent of dropouts between the ages of 16 and 24 are unemployed. And the cost of dropouts is enormous. The PTA reports that "The Committee for Economic Development, composed of leaders from two hundred major American corporations, estimates that each year's school dropouts cost the nation $240 billion in lost earnings and taxes over their lifetime. To these billions of dollars must be added the high costs of welfare, law enforcement, crime and social services needed by the dropouts."*

Receiving a degree does not guarantee a job, nor does it assure that a student is properly educated.

Minorities have been affected as well. Even though increasing numbers of black students are finishing high school, their attendance in college is dropping.

One of this country's greatest concerns is the ability to compete in an international market. Inadequate education and underprepared students will hinder America's ability to excel, both at home and abroad.

WHAT IS BEING DONE?

Public Sector

▶ President Bush met with the nation's governors for an education summit in September 1989. Many felt that the federal government's greater willingness to involve itself in the nation's education and the performance goals it established will benefit our school programs.

▶ During the 1980s, more than 50 cities established Public Education Funds to supplement public funding.

Private Sector

▶ Television as a teaching tool is becoming more widespread. About 20 million students regularly watch some type of educational shows via public broadcasting. Whittle Communication's *Channel One* and

✪ WWOR-TV ✪

Secaucus, NJ
DAILY POINT OF LIGHT RECIPIENT: DECEMBER 8, 1989

WWOR-TV was recognized for its "A+ for Kids" project, a station-wide initiative designed to look at the problems and promise of our children's education.

The project aims to inspire increased business, community and parental involvement while providing support for the teachers. On-air activities include news segments, public service announcements, and primetime specials on education. Off-air, the station has created an "A+ for Kids," teacher network, whereby outstanding teaching ideas are shared. In addition, the station adopted one of New Jersey's most troubled high schools.

Turner Broadcasting's *CNN Newsroom* feature programming designed especially for students. In some areas of the country students watch these shows in their classrooms.

▶ In an effort to involve the expertise of the private sector, Boston University now runs the Chelsea school district.

▶ Saugus High School in southern California presents varsity letters for winning top grades, as well as for athletic ability.

WHAT CAN I DO

▶ **If you are concerned about your child's education—do something about it!** If you worry about the educational system, voice your feelings. Get involved in a local PTA or other community/school organization, or contact a national education advocacy group for more information about what you can do.

▶ **Demand a proper education!** If you are a student, get involved in your educational system. Let your school administrators, teachers, parents, and civic leaders know what you think needs to be done to improve your school.

▶ **Volunteer your time, efforts, and talents.** According to a study commissioned by the U.S. Department of Education, during the 1987–1988 school year, 1 million volunteers contributed their time to 60 percent of the U.S. public schools. Contact your school board or local PTA for more information.

▶ **Teach someone to read.** Twenty-six million Americans are functionally illiterate. You can become a literacy tutor and teach people to read! Refer to the "Teaching Americans to Read" section (page 258) for more detailed information.

▶ **Get involved in your child's education.** In programs across the country, evidence shows that active parental involvement in a child's education improves student achievement. This

Education is not a priority to compete with the national defense, the trade deficit, the federal budget deficit, drugs, or AIDS. We must think of it as the solution to the rest of those problems.

—Xerox chairman DAVID KEARNS, in *Fortune* magazine, December 4, 1989.

National Committee for Citizens in Education

Marc Lacy, "Students Walk Out to Protest Conditions at Morningside," *Los Angeles Times,* 10 February 1990.

ORDINARY PEOPLE—EXTRAORDINARY ACTIONS

More than 500 students from Morningside High School in Inglewood, California, walked out of their classes to protest their substandard classroom conditions. As 16-year-old Katrina Hamilton put it, "We're tired of people writing down our concerns and not getting back to us. We're tired of people saying, 'I heard you. I heard you.' We want something done."

The students asked for more textbooks, less substitute teachers, and cleaner facilities.

W hat the best and wisest parent want for his own child, that must the community want for all its children.

—JOHN DEWEY

*Pat Ordovensky, "Mom and Dad Just Can't Sit Back," *USA Today,* 19 February 1990.

Reprinted with permission from the White House Office of National Service.

involvement ranges from volunteering at school and attending school meetings to helping with homework and encouraging your child to read.

In a *USA Today* five-day feature on education, Anne Henderson of the National Committee for Citizens in Education, says, "Programs designed with strong parental involvement produce students who perform better than otherwise identical programs that do not involve parents."*

▶ **Even if you do not have a child in school, get involved with our educational system.** Our educational system affects everybody! A National Research Council report revealed that volunteers in public schools include not only parents, but also businesspeople, retirees, and college students.

▶ **Learn about legislative issues regarding education.** Educational legislation directly affects the welfare of children and youth. For information about how your voice can be heard contact: The PTA Office of Governmental Relations, 1201 16th St, NW, Washington, DC 20036.

Ask for a copy of "A Voice for Children and Youth: The National PTA Guide to Legislative Activities."

▶ **Businesses can also participate with our schools.** Business leaders can offer their leadership expertise and resources to local school programs.

This extra effort has proved highly beneficial for both businesses and students alike.

❂ ANN DRYBURG ❂

Brownsville, PA
DAILY POINT OF LIGHT RECIPIENT: MAY 19, 1990

Ms. Dryburg, 76, has touched the lives of thousands of children.

Ms. Dryburg's father once told her to never quit school, and she never has. After 56 years of teaching, Ms. Dryburg retired from the Bethlehem-Center School District with the record for the longest teaching tenure in Pennsylvania public schools. Though now retired, Ms. Dryburg still reports to school each day, continuing to teach as a volunteer. Students are scheduled for tutoring sessions with her throughout the day. She also continues to teach a pre-algebra course and tutors a disabled child.

❂ DUKE POWER COMPANY ❂

Charlotte, NC
DAILY POINT OF LIGHT RECIPIENT: DECEMBER 29, 1989

Duke Power Company is committed to supporting quality education. The company encourages its employees to volunteer in local schools by sponsoring a school improvement program.

Its Power in Education program, started in 1984, now includes 2,300 workers who volunteer as tutors, teaching assistants, science fair judges, and school facilities inspectors. The program also offers academic scholarships to high school seniors. Over 2,500 schools have been enriched by the contribution of Duke Power Company employees.

Reprinted with permission from the White House Office of National Service.

Organizations and Resources

Council for Aid to Education
212-689-2400
A not-for-profit organization that encourages broader and more effective voluntary support of education.

Educational Resources Information Center (ERIC)
202-357-6089
Administered by the Department of Education's Office of Educational Research and Improvement, ERIC is a computerized clearinghouse of educational information. ERIC receives almost 3 million inquiries each year and responds with more than 30 million documents. The ERIC system is composed of 16 clearinghouses each devoted to a specific educational topic.

Educators for Social Responsibility (ESR)
617-492-1764
Offers workshops and other consultation to educators and parents about teaching children the critical issues related to the survival of the planet.

National Committee for Citizens in Education (NCEE)
301-997-9300/800-638-9675/ 800-NET-WORK (toll-free help line)
A nonprofit organization that promotes the involvement of parents and other citizens to improve the quality of education of the nation's children. They offer resources such as their magazine *Network for Public Schools*, together with other

information designed to inform and train concerned citizens.

National Community Education Association
703-683-6232
An association that fosters community involvement in the education system.

National Congress of Parents and Teachers (PTA)
312-787-0977
More than 6 million members strong, the PTA helps parents take an active part in the child's education. They work with local communities to strengthen their schools and have helped to establish significant child programs such as field tests of the Salk polio vaccine, AIDS education projects, and developing school hot lunch programs. Ask them about their book, *The National PTA Talks to Parents: How to Get, the Best Education for Your Child.* Contact your local PTA for more information about programs in your area.

National Education Association
202-833-4000
Almost 2 million members strong, NEA is comprised mostly of elementary and secondary school teachers. The Association deals with such issues as adequate funding for schools and teachers, self-governance in licensing and certification, and ensuring the rights of educators and students.

OTHER COMMITTED ORGANIZATIONS

Refer to the end of this part for addresses and/or phone numbers.

The American Association of School Administrators (AASA)

American Council on Education

American Federation of Teachers

Carnegie Foundation for the Advancement of Teaching

IBM Educational Systems

International Reading Association

Leadership for Quality Education, Chicago

National Association for the Education of Young Children

National Head Start Association

National Institute of Education

Recruiting New Teachers, Inc.

United Negro College Fund

U.S. Department of Education

▶ For a more comprehensive listing of associations and organizations devoted to education refer to:

▶ *The Educator's Desk Reference: A Sourcebook of Education Information and Research,* Melvyn N. Freed, Robert K. Hess, Joseph M. Ryan, Macmillan, NY, 1989.

▶ *The Education Almanac 1987–88: Facts and Figures About Our Nation's System of Education,* Leroy Goodman, editor. Reston, Va.: National Association of Elementary School Principals, 1984.

▶ *The Encyclopedia of Associations,* Detroit: Gale Research, 1989.

TEACHING AMERICA TO READ

∎ ∎ ∎

·········· Did you know?

▶ According to the U.S. Department of Education, 26 million adults age 18 and older are functionally illiterate today.

▶ The National Commission on Excellence in Education reports that 13 percent of all 17-year-olds in the United States are functionally illiterate. Among minority youth the number approaches 40 percent.

▶ More than 700,000 functionally illiterate youths graduate from high school each year.

CAN YOU READ THIS?

··

Well, 26 million Americans cannot!

WHAT IS FUNCTIONAL ILLITERACY?

According to the Coalition for Literacy, a functionally illiterate person is unable to use reading, writing, and computational skills in everyday life situations. For example, when confronted with printed materials, such as signs, telephone books, and newspapers, a functionally illiterate person would not be able to read and thus would be unable to function effectively.

A WIDESPREAD PROBLEM

Illiteracy is a prevalent problem in America and affects all sectors of society. An illiterate person will find it very difficult to get a good job. Businesses must spend extra money to educate their workers, and the government must incur the costs of financial and educational programs for those who cannot enter the workplace.

THE IMPACT OF ILLITERACY

One estimate puts the cost of welfare and unemployment compensation due to illiteracy at $5 billion annually. Besides that, millions of people are deprived of a skill that is needed for many normal daily tasks, as well as for advancement of career. Twenty-five million Americans will have to upgrade their skills in the next decade to remain competitive in the world marketplace—skills that include basic literacy.

THE REASONS FOR ILLITERACY

The reasons for illiteracy vary. Some people have minor physical or mental handicaps, such as a learning disability, or they may need eyeglasses or hearing aids. Others may have experienced emotional problems during their educational periods that distracted them from learning. Or perhaps the child was just able to slip through the education process without learning the basic skill of reading. The problem may lie with a fault of the "system"—educational, health, or parental.

Because there are so many reasons for illiteracy in this country, it must be corrected at all levels—at home, at school, and later when an adult needs to learn these basic and essential skills.

WHAT IS BEING DONE?

● ●

▶ Bell Atlantic produced the National Literary Honors television special hosted by President and Mrs. Bush.

▶ One of the goals of President Bush's Education Summit is to help every adult in America become literate by the year 2000.

▶ The public Adult Basic Education Program (ABE) teaches reading and other skills for students who are 16 years of age or more, out of school, and without a high school diploma.

▶ Since 1962, approximately 140,000 Literacy Volunteers of America have tutored more than 1,750,000 students in 350 programs in 38 states.

▶ The Coalition for Literacy is working with the Ad Council to produce a national awareness campaign to fight illiteracy.

What is life like when you can't read?

Tom can tell you.

Tom is 51, a sanitation worker in a New York City suburb. He is the father of two teenage daughters for whom he buys acid-washed denim and high tops even though he can't afford them. His day-to-day life is exhausting and defeating. Sickly as a youngster, he missed many months of school. He never caught up and quit school at twelve, still unable to read.

Yet at 51, Tom is beginning a new life.

Tom is learning to read, through Literacy Volunteers of America.

Permission of Literacy Volunteers of America.

❂ EDWARD CASTOR ❂

Wind Falls, IN
DAILY POINT OF LIGHT RECIPIENT: DECEMBER 5, 1989

Edward Castor, 47, kept a secret shared only by family and a few close friends for almost 40 years. For most of his life, he was illiterate.

As a 27-year employee of General Motors, he was reading at a third-grade level. But after encountering an embarrassing situation at work, he decided to seek help. He enrolled in a GED class sponsored by General Motors and the United Auto Workers Union and received his GED diploma. Today, he speaks out for others who share his former problem, giving lectures on literacy and teaching others how to read. In addition, he serves as the governor's appointee to the Indiana Adult Literacy Coalition.

▶ B. Dalton Bookseller launched the B. Dalton National Literacy Initiative, a $3 million corporate contributions program to help significantly reduce functional illiteracy.

▶ The Business Council for Effective Literacy promotes literacy, especially in the work force.

▶ GM and the United Auto Workers have joined together in a program to help workers learn to read and achieve their high-school equivalency diploma.

☆ ☆ THE STARS ARE SHINING! ☆ ☆
FAMOUS AUTHORS FIGHT ILLITERACY

Alice Walker, Garrison Keillor, E. L. Doctorow, Nikki Giovanni, and Pulitzer Prize-winning poet Charles Simic have joined 70 other authors to write *Words on the Page, The World in Your Hands.*

The three-book series contains material targeted for those with reading levels in the range of third through sixth grades.

WHAT CAN I DO?

▶ **Become a one-to-one literacy tutor.** Tutoring does not require a special degree. All that is required is that you be an adult with adequate reading and writing skills and that you complete a brief training course offered by your local literacy education center. Then you simply allocate a little time each week to teach basic reading skills to an adult. Contact the literacy programs in your area for more information. It may be one of the most rewarding things you have ever done.

▶ **Literacy volunteerism involves more than tutoring.** The Coalition of Literacy suggests some additional literacy volunteer opportunities: "Volunteers can become tutor trainers, and assist

Reprinted with permission from the White House Office of National Service.

❂ CAPTAIN AL LEWIS ❂
Philadelphia, PA
DAILY POINT OF LIGHT RECIPIENT: JUNE 25, 1990

Captain Lewis, who commands the 22nd District Police Department, has gone above his official duties in the community to promote literacy.

Captain Lewis has initiated a tutorial program for the young people in his neighborhood, whereby police officers tutor students in basic reading and writing. The officers meet with the students once a week at the Police Department, fostering understanding between officers and the young citizens of the community. Captain Lewis has also established a public library in response to the need to increase literacy and promote neighborhood unity. The library, located at the James Weldon Johnson Housing Project, was built by Captain Lewis and other police officers. Captain Lewis is establishing libraries at the remaining shelters and housing projects in the area.

with administrative functions such as clerical work, contribute to newsletters and develop public relations materials and strategies, or serve on an Advisory Board. Other volunteers may be interested in providing transportation for students and tutors, assisting with child care, and so on. Individual programs in your locality can let you know what their special needs are."

▶ **Contact your local library for more information.** Many libraries sponsor literacy tutorial programs and work with other education agencies to help teach people to read.

▶ **Contact one of the following organizations to see how you can help.** They will show you ways you can help fight illiteracy in your community or business. Perhaps you can find time to volunteer to teach the illiterate. Or you can show your support by making a donation to one of these groups.

Organizations and Resources

Coalition for Literacy
800-228-8813
An association of literacy organizations and other concerned groups devoted to fighting illiteracy. The National Contact Hotline (800-228-8813), established by Contact Center Inc., links potential volunteers, students, businesses, and community groups with local literacy efforts.

Contact Center, Inc.
800-228-8813
Provides a national hotline for the Coalition for Literacy and the Unsung Americans program.

Literacy Volunteers of America (LVA)
315-445-8000
A national, nonprofit organization that combats illiteracy through a network of community volunteer literacy programs.

Laubach Literacy Action (LLA)
315-422-9121
Trains volunteers to tutor adults and teens at the very lowest reading skill levels, on an individual basis.

National Literacy Hotline/ Project Literacy U.S. (PLUS)
800-228-8813
Provides information about illiteracy in the United States and offers ideas and referrals to potential literacy volunteers.

Reading Program
800-228-8813
Call this number to receive general information about learning how to tutor an illiterate person. You will also be given a number to call in your area for local programs.

U.S. Department of Education
202-732-2394
Provides statistics and other information about illiteracy.

OTHER COMMITTED ORGANIZATIONS

American Library Association
312-944-6780

Coors Literacy Hotline
800-348-2337

National Education Association (NEA)
202-833-4000

Reading Is Fundamental (R.I.F.)
202-287-3220

CRIME

...

A young woman is brutally raped in a mall parking lot. An elderly man is assaulted while walking home from the store. A car is stolen from a busy city street. An innocent child lies sprawled on his front lawn— victim of another random drive-by shooting.

Violent Crime Changing America —news item

Corky Trinidad. *Honolulu Star-Bulletin.*

CRIMES ON THE RISE

Throughout America crime is on the rise. From suburb to city and coast to coast the incidence of crime touches every citizen.

No longer is it safe to leave a car or house unlocked. Many parents wait up at night, fearful that their children will be hurt or involved in a crime. In some urban communities, kids are forced to play inside rather than risk being hit by random bullets fired on the streets. Citizens learn self-defense, carry mace, join "watch groups" and even carry guns to protect themselves.

THE FBI 1989 CRIME CLOCK

Violent Crimes	Crimes Against Property
Every 24 minutes a person is murdered.	**Every 10 seconds** there is a burglary.
Every 6 minutes someone is forcibly raped.	**Every 4 seconds** there is a larceny theft.
Every 55 seconds a person is robbed.	**Every 20 seconds** a motor vehicle is stolen.
Every 33 seconds an aggravated assault occurs.	

FBI Uniform Crime Reports, *Crime in the United States,* 1989.

THE CAUSES OF CRIME

The crime rate, especially for violent crimes, continues to soar at a record pace. The massive drug trade offers many young people the opportunity to get rich quick. Crack, heroin, and other drugs are a part of a vicious cycle, as users turn to crime to pay for more dope. Gangs resort to violence in order to protect and expand their turf. Guns are readily available, making it easier and more dangerous to accomplish their goal. And the training starts early: gangs recruit children as young as 6 to do their dirty work, making criminals the role model for children in some neighborhoods.

Drugs. Drugs play a major role in crime, especially violent crimes, in this country.

262

Lured by all the trappings of the multibillion-dollar drug industry and overtaken by the deleterious effects of addictive substances, many people are driven to criminal acts, ranging from theft to murder. High-risk/high-return drug trafficking is often accompanied by violence, affecting those involved as well as innocent victims.

The drugs themselves have their own dangerous element. Extremely strong concentrations found in the substances cause incoherence, confusion and paranoia. Lisa Sarno, who started the L.A. Crusaders, a neighborhood watch group, explains, "These guys are on drugs, they're high, they're hallucinating, they're capable of doing anything and they do."*

Many drugs are highly addictive. People are robbed, assaulted and even murdered for pocket change to pay for a "hit." Many stolen goods, such as car stereos and jewelry, are fenced for drugs. Women and men sell their bodies and women have even sold their babies for a little crack cocaine or heroin.

Gangs. To a historian, the recent phenomenon of gangs is perhaps just another chapter in a long book of violence in America. Modern U.S. cities appear in many ways to be just like their counterparts of the past. Drive-by shootings echo a reminder of underworld hit men. Gangs fight it out to determine supremacy much like the "families" in the movies. Rather than bootlegging booze, gangs now control a much bigger and more dangerous bounty—illegal drugs.

Armed with high-tech warfare such as Uzi submachine guns and other assault rifles, modern gangs seem to be a step ahead of the authorities as the violence continues unabated and the drug trade continues to flourish. Most major cities and even many smaller ones have some type of gang problem. The Los Angeles gang population has increased from 25,000 in 1980 to approximately 100,000 in 1990. Members of L.A. gangs have also spread out to other cities. Many cities across the nation, including Washington, D.C., Philadelphia, San Antonio, and Milwaukee, reported record homicides in 1989, most of them gang and/or drug related. In the same year there were 544 gang-related murders in Los Angeles.

Guns. As the crime rate increases the debate heats up over the restriction of guns. Concerned for the welfare of all, gun control advocates point to the relationships between guns and violent crimes.

Did you know? ....

According to the Justice Department:

▶ The U.S. ranks first among the industrialized nations in the number of crime victims.

▶ One in four U.S. households was the target of a violent crime or theft in 1989.

▶ In 1990 there were approximately 35 million personal and household crimes, including almost 6 million violent crimes.

Did you know? ....

▶ The Justice Department found that in 1988, 80 percent of people arrested for serious crimes had used drugs during the preceding 1 to 2 days.

▶ The FBI reports that 7.4 percent of all murders in 1989 were narcotics-related.

▶ According to the FBI, in 1989, approximately 1.4 million violent crime arrests involved the sale, manufacture, or possession of drugs.

*Tom Squitieri, "Just Another Night in Gangland USA," *USA Today* 8 December 1989.

▪▪▪▪▪▪▪▪▪▪ Did you know?

According to 1989 statistics compiled by Handgun Control, Inc:

▶ Since 1986, gunshot wounds among children ages 16 and under have increased 300 percent in urban areas.

▶ One out of every 25 admissions to pediatric trauma centers across the country today is a child with a gunshot wound.

▶ In 1987, more than 400,000 male students carried handguns to school, including 135,000 who did so on a daily basis.

▶ According to the FBI, guns accounted for 64 percent of all homicides in 1989.

E verybody's fed up with the drug trade. We are losing one or two kids per night. I refuse to step down.

—GEORGETTE WATSON, Director, Drop-A-Dime

Gun owners and others who oppose gun restriction remind gun control advocates of the Second Amendment to the Constitution, "the right to keep and bear arms." They also argue that guns do not make the criminal—crime will still exist even with stronger gun laws. Finally, they argue that criminals will circumvent the gun regulations, just as they break other laws.

☆ ☆ THE STARS ARE SHINING! ☆ ☆
"ALL IN THE SAME GANG"

More than a dozen rap music artists joined together to cut an anti-violence rap album and video.

Aimed at curbing gang violence, "All in the Same Gang" features the rhymes of Tone Loc, M.C. Hammer, N.W.A.'s Eazy-E, and Ice-T.

WHAT CAN I DO?
▪▪▪▪▪▪▪▪▪▪▪▪▪▪▪▪▪▪▪▪▪▪▪▪▪▪▪▪▪▪▪▪▪▪▪▪

▶ **Become involved!** Throughout the nation communities and citizen groups are mobilizing to fight combat violence. Realizing that the local authorities need help in fighting criminal violence, residents have joined in the battle by starting and fostering antidrug and crime education programs, forming citizen watch groups, cleaning up their neighborhoods, and campaigning for more fiscal support.

▶ **Citizen watch groups.** More than 1,000 citizen watch groups have been formed across the nation in the past few years. Citizen watch groups work closely with local authorities to help prevent crime. In some areas, residents patrol the streets, reporting suspicious activities. In other programs, citizens keep the police informed of dangerous elements. Citizen groups also sponsor block parties and neighborhood cleanups. They strive to make their communities safe places in which to live and work. Here are some examples of such groups:

▶ In Los Angeles, anti-gang groups such as L.A. Crusaders and Operation Safe Streets have been formed to protect themselves and their neighborhoods against gang violence.

▶ According to one report, 250,000 families have formed grass-roots coalitions to fight crime, especially gang-related, in Los Angeles.

▶ More than 180 citizen watch groups were started in Milwaukee in 1989, a record year for homicides in that city.

▶ Muslims in Brooklyn, New York, and Jewish groups in Crown Heights, New York, use walkie-talkies and other professional tactics to keep the streets free of drug dealers.

▶ Five members of a Minneapolis Guardian Angels patrol were awarded the city's Medal of Honor for helping to catch a murderer. There are more than 5,000 Angels throughout the nation.

▶ Grandmother Georgette Watson's "Drop-A-Dime" 24-hour anonymous crime hotline received a Daily Point of Light award for its service to the city of Boston.

▶ **Educational efforts.** Active citizen involvement to fight crime also involves bolstering the anticrime, drug, and alcohol educational programs in the community. In some instances, parents and teachers work together to encourage youths to stay drug and crime free. In others, churches reclaim their roles as community leaders by offering forums for their community members. Other groups publicize their need for more support by joining in marches and attending city council meetings.

▶ A coalition of more than 40 churches in southern California formed a community-based volunteer group to combat social problems, such as drugs and gang activity. Focus 90 (the group's name) counsels youths and families, provides drug and alcohol treatment programs, and gets involved in community cleanup programs.

▶ Los Angeles schools offer a course to fifth graders called the Alternatives to Gang Membership Program, which warns of the dangers of gangs and drugs and offers advice and alternatives.

▶ Since its premiere in April of 1988, Fox Broadcasting Company's television show, "America's Most Wanted," has been responsible for the capture of over 165 fugitives as a direct result of tips from viewers.

▶ The LA "Turn the Tide" anti-gang movement sponsored a march to alert citizens about gang problems; more than 10,000 people participated.

▶ A Chicago woman whose child was killed as a result of

Did you know? ∎∎∎∎∎∎∎∎∎∎∎

The chances that you will fall victim to a violent crime are greater than your chances of:

▶ Divorce

▶ Injury in a car accident

▶ Death from cancer

▶ Injury or death due to fire

Nationwide study by the Justice Department.

Did you know? ∎∎∎∎∎∎∎∎∎∎∎

According to the National Coalition on Television Violence:

▶ By the age of 70 the average viewer will watch over 50,000 killings on TV.

▶ By the age of 18, children will have seen more than 200,000 acts of violence on TV shows.

W e need involvement from every segment of our society—the private sector, the media, neighborhood action coalitions, the clergy, schools, parents and children all united to combat gangs and drugs.

—STEVE D. VALDIVIA, executive directory of the Community Youth Gang Services Project in L.A.

Reprinted with permission from the White House Office of National Service.

gang violence formed Mothers Against Gangs, which now has five chapters.

▶ **Contact your local police, school superintendent, and community leaders.** Ask for more information about how you can form or join a citizen crime prevention group.

❂ SHAHID SAMAD WATSON ❂

Trenton, NJ
DAILY POINT OF LIGHT RECIPIENT: DECEMBER 1, 1989

Shahid Watson, 29, founded the Grassroots Movement. This initiative, committed to ridding the streets of crack dealers, uses ordinary citizens in the fight against drugs.

The movement, a community-based mobilization effort, has organized anti-drug campouts, with the hope of keeping drug dealers out of the neighborhood during the night. In addition, the campouts bring members of the movement into tough neighborhoods, giving neighbors an incentive to come together and fight street-level drug trafficking. With Mr. Watson's help, community leaders have successfully intervened in an ongoing drug war in their neighborhood.

Organizations

Community Youth Gang Services (CYGS)—Los Angeles
213-232-7685

Compassionate Friends
708-990-0010

Crime Stoppers International
505-294-2300

Domestic Violence Hotline
800-333-SAFE

Guardian Angels
718-649-2607

National Association of Town Watch
215-649-7055

National Safety Council
312-527-4800

The National Crime Prevention Council
202-466-6272

National Council on Crime and Delinquency
415-896-6223

National Organization of Victims Assistance
202-232-6682

Parents of Murdered Children
513-721-5683

PRIDE
404-577-4500

We Tip
714-987-5005/800-78-CRIME

Youth Force Citizens Committee for New York City
212-684-6767

(Refer to "The Issue of Gun Control" for a listing of organizations that address that issue)

THE AGING OF OUR SOCIETY

■ ■ ■

A GROWING ELDERLY POPULATION

One of the greatest challenges of our society will be the care of a rapidly expanding elderly population.

The size of the elderly population will not only increase in the upcoming years, its growth will also surpass other age segments in our country. Between 1980 and 2010 the total population is expected to grow by 25 percent, whereas the number of Americans over 45 will grow by 67 percent.

CARING FOR THE ELDERLY

As people continue to live longer, the costs to our country will rise accordingly. Health-care, housing, and retirement benefits must keep pace with the aging of America.

This country is already experiencing some strain in these programs, especially because a large percentage of the elderly have low incomes. Americans under 17 and over 65 make up about one-third of the population—but they comprise nearly 60 percent of our nation's poor. About 12 percent of those 65 and over are at or below the poverty level with another 20 percent (6 million) just above it. Since many of the elderly live on fixed incomes, their risk of poverty is much greater than that of younger, working individuals. And they have twice as great a chance of staying poor because they have limited opportunities to raise their income.

Although federal health-care, food, and housing programs help the elderly, they do not pay for everything. According to the Gray Panthers, almost a third of all elderly Americans have fallen, or are in danger of falling, through the so-called "safety net" of government programs designed to protect them. For example, the elderly pay for more than 25 percent of their own health-care costs, which puts an added strain on an elderly person's ability to preserve his or her savings.

▶ According to *American Guidance for Those Over 60,* one catastrophic illness requiring extended care in a hospital or

The aging of our society will affect not just older individuals, but the lives of all Americans regardless of their ages. It will have a profound impact—economically, sociologically, and medically—on the entire nation.

—KEN SKALA, author of *American Guidance for Those Over 60.*

.... Did you know?

▶ One out of every eight Americans (or 30 million people) is 65 or older. Almost 40 percent of the elderly are 75 or older.

▶ By the year 2010, older citizens will comprise 13.9 percent of the population, or 35 million—by 2030 they will make up 21 percent of 64.3 million.

*From Ken Skala, *American Guidance for Those Over 60* (Falls Church, Va.: Sharff Publications, Inc., 1989).

nursing home "can be devastating to the elderly bringing them into the ranks of poverty, with the loss of their dignity and reason for living."

▶ The Urban Institute Reports that by 2030, the number of elderly in the United States requiring institutional care could be as high as 5.3 million.

The added burden of such care will not only tax the nation's financial resources, but it also will accentuate the problem of poverty among the aged.*

ELDERLY ABUSE

The types of elderly abuse range from fraudulent schemes and neglect to assault and even murder. Often, acts of abuse go unreported because the elderly victim is embarrassed, afraid of possible reprisals, or does not want to send a relative to jail. In fact, for every case that is reported, seven are not.

The police, human welfare agencies, and elderly advocacy organizations urge anyone who knows of a case of elderly abuse to report it to the proper authorities.

WHAT CAN I DO?

....

▶ **Learn about legislation that affects the elderly and contact your political representatives to voice your opinion.** Many political programs have a direct and indirect impact on the elderly. Although the president and other politicians vow to protect programs for the elderly, a large deficit and the competition from other programs necessitate a strong need to lobby for the elderly.

▶ **Learn about the many programs that provide services for the elderly.** Many older persons do not take full advantage of federal and state programs as well as the

---

ORDINARY PEOPLE—EXTRAORDINARY ACTIONS

Carole, 28, delivers between 15 and 20 meals a day to elderly people in the Los Angeles area. She participates in a local Meals on Wheels program in which meals are specially prepared at UCLA according to the dietary requirements of each recipient.

Volunteering in the program to Carole "is such a wonderful experience because many of the elderly don't have the energy or capacity to cook for themselves." The program ensures that the recipients will receive at least one nutritious meal a day and the added touch of personal delivery provides human contact which is often equally important to some lonely elderly citizens.

Besides the enjoyment of meeting and talking with interesting people, Carole has also gained insight to the fact that "although Los Angeles is one of the wealthiest cities in the world, there are people in your own backyard who often have to go without and depend on the charity of others."

---

services of private groups. For instance, many private groups, such as AARP, offer discounted services and products ranging from travel to prescription drugs.

▶ Contact one of the groups listed on pages 271 and 272 or refer to the book *American Guidance for Those Over 60* for more information: Sharff Publications, P.O. Box 4448, Falls Church, VA 22044. 703-533-1464; $12.95 + $2.00 postage and handling.

▶ **Help to care for the elderly.** Both young and old can help in a number of ways. Some examples are:

▶ **Volunteer in a nursing home.** Senior citizen housing and health-care facilities often need volunteers to assist nursing home staff with resident activities, meal services, and administration.

▶ **Visit sick elderly relatives or friends whenever possible.** Regular visits will lift the spirits of an older person who may be ill at home or in the hospital.

▶ **Participate in a Meals on Wheels program.** Deliver meals to senior citizens who are disabled and cannot prepare their own meals or go out to eat. The St. Vincent Meals on Wheels program in Los Angeles feeds 1,150 needy seniors daily. If there is no program in your area, perhaps you can work with a local charity and organize one.

▶ **Become a Senior Companion or volunteer at a day-care center for the elderly.** A Senior Companion (ACTION) serves the homebound elderly by helping with shopping, visiting the doctor, managing finances, and just being a friend.

▶ **If you are a retired senior citizen, there are many things you can do to stay active and involved:**

  ▶ **Encourage your club or church group to help others.** Senior citizen groups are very active in volunteering and helping others. Get your group involved in the community!

  ▶ **Teach your skills to others.** Many retired persons lecture and teach at schools, sharing their knowledge with students. You can also join a local

Did you know? ▪▪▪▪▪▪▪▪▪▪

A recent report found that 1 out of every 20 elderly persons is a victim of abuse.

Reprinted with permission from the White House Office of National Service.

 DAVID SCOTT LESSEN

Woodmere, NY
DAILY POINT OF LIGHT RECIPIENT: MAY 11, 1990

After extending his hand to a senior citizen and experiencing the joy of helping others, David Lessen approached his high school principal with a detailed proposal for "Reachout To Seniors."

This program matches high school students with senior citizens to provide senior citizens with friendship and assistance with household chores. The students help them change light bulbs, turn mattresses, reach high shelves, caulk windows, and fix broken items. In turn, the students make a friend and learn about the wisdom and experiences of senior citizens.

America is the richest and most resourceful nation on earth. Yet 33.7 million Americans—mostly the youngest and oldest among us—live in grinding poverty.

—The Gray Panthers

literacy program and teach functionally illiterate people to read and write. Or you can volunteer your services at a day-care center in your area.

▶ **For more information contact a volunteer center near you,** or contact ACTION about their Older American Program, Foster Grandparent Program, and Retired Senior Volunteer Program. The National Council on the

ORDINARY PEOPLE—EXTRAORDINARY ACTIONS
LUCY NARVAIZ—"FULL OF DRIVE"

Lucy Narvaiz does more at the age of 79 than people half her age. "My younger friends ask me where I get the energy," she explains. "I tell them it's not energy, it's drive."

And it is Lucy's drive which has led her through 70 years of helping others. When she was just nine years old, Lucy's father asked her to be the interpreter for their small community outside of Santa Fe, New Mexico. "You are lucky enough to learn English," he said. "It is up to you to help your people." So Lucy read and translated letters and accompanied residents to nearby Santa Fe when they needed assistance with language barriers.

Since Lucy started volunteering at such a young age she thought "that it was just a way of life." Indeed, it became her way of life. After attending a high school six miles from home and then raising a family, Lucy opened Senior Citizen centers in her area and was a 4-H leader for 19 years. Later she attended the college of Santa Fe, where she graduated at the age of 74. Called the "Grandmother" of the college, Lucy feels that if she "can live as an example of what people can do then it's worth it."

She put her degree to good use by tutoring Spanish speaking people and teaching English and Spanish at a community college. A few years ago, she got involved with Literacy Volunteers of America, and has been teaching Hispanic-Americans and others how to read and write.

Her aim is "to educate people so they can better their lives and go on their own." One of her students couldn't speak a word of English but now has a full time job as a bus driver with the city. Others are senior citizens who could only sign an X to their name, but who are now learning how to read and write. She volunteers at churches, senior centers and community colleges to tutor people.

"A lot of sacrifice is involved when you volunteer," she explains. "But to help people help themselves—that's pay in itself!"

And Lucy is starting to see other types of pay as well. For her invaluable service Lucy has received a number of awards, including recognition from Literacy Volunteers of America and a Daily Point of Light Award from the President.

But she hasn't let all the publicity slow her down. She still works with her community and is currently writing a book. "I'll do what it takes to accomplish my goals and I'll continue till God says, 'That's it!' "

Aging's Senior Community Service Employment Program helps senior citizens find jobs, increase their incomes, and learn new skills.

▶ **Join an organization that works for the welfare of the elderly.** As the elderly population grows the influence of these organizations will increase dramatically. Be a part of them. They exist solely to improve people's lives.

❂ RSVP SEWING CIRCLE ❂ (RETIRED SENIOR VOLUNTEER PROGRAM)

Salinas, KS
DAILY POINT OF LIGHT RECIPIENT: MAY 26, 1990

For over five years, the Sewing Circle has met once a week to "recycle" donated cloth into useful items, literally stitching together the dreams of those in need.

Volunteers have completed hundreds of quilts ranging from doll-size to queen-size bed covers. Finished quilts have covered the laps of nursing home residents and disaster victims, as well as beds at halfway houses, homeless shelters, and day care centers.

Reprinted with permission from The White House Office of National Service.

Organizations and Resources

• •

American Association of Homes for the Aging (AAHA)
202-296-5960
Represents 3,300 nonprofit senior citizen housing and health-care facilities.

American Association of Retired Persons (AARP)
202-872-4700
More than 28 million people belong to AARP, making it the largest citizens group in America. AARP is dedicated to enhancing the quality of life of our elderly population. They publish the monthly *AARP News Bulletin* and the bimonthly *Modern Maturity* magazine.

B'nai B'rith International
202-857-6580
Their Senior Citizen Housing Committee provides housing projects for the elderly of all races and religion.

Catholic Golden Age
800-233-4697/800-982-4367 (PA)
Provides numerous services for senior citizens, including supplemental insurance and product discounts.

Evangelical Lutheran Good Samaritan Society
605-336-2998

Foster Grandparent Program (FGP)
c/o ACTION 202-634-9108
FPG is a program of ACTION, the federal volunteer program. Foster Grandparents are elderly volunteers who work with children with special or exceptional needs. They work in schools for the mentally retarded, disturbed and learning-disabled children, in Head Start Programs, in juvenile detention centers, in boarding schools and foster care homes, and occasionally in a child's home.

Gray Panthers
202-387-3111
They were founded in 1970 by social activist Maggie Kuhn and five friends. Today there are more than 70,000 Gray Panthers in approximately 80 chapters nationwide fighting for the rights of the elderly and any other people who are denied their basic rights.

National Alliance of Senior Citizens, Inc. (NASC)
703-528-4380
NASC lobbies for the rights and welfare of senior citizens. They also publish *Our Age* and *The Senior Guardian*.

National Association of Area Agencies on Aging (NAAAA)
202-296-8130
Provides support services for the elderly.

National Association for the Hispanic Elderly
213-487-1922
An organization concerned primarily with the welfare of the Hispanic Elderly. Its Project Ayuda is an employment program for low-income seniors.

National Association of Meal Programs
202-547-6157

National Association of Retired Employees (NARFE)
202-234-0832
NARFE works to ensure proper retirement benefits for retired federal workers and their dependents.

National Caucus and Center on Black Aged, Inc. (NCBA)
202-637-8400
NCBA seeks to improve the quality of life for older persons, especially elderly blacks.

National Church Residences
614-451-2151

National Committee to Preserve Social Security and Medicare
202-822-9459
Lobbies to preserve the Social Security and Medicare systems. Publishes *Saving Social Security,* a monthly paper that keeps members informed about this and other programs.

The National Council on the Aging (NCOA)
202-479-1200
Resource organization for professionals serving the aged. Since 1950, service providers, educators, researchers, advocates, corporate planners, and public policy experts have looked to NCOA for training, research, information, and technical assistance required to better serve America's older population.

National Indian Council on the Aging, Inc. (NICOA)
505-888-3302
Provides services to Native American and Native Alaskan elderly.

National Institute on the Aging
301-496-1752
An agency of the National Institutes of Health, the Institute publishes information on the elderly, including research on health problems of the aging.

Older Women's League (OWL)
202-783-6686
Organization concerned with the welfare of the elderly, particularly women.

Retired Senior Volunteer Program (RSVP)
c/o ACTION 202-634-9108
ACTION's largest program, RSVP matches the interests and abilities of seniors with rewarding part-time opportunities for community service.

Save Our Security Coalition (SOS)
202-822-7848
An organization concerned mainly with protecting and improving security benefits for the elderly, including Medicare and Medicaid, and Supplemental Security Income.

Senior Companion Program (SCP)
202-634-9108
An ACTION program that links volunteers with the homebound elderly to provide companionship and care.
c/o ACTION

Salvation Army
(call your local chapter)
The Army helps senior citizens through drop-in-clubs, senior centers, housing facilities, and friendly visitations in hospitals and nursing homes. They also provide hot lunches and "meals on wheels."

MOMMA By Mell Lazarus

Courtesy of Mell Lazarus and Creator's Syndicate, Inc.

HUMAN WELFARE ORGANIZATIONS

Adam Walsh Child Resource Center
3111 South Dixie Highway
Suite 244
West Palm Beach, FL 32405
407-833-9080

Adoption Center of Delaware Valley
c/o the National Adoption Center
1218 Chestnut St.
Philadelphia, PA 19107
215-925-0200
800-TO-ADOPT

Afghanistan Relief Committee (ARC)
667 Madison Ave., 18th floor
New York, NY 10021
212-355-2931

Africare
440 R St., NW
Washington, DC 20001
202-462-3614

American Academy of Pediatrics
141 Northwest Point Blvd.
P.O. Box 927
Elk Grove Village, IL 60009
708-228-5005

Amateur Athletic Union (AAU)
3400 W. 86th St.
P.O. Box 68207
Indianapolis, IN 46268

American Association of Homes for the Aging (AAHA)
1129 20th St., NW
Suite 400
Washington, DC 20036
202-296-5960

American Association of Retired Persons (AARP)
1909 K St., NW
Washington, DC 20049
202-872-4700

American Friends Service Committee (AFSC)
1501 Cherry St.
Philadelphia, PA 19102
215-241-7000

American Association of School Administrators
Publication Department
1801 N. Moore St.
Arlington, VA 22209-9988

American Horticulture Therapy Association
"Horticulture Hiring the Disabled"
9220 Wightman Rd.,
Suite 300
Gaithersburg, MD 20879
301-948-3010
800-634-1603

American Humane Association
63 Inverness Drive East
Inglewood, CO 80112
303-792-9900

American Jewish Joint Distribution Committee (JDC)
711 Third Ave.
New York, NY 10017
212-687-6200

American Jewish World Service
1290 Ave. of the Americas
New York, NY 10104
212-468-7388

American Library Association
Cybil Moses/Peggy Barber
50 E. Heron St.
Chicago, Ill. 60611
312-944-6780

American Red Cross
17th and D St., NW
Washington, DC 20006
202-737-8300

American Red Cross Disaster Relief
PO Box 37243
Washington, DC 20013
800-453-9000

American Refugee Committee (ARC)
2344 Nicollet Ave., Suite 350
Minneapolis, MN 55404
612-872-7060

AmeriCares
161 Cherry St.
New Canaan, CT 06840
203-966-5195
800-486-4357

Association for Voluntary Surgical Contraception
122 E. 42nd St.
New York, NY 10168
212-351-2575

Athletes and Entertainers for Kids
c/o Nissan Motor Corp.

P.O. Box 191, Bldg. B
Gardena, CA 90248-0191
213-768-8493

Best Buddies
1350 New York Ave., NW,
Suite 500
Washington, DC 20005
202-347-7265

Big Brothers/Big Sisters of America
230 N. 13th St.
Philadelphia, PA 19107
215-567-7000

B'nai B'rith International
1640 Rhode Island Ave., NW
Washington, DC 20036
202-857-6580

Boys and Girls Club of America
771 First Ave.
New York, NY 10017
212-351-5900

Boys Scouts of America
1325 Walnut Hill Lane
P.O. Box 152079
Irving, TX 75015
214-580-2000

Bread for the World
802 Rhode Island Ave., NE
Washington, DC 20018
202-269-0200
800-82-BREAD

CARE
Worldwide Headquarters
660 First Ave.
New York, NY 10016
212-686-3110

Camp Fire, Inc.
4601 Madison Ave.
Kansas City, MO 64112
816-756-1950

Catholic Charities
1731 King St., Suite 2200
Alexandria, VA 22314
703-549-1390

Catholic Golden Age (CGA)
400 Lackawanna Ave.
Scranton, PA 18503

717-342-3294
800-233-4697
800-982-4367 (PA)

Catholic Relief Services
209 W. Fayette St.
Baltimore, MD 21201
301-625-2220

The Center for Budget and Policy Priorities
777 N. Capitol St., NE
Washington, DC 20002
202-408-1080

Center for Child Protection and Family Support, Inc.
209 W. Fayette St.
Baltimore, MD 21201
301-625-2220

Child Care Action Campaign
330 7th Ave., 18th floor
New York, NY 10001

Child Care, Inc.
275 Seventh Ave.
New York, NY 10001
212-929-7604

Childhelp USA
6463 Independence Ave.
Woodland Hills, CA 91367
818-347-7280
800-4-A-CHILD

Children's Defense Fund
122 C St., NW
Washington, DC 20001
202-628-8787

Children's Foundation
815 15th St., NW, Suite 928
Washington, DC 20005
202-347-3300

Children International
(a program of Holy Land
Christian Mission)
P.O. Box 419055
Kansas City, MO 64141

Child Welfare League of America
440 First St., NW, Suite 310
Washington, DC 20001
202-638-2952

Children, Inc.
P.O. Box 5382
Richmond, VA 23220
804-359-4562
800-538-5381

Children's Aid Society
150 E. 45th St.
New York, NY 10017

Children's Television Workshop
1 Lincoln Plaza
New York, NY 10023
212-595-3456

Christian Appalachian Project
322 Crab Orchard Rd.
Lancaster, KY 40446
606-792-3051

Christian Children's Fund
Box 26511
Richmond, VA 23261
804-644-4654

Church World Service and Witness
775 Riverside Drive
New York, NY 10015
212-870-2061

Clearinghouse on Homelessness Among Mentally Ill People (CHAMP)
(contact the National Resource
Center on Homelessness and
Mental Illness)

Coalition for the Homeless
500 8th Ave., Room 910
New York, NY 10018
212-695-8700

Coalition for Literacy
P.O. Box 81826
Lincoln, NE 68501

Committee on Migration and Refugee Affairs
c/o Interaction
200 Park Ave South
New York, NY 10003
212-777-8210

Community for Creative Non-Violence (CCNV)
425 Second St., NW
Washington, DC 20001
202-393-4409

The Community Nutrition Institute
2001 S St., NW
Washington, DC 20009

Community Youth Group Gang Services (CYGS)
144 S. Fetterly Ave.
Los Angeles, CA 90022
213-232-7685

Compassion International
3955 Cragwood Drive
Colorado Springs, CO
80918-7860
719-594-9900

Compassionate Friends
P.O. Box 3696
Oak Brook, IL 60522-3696

Coordination in Development (CODEL)
475 Riverside Dr., Room 1842
New York, NY 10115
212-870-3000

Council for Aid to Education
51 Madison Ave., Suite 2200
New York, NY 10110
212-689-2400

Covenant House
346 W. 17th St.
New York, NY 10011-5002
212-727-4000
800-999-9999

Crime Stoppers International
3736 Eubank, NW, Suite B4
Albuquerque, NM 87111
505-294-2300

CROP
P.O. Box 968
Elkhart, IN 46515
219-264-3102

Direct Relief International
P.O. Box 30820
Santa Barbara, CA 93130
805-687-3694

Direction Sports
117 W. Ninth St.
Los Angeles, CA 90015
213-627-9861

Educational Resources Information Center (ERIC)
Office of Educational Research and Improvement
U.S. Department of Education
Washington, DC 20208
202-357-6089

Educators for Social Responsibility (ESR)
23 Garden St.
Cambridge, MA 02138
617-492-1764

El Rescate
2675 W. Olympic Blvd.
Los Angeles, CA 40006
213-387-3284

End Hunger Network
222 N. Beverly Drive
Beverly Hills, CA 90210
213-273-3179

End World Hunger
1460 W. McNab Rd.
Fort Lauderdale, FL 33309
303-977-9700

Episcopal Church
The Presiding Bishop's Fund for World Relief, The
Episcopal Church Center
815 2nd Ave.
New York, NY 10017
800-334-7626

Evangelical Lutheran Good Samaritan Society
1000 W. Avenue North
P.O. Box 5038
Souix Falls, SD 57117-5038
605-336-2998

Families and Work Institute
330 Seventh Ave.
New York, NY 10001
212-465-2044

Family Research Council
601 Pennsylvania Ave., Suite 901
Washington, DC 20004
202-393-2100

FARM AID
Route #1, Briarcliff #2
Spicewood, TX 78669
512-264-2064

Father Flanagan's Boys Home
14100 Crawford St.
Boys Town, NE 68010
402-498-1111

Feed the Children
P.O. Box 36
Oklahoma City, OK 73101
800-367-2400
405-942-0228

Food First
145 Ninth St.
San Francisco, CA 94103
415-864-8555

Food for the Hungry
7729 E. Greenway Rd.
Scottsdale, AZ 85260
800-2HUNGER

Food Research and Action Center
1875 Connecticut Ave, NW, Suite 540
Washington, DC 20009
202-986-2200

The Fortune Society
39 W. 19th St.
New York, NY 10011
212-206-7070

Foster Grandparent Program (FGP)
c/o ACTION
The Federal Domestic Volunteer Agency
Washington, DC 20525
202-634-9108

Fraternal Order of Police
2100 Gardiner Lane,
Suite 103A
Louisville, KY 40205
502-451-2700

Freedom from Hunger Foundation
1644 Davinci Port
P.O. Box 2000
Davis, CA 95617
916-758-6200

Girls Incorporated
30 E. 33rd St.
New York, NY 10016
212-689-3700

Girl Scouts of the USA
830 3rd Ave.
New York, NY 10022
212-940-7500

Global Missions
c/o Evangelical Lutheran
Church
8765 W. Higgins Rd.
Chicago, IL 60631
312-380-2650

Goodwill
9200 Wisconsin Ave.
Bethesda, MD 20814
301-530-6500

Gray Panthers
1424 16th St., NW, Suite 602
Washington, DC 20036
202-387-3111

**The Greater Los Angeles
Partnership for the
Homeless**
221 South Figueroa St.
Los Angeles, CA 90012-2501
213-620-8922

Guardian Angels
982 E. 89th St.
Brooklyn, NY 11236
718-649-2607

Habitat for Humanity
Habitat and Church Streets
Americus, GA 31709-3498
912-924-6935

**Hadassah: Women's
Zionist Organization of
America**
50 W. 58th St.
New York, NY 10019
212-355-7900

HANDSNET
303 Potrero St., Suite 54
Santa Cruz, CA 95060
408-427-0808

**Heifer Project
International**
P.O. Box 808

Little Rock, AR 72202
501-376-6836

4-H
7100 Connecticut Ave.
Chevy Chase, MD 20815
301-961-2806

**Holy Land Christian
Mission**
2000 East Red Ridge Rd.
Kansas City, MO 64131
816-942-9150

**Homelessness Information
Exchange**
Community Information
   Exchange
1830 Connecticut Ave., NW,
4th floor
Washington, DC 20009
202-462-7551

**Housing Assistance
Council**
1025 Vermont Ave, NW,
Suite 606
Washington, DC 20005
202-842-8600

Hunger Project
Global Office
One Madison Ave.
New York, NY 10010
212-532-4255
U.S. Office
1388 Sutter St.
San Francisco, CA 94109-
5452
415-928-8700

IBM Educational Systems
P.O. Box 3900
Peoria, IL 61614

**Industrial Cooperative
Association**
249 Elm St.
Somerville, MA 02144
617-628-7330

**Institute for Community
Economics**
151 Montague City Rd.
Greenfield, MA 01301
413-774-5933

**Interaction/American
Council for Voluntary
International Action**
200 Park Ave. South
New York, NY 10003
212-777-8210

**Interchurch Medical
Assistance**
P.O. Box 429, College Ave.
New Windsor, MD 21776
301-635-6474

**Interfaith Action for
Economic Justice**
110 Maryland Ave., NE
Washington, DC 20002-5694
202-543-2800

Interfaith Hunger Appeal
470 Park Ave. South
New York, NY 10016
212-689-8460

**International Planned
Parenthood Federation
(IPPF)**
902 Broadway, 10th floor
New York, NY 10010
212-995-8800

**International Rescue
Committee**
386 Park Ave. South
New York, NY 10016
212-679-0010

**Jewish Board of Family
and Children's Services**
120 W. 57th St.
New York, NY 10019
212-582-9100

Jewish Child Care
575 Lexington Ave.
New York, NY 10022
212-371-1313

Jewish Welfare Board
15 E. 26th St., 14th floor
New York, NY 10010
212-532-4949

Johnny Alfalfa Sprout
P.O. Box 1751
Williamsport, PA 17703
717-323-7730

Junior Achievement
45 Clubhouse Drive
Colorado Springs, CO 80906
719-540-8000

Juvenile Justice and Delinquency Program
Office of Justice Programs
633 Indiana Ave., NW
Washington, DC 20531
202-724-7655

Kentucky Harvest
807 East Gray St.
Louisville, KY 40204
502-589-FOOD

Laubach Literacy Action (LLA)
P.O. Box 131
Syracuse, NY 13210
315-422-9121

Legal Aid Society
15 Park Row, 22nd floor
New York, NY 10038
212-577-3340

Literacy Volunteers of America
5795 Widewaters Parkway
Syracuse, NY 13214
315-445-8000

Love Is Feeding Everyone (LIFE)
310 N. Fairfax Ave., 2d floor
Los Angeles, CA 90036
213-936-0895

Lutheran Social Ministries Organizations
8765 W. Higgins Rd.
Chicago, IL 60631
312-380-2690

Lutheran World Relief
360 Park Avenue
New York, NY 10010
212-532-6350

MAP International
P.O. Box 50
Brunswick, GA 31521
912-265-6010

Meals for Millions
1644 DaVinci Ct.
P.O. Box 2000
Davis, CA 95617

Medical Aid for El Salvador
6030 Wilshire Blvd.
Los Angeles, CA 90036
213-937-3596

Mennonite Central Committee
P.O. Box 500
Akron, PA 17501
717-859-1151

Metro. N.Y. Coordinating Council on Jewish Poverty
9 Murray St., 4th floor
New York, NY 10007
212-267-9500

Migration and Refugee Service
c/o U.S. Catholic Conference
1312 Massachusetts Ave., NW
Washington, DC 20005
202-541-3000

Mothers Against Drunk Driving (MADD)
511 East John Carpenter
Freeway, Suite 700
Irving, TX 75062

National Abortion Rights Action League (NARAL)
1101 14th St., NW
Washington, DC 20005
202-371-0779

National Adoption Center
1218 Chestnut St.
Philadelphia, PA 19107
215-925-0200
800-TO-ADOPT

National Adoption Clearinghouse
1400 Eye St. NW, Suite 600
Washington, DC 20005
202-842-7600/1919

National Alliance to End Homelessness, Inc.
1518 K St., NW, Suite 206
Washington, DC 20005
202-638-1526

National Alliance of Senior Citizens (NASC)
2025 Wilson Blvd.

Arlington, VA 22201
703-528-4380

National Association of Area Agencies on Aging (NAAAA)
1112 16th St., NW,
Suite 1000
Washington, DC 20036
202-296-8130

National Association for the Education of Young People
1834 Connecticut Ave., NW
Washington, DC 20009
202-237-8777

National Association for the Hispanic Elderly
2727 W. 6th St., Suite 270
Los Angeles, CA 90057
213-487-1922

National Association of Meal Programs
202-547-6157

National Association of Retired Employees (NARFE)
1533 New Hampshire Ave.,
NW
Washington, DC 20036
202-234-0832

National Association of Town Watch
P.O. Box 303
Seven Wynnewood Rd.,
Suite 215
Wynnewood, PA 19096
215-649-7055

National Benevolent Association of the Christian Church
11780 Borman Drive
St. Louis, MO 63146
314-993-9000

National Catholic Disaster Relief Committee
(see Catholic Charities)

National Caucus and Center on Black Aged, Inc. (NCBA)
1424 K St., NW, Suite 500

Washington, DC 20005
202-637-8400

National Center for Missing and Exploited Children
2101 Wilson Blvd., Suite 550
Arlington, VA 22201
703-235-3900
800-843-5678
800-826-7653 (hearing impaired)

National Child Day Care Association
1501 Benning Rd., NE
Washington, DC 20003
202-397-3800

National Children's Advocacy Center
106 Lincoln St.
Huntsville, AL 35801
205-533-5437

National Church Residences
2335 N. Bank Drive
Colombus, OH 43220
614-451-2151

National Coalition Against Domestic Violence
P.O. Box 34103
Washington, DC 20043-4103
202-638-6388

National Coalition for the Homeless
1621 Connecticut Ave., NW
Suite 400
Washington, DC 20009
202-265-2371

National Committee for Adoption
419 7th St., NW
Washington, DC 20004
202-638-0466

National Committee for Citizens in Education (NCEE)
10840 Little Patuxent
Parkway, Suite 301
Columbia, MD 21044
301-997-9300
800-638-9675

National Committee for the Prevention of Child Abuse
332 S. Michigan Ave.
Chicago, IL 60604
312-663-3520

National Committee for World Food Day
1001 22nd St., NW
Washington, DC 20437
202-653-2404

National Committee to Preserve Social Security and Medicare
2000 K St., NW, Suite 800
Washington, DC 20006
202-822-9459

National Community Education Association
119 N. Payne St.
Alexandria, VA 22314
703-683-6232

National Congress of Parents and Teachers (PTA)
700 North Rush St.
Chicago, IL 60611
312-787-0977

National Council on the Aging, Inc.
600 Maryland Ave., SW,
West Wing 100
Washington, DC 20024
202-479-1200

National Council on Crime and Delinquency
77 Maiden Lane, 4th floor
San Francisco, CA 94180
415-896-6223

National Council for Jewish Women
53 W. 23rd St.
New York, NY 10010
212-645-4048

National Council of Retired Peace Corps Volunteers (NCRPCV)
2119 S St., NW
Washington, DC 20008-4011
202-462-5938

National Council of Senior Citizens (NCSC)
925 15th St., NW
Washington, DC 20005
202-347-8800

National Court Appointed Special Advocates Association (NCASAA)
909 N.E. 43rd St., Suite 202
Seattle, WA 98102

National Crime Prevention Council
1700 K St., NW 2d floor
Washington, DC 20006
202-466-6272

The National Easter Seal Society
70 East Lake Street
Chicago, IL 60601
312-243-8400

National Education Association
1201 16th St., NW
Washington, DC 20036
202-822-7200

National Head Start Association
1309 King St., Suite 200
Alexandria, VA 22314
703-739-0875

National Health Care Campaign
P.O. Box 27434
Washington, DC 20038
202-639-8833

National Housing Institute
439 Main St
Orange, NJ 07050
201-678-3110

National Indian Council on Aging, Inc. (NICOA)
6400 Uptown Blvd., NE,
Suite 510W
Albuquerque, NM 87110
505-888-3302

National Institute on the Aging
9000 Rockville Pike
Bldg. 31, Room 5C35

Bethesda, MD 20892
301-496-1752

National Literacy Hotline
800-228-8813

National Low Income Housing Coalition
1012 14th St., NW,
Suite 1006
Washington, DC 20005
202-662-1530

National Law Center on Homelessness and Poverty
918 F. St., NW, Suite 412
Washington, DC 20004
202-638-2535

National Low Income Housing Coalition
1012 14th St., NW,
Suite 1006
Washington, DC 20005
202-662-1530

National Network of Runaway and Youth Services
1400 I St., NW, Suite 330
Washington, DC 20005
202-682-4114

National Organization for Victims Assistance
1757 Park Rd., NW
Washington, DC 20010
202-232-6682

National Organization for Women (NOW)
1000 16th St., NW
Washington, DC 20036
202-331-0066

National Resource Center on Child Sexual Abuse
107 Lincoln St.
Huntsville, AL 35801
800-KIDS-006

National Resource Center on Homelessness and Mental Illness
Policy Research Associates, Inc.
262 Delaware Ave.
Delmar, NY 12054
800-444-7415

National Resource Center on Special Needs Adoption
P.O. Box 337
Chelsea, MI 48118
313-475-8693

National Safety Council
444 N. Michigan Ave.
Chicago, IL 60611
312-527-4800

National Student Campaign Against Hunger and Homelessness (NSCAHH)
29 Temple Pl.
Boston, MA 02111
617-292-4823

National Volunteer Clearinghouse for the Homeless
Operated by the Community for Creative Non-Violence (CCNV)
425 2nd St., NW
Washington, DC 20001
202-722-2740
800-HELP-664

National Volunteer Hotline
Operated by the Community for Creative Non-Violence (CCNV)
425 2nd St., NW
Washington, DC 20001
202-722-2740
800-HELP-664

Nazareth Literary and Benevolent Association
SCN Center
Nazareth, KY 40048
502-348-1555

Network
National Catholic Social Justice Lobby
806 Rhode Island Ave., NE
Washington, DC 20018
202-526-4070

OURS, Inc.
3307 Highway 110 North
#203
Minneapolis, MN 55422

Overseas Development Network (ODN)
2940 16th St., #110
San Francisco, CA 94103
415-431-4204

Oxfam America
115 Broadway
Boston, MA 02116
617-482-1211

Parents of Murdered Children
100 East Eighth St., B41
Cincinnati, OH 45202
513-721-5683

Peace Corps
P-301
Washington, DC 20526
800-424-8580

The Pearl S. Buck Foundation
Green Hills Farm
Perkasie, PA 18944
215-249-0100

Plan International
(formerly Foster Parents Plan)
155 Plan Way
Warwick, RI 02886
800-556-7918

Planned Parenthood Federation of America
810 Seventh Ave.
New York, NY 10019
212-541-7800

Plenty USA
P.O. Box 2306
Davis, CA 95617

Population Council
1 Dag Hammarskjold Plaza
New York, NY 10017
212-644-1300

Population Crisis Committee
1120 19th St., NW, Suite 550
Washington, DC 20036
202-659-1833

Population Institute
110 Maryland Ave., NE
Washington, DC 20002
202-544-3300

Population Reference Bureau, Inc.
1875 Connecticut Ave., NW
Suite 520
Washington, DC 20009
202-483-1100

Presbyterian Church (USA)
Central Treasury Service
100 Witherspoon
Louisville, KY 40202

Presiding Bishop's Fund for World Relief (PBFWR)
815 2nd Ave.
New York, NY 10017
212-867-8400

Project Hope
(People to People Health Foundation)
Carter Hall
Millwood, VA 22646
703-837-2100

Older Women's League (OWL)
1235 G St., NW,
Lower Level B
Washington, DC 20005
202-783-6686

Reading Is Fundamental (R.I.F.)
P.O. Box 2344
Washington, DC 20024

Recruiting New Teachers
617-489-6000
800-45-TEACH

Results
245 2nd St. NE
Washington, DC 20002
202-543-9340

Retired Senior Volunteer Program (RSVP)
c/o ACTION
The Federal Domestic
Volunteer Agency
Washington, DC 20525
202-634-9108

Salvation Army
National Headquarters
799 Bloomfield Ave.

Verona, NJ 07044
201-239-0606

Save the Children
50 Wilton Rd.
Westport, CT 06880
203-226-7272
800-243-5075

Save Our Security Coalition (SOS)
1221 16th St., NW, Suite 222
Washington, DC 20036
202-822-7848

Second Harvest
116 S. Michigan Ave., Suite 4
Chicago, IL 60603
312-263-2303

Seeds
222 East Lake Drive
Decatur, GA 30030
404-371-1000

Senior Companion Program (SCP)
c/o ACTION
The Federal Domestic
Volunteer Agency
Washington, DC 20525
202-634-9108

Senior Gleaners, Inc.
3185 Longview Drive
North Highlands, CA 95660
916-971-1530

Seva Foundation
108 Spring Lake Drive
Chelsea, MI 48118
313-475-1351

Share Our Strength (SOS)
733 15th St., NW, Suite 700
Washington, DC 20005
800-222-1767
202-393-2925

Special Olympics Intl.
1350 New York Ave., NW
Suite 500
Washington, DC 20005
202-628-3630

St. Vincent Meals on Wheels
P.O. Box 57992

2131 West Third St.
Los Angeles, CA 90057-9900

United Jewish Appeal Federation
99 Park Avenue
New York, NY 10016
212-818-9100

United Jewish Appeal
130 E. 59th St.
New York, NY 10022
212-980-1000

United Nations Disaster Relief Fund
Room 2395 Secretariat
Building
One U.N. Plaza
New York, NY 10037

United Negro College Fund
500 E. 62nd St.
New York, NY 10021
212-326-1118

United Planning Organization
810 Potomac Ave., SE
Washington, DC 20003-3698
202-546-7300

U.S. Committee for Refugees
1025 Vermont Ave., NW
Suite 920
Washington, DC 20005
202-347-3507

UNICEF
3 U.N. Plaza
New York, NY 10017
212-326-7000

United States Committee for UNICEF
331 East 38th St.
New York, NY 10016
212-686-5522

United Support of Artists for Africa/USA for Africa/Hands Across America
6151 W. Century Blvd.
Los Angeles, CA 90045
213-670-2700

U.S. National Committee for World Food Day
1001 22nd St., NW
Washington, DC 20437
202-653-2404

United Way
701 N. Fairfax St.
Alexandria, VA 22314-2045
703-836-7100

Volunteers in Technical Assistance coordinating data for the Federal Emergency Management Agency (FEMA)
1815 N. Lynn St.
Washington, DC 22209
800-456-1675

Simon Wiesenthal Center
9760 W. Pico Blvd.
Los Angeles, CA 90035
213-553-90367

WE TIP, Inc.
P.O. Box 1296
Rancho Cucamonga, CA 91730
714-987-5005

World Hunger Education Service
3018 4th St., NE
Washington, DC 20017
202-268-9503

World Hunger Year
261 W. 35th St., Room 1402
New York, NY 10001-1906
212-629-8850

World Relief
P.O. Box WRC
Wheaton, IL 60189
708-665-0235

World Vision
P.O. Box 5002

Monrovia, CA 91016-9918
800-444-2522

Youth Force/Citizens Committee for New York City
3 West 29th St.
New York, NY 10001
212-684-6767

YMCA-USA
101 N. Wacker Drive
Chicago, IL 60606
312-977-0031

YWCA of the USA
726 Broadway
New York, NY 10003
212-614-2700

Zero Population Growth
1400 16th St., NW #320
Washington, DC 20036
202-332-2200

Ralph Waldman

National Coalition for the Homeless.

HUMAN RIGHTS

• • •

**Concern for human rights is growing
gradually around the world. It is like a
wide, shallow river spreading slowly across
a dry plain.**

• • •

—JOHN HEALEY, Executive Director, Amnesty International USA

The Changing Scene

• • •

A·M·N·I·S·T·I·A
I·N·T·E·R·N·A·C·I·O·N·A·L

AMNESTY INTERNATIONAL
322 Eighth Avenue
New York, NY 10001

Amnesty International USA

A WAVE OF FREEDOM

The end of the 1980s may well be remembered as a pivotal time for democracy and freedom across the world. Movements toward democracy and away from repression occurred from Nicaragua to Czechoslovakia. Andrei Sakharov and Nelson Mandela, themselves symbols of freedom in oppressive nations, were released from internal exile. The Berlin Wall toppled. Chinese students challenged a restrictive government and the Romanians toppled a ruthless dictator.

The Freedom House, a New York–based human rights group, reports that for the first time in their 18-year freedom survey more countries are free than not free. According to their 1989 survey, out of 5.2 billion people in the world, 2 billion live in freedom, 1.2 billion live in "partly free" areas, and 2 billion are "not free."*

Nonetheless, although the decade ended with a positive note toward human rights, much of the world still suffers from a loss of political and civil liberty, as well as from economic and social deprivation. Amnesty International reports that in 1988 more than half of the 135 countries studied for human rights violations disallow freedom of speech, more than a third torture their political prisoners, and a large number kidnap and murder their citizens. Almost a billion people live in poverty and in many countries a large percentage of the population are unemployed.

Although considered a "free" country, the United States is not exempt from human rights abuses. U.S. citizens still fight against discrimination due to their ethnic and religious background, gender, or sexual preference. The country is divided over the question of freedom of choice versus the rights of an unborn life. War veterans, men and women who fought for the rights of humans throughout the world, experience a violation of their own rights by their fellow countrymen and government by not being awarded their due respect or their due medical care.

"Liberty Marches Across the Map," *U.S. News & World Report* 8 January 1990.

THE HUMAN RIGHTS MOVEMENT

The global human rights movement, slightly more than 40 years old, is experiencing a tidal wave of international support. Marked by the Universal Declaration of Human Rights on December 10, 1948, and reinforced by "Human Rights Now!," a global concert tour sponsored by Reebok International and attended by approximately 1.5 million people in 19 cities on five continents, the call for human rights is being heard throughout the world.

The United States is at the forefront of the human rights movement, energized by concerned individuals and politicians alike. U.S. political leaders incorporate human rights issues in their policies with other countries. President Jimmy Carter stated that "Human rights is the soul of our foreign policy." During the May 1988 Summit meeting in Moscow, President Reagan reminded Soviet leader Gorbachev of his country's human rights abuses, when he stated that there was no reason why the Soviet Union could not release all people still imprisoned for expressing their political or religious beliefs. Human rights abuses in South Africa determined U.S. policies toward that country.

Thousands of human rights advocacy groups were formed and gained strength during the 1980s. Many of these organizations and their movements exert considerable power in the political arena as they have been responsible for providing a voice of conscience to our leaders and the rest of the world.

LOOKING AHEAD

Above all, the United States prides itself as a free nation. We must not forget, however, that freedom for a country as well as freedom for an individual cannot be taken for granted. History reveals that the quest for liberty is accompanied by the heroic actions of concerned and devoted people. Similarly, once achieved, an equal amount of energy must be applied to insure its safety. The liberation of Kuwait by the Allied Coalition serves as a vivid example of the type of energetic devotion to freedom. Perhaps it is the basic tenet of this fact that requires America not only to uphold freedom here, but also throughout the rest of the world.

SIT DOWN AND WRITE

AMNESTY INTERNATIONAL
322 Eighth Avenue
New York, NY 10001

Amnesty International USA

Human Rights Violations Throughout the World

■ ■

• • •

POLITICALLY OPPRESSED

■ ■ ■

We could always tell when international protests were taking place . . . the food rations increased and the beatings were fewer. Letters from abroad were translated and passed around from cell to cell, but when the letters stopped, the dirty food and repression started again.

> —A released prisoner of conscience from Vietnam in an Amnesty International newsletter.

PRISONERS OF CONSCIENCE

Even as a wave of freedom spreads across the planet, thousands of people are still detained, incarcerated, and tortured in prison cells throughout the world. Amnesty International explains that these "prisoners of conscience" are "men and women who are imprisoned anywhere for their beliefs, color, sex, ethnic origin, language, or religion." According to the human rights advocacy group, the "horrors of torture and political detention are everyday incidents in fully one-third of the world's countries."

Political Prisoners. In countries such as Colombia, Peru, Guatemala, and Brazil, countless people die for opposing the political regime. African countries like Ethiopia, the Sudan, and Somalia use torture, mutilation, and starvation to punish and control supporters of insurgent forces. The world got a firsthand look at how a repressive country treats its peaceful protesters during the demonstrations and ensuing tragedy in China. More than 1,000 people were murdered in Tiananmen Square by heavily armed Chinese forces. According to the June 4th Foundation, a group concerned with the rights of Chinese citizens, at least 6,000 have already been arrested, and these prisoners face execution, imprisonment or long sentences in the government's "political re-education" facilities. And the atrocities committed against the people of Kuwait and Iraq by Iraqi soldiers serve as an extreme example of human rights violations.

Violations of Basic Rights. In many cases people are jailed for violating even the most basic human rights, such as freedom of speech and freedom of religion. Often, charges are fabricated or trumped up, speedy and fair trials are denied, and sentences are unduly long and harsh. A Chinese man was given a 10-year sentence for painting an unauthorized slogan on a wall. A Brazilian spent 15 years in prison for stealing a bike. In some countries people simply disappear for no known reason, and others are rounded up and executed by death squads.

Prisoner Treatment. The prison conditions and the treatment of prisoners is of major interest among human rights advocates. Abuses within prisons and jails include inhumane living conditions, overcrowding, lack of proper food and medical care, and torture.

A *U.S. News & World Report* writer toured some of Brazil's prisons with two representatives of Human Rights Watch. He reports that "the shortage of prisons in Brazil leads to all the horrors that result from gross overcrowding and forcing inmates to serve long sentences in scrofulous police lockups designed as short-term holding facilities. Some inmates spend years in fetid semidarkness, never going outside for exercise or to breathe fresh air."*

A 16-year-old Turkish woman was tortured, raped, and sexually abused by Turkish police for no apparent reason. She described her treatment in an Amnesty International newsletter: "They made me stand on a chair, put blankets across my arms, and tied me to a cross with ropes. When they took away the chair, I was hanging by my arms." Four months later she was released.

HUMAN RIGHTS VIOLATIONS IN THE UNITED STATES

The United States is not exempt from human rights abuses. Human rights advocates cite capital punishment, the treatment of immigrants who seek asylum, and overcrowded pris-

Amnesty International USA

*Michael Satchell, "The Just War That Never Ends," *U.S. News & World Report,* 19 December 1988.

·········· Did you know?

▶ Human-rights monitors from groups such as Human Rights Watch inspect prisons and report on cases of violation of human rights, such as unhealthy living conditions, arrests, and detention without cause or trial, overcrowding, and torture.

ons as examples of human rights abuses in this country.

Amnesty International has started the Campaign to Abolish the Death Penalty to protest capital punishment. In terms of immigration, Peter Duffy, head of Amnesty International, believes that a country should have an immigration policy, but it should also be fair to those who seek asylum. Human Rights Watch executive director Aryeh Neier points out the problems in our overcrowded prisons: "We have about 900,000 people in prisons and jails, one of the highest rates of incarceration anywhere in the world—and the violence there is terrifying."*

Although the United States may have one of the best records in the protection of human rights, it is not perfect.

"... They made me stand on a chair, put blankets across my arms, and tied me to a cross with ropes. When they took away the chair, I was hanging by my arms."

Saadet Akkaya was 16 years old when she was tortured, raped and sexually abused by Turkish police.

Arrested in April 1988, Saadet was tortured for 15 days until she confessed to activities about which she knew nothing. When brought to court, she told of the torture she had suffered in detention:

"I was taken downstairs blindfolded, while being beaten and kicked, to a dark room. I was interrogated by seven or eight policemen who were shouting and swearing ..."

"They took off my coat, blouse and bra. They made me stand on a chair, put blankets across my arms, and tied me to a cross with ropes. When they took away the chair, I was hanging by my arms."

Next the police took off her skirt and underwear and sexually assaulted her as she hung naked on the cross. On the orders of one policeman, she was removed from the cross and then raped by another policeman.

Saadet Akkaya lodged a formal complaint against her torturers with the Istanbul Criminal Court, but the Turkish court refused even to consider her complaint.

The fact is that torture of political prisoners is a commonplace practice in Turkey today. Many of the more than 200,000 political prisoners arrested in Turkey since 1980 have made serious allegations of torture.

Virtually no one escapes the horror and degradation of torture. Neither the old, nor the sick, nor the young are spared. Young women and men are tortured in front of each other.

Saadet Akkaya was released in August 1988.

BUT ... at this very moment, thousands of other men, women and even children cringe in dark cells waiting to hear the footsteps of their torturers. Please help them.

♲ Recycled Paper

*Wendy Buchert, "Trends in Human Rights Provide Hope for Change," *USA Today*, 10 April 1990.

Amnesty International USA

SIGNS OF IMPROVEMENT

Although human rights violations still plague many parts of the world, there are some signs of improvement.

▶ Democratic governments replaced repressive regimes in Latin America and Eastern Europe, freeing political prisoners and establishing governments with more humane policies.

▶ Three-quarters of the Soviet Union's political prisoners have been released.

▶ South Africa set free its most famous prisoner, Nelson Mandela, and in the early 1990s, Pretoria began to move toward abolishing apartheid by releasing other prisoners and loosening restrictions on blacks and coloreds.

Mr. Neier points out that "in many countries, we've seen the disappearance of the phenomenon of the political prisoner. Now, Cuba is virtually alone in Latin America in having any prisoners who are held for non-violent dissent. In other countries of Latin America, there were great numbers of political prisoners in previous years."*

Many advocates are hopeful that as the world's governments shift toward a more democratic framework, human rights violations will disappear together with the failed policies of authoritarian regimes.

Today, people are still being tortured and murdered because they are Jewish . . . or Catholic . . . or of another religion that their government doesn't approve of . . . or because they peacefully work for freedom and human rights within their country. Torture is used by governments to squash political opposition, to get false confessions, to force information out of victims, and to intimidate the citizens of a country.

In my own case, I was held without charge for 18 months and tortured—including undergoing electric shock treatments.

I was a practicing attorney in Argentina, engaged with many of my clients in bringing court action to stop the torture of prisoners. My tormentors tried to force me to reveal the names of my colleagues and information about my clients and their families.

In 1977, thanks mostly to the efforts of Amnesty International, I was released. I was one of the lucky ones.

—Juan Mendez, in Amnesty International newsletter, AIUSA.

*Wendy Buchert, "Trends in Human Rights Provide Hope for Change," *USA Today*, 10 April 1990.

TWO GROUPS OF ENDANGERED NATIVE AMERICANS

Kieron Dwyer

Organizations

Amnesty International
212-807-8400
Amnesty International is a worldwide movement of people acting on the conviction that governments must not deny individuals their basic human rights. They work to help free prisoners of conscience, to end torture and executions, and to ensure fair and prompt trials. This organization was awarded the 1977 Nobel Peace Prize for its efforts in promoting global observance of the United Nations' Universal Declaration of Human Rights.

Freedom House
212-473-9691
An organization concerned with civil and political freedom throughout the world. The Freedom House survey monitors political rights and civil liberties in 167 nations, classifying areas on their annual Map of Freedom as Free, Partly Free, or Not Free.

Human Rights Internet
613-564-3492
An international clearinghouse for human rights information. They gather and publish a broad array of information, including the *Human Rights Internet Reporter* and the *North American Human Rights Directory*.

Human Rights Watch
202-371-6592
An organization that promotes and monitors human rights worldwide. Human Rights Watch serves as an umbrella organization to Africa Watch, Asia Watch, Americas Watch, Middle East Watch, Helsinki Watch, and the Fund for Free Expression.

International League for Human Rights
212-684-1221
The group monitors human rights conditions and reports them to the United Nations and the public. The League concentrates in Latin America and Eastern Europe and publishes the *Human Rights Bulletin*.

June 4th Foundation
Named after the bloodiest day of the Beijing tragedy, the Foundation supports the rights of the Chinese people.

Lawyers Committee for Human Rights
212-629-6170
Monitors human rights violations across the world. Encourages younger members and letter-writing campaigns.

APARTHEID

...

THE APARTHEID SYSTEM

The apartheid system institutionalizes racism by creating separate political institutions for each of the racial groups in South Africa. Blacks are not considered permanent citizens of South Africa; rather they are required to live in specific areas called homelands—areas considered independent countries by the South African government—or in segregated townships that surround "white-only" urban areas. Approximately 13 million blacks live in the homelands, whereas 11 million reside in townships. Blacks are not permitted to vote and they must have specific passes to travel and work in "white-only areas."

Protests of these and many other abuses of human rights by such groups as the African National Congress and the United Democratic Front have resulted in mass arrests, torture, and death for countless blacks.

South Africa Racial Breakdown

Mixed race	3 million
Asian	1 million
White	5 million
Black	24 million
Total	33 million

The nation of South Africa epitomizes the extreme racial discrimination that exists in many parts of the world. Although whites make up only 15 percent (or 5 million) of the total population of this country, they are more powerful and enjoy much more freedom than the blacks, Asians, and mixed-race people who make up the majority of the population.

The flagrant violations of human rights imposed against blacks and other nonwhites by the white-controlled government has fostered a lower standard of living for all nonwhites in that country. Blacks lag the white minority in many areas of life, including health, housing, education, and income.

Health. Most whites receive better health care than blacks. The infant mortality rate is 75 per 1,000 for blacks, versus 11 per 1,000 for whites. Blacks live an average of 58 years, whereas whites live approximately 71 years.

I went to jail 27 years ago, and I could not vote. And 27 years later I still cannot vote.

—NELSON MANDELA

'Now is the time'

Copyright © 1990, *USA Today*. Reprinted with permission.

291

Housing. There is a severe shortage of housing for blacks. Outside of the black homelands, blacks need more than 2 million housing units.

Education. Blacks in South Africa do not receive the same quality education as whites. One hundred percent of the white population are considered literate, whereas only half of the black population can read. This is partially due to a lack of resources allocated for teachers. In black schools, the average class size is 41 students, whereas in white schools, the average number of students is 16.*

Income. The disparity of average per capita income illustrates another difference between whites and the blacks in South Africa. In 1987, excluding four independent homelands, blacks earned an average salary of $1,467 per year. Whites earned almost five times that amount, averaging $7,276 per person.**

OTHER FORMS OF OPPRESSION IN SOUTH AFRICA

The apartheid government of South Africa is involved in wars with its neighbors, including Mozambique, Angola, and Nambia. Although some of these conflicts have been resolved, the South African government's involvement in these countries helped create poverty, homelessness, and hunger in these nations. These conflicts drained enormous amounts of money, cost many lives, and affected each country's ability to allocate resources to people in need.

CHANGING THE COURSE OF APARTHEID

Fortunately, in recent years some of the apartheid government's oppressive policies have been eased. This is due to a number of factors, including international pressure and a shift in the power base of the conservative party.

Most notably, in February 1989, the South African government led by President Frederik W. de Klerk took sweeping actions to change the course of apartheid. These actions included the release of Nelson Mandela, a longtime political prisoner; a lifting of a 30-year-old government ban on the African National Congress; a legalization of the South Afri-

*South Africa Institute on Race Relations; Carnegie Endowment for International Peace

**Ibid.

can Communist Party and the Pan-Africanist Congress; and a removal of 150 names from a list of people who may not be quoted or published in South Africa.

Nonetheless, until South Africa completely abolishes its apartheid system and gives equal rights to all its citizens, it will serve as a blatant symbol of the oppression and violation of the rights of all humans.

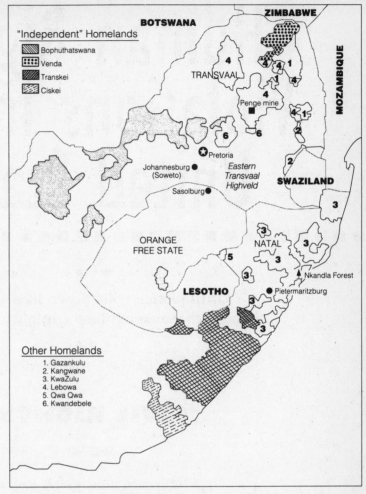

Worldwatch papers #95. Worldwatch Institute.

Organizations and Resources

The Africa Fund
212-962-1210

American Friends Service Committee
215-241-7000

Fund for a Free South Africa
617-267-8333

Interfaith Center on Corporate Responsibility
212-870-2295

South Africa Project
c/o Lawyers' Committee for Civil Rights Under Law
202-371-1212

South Africa Support Project
202-332-2009

Student Coalition Against Apartheid and Racism
202-483-4593

TransAfrica
202-547-2550

Washington Office on Africa
202-546-7691

Human Rights Violations in the United States

• • •

Until justice rolls down like waters and righteousness like a mighty stream.

• • •

—DR. MARTIN LUTHER KING, JR.

CIVIL RIGHTS

• • •

Although many people look back to the 1960s and 1970s as a time for civil rights protests and subsequent reform, the battle still rages on. Discrimination has not disappeared in this country. And the overall economic gains of minorities lag behind those of whites.

DISCRIMINATION

Minorities face discrimination in many aspects of their lives. In two *USA Today* polls, 60 percent of the blacks surveyed feel that racism intrudes on their daily lives, and only 41 percent think that opportunities will improve over the next 10 years. Conversely, 60 percent of the whites questioned feel they are less prejudiced than the "average person."*

Perceptions of Prejudice. Although the perception of the degree of prejudice differs among blacks and whites, discrimination against blacks and other minorities in the workplace, housing, education, and other matters continues in this country. A 1989 *Washington Post*-ABC News poll found that 52 percent of blacks surveyed reported housing discrimination and 37 percent reported discrimination in education.

Hate Crimes. Alarming incidences of violent acts of prejudice are on the rise. Racial hate crimes directed toward almost every racial minority have increased across the nation. In 1989, the Los Angeles County Commission of Human Relations documented more hate crimes—those motivated by race, religion, or sexual orientation—than in any other year in the decade. Crimes against race increased by 75 percent, religious groups by 12.6 percent, and sexual orientation by 41 percent from the previous year.*

HATE CRIMES ON THE RISE

Mulegeta Seraw, an Ethiopian college student, was beaten to death with a baseball bat in an attack by three Skinheads in Portland, Oregon.

In the early morning hours of November 13, 1988, two of Seraw's friends had just dropped him off in front of the modest apartment where he lived when they heard shouting and racial slurs.

Looking back, they saw three white youths surrounding Seraw. One was beating his head with a baseball bat. Seraw's friends rushed to his aid, but they too were beaten unmercifully by the Skinhead attackers.

In less than three minutes, Mulegeta Seraw lay sprawled in the street, brain dead. A few hours later in the hospital, all remaining signs of life would cease.

Throughout the decade, but especially in the past few years, violent actions spurred by hate, fear, and prejudice plagued the nation. White youths attacked and killed a black teenager who had ventured into their Brooklyn neighborhood. Skinheads in Portland, Oregon, attacked a 15-year-old Hispanic girl, slashing her face. Other similar hate-motivated groups attacked homosexuals in various parts of the country.

These actions polarize minority groups, making it more difficult to ease racial tension and leading to further acts of fear and hate.

OVERALL WELFARE OF MINORITIES

Minority advancement has made only modest gains in the last few decades. In fact, when compared with the white majority in this country the overall welfare of minorities has actually declined. *One-Third of a Nation,* a report by the Commission on Minority Participation, reveals that blacks, Hispanics, American Indians, and Asian Americans have lagged behind whites in health, income, and education. These factors con-

*LA County Commission on Human Relations as reported in the *Los Angeles Times,* 23 February 1990. Reported in Southern Poverty Law Center Klanwatch Project.

·········· **Did you know?**

► The Southern Poverty Law Center's Klanwatch Project stands up to, exposes, and takes legal action against the Klan.

The Klanwatch Project

of the
Southern Poverty Law Center

"Bringing the Klan to Justice."

400 Washington Avenue
Montgomery, Alabama 36104

Klanwatch Project/SPLC

tribute to a cycle of destitution for minorities in the United States.

Health. Many minorities do not receive proper health care. Note the following statistics:

► An October 1989 House Select Committee on Children, Youth and Families report finds that 1 in 8 Latino mothers and 1 in 9 black mothers received only late prenatal care or none at all. That compares with a national average of 1 in 17.

► The Infant Mortality Rate (IMR) measures the rate per thousand babies that die each year before the age of 1. It is a prime indicator of a population's overall health. According to the U.S. Census Bureau, the 1988 IMR for whites was 8.5. That same year, the IMR for blacks was more than twice that at 17.6.

► In 1988, blacks lived an average of 69.2 years, more than 6 years less than whites, according to the U.S. Census Bureau.

Income. On average, minorities make less money than whites. The 1989 median white family income is more than 1.5 times that of Latino families and 1.78 times greater than that of black families, according to the U.S. Census Bureau. The median white family made almost $36,000 in 1989, versus $23,449 for Latino families and $20,209 for black families.

The percentage of people below the poverty level is much higher for minorities than for the white majority population. In 1989, 12.8 percent of the U.S. population, or more than 31 million people, lived below poverty levels. Categorizing that number by race, the statistics for minorities appear quite disproportionate: Almost 31 percent of the total 1989 black population and 26 percent of the Hispanic population lived in poverty, versus 10 percent of the total white population.

Especially affected are children. The U.S. Census Bureau finds that in 1989, 43.7 percent of all black children under the age of 18 and 36.2 percent of all Hispanic youths live in poverty.

Another minority group that faces poverty is Native Americans. Not only do they have the poorest health and shortest life expectancies of almost any Americans, they also live in some of the worst housing conditions with the highest unemployment and the lowest per capita income.

Education. Proper education for minorities is another area of concern. According to the PTA, the "dropout rate for blacks is almost twice as high as for whites, and approximately 45 percent of all Hispanic students drop out of school. In large cities the dropout rate for Native Americans may be as high as 85%, for Hispanics 75% and for blacks 50%."[*] Moreover, finishing high school does not guarantee higher education. From 1976 to 1988 the number of blacks and Latino high school graduates entering college declined.

These statistics are not encouraging for the welfare of minorities in this country. According to author Melitta Cutright, "Statistics indicate that if you belong to a minority group or are from a non-English–speaking family, you are more likely to live in poverty, drop out of school, have a teenage pregnancy and be a single parent"[**]

SOME PROGRESS HAS BEEN MADE

Many members of the minority community are beginning to hold high positions in our society, as professionals and politicians. For instance, in the last 20 years the number of elected officials has increased fivefold, and the number of congressional representatives has more than doubled. In 1989, Douglas Wilder was elected as the first black governor of Virginia, and David Dinkins was elected as the first black mayor of New York City. During the 1988 presidential primaries, Jessie Jackson made a serious bid for the Democratic party presidential nomination. And General Colin Powell, as head of the United States Joint Chiefs of Staff, holds one of the most powerful positions in our nation.

Nonetheless, these gains and many others do not overshadow the increasing percentage of minorities who strive for equal opportunities to advance in our society.

20 years 1970–1990

Standing firm for justice

For more information write or call:
Native American Rights Fund
1506 Broadway
Boulder, Colorado 80302
303/447-8760

ORDINARY PEOPLE—EXTRAORDINARY ACTIONS

Ayinde Jean-Baptiste is a bit ahead of his time. Although he is just six years old he is in the third grade and actually tests above sixth-grade levels.

Besides his studies, Ayinde is very interested in the rights of all citizens. In June 1989 he received the N.A.A.C.P. Presidential Award for community services and in November 1989 he attended the dedication of the Civil Rights Memorial in Montgomery, Alabama, where he recited Dr. Martin Luther King Jr.'s "I Have A Dream Speech" to a crowd of 7,000.

[*]Melitta Cutright, *The National PTA Talks to Parents* (Garden City, N.Y.: Doubleday, 1989), 247.

[**]Cutright, *The National PTA Talks to Parents*, 247.

▪▪▪▪▪▪▪▪▪▪ Did you know?

The population of minorities in this country is rapidly increasing, especially among the Hispanic population.

▶ In 1988, almost one out of every five people was a "minority."

▶ By the year 2000, this ratio will approach one in three.

▶ In Los Angeles, about half of the graduating high-school class of the year 2000 will be Hispanic and by the year 2010 half of California will be composed of "minorities."

From Southern Poverty Law Center, *Law Report,* January 1990, with permission from Ayinde Jean-Baptiste.

Here is an excerpt from a letter Ayinde wrote to the Southern Poverty Law Center expressing his feelings about the Memorial dedication:

Dear Mr. Dees,

....

How are you doing? I am fine, and so is my family. My cold is much better. Thank you for bringing me out there to Alabama to speak at the Civil Rights Memorial.

I enjoyed being out there, especially meeting Martin Luther King III and Rosa Parks. When Martin spoke, his tone reminded me of his father, Dr. King, who is one of my heroes.

When I grow up I want to become a lawyer like you, and my father will become, to keep Freedom fighters out of jail. I also want to become a scientist, a great leader like Dr. King, and the president of the United States. I will make sure that everyone has: Food, clothes, money, a house, and a good school to go to.

I was elated to be at the Civil Rights Memorial to send a message that even though some of us have fallen, the struggle is still not over!

Sincerely,
Ayinde Jean-Baptiste

Organizations

●●

American Civil Liberties Union (ACLU)
212-944-9800
The ACLU's stated mission is to make sure that the Bill of Rights (amendments to the Constitution that guard against unwarranted government control) are preserved for each generation. They work with any and all persons denied such rights, including racial minorities, homosexuals, mental patients, prisoners, soldiers, children in the custody of the state, the handicapped, and Native Americans.

American Indian Relief Council
703-347-0350
A project of the Famine Relief Fund, the group helps American Indians, including the Sioux who live on the Rosebud Reservation, where 60 percent of the families live below the poverty level and whose per capita income is about $100 per month.

Christic Institute
202-797-8106
Founded in 1980, the center grew out of the work of the investigative, legal and public education team that won the Karen Silkwood case—a case that alerted the public to the dangers of nuclear radiation in the workplace. The center has established a solid track record of taking on controversial social justice cases—and winning.

Congress of Racial Equality (CORE)

718-434-3580
Founded in 1942, CORE is one of the oldest national civil rights groups in America. CORE has established a noteworthy record of finding solutions to the most difficult problems facing minorities: formulating the most pragmatic positions on important civil rights issues; instituting many successful actions to bring about social, political, and economic change for the underprivileged, and leading the United States toward true equality.

Japanese American Citizens League

415-921-5225
Advocates civil rights for Asian Americans.

LULAC—League of United Latin American Citizens

702-737-1240
Since 1929, LULAC has worked to provide Hispanic citizens with proper education, jobs, and civil rights.

Martin Luther King, Jr., Center for Nonviolent Social Change

404-524-1956
Coretta Scott King is founding president and CEO. The center convened the First International Congress of Nonviolent Movements in 1991, bringing leaders of freedom movements from more than 100 nations to Atlanta for a conference on freedom and human rights.

National Association for the Advancement of Colored People (NAACP)

The NAACP works to ensure the political, educational, social, and economic equality of minority citizens, achieve equality of rights, and eliminate racial prejudice among U.S. citizens. With more than 1,500 branches, the NAACP offers programs such as the Back to School/Stay in School program and the ACT/SO program, which fosters educational excellence.

NAACP Legal Defense and Education Fund

212-219-1900
Provides legal support to blacks, other racial minorities, and women in cases of discrimination and other violations of civil rights.

National Council of Negro Women, Inc. (NCNW)

703-684-5733
A coalition of 32 national organizations that seeks to improve the quality of life for black women, their families, and communities in the United States and Africa.

National Center for Urban Ethnic Affairs (NCUEA)

202-232-3600
NCUEA promotes policies that assist multicultural and multiethnic understanding.

National Urban League

212-310-9000
Offers programs to help minorities gain equal opportunities in all sectors of society.

Native American Rights Fund (NARF)

303-447-8760
A nonprofit Indian rights legal organization that dedicates itself to the legal rights of Indian people.

Southern Poverty Law Center

205-264-0286
Since 1971, the Southern Poverty Law Center has protected and advanced the legal rights of poor people and minorities.

OTHER COMMITTED ORGANIZATIONS

Anti-Defamation League of B'nai B'rith

212-490-2525

Center for Democratic Renewal

404-221-0025

Center for Third World Organizing

415-654-9601

Commission for Racial Justice

216-736-2100

Council on Interracial Books for Children

212-757-5339

Leadership Conference on Civil Rights

202-667-1780

Mexican American Legal Defense and Education Fund (MALDEF)

415-543-5598

National Alliance Against Racist and Political Repression

212-406-3330

National Institute Against Prejudice and Violence

301-328-5170

National Council of La Raza

202-289-1380

National Council of Negro Women, Inc. (NCNW)

202-659-0006

National Puerto Rican Coalition

202-223-3915

Simon Wiesenthal Center

213-553-9036

Southern Christian Leadership Conference
404-522-1420

Student Coalition Against Apartheid and Racism
202-483-4593

United Negro College Fund
212-326-1118

WOMEN'S RIGHTS

■ ■ ■

"You've come a long way, baby!" is a familiar phrase describing the Women's Movement today. However, it only tells part of the story. Many women in this country still encounter violations of their rights in both the home and the workplace. Although political legislation, organizational efforts, and popular support have all helped to ensure the rights of women, many issues remain to be solved.

IN THE WORKPLACE

The issues that women confront in the workplace include sexual harassment and discrimination, pay equity, access to non-traditional jobs, and protection during and after pregnancy.

Sexual discrimination. There are still many reported and unreported cases of sexual harassment at the workplace; in 1990 more than one-third of the job discrimination cases reported to the Equal Opportunity Commission were gender-

"Peanuts" reprinted by permission of UFS, Inc.

based. These cases of discrimination make it more difficult for women to achieve overall equality in the workplace.

Getting the right job in the first place remains a problem for some women. Although Affirmative Action and pressure from women's groups have helped to alleviate some sexual discrimination, women still find themselves placed in stereotypical job roles. These traditional "women's jobs" frequently pay lower than jobs usually held by men.

Equal pay. Although the salary gap between sexes has begun to narrow, it is far from equal. In 1986, the average woman earned a little more than $16,000 a year, whereas men averaged just over $25,000. In other words, women earned on average 64 cents for every dollar a man made.

For the most part, however, the salary discrepancy is not due to employers paying women less for the same job. Instead, the earnings gap results from the type of job. The number of women entering the work force has increased dramatically, yet many women hold lower-paying jobs. For instance, 98 percent of all secretaries are women, and secretaries average just over $14,500 a year. On the other hand, mail carriers are predominantly men—who take home more than $23,000 each year.*

In essence, women still dominate traditional "women's jobs," such as cashiering, waitressing, nursing, and teaching. And these jobs simply pay less on the average than the jobs men normally hold. Therefore, the earnings gap will not narrow appreciably until more women move into "men's jobs" and vice versa.

Some progress is being made, however. In 1985, 17 percent of all doctors, 44 percent of all accountants, and 18 percent of all lawyers were women. And many women are now pursuing entrepreneurial careers. According to the Census Bureau, women now own more than three million businesses, indicating a whopping 300 percent increase since 1979. Moreover, women are now starting to fill top-level corporate and political positions. More women own or run multimillion dollar corporations than ever before. And the number of women judges, legislators, and mayors has risen impressively.

The working mother. A Gallup Poll reports that almost two-thirds of the men and women surveyed believe that it is now harder for women to combine jobs and family.

Although it is now quite common for women to work

*Clare McHugh, "Letter to the Past," *Scholastic Update,* 18 May 1987.

WOMEN IN GOVERNMENT (AS OF 1986)

	National Legislature	Executive Cabinet
Norway	34%	47%
USSR	33%	none
Sweden	32%	24%
Finland	31%	18%
Denmark	27%	14%
Iceland*	15%	10%
Australia	11%	4%
Canada	10%	16%
Ireland	8%	7%
Israel	8%	5%
Italy	7%	3%
United States	5%	8%

*In its April, 1987, elections Iceland doubled the number of women in its national legislature.

Source: Country Embassies, Consulates, and Missions; Congressional Caucus for Women's Issues (U.S.).

Compiled by Karen Berry for *Ms.* magazine, July/August 1987

While working on this Anniversary Issue, I met with a businessman for advice on economic trends.

"You must be very happy," he said, while his butler served us breakfast in his elegant boardroom. "The Women's Movement has succeeded, and now you can go on to something else."

"What makes you think it's over?" I asked politely. After all, I was about to eat this man's scrambled eggs.

"Why, I see women everywhere now," my host explained. "They're working in my bank, my investment house, my ad agency—everywhere. I can see more of them all the time."

I thought about pointing out that the women he saw were not anywhere near his own level, and were certainly not corporate presidents or other authorities he himself might report to, but I thought he would just say that women had not been "in the pipeline" long enough; as if change were automatic and talent would always be rewarded.

"Do you think," I asked instead, "that men are doing housework and raising children as much as women are?"

"My God, no," said my host, appalled. "Is *that* what you want? That will never happen!"

© Gloria Steinem, Editorial, *Ms.* magazine, July/August 1987.

---

and raise children (more than half of women with infants under age 2 work), a mother constantly encounters problems along the way. Betty Friedan, author of *The Feminine Mystique,* explains. "The women's movement made new opportunities available, but when working women work 40 to 80 hours a week on the job in addition to working at home, then life is much more difficult."*

To further complicate matters, many working women now find themselves having to take care of an elderly parent along with the kids. This extra function is creating a situation that society is just starting to recognize. Moreover, if a mother (or a father) chooses to spend more time with the children than at work, he or she may find themselves on the infamous "mommy track"—a career path that lags behind one's peers.

Although the struggle to meet the needs of the family and the demands at the workplace is becoming increasingly more difficult, little has been done to alleviate the strain. America lags behind many other nations in terms of prenatal care, child sick leave, and day care.

The Pregnancy Discrimination Act of 1978 requires employers to treat pregnancy as a short-term illness or disability.

*U.S. News & World Report, 12 February 1990.

A woman may take some time off before, during, and after the pregnancy; however, companies do not have to pay a pregnant employee for an extended leave of absence. And if the woman takes off too much time, she may risk being replaced. Currently, only a handful of states require employers to guarantee women their jobs if they leave work to have a child.

Also, the United States is the only industrialized Western nation without a national child-care policy. Even if a woman wants to work and have a child, she may be unable to find or afford proper day care. This puts an extra burden on the many households in which both parents must work. Although Congress is working on a plan and many businesses are establishing their own programs, child day care is still a high-priority issue that is not yet properly resolved.

OUTSIDE THE WORKPLACE

Women face difficulties outside the workplace as well, such as equal treatment during divorce, protection from domestic violence, and preserving their right to have an abortion.

Divorce. The rising number of divorces in this country has put this issue high on the list of concerns for women. Although most courts attempt to divide assets equally and provide a fair amount of alimony and other support, many divorced women still receive unequal settlements and face difficult economic situations. According to statistics compiled in 1989 by the National Coalition Against Domestic Violence, in the first year after a divorce, a woman's standard of living

Did you know? ∙∙∙∙∙∙∙∙∙∙

▶ In Los Angeles, companies such as Paramount Pictures and Arthur Anderson offer on-site day care for employees' children.

▶ Washingtom law firm, Arnold & Porter, offers on-site child care for $20.00 per day for its employees.

▶ In Arcadia, CA, the Methodist Hospital provide nursery and preschool service for all 1,200 of it employees on a wait-list basis.

IF YOU WANT TO HEAR
WHAT WOMEN ARE SAYING AROUND THE WORLD . . .

LISTEN REAL LOUD
News of Women's Liberation Worldwide

Nationwide Women's Program · American Friends Service Committee

American Friends Service Committee

MATERNAL MORTALITY RATES

Maternal Mortality Rates (per 100,000 live births, 1982)

Canada	● 1.9
Israel	● 3.1
Hong Kong	● 3.5
Sweden	● 4.3
Finland	● 4.5
Ireland	● 5.6
Netherlands	● 6.4
England & Wales	● 6.7
Kuwait	● 7.4
Belgium	● 7.5
United States	● 7.9

Source: 1985 Demographic Yearbook (UN).

INFANT MORTALITY RATES

Deaths of infants under one year of age per 1,000 live births as of 1986

Finland, Japan, Iceland	● 6.2
Sweden	● 6.3
Denmark, Switzerland	● 7.7
Norway	● 7.9
Netherlands	● 8.3
Canada	● 8.5
France	● 8.5
Hong Kong	● 9.2
Singapore	● 9.4
Australia	● 9.6*
Ireland	● 9.8
England & Wales	● 10.1
East Germany	● 10.3
West Germany	● 10.3
United States	● 10.6†

*In 1982 aboriginal infant mortality rates were estimated at 30 per 1,000 live births.

†In 1981 infant mortality rates in ten urban, poor areas ranged from 16.7 to 32.5 per 1,000 live births.

Sources: Demographic Office of UNICEF; Economic and Social Council of the United Nations; "Sisterhood Is Global."

Compiled by Karen Berry for *Ms.* magazine, July/August 1987.

*Barbara Mart, National Coalition Against Domestic Violence Fact Sheet, October 1988.

drops by 73 percent, while a man's improves by an average of 43 percent. For many divorced women the burden of caring for children and holding a job is taking its toll. Almost half of the low-income families in the United States are headed by women.

Protection against violence. Physical attacks against women are on the rise both in and out of the home.

▶ The Bureau of Justice Statistics estimates that 3 out of 4 women will be victims of at least one violent attack during their lifetime. (A violent attack involves rape or attempted rape, robbery or attempted robbery, assault or attempted assault.)

▶ The 1989 FBI Uniform Crime Statistics report finds that on average 1 woman is raped every 6 minutes.

But the incidence of sexual violence against women may be much higher. Sexual assaults are still reported less frequently to the authorities than any other violent act.

Women not only have to worry about attack from an intruder; millions of women are victims of battery, or violence from a husband or partner in the home.

▶ A minimum of 1.8 million women are assaulted by a spouse or partner at least once a year (not including minor violence), according to the Family Research Laboratory 1985 National Family Violence Survey.

▶ The 1987 FBI Uniform Crime Reports found that 30 percent of female homicide victims were killed by their husbands or boyfriends.

▶ On average, 10 women are killed each day by their batterers, according to a 1987 National Organization for Women report.

According to former Surgeon General C. Everett Koop battery is the single most significant cause of injury to women in this country. Yet many cases of domestic violence go unreported. Many victims keep silent because of embarrassment or fear for their safety. Research over the last 10 years finds that women who leave their batterers are at a 75 percent greater risk of being killed by the batterer than those who stay with them.*

The right to choose. One very important issue that has a direct effect on women is the right to choose to have an abortion. When the U.S. Supreme Court ruled on *Webster v. Reproductive Health Services* the abortion question was reopened and handed back to the states to resolve. Since that decision, there has been an outpouring of public opinion on both sides of the issue, and reproductive freedom has again become a primary issue for women. See "Abortion—Whose Choice?" (page 311) for further discussion.

Copyright © 1989, *USA Today*. Reprinted with permission.

The Movement Today

Many opinions have been voiced concerning the current status of the Women's Movement. Some feel that the feminism of the 1960s and 1970s lost ground to the conservatism of the 1980s. But they argue, women "have come a long way" and further gains will inevitably take hold.

Others believe that the Movement has just taken on new issues. Ohio State historian Susan Hartmann suggests that the next stage of the Movement will focus on such issues as care for dependents—both children and parents—and combating violence against children.*

This new focus signals a different phase for movement. Gloria Steinem explains this "second wave":

> The suffragist and abolitionist movements of the First Wave took more than a century to win a legal and social identity as citizens and human beings for everyone in this country who was not white and male. Now we are in the second full decade of an even more complex struggle for legal and social equality, regardless of sex or race.**

The Women's Movement thus focuses on a broader goal—that of total equality for all.

*U.S. News & World Report, 12 February 1990.

**Gloria Steinem, "Looking to the Future," *Ms.* magazine, July/August 1987.

Organizations

• •

Women's rights organizations undertake many important issues. Many provide legal representation, give advice and counsel, lobby for better legislation, and educate the public about women's issues.

American Civil Liberties Union
(Women's Rights Project)
212-944-9800

Concerned Women for America
202-488-7000

Domestic Violence Hotline
800-333-SAFE

Equal Rights Advocates (ERA)
415-621-0505

Federally Employed Women (FEW)
202-638-4404

Fund for the Feminist Majority
703-522-2214

National Coalition Against Domestic Violence
202-638-6388

National Coalition of 100 Black Women, Inc.
212-974-6140

National Commission of Working Women
202-737-5764

National Council of Negro Women, Inc. (NCNW)
703-684-5733

National Organization for Women (NOW)
202-331-0066

National Women's Abuse Prevention Project
202-857-0216

National Women's Political Caucus
202-347-4456

Women's Equity Action League (WEAL)
202-638-1961

Women's Action Alliance
212-532-8330

Women's Legal Defense Fund
202-887-0364

GAY RIGHTS

###

They gave me a medal for killing two men—and a discharge for loving one.

—Tombstone inscription of Leonard Matlovich, Gay Vietnam Veteran

It is estimated that about 25 million Americans are gay. But even though gay men and women represent a significant percentage of the country's population, they are often denied their basic civil rights.

Many gays experience discrimination in the workplace, while seeking employment, and even in housing. Some of this bias results from fear of AIDS, whereas other bias is a result of ignorance and anger about a gay person's lifestyle choices. For whatever reason, discrimination exists. Gay persons are banned from the military, excluded from many of the same legal rights that heterosexuals enjoy, and in some cases harassed and physically attacked simply because of their sexual preference.

AIDS

The fear and ignorance of AIDS has been a scourge for the gay population. When AIDS first appeared in the early 1980s, gay men faced two plagues. One was the AIDS virus, which spread rapidly throughout the gay community, and the other was society's equally vicious discriminatory backlash.

The AIDS epidemic brought an unknown and deadly disease to the gay population; this illness changed the lifestyle

306

of the entire community and took the lives of many of its members. By the end of 1989, more than 50,000 homosexuals had died of AIDS and a much larger number were infected with the HIV virus. Living and dying with AIDS became commonplace as many gays lost close friends and loved ones, and many more lived in fear of the disease's ruthless attack.

But gay men had more to fear than the disease itself. With AIDS came an onslaught of hatred and discrimination against the entire gay community. Some people blamed gays for creating and fostering the disease. As a result, gay men experienced discrimination in areas ranging from housing to the workplace, regardless of whether they had AIDS. And a person who developed AIDS not only has to fight the disease, but also has to struggle to keep his job, his medical insurance, and even his family and peers.

If one could find anything positive about the effect of AIDS on the gay community, it would be that the disease helped bring gays together. Gay health and support groups and legislative and advocacy organizations were formed and strengthened as a result of the detrimental effect of AIDS. These groups not only have fostered help for those with AIDS, but they also provide a resurgence of energy directed toward helping gays in all areas of life.

DISCRIMINATION IN THE MILITARY

As a matter of policy, the U.S. military bars homosexuals from service. Although it has not been proven that a gay person would not make a good soldier, the Defense Department believes that "the presence of such members adversely affects the ability of the armed forces to maintain discipline, good order, and morale."[*] Nevertheless, even though the Department of Defense pursues a strict policy against homosexuals, one study suggests that 1 out of 10 servicemen and women are gay. And even though many of these gay army members make good soldiers, the military discharges about 1,700 officers and enlisted men and women for homosexuality each year.

Being charged with homosexuality can be a very unpleasant experience. An accused gay soldier may face onerous hearings, court-martial, discharge, and even prison. So a gay soldier must hide his or her sexual preferences, or suffer embarrassing and sometimes dire consequences.

[*]Peter Cary, "The Pentagon's Fight to Keep Gays Away," *U.S. News & World Report,* 20 November 1989.

LEGISLATIVE BARRIERS

The United States still has more laws directed against gays than enacted to protect them. Laws against sodomy are still in existence in almost half the states in this country. Conversely, only two states—Wisconsin and Massachusetts—have passed legislation protecting the rights of gays. Ironically, a gay person may stand a better chance of being charged of having sex than being protected against discrimination.

FAMILY MATTERS

Gay men and lesbians also want to enjoy the same rights as their heterosexual counterparts, including marriage, child custody and adoption, and other spousal rights such as Social Security and insurance benefits, inheritance, and matters of credit. Even though countless homosexual men and women live together and an estimated 3 to 5 million are parents who have had children in previous heterosexual relationships, they are often denied these rights.

Many gay and lesbian couples have custody of their children, whereas others adopt them. And in some cases, lesbians have become parents through artificial insemination. And although their desire to live "normally" is outpacing society's acceptance of these matters, their actions are forcing the courts to confront legal issues regarding gays and the family. Seven U.S. cities have enacted "domestic partnership" legislation, which is similar to basic spousal laws. In November 1989, San Francisco voters passed a local ordinance which gives legal recognition to unmarried couples, homosexual or heterosexual. This type of legislation helps answer legal questions about unmarried partnerships and, as one person explains it, acts as "the completion of a process of self-acceptance, of healing, to be able to publicly say, 'This is who I am and this is the person I love.' "*

ANTI-GAY VIOLENCE

Homophobia takes many forms, but the most vicious type is the verbal and physical harassment of gays. Attacks against gays are on the rise throughout the country. In 1986, more than 4,500 attacks on gay men and women were reported in the United States, and that represents only the number of *reported* cases. New York's Gay and Lesbian Anti-Violence Project believes that only 2 out of 10 victims actually report

*"Not Quite a Wedding, but Quite a Day for Couples by the Bay," *New York Times*, 15 February 1991.

these crimes. The other 80 percent keep quiet for a number of reasons, including adverse publicity, fear of possible recrimination, and distrust of the police.

The types of "hate" attacks range from verbal harassment and threats of violence to physical and sexual abuse. Gay men and women throughout the country are threatened, beaten up, and in extreme cases even killed. In fact, physical violence against gays has actually been given a name—"gay bashing."

Although the rise in anti-gay violence matches that of crimes against race and religion, it has not received the same level of attention. Gay advocacy groups charge that some human rights groups do not embrace the homophobic problem as forcefully as they do racial and religious incidents. Matt Foreman, of the New York Gay and Lesbian Anti-Violence Project, explains that "Anti-gay violence is still acceptable because, while leaders decry racial and religious bigotry, they ignore violence against gays and lesbians."*

And besides being ignored by human rights leaders, some argue that in the eyes of our society violence directed against a person because of his or her sexual lifestyle is not as "bad" as violence aimed at a person of a different color or God. The New York Governor's Task Force on Bias-Related Violence reports that gays and lesbians are viewed by straight white teenagers as legitimate targets that can be openly attacked. Darrell Yates Rist, cofounder of the Gay and Lesbian Alliance Against Defamation, points out that "Bigotry against homosexual men and women never incites broad public outrage, regardless of the grotesque form the hatred takes."**

Hunter Madsen, coauthor of *After the Ball,* a book about the gay revolution, compares the gay movement to the black civil rights movement and comments on the state of the gay movement today. "The gay movement hasn't got nearly so far as the black civil rights movement. Yes, our lifestyle is now 'public'—in highly restricted urban areas—but coast to coast, hatred and contempt for gays aren't far from where they were 25 years ago."†

So until a crime against a gay person is recognized as a violation of *human* rights, society will be content to look the other way and homophobia will continue to flourish.

I was amazed to learn that many people die each year in anti-gay attacks, and thousands more are left scarred emotionally and physically. . . . Prejudice hurts . . . kills. Don't be a part of it.

—BOB HOPE, in a public service announcement.

*Editorial, "Legitimate Targets," *The Progressive,* September 1990.
**Darrell Yates Rist, "Homosexuals and Human Rights," *The Nation,* 9 April 1990.
†*Time* magazine, "Is the Gay Revolution a Flop?" July 10, 1989, p. 56

Organizations

● ●

**ACLU National Gay
Rights Project**
213-487-1720

Fund for Human Dignity
212-529-1600

**Gay and Lesbian
Advocates and Defenders**
617-426-2020

**Gay & Lesbian Alliance
Against Defamation
(GLAAD)**
212-966-1700

**Gay/Lesbian National
Crisisline**
212-807-6016/800-221-7044

Gay Rights Advocates
415-863-3622

**Gay Rights National
Lobby**
202-546-1801

Homosexuals Anonymous
800-253-3000

**Lambda Legal Defenses &
Education Fund**
212-944-9488

**Lesbian Mothers National
Defense Fund**
206-282-5798/206-284-2290

**National Coalition of
Black Gays**
202-387-8096

**National Educational
Foundation for Individual
Rights**
c/o Lesbian Rights Project
415-441-2629

**National Federation of
Parents & Friends of Gays**
202-726-3223

National Gay Task Force
212-741-5800/202-332-6483

● ●

VETERANS' RIGHTS

■ ■ ■

Unlike other veterans, the brave boys who went to Vietnam had to endure two wars. The first war was the battle waged in swamps and jungles abroad. The second was fought for respect and recognition at home. With the passage of time, they have won the battle for the hearts of their countrymen. And in my view it's about time.

—PRESIDENT GEORGE BUSH, November 1989

There are more than 27 million veterans, including 1.2 million women, in the United States and Puerto Rico. These men and women served the United States during World War I, World War II, the Korean and Vietnam Wars, as well as during times of peace. They fought to uphold and protect the rights of Americans, and also those of many others around the world.

After serving their country many vets have successfully reentered society. However, a significant number of veterans have had difficulty in finding employment, receiving adequate medical care, and obtaining their rightful benefits. Many suffer mental and physical disabilities as a result of war activities, including the emotional strain, the effects of Agent Orange exposure, and the symptoms of post-traumatic stress disorder.

These problems and others put pressure on their personal lives, in many cases leading to divorce, alcohol and drug abuse, and loss of job or failure to find suitable employment.

Many veteran organizations—public and private—help vets deal with medical, financial, and emotional difficulties. These groups provide outreach services for homeless vets (as many as 30 percent of the homeless population are veterans); secure benefits, services, and programs for disabled veterans and their families; help vets in financial need; and strive to find them appropriate employment. Some organizations devote much of their resources to such issues as trying to free prisoners of war and securing Agent Orange compensation.

The Persian Gulf War serves as an excellent example of the critically important role that the men and women of the United States Armed Forces play in protecting human rights here and abroad. Hopefully, this new dose of patriotism will remind the nation to treat all of its veterans with the respect that they deserve.

Organizations

American Veterans of WWII, Korea, and Vietnam (AMVETS)
301-459-9600

Department of Veterans Affairs (DVA)
202-233-2706

Disabled American Veterans (DAV)
606-441-7300

Jewish War Veterans of the USA (JMV)
202-265-6280

National Association of Concerned Veterans (NACV)
203-397-4329

Paralyzed Veterans of America (PVA)
202-872-1300

Regular Veterans Association of the U.S. (RVA)
512-389-2288

Veterans of Foreign Wars (VFW)
816-756-3390

Veterans of the Vietnam War
717-825-7215

Vietnam Veterans of America (VVA)
202-332-2700

Vietnam Women's Memorial Project
202-328-7253

ABORTION—WHOSE CHOICE?

■ ■ ■

CHIPPING AWAY AT *ROE* V. *WADE*

A July 1989 U.S. Supreme Court decision ruled that Missouri could limit the use of public facilities and funds for abortions. This ruling chipped away at the landmark 1973 *Roe* v. *Wade*

Women don't have abortions they want. They have abortions they need.

—KATE MICHELMAN, executive director, National Abortion Rights Action League

Cynthia Johnson/Time Magazine.

decision that legalized the abortion procedure, gave states new authority to regulate abortion, and reopened the abortion debate as each state began reviewing its own abortion laws.

OPEN FOR DEBATE

Pro-choice advocates and antiabortion activists took advantage of this turn in abortion law and the resulting publicity by beginning intense national campaigns to herald their causes. The country quickly became divided on the issue, as abortion became a question not only of personal choice, but also a matter of federal or state laws and of political philosophy.

THE ABORTION ISSUE

The abortion issue crosses many boundaries and involves many topics. Surrounding the abortion issue are the very tough questions of rights and morality. Within the debate stands a variety of topics that are also being vigorously discussed, such as questions concerning birth control measures, sex education, pregnancy counseling, prenatal care, and adoptive services.

The debate also touches upon issues of parental involvement—both in terms of family planning and in notification of a minor's abortion.

Other volatile issues include the worldwide role of churches in contraception and abortion, sterilization, abortion pills, and the use of aborted fetuses for medical science.

Finally, some legal "hot potatoes" being decided in various states are age limits for abortion, funding, waiting periods, consent from spouses and parents, the cutoff date for an abortion, and abortion in cases of rape, endangerment of the mother's life, or deformities in the fetus.

THE DEBATE HEATS UP

These issues and others make the abortion issue highly charged and extremely complex. Abortion taps into the deepest realms of conscience and personal rights; it touches virtually every citizen, regardless of sex or race and reaches across the boundaries of state, party, and law.

For these reasons and others the question of abortion and choice has catapulted to one of the most controversial, vocal, and powerful issues of the day. Millions of people listen to the arguments, do some intense soul searching, and try to answer some very tough questions. Hundreds of thousands of people attend rallies, fund-raisers, and work for the group of their choice. Politicians, judges, and executives fully understand how their stance on the issue will direct the course of their campaigns, change the nature of laws, and influence the opinions of stockholders, employees, and clients. Numerous organizations have emerged or have been greatly strengthened, finding themselves in a national spotlight and vigorously pursued by an anxious media following.

PERSONAL AND POLITICAL DECISIONS

As the legislators ultimately decide the laws governing abortion in this country, much attention has been directed toward the protection of rights. Right-to-Life groups argue that the unborn fetus has its own rights and that abortion kills the fetus against its will. Pro-choice groups argue that a woman has the right to make her own choice about her body and the right to privacy in doing so.

Somewhere within the debate each individual must balance legal and civil statutes with his or her own personal morality.

A hospital should be an institution of healing and not killing.

—THE REV. HENRY PATINO, Miami antiabortion protester

Trippett

Organizations

RIGHT-TO-LIFE AND RELATED GROUPS
American Life League
703-659-4171

Americans United for Life
312-786-9494

National Right to Life Committee
202-626-8800

Operation Rescue
607-723-4012

Pro-Life Action League
312-777-2900

PRO-CHOICE AND RELATED ORGANIZATIONS

American Civil Liberties Union
212-944-9800

Center for Population Options
202-347-5700

Fund for the Feminist Majority
703-522-2214

National Abortion Federation (NAF)
202-667-5881

National Abortion Rights Action League (NARAL)
202-408-4600

National Organization for Women (NOW)
202-331-0066

Physicians for Choice c/o Planned Parenthood
212-541-7800

Planned Parenthood (PPFA)
212-541-7800

Religious Coalition for Abortion Rights
202-543-7032

THE GUN CONTROL ISSUE

■ ■ ■

The finger pulls the trigger, but the trigger may also be pulling the finger.

—DR. LEONARD BERKOWITZ, author of *Aggression*

Criminals, unfortunately, don't obey the law.

—CHARLES H. CUNNINGHAM, NRA

"I didn't know my dad's gun was loaded . . . and I shot her, I didn't mean to . . . Please don't be dead."

—10-year-old SEAN SMITH, of Miramar, Florida, on a 911 recording after he accidentally shot his 8-year-old sister.

Like gunfighters facing off at the OK Corral, the debate over gun control divides the country into two separate camps. On one side stands the gun owner, who feels that it is his or her right to own a gun. An estimated 50 to 60 million households own at least one gun. The majority of these gun owners use these weapons responsibly for sport and protection.

On the other side is the gun-control advocate, who believes that restrictions on gun ownership will curb violence and needless deaths. These people point out that death due to gunfire is the sixth most frequent cause of death to those Americans under the age of 65.

Fueling the controversy are a number of factors. Crimes, violence, and deaths involving guns are reaching alarming levels. The youth of this nation are being recklessly murdered by guns. Instances of psychopaths armed with assault rifles have made parents fearful of letting their children play on the streets. Drive-by shootings are commonplace in many large cities; gang members shoot without conscience, not caring if children or other bystanders fall victim to their turf battles.

GUN DEATHS ON THE RISE

Gun-control advocates point to the tragic number of deaths each year involving guns. For instance, according to the National Center for Health Statistics, more than 32,200 Americans died in 1987 from accidents, homicides, and suicides involving guns. Moreover, the number of gun deaths is rising, especially among our youth. The FBI reports that the teen death rate from guns increased 97 percent from 1984 to 1988. In 1987 alone, 3,392 youths were killed by gun violence, according to the NCHS.

Many of these deaths are accidental—resulting from improper training or inadequate supervision. For instance, NCHS reports that each year more than 450 youths die from accidental shootings.

Gun-control advocates argue that mandated training programs and restrictions on ownership will cut the number of these senseless deaths. Gun owners agree that gun education is important but differ on how to implement it. They point out that the shootings account for only 2 percent of all accidental deaths in this country and that 99.9 percent of all households with a gun are responsible owners.

GUN BANS AND CRIME

Gun-control proponents believe that waiting periods, personal history checks, required training, and bans on certain types of weapons will decrease the number of crimes involving guns. Under tighter regulations criminals and other unstable persons will not be able to purchase guns, therefore putting a halt to potentially dangerous activities.

Charles H. Cunningham of the NRA argues that "criminals, unfortunately, don't obey the law." They will be able to obtain a gun or another weapon if they want to commit a crime. Gun ownership rights groups feel that authorities should focus their attention on stronger crime control, including tougher prison sentences and increased funding for police forces, instead of gun regulations.

ASSAULT RIFLES

Assault rifles, more suitable for combat than protection or hunting, can be easily bought by almost anyone.

Gun-control groups believe that banning assault weapons will help prevent many deaths, whereas gun advocates argue that banning guns of any nature will not affect crime. Criminals will be able to obtain assault-type weapons not restricted by new laws, or will use other guns to commit crimes.

CHILDREN AND GUNS

America's children stand in the cross fire of the gun debate. The Center to Prevent Handgun Violence reports that every day, 10 American children ages 18 and under are killed in handgun suicides, homicides, and accidents, and many more are wounded.

Some children become innocent victims to brutal drive-by shootings. In 1987, 1 out of every 10 children who lost their lives before age 20 was a gunshot victim, according to the NCHS. Rival gang members invade each other's turf, firing indiscriminately at anything that moves. Sadly, children who live in these areas risk their lives when playing outside; and they are even at risk in their own homes.

School is not a safe haven either. Gun-wielding psychopaths have opened fire on school playgrounds—and many students themselves carry guns. The National School Safety

Did you know? ....

On average, in the United States:

Every 2.5 minutes—a person is injured by a gun.

Every 3 hours—a teenager commits suicide by use of a gun.

Every day—a child is killed by a gun.

Every year—30,000 people are murdered, shot by a gun, 1,500 people die as a result of gun accident, and 12,000 people commit suicide using a gun.

Editorial, "Waiting Period Can Curb Handgun Toll," *USA Today,* June 13, 1990.

.... Did you know?

▶ According to L.A. Sheriff Deputy Ken Evers, Operation Safe Streets, "Assault weapons are the weapon of choice for gang members."

▶ Rapid fire from an assault rifle killed 5 children and wounded 29 others in a California schoolyard.

▶ James Edward Pough, 42, used a semiautomatic rifle to gun down eight people in a Jacksonville, FL, auto loan office.

▶ Purchases of the AK-47-type assault rifles increased from 4,000 a year in 1985 to 40,000 in 1988.

Center reports that an estimated 135,000 male students carried guns to school daily in 1987, and another 270,000 carried handguns at least once. In some parts of the nation, risks at school are now almost as great as risks in the street. According to the Center to Prevent Handgun Violence, at least 71 students and teachers nationwide were killed with guns on school campuses between 1985/86 and 1989/90 school years. Another 201 were wounded by gunfire and at least 242 were held hostages at gunpoint.

The home can be equally as dangerous for children. More than 25 million households own handguns and half keep them loaded. Improper care of guns kept in the home has led to many tragic deaths. One child is killed every day in the United States in accidental shootings and 10 are injured, claims the Center to Prevent Handgun Violence. Sadly, most—if not all—of these senseless deaths could be prevented by responsible adult care and supervision of their firearms.

A QUESTION OF RIGHTS

Many gun owners point to the Second Amendment, which states that "the right of the people to keep and bear arms, shall not be infringed." They argue that every citizen has the right to own a gun for sport and to protect his or her home. Opponents, however, believe that the Second Amendment applies only to the state and its militia, not to each and every citizen.

Gun-control advocates feel that owning a gun may be the right of every American, but it is actually only the right of every responsible American. It is hoped that effective gun control laws will weed out the irresponsible persons, curbing potential violence and needless accidents.

Q. WHAT DO THESE CHILDREN HAVE IN COMMON?

....

Scott Feltner, 10 (Orlando)
Erin Smith, 8 (Miramar)
Evie Sue Hagan, 4 (Orlando)
Walter Jones, 12 (Ocala)
Silvio, 4 (Tampa)

A. They are five children who were shot with handguns by other children, three fatally, in a one-week period in Florida.

Center to Prevent Handgun Violence.
National Safety Council

THE FUTURE

The question of whether authorities have the right to restrict the purchase and use of guns affects many Americans. Most gun-control groups do not seek a complete denial of guns for

A Child A Day Is <u>Killed</u> With A Handgun

Let's Keep Handguns Out Of The Wrong Hands

Center To Prevent Handgun Violence

citizens. They argue mostly for stricter controls on the purchase and use of firearms. Gun-ownership advocates do not want to have their Constitutional rights infringed upon and object to suffering for the irresponsible actions of a small percentage of gun users.

Although both groups disagree on the issue of whether strict gun regulation will deter crime, they agree that proper gun training is essential to prevent accidental tragedies.

Over time it is hoped that some type of common ground will be found, where the rights of all people are protected and needless violence is prevented.

Did you know? ⋯⋯⋯⋯

In 1988, gun accidents were the fifth-leading cause of accidental death for children ages 14 and under.

Organizations

GUN-CONTROL ADVOCACY GROUPS

Center to Prevent Handgun Violence
202-289-7319

Educational Fund to End Handgun Violence
202-544-7227

Handgun Control, Inc.
202-898-0792

National Coalition to Ban Handguns
202-544-7190

GUN-OWNERSHIP ADVOCACY GROUPS

National Rifle Association
202-828-6000

Citizens Committee for the Right to Keep and Bear Arms
206-454-4911

Second Amendment Foundation
206-454-7012

WHAT CAN I DO?

▶ **Realize that individual actions help.** Voicing your opinion through such actions as letter writing, protest marches, and supporting human rights groups epitomizes the foundation of

"I DIDN'T SPEAK UP"

Martin Neimoeller, a German Lutheran pastor who was arrested by the Gestapo and sent to a concentration camp in Dachau in 1938, wrote this piece about individual action:

"In Germany, the Nazis first came for the communists, and I didn't speak up because I wasn't a communist. Then they came for the Jews, and I didn't speak up because I wasn't a Jew. Then they came for the trade unionists, and I didn't speak up because I wasn't a trade unionist. Then they came for the Catholics, and I didn't speak up because I was a Protestant. Then they came for me, and by that time there was no one left to speak for me."

He was freed by the Allied forces in 1945.

the human rights movement. Millions of people long for the day in which these rights will also be theirs.

▶ Dr. Charles Moody, Sr., vice provost for minority affairs at the University of Michigan, believes that every individual can do something to battle racism. "I think people as individuals can do something about [racism] by looking at themselves and trying to change that part of the institution or community that they have control over. All of us have control over some part of it, even if it is just ourselves."*

▶ When asked about his feeling on helping the cause of human rights, the musician Sting replied, "We're only entertainers. But with a song we can affect how people think about the world."**

▶ Judith Nicastro formed the National Abortion Rights Action League campus chapter at University of Washington. Similar groups have formed at other colleges.

▶ An Amnesty International memo describes the importance of individual action in helping political prisoners:

> When you do something to help a prisoner of conscience or to try to save someone from torture, you are doing something of incalculable value—even if it may seem very modest to you. You are taking a stand for human dignity. You are saying that you refuse to accept the torture, the humiliation and the silencing of another human being. In the face of cruelty and the arrogant abuse of limitless power, you are proving—by personal example—to both the victims and their tormentors that compassion, justice and human love are still alive.

▶ **Learn about human rights issues.** One of the best ways to become better informed about a particular issue is to contact one or more human rights advocacy groups and ask for information about their cause, including a publications list. For example:

▶ The Research, Information, and Publications Department of the International Defense and Aid Fund provides authoritative, comprehensive, and well-documented information about the issue of apartheid. By simply contacting IDAF you will receive a booklet containing many informative references on the subject of apartheid.

▶ Ask your local colleges, adult education programs, and college extension courses about classes on human rights and related subjects. For example, USC sponsors a theme semester, during which 20 courses are wholly or partly devoted to the study of South Africa and its apartheid system. The courses have a total enrollment of 1,030 students. Included are courses in business, film, international relations, religion, urban planning, and education.

▶ The Council on Interracial Books for Children provides lists of books that help create a common bond between races.

▶ As with many other causes, you can learn more by reading the daily newspaper, listening attention to the news, and doing research in a public library.

▶ **Support human rights organizations through volunteerism and donations.** Many human rights advocacy groups are self-funded and rely solely on the contributions and volunteerism of interested individuals. Activities range from answering phone calls to organizing rallies to running local chapters. Those who contribute perform a valuable service to the organization and the people they represent.

▶ **Support the many programs of human rights groups.** Human rights groups are well organized and pursue many avenues of activism. Contact an organization of interest and ask about their programs.

▶ **Contact your political representatives.** Many human rights causes need the support of politicians to gain funding and bring attention to human rights issues. Every issue, from abortion to the rights of minorities, involves legislation and requires political leadership.

▶ Organizers such as the Vietnam Veterans of America are working hard to enact legislation to mandate com-

Did you know? ▪▪▪▪▪▪▪▪▪▪▪

▶ Members of Disabled American Veterans local chapters and Auxiliary Units volunteer at VA hospitals, clinics, and nursing homes. In 1988, these members donated 1.9 million hours to VA Voluntary Service. These actions help both the DAV and the many veterans who need support and care.

▪▪▪▪▪▪▪▪▪▪ Did you know?

▶ The Congress of Racial Equality's Equal Opportunity Affairs department helps solve job discrimination complaints.

▪▪▪▪▪▪▪▪▪▪ Did you know?

▶ The Native American Rights Fund dedicates 100 percent of its time to legal cases of importance to all Indian people. They have helped dozens of tribes protect their treaty-guaranteed fishing, hunting, and water rights.

pensation of certain disabilities caused by Agent Orange. Rep. Patricia Schroeder (D-Colo.) and Rep. Olympia Snowe (R-Maine) introduced two bills intended to refocus federal commitment in contraceptive research. Your support will help these and other causes.

▶ **Protest human rights violations here and abroad, and support the human rights movement.** Because the human rights movement is so broad in nature, there are countless causes to choose from. Decide what interests you and then find out ways you can help. For instance:

▶ Thousands of people across the country annual attend marches and other celebrations to commemorate Martin Luther King Jr.'s birthday.

▶ To help calm rising racial tension, Boston minister Charles Stith organized vigils in 21 cities, and asked political, business, and civic leaders, as well as citizens, to sign a pledge to support racial harmony, justice, and equality.

▶ More than 1.5 million people in 19 cities on five continents participated in the Reebok International-sponsored and Amnesty International-produced Human Rights Now! concert tour in 1988.

▶ Hundreds of thousands of people have attended pro-life and pro-choice rallies across the country to herald their causes.

▶ Students and others formed rallies at college campuses to protest the investment policies of their college endowment funds. In many cases this led to a divestment of the securities of companies that did business in South Africa.

▶ Local religious congregations in San Francisco and Detroit protested detentions of political prisoners in South Africa by meeting on Soweto Sunday, June 12. They showed their support by signing covenants to pledge continued work against apartheid and singing songs to herald the cause of freedom.

▶ **Write letters to protest the detention and treatment of political prisoners throughout the world.** Amnesty International employs one of the best known and most effective letter-writing campaigns aimed to help prisoners of conscience. As an example, more than 10,000 people wrote letters on behalf of a Spanish prisoner whose case was announced at the launch of the Campaign to Abolish Torture. As a result of the campaign, the king of Spain ordered an investigation.

OUTPOURING OF LOVE FOR VETERANS

DEAR READERS:

Well, you did it again, and there are no words to adequately thank you. I'm talking about your generous response to the second annual Valentines for Vets program. It was a stunning success. Last year, we were thrilled to receive 1.5 million valentines. This year the count was nearly 5 million.

At Hines Veterans Administration Hospital in Chicago, the central mailing point, more than 100 volunteers worked hard and long for three weeks to box the valentines and ship them to the other 171 VA hospitals and medical centers around the nation. More volunteers were on hand at these facilities to distribute the valentines to patients. More than 2,300 boxes, each containing 2,000 valentines, were mailed to about 50,000 hospitalized veterans. That's about 90 valentines for every patient!

Cards and letters arrived from individuals, schools, churches, community organizations and businesses all over the world, including Saudi Arabia, Taiwan, Australia, Tokyo, Canada, the Philippines and Germany.

Teachers once again made this celebration a class project. Thousands of children sent brightly decorated, hand-made cards and wrote letters. Many enclosed poems and pictures of themselves and their pets. Several schools made banners and posters that the vets tacked up in the wards.

Readers sent beautiful hand-made afghans, quilts, pillows, bedroom slippers and floral arrangements. It was obvious that a great many people spent a lot of time and money to make our veterans feel loved on Valentine's Day.

So, thank you, dear readers, for helping me bring so much pleasure to thousands of veterans. We must never forget that they fought for our freedom, and we owe them a debt that can never be repaid.

—ANN LANDERS

Did you know? ··········

▶ Amnesty International's Freedom Writers is a network of individuals who write letters on behalf of prisoners. Members of the Urgent Action Network send airmail letters and telegrams to assist individuals in immediate danger of torture and execution.

Creator's Syndicate

Since it was founded in 1961, Amnesty International has worked on behalf of more than 25,000 prisoners around the world. In 1988, 150 of the prisoners of conscience adopted by groups in the United States were released. Here are examples of how effective these letters are. A released prisoner of conscience from Paraguay says:

For years I was held in a tiny cell. My only human contact was with my torturers . . . My only company were the cockroaches and mice . . . On Christmas Eve the door to the cell opened and the guard tossed

HUMAN RIGHTS NOW!

THE UNIVERSAL DECLARATION OF HUMAN RIGHTS

1948–1988

YOUR PASSPORT TO HUMAN RIGHTS

IN 1948, GOVERNMENTS TOOK A HISTORIC FIRST STEP BY ADOPTING **THE UNIVERSAL DECLARATION OF HUMAN RIGHTS.**

TODAY, YOU CAN TAKE THE NEXT STEP. ADD YOUR NAME TO THE DECLARATION AND URGE THAT IT BE RESPECTED WORLDWIDE. SEND YOUR SIGNATURE TODAY.

THIS IS YOUR PASSPORT TO HUMAN RIGHTS.

SIGN IT!
READ IT!
KEEP IT!
RESPECT IT!

Amnesty International USA

in a crumpled piece of paper. It said, "Take heart. The world knows you're alive. We're with you. Regards, Monica, Amnesty International." That letter saved my life.

By helping the human rights movement you will not only benefit those deprived of basic rights, you will also be giving power to the movement as a whole.

HUMAN RIGHTS ORGANIZATIONS

Account For POW/MIAs
280 Wheatley Road
Old Westbury, NY 11568
516-626-0800

The Africa Fund
198 Broadway
New York, NY 10038
212-962-1210

Americas Watch
(see Human Rights Watch)

American Civil Liberties Union
132 W. 43rd St.
New York, NY 10036
212-944-9800

ACLU National Gay Rights Project
6333 S. Shatto St., Suite 207
Los Angeles, CA 90048
213-487-1720

American Friends Service Committee
1501 Cherry St.
Philadelphia, PA 19102
215-241-7000

American Indian Relief Council
(project of Famine Relief Fund)
P.O. Box 226
Warrenton, VA 22186-9852
703-347-0350

American Life League
P.O. Box 1350
Stafford, VA 22554
703-659-4171

American Veterans of WWII, Korea, and Vietnam (AMVETS)
4647 Forbes Blvd.
Lanham, MD 20706
301-459-9600

Americans for Democratic Action
815 15th St., Suite 711
Washington, DC 20005
202-638-6447

Americans United for Life
343 Dearborn St., Suite 1804
Chicago, IL 60604
312-786-9494

Amnesty International, USA
322 Eighth Ave.
New York, NY 10001
212-807-8400

Anti-Defamation League of B'nai B'rith
823 United Nations Plaza
New York, NY 10017
212-490-2525

Asia Watch
(see Human Rights Watch)

Center for Democratic Renewal
P.O. Box 50469
Atlanta, GA 30302
404-221-0025

Center for Population Options
1012 14th St., NW
Suite 1200
Washington, DC 20005
202-347-5700

Center for Third World Organizing
3861 M.L. King Jr. Way
Oakland, CA 94609
415-654-9601

The Center to Prevent Handgun Violence
1225 Eye St., NW, Suite 1100
Washington, DC 20005
202-289-7319

Christic Institute
1324 N. Capitol St., NW
Washington, DC 20002
202-797-8106

Citizens Committee for the Right to Keep and Bear Arms
12500 NE Tenth Pl.
Bellevue, WA 98005
206-454-4911

Clergy and Laity Concerned
198 Broadway
New York, NY 10038
212-964-6730

Concerned Women for America
370 L'Enfant Promenade, SW, Suite 800
Washington, DC 20024
202-488-7000

Commission for Racial Justice
700 Prospect Ave., 7th floor
Cleveland, OH 44115
216-736-2100

Congress of Racial Equality (CORE)
1457 Flatbush Ave.
Brooklyn, NY 11210
718-434-3580

Council on Interracial Books for Children
1842 Broadway, Room 500
New York, NY 10023
212-757-5339

Department of Veterans Affairs (DVA)
810 Vermont Ave., NW
Washington, DC 20420
202-233-4000

Disability Rights Center
2500 Q St., NW, Suite 121
Washington, DC 20007
202-337-4119

Disability Rights Education Fund
2212 Sixth St.
Berkeley, CA 94710
415-644-2555

Disabled American Veterans
3725 Alexandria Pike
Cold Spring, KY 41076
606-441-7300

Educational Fund to End Handgun Violence
Box 72
110 Maryland Ave., NE
Washington, DC 20002
202-544-7227

Equal Rights Advocates
1370 Mission St., 3rd floor
San Francisco, CA 94103
415-621-0505

Federally Employed Women (FEW)
National Press Building, Room 481
Washington, DC 20045
202-638-4404

Freedom House
48 East 21st St.
New York, NY 10010
212-473-9691

Fund for a Free South Africa (FreeSA)
729 Boylston St., 5th Floor
Boston, MA 02116
617-267-8333

Fund for Human Dignity
666 Broadway 4th floor
New York, NY 10012
212-529-1600
800-221-7044

Fund for the Feminist Majority
1600 Wilson Blvd., Suite 704
Washington, DC 22209
703-522-2214

Gay and Lesbian Advocates and Defenders
2 Park Square
Boston, MA 02116
617-426-2020

Gay & Lesbian Alliance Against Defamation (GLAAD)
99 Hudson St., 14th floor
New York, NY 10003
212-966-1700

Gay/Lesbian National Crisisline
212-807-6016
800-221-7044

Gay Rights Advocates
540 Castro St.
San Francisco, CA 94114
415-863-3622

Gay Rights National Lobby
P.O. Box 1892
Washington, DC 20013
202-546-1801

Green Committees of Correspondence National Clearinghouse
145 Ninth St.
San Francisco, CA 94103
415-864-8555

Gray Panthers Project Fund
311 S. Juniper St., Suite 601
Philadelphia, PA 19107
215-545-6555

Hadassah: Women's Zionist Organization of America
50 W. 58th St.
New York, NY 10019
212-355-7900

Handgun Control, Inc.
1225 I St., NW, Suite 1100
Washington, DC 20005
202-898-0792

Human Rights Internet
Harvard Law School
Cambridge, MA 02138
617-495-9924

Human Rights Watch
1522 K St., NW, Suite 910
Washington, DC 20005
202-371-6592

Institute for Policy Studies/Transnational Institution (IPS)
1601 Connecticut St., NW
Washington, DC 20009
202-234-9382

International League for Human Rights
432 Park Ave. South
New York, NY 10016
212-684-1221

Japanese American Citizens League
1765 Sutter St.

San Francisco, CA 94115
415-921-5225

Jewish War Veterans of the USA (JWV)
1811 R St., NW
Washington, DC 20009
202-265-6280

June 4th Foundation
1300 19th St., NW,
Suite 350
Washington, DC 20036

Lambda Legal Defenses & Education Fund
132 W. 43rd St.
New York, NY 10036
212-944-9488

Lawyers' Committee for Civil Rights Under Law
1400 I St., NW, Suite 400
Washington, DC 20005
202-371-1212

Lawyers Committee for Human Rights
330 Seventh Ave.,
10th floor North
New York, NY 10001
212-629-6170

Leadership Conference on Civil Rights
2027 Massachusetts Ave., NW
Washington, DC 20036
202-667-1780

The League of Women Voters USA
1730 M St., NW
Washington, DC 20036
202-429-1965

LULAC—League of United Latin American Citizens
900 E. Karen St., Suite C215
Las Vegas, NV 89109
702-737-1240

Lesbian Mothers National Defense Fund
2446 Lorentz Pl., N.
Seattle, WA 98109
206-282-5798
206-284-2290

Martin Luther King Jr. Center for Nonviolent Social Change
449 Auburn Ave., NE
Atlanta, GA 30312
404-524-1956

Mexican American Legal Defense and Education Fund (MALDEF)
182 2nd St., 2nd floor
San Francisco, CA 94105
415-543-5598

National Abortion Rights Action League (NARAL)
1101 14th St., NW, 5th floor
Washington, DC 20005
202-408-4600

National Association for the Advancement of Colored People (NAACP)
4805 Mt. Hope Drive
Baltimore, MD 21215
301-358-8900

NAACP League Defense and Education Fund
99 Hudson St.
New York, NY 10013
212-219-1900

National Abortion Federation (NAF)
1436 U St., NW, Suite 103
Washington, DC 20009
202-667-5881

National Alliance Against Racist and Political Repression
11 John St., Room 702
New York, NY 10038
212-406-3330

National Association of Concerned Veterans (NACV)
c/o Jack Mordente
Veterans Office
501 Crescent St.
Southern Connecticut State University
New Haven, CT 06515
203-397-4329

National Center for Urban Ethnic Affairs (NCUEA)
Box 20 Cardinal Station
Washington, DC 20064
202-232-3600

National Coalition Against Censorship
Two West 64th St.
New York, NY 10023
212-724-1500

National Coalition of 100 Black Women, Inc.
50 Rockefeller Plaza
Concourse Level, Room 46
New York, NY
212-974-6140

National Coalition to Abolish the Death Penalty
1419 U St., NW
Washington, DC 20009
202-797-7090

National Coalition to Ban Handguns
100 Maryland Ave., NE
Washington, DC 20002
202-544-7190

National Coalition of Black Gays
P.O. Box 57236
West End Station
Washington, DC 20037
202-387-8096

National Commission of Working Women
Center for Women and Work
1211 Connecticut Ave., NW
Washington, DC 20036
202-737-5764

National Council of La Raza
810 First St., NE, 3rd floor
Washington, DC 20002
202-289-1380

National Council of Negro Women, Inc. (NCNW)
1211 Connecticut Ave., NW,
Suite 702
Washington, DC 20036
202-659-0006

National Educational Foundation for Individual Rights
c/o Lesbian Rights Project
1370 Mission St.
San Francisco, CA 94103
415-441-2629

National Federation of Parents & Friends of Gays
5715 16th St., NW
Washington, DC 20011
202-726-3223

National Gay and Lesbian Task Force
1517 U St., NW
Washington, DC 20009
202-332-6483

National Institute Against Prejudice and Violence
525 W. Redwood St.
Baltimore, MD 21201
301-328-5170

National Organization for Women (NOW)
1000 16th St., NW
Washington, DC 20036
202-331-0066

National Puerto Rican Coalition
1700 K St., NW, Suite 500
Washington, DC 20006
202-223-3915

National Rifle Association
1600 Rhode Island Ave., NW
Washington, DC 20036
202-828-6000

National Right to Life Committee
419 Seventh Ave., NW,
Suite 500
Washington, DC 20004
202-626-8800

National Urban League
500 E. 62nd St.
New York, NY 10021
212-310-9000

National Women's Political Caucus
1411 K St., NW, Suite 1110

Washington, DC 20005
202-347-4456

Native American Rights Fund
1506 Broadway
Boulder, CO 80302
303-447-8760

Operation Rescue
P.O. Box 1180
Binghamton, NY 13902
607-723-4012

Paralyzed Veterans of America (PVA)
801 18th St., NW
Washington, DC 20006
202-872-1300

People for the American Way
2000 M St, NW, Suite 400
Washington, DC 20036
202-467-4999

Physicians for Choice
c/o Planned Parenthood
810 Seventh Ave.
New York, NY 10019
212-541-7800

Planned Parenthood Federation
810 Seventh Ave.
New York, NY 10019
212-785-3351

Pro-Life Action League
6160 N. Cicero, #210
Chicago, IL 60646
312-777-2900

Regular Veterans Association of the U.S. (RVA)
RVA Bldg. 219
2470 Cardinal Loop
Del Valle, TX 78617
512-389-2288

Religious Coalition for Abortion Rights
100 Maryland Ave. NE,
Suite 307
Washington, DC 20002
202-543-7032

Second Amendment Foundation
James Madison Bldg.
12500 NE Tenth Pl.
Bellevue, WA 98005
206-454-7012

Seventh Generation Fund for Indian Development
P.O. Box 10
Forestville, CA 95436

Simon Wisenthal Center
9760 W. Pico Blvd.
Los Angeles, CA 90035
213-553-9036

South Africa Foundation
1225 19th St., NW, Suite 700
Washington, DC 20036
202-223-5486

South Africa Project
c/o Lawyers' Committee for
Civil Rights Under Law
1400 I St., NW, Suite 400
Washington, DC 20005
202-371-1212

South Africa Support Project
P.O. Box 50103
Washington, DC 20004
202-332-2009

Southern Christian Leadership Conference
334 Auburn Ave., NE
Atlanta, GA 30303
404-522-1420

Southern Poverty Law Center
400 Washington Ave.

Montgomery, AL 96104
205-264-0286

TransAfrica
545 8th St., SE, #200
Washington, DC 20003
202-547-2550

United Jewish Appeal
99 Park Avenue
New York, NY 10016
212-818-9100

United Jewish Appeal Federation
130 E. 59th St.
New York, NY 10022
212-980-1000

United Jewish Fund
6505 Wilshire Blvd.
Los Angeles, CA 90048
800-553-9474, Ext. 4050

United Negro College Fund
500 E. 62nd St.
New York, NY 10021
212-326-1118

U.S. Corporate Council on South Africa
c/o Mobil Oil Corporation
150 E 42nd St.,
Room 19W901
New York, NY 10017

Veterans of Foreign Wars (VFW)
VFW Bldg.
Kansas City, MO 64111
816-756-3390

Veterans of the Vietnam War

2090 Bald Mtn. Rd.
Wilkes-Barre, PA 18702
717-825-7215

Vietnam Veterans of America
1224 M St., NW
Washington, DC 20005
202-628-2700

Vietnam Veterans Foundation of America
2001 S St., NW, Suite 740
Washington, DC 20009
202-483-9222

Vietnam Women's Memorial Project
202-328-7253

Washington Office on South Africa
110 Maryland Ave., NW,
Suite 112
Washington, DC 20002
202-546-7961

Women's Action Alliance
370 Lexington Ave., Room 601
New York, NY 10017
212-532-8330

Women's Equity Action League (WEAL)
805 15th St., NW, Suite 822
Washington, DC 20005
202-638-1961

Women's Legal Defense Fund
2000 P St., NW
Washington, DC 20036
202-887-0364

HEALTH

• • •

The volunteers and the scientists are in partnership—like a family relationship. And that's what characterizes this remarkable family of people who have come together to improve human life and make this a better world in which to live.

• • •

—JONAS SALK, on the March of Dimes

Today's Critical Health Issues

Virtually everyone in this country is in some way affected by the health-care issue. The health industry employs millions of workers, from nurses and doctors to scientists. The health insurance industry spends billions of dollars every year on the care and treatment of our citizens. Each year businesses lose billions of dollars worth of productivity from absent or ineffective workers who become sick or disabled.

As a result of the far-reaching capabilities of the health-care industry and the wonders of high technology, people are living longer and more healthy lives. Modern surgical techniques, the increased focus on diet and fitness, and a wide array of drugs and other remedies have helped raise life expectancy by many years. And an emphasis on a healthy lifestyle has helped many to raise people's consciousness.

Nonetheless, just as certain lifestyles help prevent health problems, others cause them. Alcohol and drug abuse ruin the lives of millions of people and cost taxpayers billions of dollars. Unhealthy diets help make heart disease the leading killer of Americans. Smoking has led to a 161 percent increase in lung cancer among men, and 396 percent for women, from the mid-1950s to the mid-1980s. And many other health problems may not be directly caused by the actions of individuals, but their symptoms are aggravated by unhealthy pursuits.

Many charitable organizations have been created in response to the urgent need for treatment and cures of the significant health problems facing society today. These groups provide invaluable services for those who are afflicted with certain illnesses by helping them live as normally as possible. They promote better lifestyles to prevent greater problems in the future. And they spend incredible amounts of resources in trying to find cures.

These groups need the support of the public to fund and

carry out their activities. Pledging money to the *Jerry Lewis Telethon for Muscular Dystrophy,* adding your name to a bone marrow donor list, and buying groceries for an AIDS sufferer are just a few of the countless ways you can help.

This section should give you an even greater appreciation of the efforts of the millions of people who dedicate themselves to making us healthier, and you may be inspired to find a way to become involved as well.

ALCOHOL AND DRUG ABUSE
∎ ∎ ∎

A PERVASIVE PROBLEM
Most people will agree that drug and alcohol abuse stand high on the list of problems facing our society today.

And although the number of illicit drug users among young adults in the United States has declined in the past few years, it is still the highest percentage in the industrialized world.

IMPACT ON SOCIETY
Substance abuse affects society in a myriad of ways. Those with drug and alcohol dependencies experience problems in many aspects of their lives, including health, jobs, education, and personal relationships. Deaths and injuries from alcohol and/or drug abuse are alarmingly high.

Chances are that even those without an alcohol or drug problem will be affected in one way or another by a substance abuser. The National Council on Alcoholism finds that about 2 out of every 5 people in the United States will be in an alcohol-related highway crash in their lifetime. And if you are lucky enough to escape injury on the road you still may become a victim of an alcohol- or drug-related crime.

SUBSTANCE ABUSE AND CRIME
The number of alcohol- and drug-related crimes have dramatically increased in the past decade.

Although total use of drugs is on the decline, those who are still using drugs use them in greater quantities.

Did you know? ∙∙∙∙∙∙∙∙∙∙∙

► In 1985, about 10 percent of the U.S. population, or 18 million adults (18 or older) had alcohol problems.

► A National Council on Alcoholism report finds that approximately one out of four American homes has been affected by an alcohol-related problem.

► A 1985 study found that at least 22 million persons had tried cocaine and approximately 18 million had used marijuana in the month before the survey was taken.

► In fact, 15 to 18 percent of the population will exhibit a dependence problem with alcohol or other drugs at some time during their life.

From *The Fact is . . .* Office of Substance Abuse Prevention, October 1988; The National Council on Alcoholism, Inc.

▶ The National Center for Statistics and Analysis reports that traffic crashes are the single greatest cause of death for every age between the ages of 5 and 32. Almost half of these fatalities are a result of alcohol-related crashes.

▶ According to the General Estimates System, in 1989 approximately 345,000 people suffered injuries in car crashes that police reported had alcohol present—that averages to one person every one and a half minutes!

▶ The National Institute of Alcohol and Alcohol Abuse estimates that alcohol is directly or indirectly attributable for almost 1 out of every 20 deaths in the United States.

▶ In 1989 one person died on average every 23 minutes in a car crash that involved alcohol, according to the National Highway Traffic Safety Administration.

AFFECTING THE INNOCENT

The users of alcohol and other drugs are not the only ones affected. The families and friends of substance abusers suffer as well. The 7 million children of alcoholics in this country experience stressful lives, often accompanied by abuse and neglect. According to the National Committee to Prevent Child Abuse 1 out of every 13 children with a substance-abusing parent is seriously abused each year. These negative experiences often lead them to alcohol and drugs and the problems that accompany substance abuse.

The rise in the number of babies born addicted to drugs is also highly disturbing. According to the National Association for Perinatal Addiction Research and Education, each year an estimated 375,000 newborn infants are exposed to drugs in the womb.

A fetus exposed to cocaine and other drugs may be born with medical and behavioral problems. One report cites crack cocaine addiction and inadequate prenatal care as the two main reasons why more babies are born at weights less than 5.5 pounds and are chemically dependent.

Children born with these problems are often abandoned because their addicted mothers cannot care for them, placing a great burden on the adoption and foster-care system. Often the drugs impair their motor and mental skills and cause abnormal behavior, making it more difficult for these children to be placed.

THE COSTS

The abuse of drugs and alcohol takes a huge economic toll on the United States. Each year the costs of treatment and other medical claims, accidents, thefts, and lost productivity add up to a staggering amount and place a tremendous strain on businesses and the government.

As alcohol- and drug-related problems continue, businesses and the government will be burdened with having to pay for the high costs associated with the dilemma.

WHAT CAN I DO?
··

▶ **Parents must be educated and informed!** Parents must learn about alcohol and drugs so they can detect problems with their children. The Get Involved Before Your Kids Do program in Apelton, WI, received a Daily Point of Light award for their work in parental education.

GET INVOLVED BEFORE YOUR KIDS DO

Appleton, WI
DAILY POINT OF LIGHT RECIPIENT: JANUARY 24, 1990

"Get Involved Before Your Kids Do," developed by Aid Association for Lutherans, recognizes that parents are the first and best protection against teenage substance abuse.

This initiative is composed of "Get Involved" workshops and community outreach events. The workshops encourage parents to talk with their children about alcohol and drugs, set family rules, assess their own behavior with respect to alcohol and drugs, and "network" with other parents. Community events include alcohol-free parties for high school students, sponsoring speakers, and funding local Students Against Driving Drunk projects.

Reprinted with permission from the White House Office of National Service.

Contact one of the many organizations listed on pages 333–335 and tell them you want to become better informed. Or contact your local school administrators or local authorities and ask them about programs designed to educate parents about drug and alcohol abuse in your area.

▶ **Start educating your children about substance abuse at an early age.** Parents must learn about drug and alcohol abuse and discuss it with their children. The National Institute on Drug Abuse claims that parents are the best protection against drug abuse. Alcohol and drug abuse prevention means helping your children build a resistance to abusing drugs so that they never begin. It means stopping drug abuse before it starts.

▶ Contact the National Clearinghouse for Alcohol and Drug Information for their flier, *Parents: What You Can Do About Alcohol and Drug Abuse.*

▶ **Know the signals.** Parents should learn to detect the possible early warning signs that may indicate their child is involved with drugs or alcohol. Such behavior includes:

   ▶ An abrupt change in mood or attitude.
   ▶ A sudden decline in attendance or performance at work or school.
   ▶ Associating with a new group of friends, especially with those who use drugs.

Did you know? ----------

▶ In 1989, the National Institute on Drug Abuse reported record increases in the numbers of hospitals treating emergency drug cases.

▶ The Drug Abuse Warning Network found that there were more than 46,000 cocaine-related medical emergencies in 1989—five times the number reported in 1984. Medical emergencies involving crack increased 28 times during that time period, to over 15,000 cases in 1989.

Did you know? ----------

▶ An FBI crime report finds that arrests of youths age 16 or under for dealing in cocaine and heroin has risen from 1 in 50 in 1984 to 1 in 5 in 1989.

▶ A government study finds that alcohol abuse is involved in 60 percent of murders, 30 percent of suicides, more than 70 percent of assaults, 50 percent of rapes, and up to 40 percent of child abuse fatalities.

The chance that your kid will die in a [drinking and driving] accident is small, but when it happens to your kid, it's 100 percent.

—TRISHA ROTH, Antialcohol activist

To learn more about detecting substance abuse contact PRIDE or another organization listed at the end of this section.

DRUG AND ALCOHOL INFORMATION FOR PARENTS

▶ **Seek Help.** If you have a problem with drugs and alcohol, seek professional help. If you are a child or an adult who is

DRUG	PHYSICAL APPEARANCE	RELATED PARAPHERNALIA	SIGNS AND SYMPTOMS OF USE	PHYSICAL EFFECTS
Tobacco	Dried Leaves		Smokey smell	Possible lung cancer, heart disease
Alcohol	Clear or amber color	Flask, bottles, cans	Slurred speech; staggering; nausea; clammy, cold skin; low body temperature	Liver, kidney, cardiovascular and digestive tract damage
Marijuana	Oregano	Rolling papers; pipes; baggies; clips	Slowed reactions; tired look; red eyes; cough; sore throat; changes in eating habits; decreased attention span	Brain and reproductive system damage
Cocaine	Artificial sweetner	Razor blade; straws; glassy surfaces	High strung; changes in eating habits; dilated pupils; sweat; euphoria; anxiety	Deviated septum; psychosis; depression; oily skin; respiratory problems
Crack	Pieces of broken chalk	Pipe; glass vials; colored stoppers; small screens	Nausea, weight loss; anxiety, paranoia; black phlegm	Lung damage; psychosis; depression; oily skin; respiratory problems
Diet Pills	Capsules or tablets		Up, active; alert	Irritable, restless; psychosis; depression
Amphetamines	Capsules or tablets		Hyperactive; dilated pupils, loss of appetite; compulsive behavior; headaches; talkativeness	Psychotic symptoms; malnutrition; skin disorders; depression
Barbiturates	Capsules or tablets		Relaxed, slurred speech; impaired coordination; distorted vision; low blood pressure	Liver damage
Heroin	White or brown powder	Syringe; spoon; lighter; needles; medicine dropper	Scars along veins; decreased coordination; flushing; watery eyes; itch; constricted pupils	Loss of skin color; lethargy; mental deterioration
LSD		Blotter papers; window panes	Disorientation; attention deficits; nausea; goose bumps; clammy hands; chills; recklessness	Panic; depression, psychosis
PCP	White Powder	Tin foil	Increased physical strength; dizziness; involuntary eye movement; paranoia	Memory and speech difficulties, unusual and audial hallucinations
Ecstasy (MDMA)	Pill or powder		Euphoria; nausea; confusion; profuse sweating; high blood pressure	Psychosis; brain damage
Inhalants	Liquid or a gas	Cleaning rags; empty spray cans; tubes of glue	Bad breath; uncoordination; changes in eating habits; flushed; headaches; red eyes; nausea	Liver, kidney; brain and nervous system damage

PRIDE Parent Primer c/o PRIDE, 50 Hurt Plaza, Suite 210, Atlanta, GA 30303

affected by someone else's drug or alcohol problem, contact a local support group.

▶ **Get involved in your local school and community programs.**

  ▶ According to *USA Today,* nationwide 99 percent of all high schools and 87 percent of elementary schools offer antidrug classes.

  ▶ Community-based antidrug watch groups are being formed across the nation. For instance, MAD DADS (Men Against Destruction/Defending Against Drugs and Social Disorder) has about 450 chapters. Groups such as MAD DADS sponsor community block parties, patrol and clean up their neighborhoods, and help with drug treatment, job training, and "surrogate" dad programs.

▶ **Volunteer your time, energy, and money.** Organizations that work to combat alcohol and other drug problems offer direct services, publish information, and lobby for effective legislation. There are numerous ways to get involved. Contact any such organization and ask what you can do.

Did you know? ....

▶ A 1989 Gallup poll commissioned by the Institute for a Drug-Free Workplace found that 1 in 3 workers had knowledge of a co-worker using illegal drugs before or after work.

▶ According to the Employee Assistance Professionals Association, substance abusers are late to work three times more often than the average employee and are 16 times more likely to be absent from work.

Organizations and Resources

ALCOHOL & DRUGS

ACTION
202-634-9108
VISTA volunteers of the ACTION program help low-income families by addressing problems such as the abuse of drugs and alcohol. Consult the section on Volunteerism for more information.

National Clearinghouse for Alcohol and Drug Information (NCADI)
301-468-2600
The Federal Resource for alcohol and drug information; it is sponsored by the Office for Substance Abuse Prevention of the U.S. Department of Health and Human Services. NCADI

works with and through Regional Alcohol and Drug Awareness Resource (RADAR) Network Centers located in almost every state. It offers numerous publications and services concerning AIDS and alcohol and drug addiction, such as *Drug Use in America: What You Can Do About It,* and it distributes research from organizations such as the National Institute for Drug Abuse (NIDA) and the Office for Substance Abuse Prevention (OSAP)

Office for Substance Abuse Prevention (OSAP)

Created by the Anti-Drug Abuse Act of 1986 to lead the federal government's efforts to reduce the demand for illicit drugs and prevent alcohol and other drug problems in the United States. Information about OSAP and OSAP publications may be obtained through the National Clearinghouse for Alcohol and Drug Information. Ask for a copy of *What You Can Do About Drug Use in America.*

ALCOHOL

Alcoholics Anonymous (AA)

(Call your local chapter) AA and Narcotics Anonymous are 12-step chapters for those seeking to end their dependence on alcohol and other drugs. There are chapters in almost every city; phone numbers are usually listed under "Alcohol" in the white and *Yellow Pages,* or contact NCA.

Al-Anon/Alateen

212-302-7240.
Al-Anon offers support for adults affected by someone else's drinking. Alateen offers support for adolescents. Phone numbers are listed under "alcohol" in the white and *Yellow Pages,* or contact NCA.

American Council on Alcoholism (ACA)

301-931-9393
An association that promotes the importance of proper education to prevent alcoholism.

Children of Alcoholics Foundation, Inc.

212-754-0656
An organization created to assist children of alcoholic parents.

Mothers Against Drunk Driving (MADD)

MADD mobilizes victims and their allies to establish the public conviction that impaired driving is unacceptable and criminal, in order to promote corresponding public policies, programs, and personal accountability. MADD's youth education programs and safe driving programs such as New Years, K.I.S.S. (Keep It a Safe Summer) have helped to educate the public about the dangers of drinking and driving.

National Association of Addiction Treatment Providers, Inc.

714-837-3038
Represents 450 nonprofit and profit-making alcohol treatment centers across the country.

National Association for Children of Alcoholics (NACoA)

714-499-3889
Offers support for children of alcoholics.

National Council on Alcoholism (NCA)

800-CALL-NCA
(also the National Council on Alcoholism and Drug Dependence Inc.—NCADD) NCA is the national nonprofit organization dedicated to combating alcoholism, other drug addictions, and related problems. Founded in 1944, NCA's major programs include prevention and education, public information, medical-scientific information, public

policy advocacy, conferences, and publications. NCA sponsors the National Alcohol Awareness Month in April and the National Fetal Alcohol Syndrome (FAS) Awareness Week. NCA also conducts the National Alcoholism Forum, the nation's first general-interest conference on alcoholism.

National Institute on Alcohol Abuse and Alcoholism (NIAAA)

800-729-6686/in M.D. 301-468-2600
An agency of the U.S. Department of Health and Human Services, NIAAA publishes research about alcoholism, including *Alcohol Health and Research World,* a quarterly magazine.

DRUGS

Drug Abuse Resistance Education (D.A.R.E.)

800-223-DARE (offers information about starting or joining a local DARE chapter or to donate money); 800-TALK-KFC (a recorded message about DARE and how to get involved). Their in-school drug education program provides information about drug abuse for parents and children and offers ways to get involved in fighting drug abuse.

Families Anonymous

818-989-7841/800-736-9805
A support group for the families and friends of people who have problems with drug abuse.

Narcotics Anonymous

Call your local chapter or call 818-780-3951
Modeled after Alcohol Anonymous, Narcotics Anonymous is a national

support group for those with drug-abuse problems.

National Institute on Drug Abuse (NIDA)
800-729-6886/in M.D. 301-468-2600 or 301-443-6500
Established in 1974, the Institute has 240 full-time employees and an annual budget of approximately $150 million in fiscal 1987. NIDA's role in the Anti-Drug Abuse Act of 1986 is to develop more effective ways of preventing and treating drug abuse. Information about NIDA and NIDA publications may be obtained through the National Clearinghouse for Alcohol and Drug Information.

National Parents' Resource Institute for Drug Education (PRIDE)
800-67-PRIDE
A private, nonprofit organization whose goal is to stem the epidemic of drug use, especially among adolescents and young adults, by dissemination of accurate health information, as well as the formation of parent and youth networks. Ask for publications such as *Drugs of Abuse Digest: A Prevention Guide for the Family, School, and Workplace.*

Phoenix House
212-595-5810
This is now the nation's largest, private nonprofit drug abuse services agency, Phoenix has both residential and outpatient treatment units for adults and adolescents.

OTHER COMMITTED ORGANIZATIONS

American Council for Drug Education
301-294-0600

Drug Abuse Information and Referral Line
800-662-HELP

Just Say No Foundation
800-258-2766

National Cocaine Hotline
800-262-2463/800-COCAINE

National Federations of Parents for Drug-Free Youth
314-968-1322

National Institute on Drug Abuse Helpline
800-843-4971

National Prevention Network
202-783-6868

National Safety Council
312-527-4800

Toughlove
215-348-7090

Women for Sobriety
215-536-8026

AIDS

■ ■ ■

WHAT IS AIDS?

Acquired Immune Deficiency Syndrome (AIDS) impairs the body's normal ability to resist serious diseases and infections. The disease is caused by a virus—the human immunodeficiency virus (HIV)—that is spread through the exchange of bodily fluids during intimate contact or exposure to the blood of an infected person, such as through the sharing of contaminated syringes.

A person infected with the HIV may or may not develop AIDS after a period of years. If AIDS is developed, the virus will attack that person's immune system and diminish his or her ability to fight other diseases, such as pneumonia, meningitis, and cancer.

At present, there is no known cure for AIDS; however,

For the rest of history, people will look back on how we respond to the AIDS epidemic today.

—PAUL MONETTE, author of *Borrowed Time: An AIDS Memoir* (nominated for the 1988 National Book Critics' Circle Award)

some drugs have been developed that slow or impede the disease's progress, allowing an infected person a chance to live a longer and healthier life.

WHO GETS AIDS?

Anyone can get AIDS. Although in the early 1980s a majority of the reported AIDS cases resulted from high-risk sex between homosexual men, the disease now increasingly affects drug users and heterosexual men and women.

At the Fifth International Conference on AIDS in Montreal, scientists reported that the epidemic is shifting away from gay men to intravenous drug users, their sexual partners, and their children. IV drug users now account for 27 percent of the AIDS cases in the United States.

And although in the United States the female-to-male ratio of victims is 1 to 13, in Africa it is one-to-one, suggesting greater risk to men and women heterosexuals. A 1989 Gallup poll suggests that 6 million young, single women risk contracting AIDS because of unsafe sexual behavior.

AIDS COUNT

Counting the number of people worldwide with AIDS is not an exact science. Many countries do not have the facilities to accurately test and count those people with the disease. Moreover, many people who are infected with the HIV virus do not yet show symptoms of the disease. Organizations therefore make conflicting estimates.

THE HIGH COSTS OF AIDS

According to the American Foundation for AIDS Research, in 1991 the United States will spend up to $13 billion in direct medical care for AIDS patients—and will have lost more than $55.6 billion in productivity.

These numbers will be dwarfed by the amount of money that will have to be spent on future AIDS cases. In the United States alone,

⭐ ⭐ **THE STARS ARE SHINING!** ⭐ ⭐

MADONNA ASKS, "PLEASE JOIN ME AND MY FRIENDS."

In an advertisement in *Daily Variety* the singer showed her support for a benefit to raise money for Hollywood Helps, a group that gives financial support to entertainment people with AIDS.

Other celeb's involved include Liz Taylor, Gene Hackman, Jack Nicholson, and Arnold Schwarzenneger.

some estimate that 1.5 million people have been infected by the virus but have not yet contracted AIDS.

THE CHALLENGE AHEAD

The worldwide AIDS epidemic represents such an immense challenge that it requires concerted effort from all sectors of society. According to Dr. Jonathan Mann, "The gap between the pace of the epidemic and the prevention and control efforts is threatening to widen. Even though we can say today for the first time that activities against AIDS are now under way in every country in the world, we are locked in a race for control of an epidemic as fatal as any the world has ever known."*

Although government spending on AIDS research and education has increased, even more is needed. In 1989 the U.S. government spent $1.3 billion for AIDS research. The developing world, however, has less to spend and therefore has the potential for a much bigger problem. There are 5 million intravenous drug users in the world, and 100 million persons who contract sexually transmitted diseases each year. Many of the lesser developed countries do not have enough money to feed their citizens, let alone protect them from AIDS. According to Dr. Mann, "the combined AIDS expenditures for CA and NY exceed the resources currently available for AIDS in the entire developing world."

Did you know? ············

AIDS currently kills one American every 30 minutes.

*Editorial, "Warning Flags on AIDS," *Los Angeles Times*, 11 November 1989.

WHAT CAN I DO?
●●●

Reprinted with permission from the White House Office of National Service.

▶ Contact your local AIDS support organization and ask how you can get involved. People with AIDS often have to battle more than their disease. Often, they lose their jobs and insurance benefits, and have trouble obtaining medical, social, and even spiritual services.

✪ PHILLIP A. WILEY ✪
Broken Arrow, OK
DAILY POINT OF LIGHT RECIPIENT: MAY 5, 1990

Mr. Wiley has devoted his life to helping others like himself who carry the HIV virus or are AIDS patients.

For more than three years, he has provided emotional support to patients and their families, and has assisted with transportation to medical appointments, meal preparation, and shopping. He receives referrals from local families, and contacts the individuals by telephone to obtain their permission to establish person-to-person contact.

Did you know?

Jonathan Mann, director of the WHO program on AIDS, predicts that the 1990s will bring 10 to 20 million new cases of HIV infection and 5.4 million new AIDS cases throughout the world.

FACT: SO FAR, THERE IS NO VACCINE FOR HIV OR A CURE FOR AIDS.

Some medicines have prolonged the lives of people with AIDS. But no cure or vaccine is in sight.

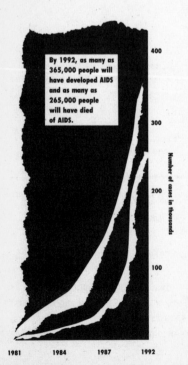

By 1992, as many as 365,000 people will have developed AIDS and as many as 265,000 people will have died of AIDS.

Number of cases in thousands

400

300

200

100

1981   1984   1987   1992

Courtesy of The American Red Cross

Many organizations help those with AIDS adjust to a different and difficult life ahead. For example:

▶ AIDS Project Los Angeles is the area's largest and most comprehensive provider of care and services to people with AIDS and AIDS-related illnesses. They find lawyers, doctors, and ministers, and provide food, counseling and even housing. Approximately 1,500 volunteers and staff members help more than 2,000 neighbors with AIDS. The Buddy Program provides priceless social, practical, and emotional support on a one-to-one basis. The Necessities of Life Food Program provides groceries on a weekly basis for those in need.

▶ The life-affirming AIDS ACTION programs of the Gay and Lesbian Community Services Center in Los Angeles concentrate on prediagnostic services to slow the HIV virus and provide effective outreach to high-risk people, trying to prevent them from getting the virus.

▶ Look for organizations such as APLA and AIDS AC-

ORDINARY PEOPLE—EXTRAORDINARY ACTIONS

RYAN WHITE: A TRUE AMERICAN HERO

In 1984, Ryan White was a normal teenage boy attending the seventh grade in Kokomo, Indiana. Although he had hemophilia, he acted much the same as other teens in his class. Life for Ryan changed, however, when he contracted AIDS from a clotting agent used to treat his hemophilia.

After a stay in the hospital, Ryan was eager to return to his school. It turned out, sadly, that his school was not eager to reaccept Ryan. Fearful of the welfare of other students, the school superintendent and some of the students' parents tried to block Ryan from coming back.

After lawsuits and much national publicity, it was determined that Ryan could return. However, Ryan and his family decided to move to Cicero, Indiana, where they were welcomed with open arms.

The ignorance and the fear from the Kokomo situation led Ryan to speak out about AIDS even while he was battling for his own life. He became a national spokesman for AIDS—meeting members of Congress, acting as a fundraiser and talking to schoolchildren across the country. A 1989 TV movie, *The Ryan White Story*, was made about his life. With all the attention Ryan met and touched a lot of people, even befriending celebrities such as Olympic swimmer Greg Louganis and singer Michael Jackson.

Although Ryan died in 1990 at the age of 18, he will not be remembered only as a boy who died of AIDS. Instead, what remains in our memory is a story of courage, about a young man who taught the country about compassion and who showed a nation how to live.

TION programs in your community. The care of AIDS patients is complex and always undermanned so there are many ways you can help.

APLA'S NECESSITIES OF LIFE PROGRAM

Stan faltered slightly as he stepped into the large, warehouse-like room. Never before in his life had he felt so helpless. He was short of breath; his pulse was racing; even his legs were weak this morning.

And then, a smiling face appeared—seemingly out of nowhere. As she sat him down in a chair his trepidation began to subside. Gently, she helped him fill out the forms. Soon, four bulging grocery bags were carried to his car.

Courtesy of AIDS Project Los Angeles, 213-962-1600.

▶ **Some other ways to volunteer include:**
   ▶ Answer AIDS hot lines and help teach others about HIV and AIDS.
   ▶ Help people with AIDS by shopping for them or bringing meals to their homes.
   ▶ Help raise funds to fight this epidemic.
   ▶ Sponsor a blood drive or donate blood. Blood donations from health volunteers help save lives.
   ▶ Work with AIDS advocacy groups to help bring about better AIDS legislation.
   ▶ For an excellent book about AIDS volunteerism, read *Simple Acts of Kindness: Volunteering in the Age of AIDS.* Contact the Publications Department, United Hospital Fund, 55 Fifth Ave., New York, NY 10003 ($5.00 each plus $2.50 postage and handling).

Did you know? ▪▪▪▪▪▪▪▪▪▪

▶ The Centers for Disease Control reports that by November 30, 1989, 115,158 cases and 68,441 deaths in the United States have been documented (the total number of cases is more than double the 1987 figure).

▶ By 1992, the Public Health Service forecasts that 365,000 Americans will have been diagnosed with AIDS, and that 263,000 of those people will have died.

We Hold. We Hug. We Cry.

What I fear most is that these babies will not be touched and loved.

Illustrations by Don Herron from *Simple Acts of Kindness: Volunteering in the Age of AIDS.*

❖ RUTH BRINKER ❖

San Francisco, CA
Daily Point of Light Recipient: June 11, 1990

Ms. Brinker, 69, has dedicated her life to making the lives of those with AIDS more comfortable.

In 1985, she founded Project Open Hand. Each morning she would purchase vegetables, cook them in a church kitchen, and deliver the meals to seven clients. Today, Project Open Hand operates seven days a week, 365 days a year, delivering a hot evening meal and the next day's bag lunch to individuals who have grown too weak and impoverished to provide for themselves. More than 900 volunteers help Ms. Brinker prepare fresh meals and deliver them to over 1,000 individuals each day.

Reprinted with permission from the White House Office of National Service.

▶ **Learn more about AIDS education and help fund AIDS research.** Dr. Joel Weisman, chairman of the American Foundation for AIDS Research, explains the importance of education and research: "When all is said and done, two things—only two things—will put an end to the epidemic: research and education. Research to find treatments and a vaccine. Education to stop the spread of the disease until a vaccine is found."

AIDS education should start at an early age. According to C. Everett Koop, former Surgeon General of the United States, "Education about AIDS should start in early elementary school and at home so that children can grow up knowing the behavior to avoid to protect themselves from exposure to the AIDS virus."

Organizations and Resources

Drug Abuse Treatment Information and Referral Line—National Institute on Drug Abuse
800-662-HELP

National AIDS Hotline
800-342-AIDS/800-342-2437
800-344-7432/800-344-SIDA
(Spanish speaking)
800-243-7889/800-AIDSTTY
(for hearing impaired)
Contracted by the Centers for Disease Control, and administered by the American

Social Health Association, the hotline personnel answer general questions about AIDS, provide free literature, and refer individuals to AIDS support groups in local areas. Also gives a hotline number for each state.

National AIDS Information Clearinghouse (NAIC)
800-458-5231
Initiated in October 1987, by the U.S. Public Health Service,

Centers for Disease Control (CDC), as part of its national information and education plan in response to the public health threat posed by AIDS. NAIC is a centralized resource providing accurate and current information on AIDS programs and services. Ask for their many publications including the *AIDS and Deafness Resource Directory* and the *CDC Plan for HIV Prevention: A Blueprint for the '90s* (free).

National Sexually Transmitted Diseases Hotline—American Social Health Association
800-227-8922

Public Health Service Information Line
800-TRIALS-A (for help finding different drugs)

OTHER COMMITTED ORGANIZATIONS

AIDS Action Council
202-293-2886

AIDS Coalition to Unleash Power (ACT UP)
212-533-8888

AIDS Project Los Angeles (APLA)
213-380-2000

American Association of Physicians for Human Rights
415-255-4547

American Medical Association
312-464-5000

American Foundation for AIDS Research (AMFAR)
213-857-5900

American Red Cross AIDS Education Office
(Contact your local Red Cross office)

American Social Health Association
800-342-2437

Citizens Commission on AIDS
212-925-5290

Gay Men's Health Crisis (GMHC)
212-807-6664/212-807-6655

The Gay and Lesbian Community Services Center/AIDS ACTION Programs
213-464-7400

Hispanic AIDS Forum c/o APRED
212-966-6336

National Association of People with AIDS
202-898-0414

National Gay and Lesbian Task Force
202-332-6483

Pediatric AIDS Foundation
213-395-9051/800-488-5000

San Francisco AIDS Foundation
415-864-5855

RESOURCE MATERIALS

AIDS School Health Education Subfile
A computerized subfile of the Combined Health Database, which contains information about AIDS programs, curricula, guidelines, policies, regulations, and other materials. 800-468-0908; BRS Information Technologies, 1200 Route 7, Latham, NY 12110.

American Foundation for AIDS Research
Publishes an AIDS directory that rates and reviews educational materials. *Learning AIDS* lists films, pamphlets, videos, and other educational data. R. R. Bowker, NY—distributor

How to Talk to Your Children about AIDS
Send self-addressed legal-size, stamped envelope to SIECUS (Sex Information and Education Council of the U.S.) SIECUS/NYU Brochure, 130 W. 42nd St., Suite 2500, NY, NY 10036 Attn: Publications (free).

AIDS and the Education of our Children
A guide for parents and teachers, U.S. Department of Education. For a free copy write Consumer Information Center, Dept. ED, Pueblo, CO 81009.

Educators' Guide to AIDS and other STD's
Stephen R. Sroka, 1987; Health Education Consultants, 1284 Manor Park, Lakewood, OH 44107 (216) 521-1766; $25.00

AIDS: What You Should Know
Linda Meeks and Philip Heit, 1987. Merrill Publishing Co, P.O. Box 508, Columbus, OH 43216 (800) 848-6205; Student's guide $3.95; Teacher's guide $6.00.

Instructional Outcomes for AIDS Education
1987 Office of Health Information, State Dept. of Education, 22 Hayes St., Providence, RI 02908; (401) 277-2651. (free)

Confronting AIDS: Directions for Public Health
Health Care and Research, 1986, National Academy Press Bookstore, 2101 Constitution Ave., NW, Washington, DC 20418; (202) 334-3313; $24.95

AIDS: Impact of the Schools
Roberta Weiner, 1986, Education Research Group, Capitol Publications, 1101 King St., Alexandria, VA 22314; (703) 683-4100; $45.50.

Bill: A Special Story
A video that provides a study of how employers and coworkers can provide support to employees with AIDS. Write the Council on Foundations, 1828 L St., NW, Washington,

DC 20036-5168; $35 for members/$50 for nonmembers.

Simple Acts of Kindness
Testimonials from volunteers

and how to get involved. Publications Program, United Hospital Fund, 55 Fifth Ave., NY, NY 10003; $5.00 + $2.50 shipping.

AIDS Prevention Guide: For Parents and Other Adults Concerned about Youth
National AIDS Information Clearinghouse; 800-458-5231

CANCER

■ ■ ■

...... Did you know?

▶ In 1991 about 1.1 million people will be diagnosed as having cancer and about 514,000 will die of the disease—that is one person every 63 seconds.

▶ Cancer causes one out of every five deaths in America. It is the second leading cause of death in this country, behind heart disease.

American Cancer Society

WHAT IS CANCER?

Cancer is a large group of diseases characterized by uncontrolled growth of abnormal cells. If the spread is not controlled or checked, it can result in death.

There are many different types of cancer that attack different areas of the body, requiring a range of different treatments. The major types of cancer are: lung, colon-rectum, breast, prostate, urinary (including bladder and kidney), uterus, oral, pancreas, leukemia, ovary, and skin.

Some types of cancer are more serious than others. However, many cancers can be cured if detected and treated promptly. Acute lymphocytic leukemia, a childhood disease that was often fatal, can be cured at least 50 percent of the time. Hodgkin's disease, if treated early, can be cured in almost 80 percent of all cases. In fact, about 40 percent of Americans diagnosed with cancer will be alive in five years because of early prevention and proper treatment.

WHAT CAUSES CANCER?

Causes of cancer vary. However, 30 percent of all cancers are directly related to the use of tobacco, either alone or in conjunction with excessive consumption of alcohol, according to the American Cancer Society. Also, it is believed that diet may be responsible for as much as 35 percent of all cancer deaths.

CANCER'S SEVEN WARNING SIGNALS

Change in bowel or bladder habits
A sore that does not heal
Unusual bleeding or discharge
Thickening or lump in breast or elsewhere
Indigestion or difficulty in swallowing
Obvious change in wart or mole
Nagging cough or hoarseness

WHAT CAN I DO?

•••

▶ **Donate money to research.** Organizations such as the American Cancer Society (ACR) and the American Institute for Cancer Research (AICR) grant funds for cancer research to help find a way to prevent, control, and cure cancer.

For instance, in fiscal 1990, ACS made grants totalling more than $80 million and as of 1991, ACS has invested more than 1.3 billion to cancer research. As of fiscal 1990, AICR helped stimulate basic research in diet and cancer at more than 99 universities, hospitals, and research centers located in 34 states and 3 foreign countries.

▶ **Contact a cancer prevention organization and ask how you can help.** Volunteers are needed to support education and research in cancer prevention, diagnosis, detection, and treatment.

▶ **Help victims of leukemia and other cancers. Have your blood tested for a bone marrow match.** A high percentage of certain types of cancer cases can be cured through a bone marrow transplant. The transplant is a simple procedure that does not harm the donor and may save the life of a recipient. See "Other Ways to Help" or contact the Life-Savers Foundation or the National Bone Marrow Donor Registry for more information.

Chanté Wouden. From "Candlelighters," Child Cancer Foundation Youth Newsletter, Summer 1989.

▶ **Learn more about cancer, including how to prevent and detect it.** The Institute for Cancer Research publishes a free booklet, *Get Fit, Trim Down,* which discusses diet and cancer. Memorize the American Cancer Society's seven warning signs of cancer.

Organizations and Resources

American Cancer Society (ACS)
800-ACS-2345
A voluntary organization dedicated to the control and eradication of cancer, ACS has programs of research, education, and service to the cancer patient. Ask about Cansurmount, a program that links people who have had cancer with cancer patients; and I Can Cope, an 8-week patient education program about living with cancer.

The American Institute for Cancer Research (AICR)
202-328-7744/800-843-8114
A nonprofit, tax-exempt organization whose primary purpose is to provide funding for research as it relates to cancer prevention and treatment.

Cancer Research Institute
800-99-CANCER
Helps fund medical scientists around the world.

Life-Savers Foundation
800-654-1247

Links potential bone marrow donors with leukemia patients who need a bone marrow transplant. For more information refer to the "Other Ways to Help" section.

National Cancer Institute
800-4-CANCER/800-538-6070 AL/202-636-5700 DC/808-524-1234 HI
An agency of the National Institutes of Health, the Institute funds research and publishes information intended for the general public, researchers, and professionals.

OTHER COMMITTED ORGANIZATIONS

American International Hospital Cancer Program
800-FOR-HELP

Association for Brain Tumor Research
312-286-5571

Association for the Care of Children's Health
202-244-1801

Cancer Care
212-302-2400

CAN HELP
206-437-2291

CITY OF HOPE
213-626-4611

Compassionate Friends
312-990-0010

Federation for Children with Special Needs
617-482-2915

Leukemia Society of America
212-573-8484

National Foundation for Cancer Research
301-654-1250

National Leukemia Association
516-741-1190

Ronald McDonald House
619-292-7413

St. Jude Children's Research Hospital
901-522-9733

OTHER SERIOUS DISEASES AND HEALTH PROBLEMS

■ ■ ■

On the following pages is a listing of various diseases and health problems affecting Americans. It is by no means a complete list, nor does it provide an in-depth description of the disease, its causes, and potential solutions. Rather, a brief explanation of the disease and its impact is given. You are then referred to national organizations dedicated to finding a cure for the disease and to making life better for those who have it.

If you would like more information, refer to *Health Care U.S.A.,* by Jean Carper (Prentice Hall Press, NY). This is a comprehensive book giving detailed descriptions of the health problems with referrals to treatment centers, research centers, organizations, and other resources. Or consult the *Encyclopedia of Associations* (Gale Research), which lists and details more than 22,000 national and international nonprofit trade and professional associations, including organizations in the health field.

Another good book is the *American Medical Association Family Medical Guide* (New York: Random House, 1987), which provides up-to-date information on the symptoms, risks, and treatment of more than 650 diseases and disorders.

Muscular Dystrophy Association

ALZHEIMER'S DISEASE

This disease attacks the brain, resulting in impaired memory. Alzheimer's disease is the fourth leading cause of death in adults. An estimated 4 million Americans suffer from Alzheimer's, and more than 100,000 die from AD each year.

According to the Alzheimer's Disease and Related Disorder Association, AD affects men and women equally, and usually strikes those over 65, although it can also affect people in their forties and fifties.

Organizations

Alzheimer's Disease and Related Disorders Association (ADRA)
312-853-3060

National Institute on Aging
301-496-1752

THE WHITE HOUSE, May 22, 1990 — The President today named Project Child of Boca Raton, Florida, as the one hundred forty-ninth "Daily Point of Light." Project Child is a program developed by the National Down Syndrome Society.

National Down Syndrome Society

ARTHRITIS

Arthritis in its many forms afflicts approximately 37 million Americans. It affects 200,000 children and more than 15 million people age 65 or older. Arthritis is the inflammation of the joints and connective tissues, and causes discomfort, pain, and crippling. There are more than 100 different forms of arthritis. Osteoarthritis, the most common type, generally affects older people and gets progressively worse with age. Rheumatoid arthritis usually affects people in the 20 to 40 age group, occurring most commonly in women. In some cases it causes severe crippling.

Organizations

The Arthritis Foundation
404-872-7100

Arthritis Institute
703-553-2431

The National Institute of Arthritis and Musculoskeletal and Skin Diseases
301-496-8188

The American Lupus Society
213-542-8891

The Lupus Foundation of America
301-670-9292
800-558-0121

United Scleroderma Foundation
408-728-2202

BIRTH DEFECTS

According to the March of Dimes Foundation, a birth defect is an abnormality of structure, function, or body chemistry, whether genetically determined or the result of environmental interference before birth. It may be present at or before birth, or it may appear later in life. More than a quarter-million infants are born with physical or mental damage every year in the United States. Birth defects thus strike 1 out of every 14 infants. Another half-million potential lives are destroyed by miscarriages and stillbirths every year, largely because of faulty fetal development.

Birth defects affect people after birth as well. About 1.2 million infants, children, and adults are hospitalized each year for treatment of birth defects; more than 60,000 Americans of all ages die every year as the result of birth defects.

Birth defects represent one of our nation's most serious child health problems. It accounts for 30 percent of admissions to pediatric hospitals, and consumes billions of dollars in medical care costs. It also exacts a toll in human suffering and anguish—for the child, a lifetime of health problems; for the parents, the shattered hope of a healthy child.

Birth defects can be caused by prematurity. A baby born prematurely, with a birthweight less than 5.5 pounds, may face serious health problems, including respiratory distress syndrome (RDS), which can be fatal. Birth defects may also be genetically caused, such as cystic fibrosis; or they may be caused by environmental factors, such as fetal alcohol syndrome.

Birth defects affect mental and physical development, as with Down's syndrome; bone structure, as with spina bifida; and body organs, as with congenital heart disorders. Many birth defects, such as Huntington's chorea, don't take their toll until adulthood.

Organizations

Cleftline
800-242-5338
800-24-CLEFT

Cystic Fibrosis Foundation
800-344-4823

Huntington's Disease Society of America
212-242-1968

March of Dimes Birth Defects Foundation
914-949-7166
914-428-7100

Muscular Dystrophy Association
800-223-6666

The National Easter Seal Society
312-726-6200
800-221-6827

National Down Syndrome Congress
800-232-6372

National Down Syndrome Society
800-221-4602
212-460-9330

Spina Bifida Association of America
800-621-3141

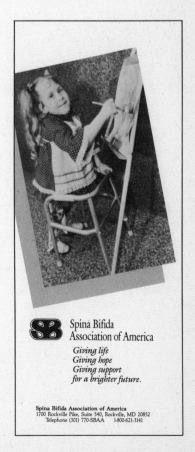

Spina Bifida
Association of America
Giving life
Giving hope
Giving support
for a brighter future.

Spina Bifida Association of America
1700 Rockville Pike, Suite 540, Rockville, MD 20852
Telephone (301) 770-SBAA   1-800-621-3141

BLINDNESS AND OTHER VISION PROBLEMS

According to the Braille Institute, an estimated 2.25 out of every 1,000 persons in the United States are born without sight, or develop legal blindness within their lifetimes. An additional 7.2 out of every 1,000 individuals develop a visual impairment so severe that it cannot be corrected by normal prescription lenses.

More than 11 million people have visual impairment; 1.4 million Americans are severely impaired and 500,000 are legally blind, meaning that they do not have 20/200 vision

Guide Dog Foundation for the Blind, Inc.

even with the use of eyeglasses or contact lenses. The National Society to Prevent Blindness estimates that one American goes blind every 11 minutes.

Organizations

American Brotherhood for the Blind
301-659-9314

American Council of the Blind
800-424-8666

American Foundation for the Blind
212-620-2000

American Printing House for the Blind
502-895-2405

Braille Institute
213-663-1111

Christian Record Braille Foundation
402-488-0981

Guide Dogs for the Blind
415-499-4000

Guide Dog Foundation for the Blind, Inc.
516-265-2121
800-548-4337

Jewish Guild for the Blind
212-769-6200

Job Opportunities for the Blind (J.O.B.)
800-638-7518

National Association for the Visually Handicapped, Inc.
212-889-3141

National Society to Prevent Blindness
800-221-3004

National Camps for Blind Children
402-488-0981

National Federation of the Blind
301-659-9314

Perkins School for the Blind
617-924-3434

Recording for the Blind, Inc.
609-452-0606

RP Foundation Fighting Blindness
301-225-9400
9409(TDD)
800-638-2300

Seeing Eye, Inc.
201-539-4425

CEREBRAL PALSY

Cerebral palsy is a partial or complete paralysis of the muscles caused by a permanent brain defect or an injury occurring before, during, or after birth. The symptoms range from slight awkwardness to severe paralysis, physical handicaps, and/or mental retardation. It strikes more than 3,000 infants and approximately 500 preschool-aged children each year. According to the United Cerebral Palsy organization, approximately 500,000 to 700,000 Americans have one or more of the symptoms of the disease.

Organizations

**National Easter Seal
Society, Inc.**
312-726-6200 (Voice)
800-221-6827 (TDD)

United Cerebral Palsy
800-872-5827

CYSTIC FIBROSIS

Cystic Fibrosis is a genetic (inherited) disease that affects approximately 30,000 Americans and occurs in about 1 of every 2,000 births. One in 20 people, or almost 17 million Americans, carry the gene (although a much smaller number of people get CF). CF affects the function of certain types of cells in the exocrine (outward-secreting—mucus, sweat, and saliva) glands.

Individuals with cystic fibrosis produce an abnormal amount of thick, sticky mucus that clogs and blocks the bodily channels and interferes with breathing. Death often results from complications.

Organizations

**The Cystic Fibrosis
Foundation**
800-FIGHT-CF

DIABETES

Diabetes affects approximately 11 million Americans. It is the seventh leading cause of death by disease in this country, causing 150,000 deaths annually and striking 500,000 Americans each year. It is estimated that diabetes costs about $20 billion annually in health care expenses.

Type I diabetes occurs mainly in young people. In these cases the pancreas produces little or no insulin. Type II diabetes usually affects those over 40. In this form the output of insulin is inadequate for the body's needs.

Symptoms include excessive urination, perpetual thirst, loss of energy, and potential complications of the circulatory system primarily affecting the kidneys, heart, and eyes.

Organizations

**American Diabetes
Association**
703-549-1500
800-232-3472

Joslin Diabetes Center

**Juvenile Diabetes
Foundation**
212-889-7575
800-223-1138

American Diabetes Association

**Who We Are,
What We Do**

Reprinted with permission from "Who We Are, What We Do." Copyright © 1988 by American Diabetes Association, Inc.

National Diabetes Information Clearinghouse
301-468-2162

National Institute of Diabetes, Digestive and Kidney Diseases
301-496-3583

PEOPLE WITH DISABILITIES

Helping people with disabilities is a broad subject because it includes all types of disabilities with many different causes. Many diseases, including multiple sclerosis or stroke, may leave an individual paralyzed or partially disabled. An injury may cause broken bones, burns, or paralysis, requiring extensive rehabilitation. The term *handicapped* refers to someone who has an inborn or acquired physical or mental handicap that interferes with the body's normal functions.

People with mental retardation constitute one of America's largest groups of citizens having disabilities. Approximately 3 percent of the population, or 7.5 million Americans, are mentally retarded or have some type of developmental disability. Each year in the United States 100,000 babies are born with mental retardation. Mentally retarded people generally have IQ levels of 70 or lower; they may not always show physical signs of their handicap.

A person with developmental disabilities may have a learning disorder such as dyslexia, which is a blockage of the ability to read. Dyslexic persons often reverse words and letters. Autism is a mental disorder that is marked by extreme withdrawal into fantasy. Many autistic children are mentally retarded, but there are some who possess exceptional abilities. Schizophrenic children are frequently autistic.

SPECIAL OLYMPICS: UNITING THE WORLD UNIFIE LE MONDE UNIE DO AL MUN

Special Olympics International

Organizations

American Horticultural Therapy Association
301-948-3010

Association for Children and Adults with Learning Disabilities
412-341-8077
412-341-1515

Association for Retarded Citizens of the United

States
817-261-6003

Best Buddies
202-347-7265

Clearinghouse on the Handicapped
202-732-1241

HEATH (Higher Education and the Handicapped)
800-544-3284

National Down Syndrome Congress
800-232-6372
708-823-7550

National Down Syndrome Society
800-221-4602
212-460-9330

National Easter Seal Society, Inc.
800-221-6827

National Information Center for Handicapped Children and Youth
703-893-6061

National Handicapped Sports and Recreation Association (NHSRA)
301-652-7505

National Organization on Disability (NOD)
800-248-2253

National Rehabilitation Information Center
800-346-2742

The National Society for Children and Adults with Autism
301-565-0433

National Spinal Cord Injury Association
800-962-9629
617-935-2722

North American Riding for the Handicapped Association
303-452-1212

The Orton Dyslexia Society
301-296-0232
800-ABC-D123

Special Olympics
202-628-3630

Stifel Paralysis Research Foundation
201-467-5915

EPILEPSY

According to the Epilepsy Foundation of America, approximately 1 percent of the population, or almost 2.5 million Americans, are affected by epilepsy, a nervous system disorder that is caused by a problem in communication between the brain's nerve cells.

Petit mal seizure is a type of epileptic seizure that causes a brief loss of consciousness. They are most common in children and adolescents. It usually does not persist after adolescence. Grand mal epilepsy is much more dramatic. A characteristic grand mal seizure involves convulsions of the body and the stopping of breathing accompanied by unconsciousness. The patient usually has no recollection of the seizure after regaining consciousness.

Organizations

Epilepsy Foundation of America
301-459-3700

National Easter Seal Society, Inc.
800-221-6827

HEARING PROBLEMS

The National Information Center on Deafness reports that an estimated 21 million Americans, or almost 9 percent of the population, suffer from a hearing loss. Hearing loss affects both young and the old. According to the Association for Hearing and Speech Action, 3 out of 100 schoolchildren have a hearing impairment, and 43 percent of all deaf Americans are age 65 or older.

Organizations

The Alexander Graham Bell Association for the Deaf
202-337-5220 (voice/TTD)

American Society for Deaf Children
301-585-5400

Association for Hearing and Speech Action
800-638-8255

National Association of the Deaf
301-587-1788 (voice/TTY)

National Information Center on Deafness
202-651-5051/
202-651-0505 (TTY)

HEART AND CARDIOVASCULAR DISEASE

Heart disease is the leading killer of Americans, accounting for almost one-half of all deaths each year. More than 68 million people, about one-quarter of the population, suffer from cardiovascular disease.

Heart attacks kill more than half a million persons each year. According to the American Heart Association, cardiovascular diseases take a life every 32 seconds.

Organizations

Call your local American Heart Association

The Coronary Club, Inc.
216-444-3690

National Heart, Lung and Blood Institute
301-496-4236

KIDNEY AND LUNG DISEASES

More than 12 million Americans are affected by kidney and urinary tract diseases, and approximately 9 million have lung disease. Both organs are crucial to the body, and diseased heart or lungs can result in death.

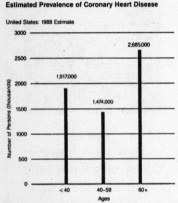

Estimated Prevalence of Coronary Heart Disease

United States: 1988 Estimate

NOTE: Of those with coronary heart disease, 52.2% are male and 47.8% are female; and 88.2% are white, 9.5% are black and 2.4% are of other races.

Source: National Health and Nutrition Examination Survey II Data, National Center for Health Statistics, U.S. Public Health Service, DHHS and the American Heart Association.

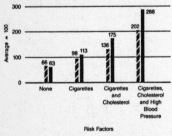

Danger of Heart Attack by Risk Factors Present
Example: 55-year-old male and female

This chart shows how a combination of three major risk factors can increase the likelihood of heart attack. For purposes of illustration, this chart uses an abnormal blood pressure level of 150 systolic and a cholesterol level of 260 in a 55-year-old male and female.

Source: Framingham Heart Study, Section 37: The Probability of Developing Certain Cardiovascular Diseases in Eight Years at Specified Values of Some Characteristics (Aug. 1987).

Reproduced with permission from "1991 Heart and Stroke Facts," 1990. Copyright American Heart Association.

Organizations

American Kidney Fund
800-638-8299
800-492-8361(MD)

American Lung Association
212-315-8700

National Association of Patients on Hemodialysis and Transplantation
212-619-2727

National Heart, Lung and Blood Institute
301-496-4236

National Institute of Diabetes, Digestive, and Kidney Diseases
301-496-3583

National Kidney Foundation
212-889-2210

MENTAL ILLNESS

In a National Institute of Mental Health nationwide survey of adults, 13 percent were shown to have mental disorders requiring diagnosis and treatment. Mental illness varies in types and degrees. Depression is one of the more common mental disorders. An estimated 15 percent of the population are likely to experience at least one period of depression severe enough to require medical treatment.

Other mental disorders include schizophrenia, phobias and anxieties, hysteria, compulsions and obsessions, and personality disorder.

Mental disorders can lead to family and job-related problems, including abuse of spouse and children, and in some instances suicide. Approximately 200,000 people in the United States attempt suicide each year, with more than 27,000 succeeding.

Organizations

American Mental Health Fund
703-573-2200

National Alliance for the Mentally Ill (NAMI)
703-524-7600

National Depression and Manic Depression Association
312-642-0049

National Institute of Mental Health
301-443-4513

National Mental Health Association
703-684-7722

HELP and HOPE

MDA®
Muscular Dystrophy Association
National Headquarters / 3561 East Sunrise Drive
Tucson, AZ 85718 / (602) 529-2000

MULTIPLE SCLEROSIS (MS)

An estimated 250,000 Americans suffer from multiple sclerosis, a neurological disorder that generally affects young adults. The disease destroys myelin, a protective coating that surrounds the brain and spinal cord. Symptoms range from vision disorders and loss of coordination to partial and complete paralysis.

Organizations

**National Multiple
Sclerosis Society**
212-986-3240
800-624-8236

NEUROMUSCULAR DISEASES

The best known type of neuromuscular disease is muscular dystrophy, a term that designates a group of hereditary muscle-destroying disorders, which vary in inheritance pattern, age of onset, initial muscles attacked, and rate of progression. The most common and fatal childhood form of the disease, Duchenne muscular dystrophy, causes progressive wasting and weakening of the skeletal muscles and strikes primarily boys.

More than a million Americans are affected by these and 31 other neuromuscular diseases. Research funded by the Muscular Dystrophy Association is rapidly uncovering the genetic causes of many neuromuscular conditions, but as yet there is no cure or treatment for most of these disorders.

Organizations

**Muscular Dystrophy
Association**
(602) 529-2000
1-800-223-6666

PARKINSON'S DISEASE

Parkinson's disease affects approximately 1 million Americans, usually those over 60 years of age. The disease causes muscle stiffness, loss of coordination, impaired handwriting, and tremors.

Organizations

**American Parkinson's
Disease Association**
718-981-8001

**Parkinson's Disease
Foundation**
212-923-4700

**Parkinson's Educational
Program USA**
800-344-7872

**United Parkinson
Foundation**
312-664-2344

SICKLE-CELL ANEMIA

Sickle-cell anemia is an incurable blood disease that almost always affects people of African descent. Approximately 1 in every 1,000 African Americans has sickle-cell anemia. The sickle cell is an abnormally shaped red blood cell that obstructs blood flow and reduces normal oxygen supplies to the tissues and organs.

Symptoms include joint pain, acute stomach pain, and possible blood clots in the vital organs.

Organizations

Sickle Cell Disease Branch
301-496-6931

OTHER WAYS TO HELP

∎ ∎ ∎

GET IN TOUCH WITH A HEALTH ORGANIZATION

There are many ways to help people who are suffering from medical disorders. If you are interested in helping to find a cure for a certain disease, you can donate your time and money to one of the many organizations listed in this section.

Besides research, health organizations are involved in many areas of need. Some groups lobby for increased political support and funding. Others provide services to improve the lives of those afflicted with an injury or disease. Certain organizations link people who are concerned with a disease with other people who have had similar experiences.

To learn more about a health disorder that may be of special interest to you, read through this section and contact one of the many organizations listed at the end.

WHAT WILL MY DONATION PAY FOR?

YOUR GENEROUS DONATION:

Will help the Muscular Dystrophy Association achieve a victory over deadly muscle diseases.

Will help find a cure for multiple sclerosis (MS), a debilitating and emotionally draining disease that has stricken more than 250,000 people.

Will help the March of Dimes prevent birth defects that strike more than a quarter-million newborn infants each year.

Provides groceries and other basic necessities for an AIDS patient.

Buy a talking calculator for classroom use at the Braille Institute.

Can buy a lifetime for the 6,600 children who will get cancer this year (American Cancer Society).*

SOME OTHER IDEAS

Listed here are some other ways to volunteer your time and energy.

▶ **Volunteer in your local hospital, nursing home, rehabilitation center, and hospice.** Health-care facilities rely heavily on the efforts of volunteers. Working in patient and nonpatient areas can be very rewarding. In *Simple Acts of Kindness: Volunteering in the Age of AIDS,* James H. Sugarman relates his experiences of volunteering:

> As a volunteer, I have learned a great deal from this type of work. I have personally learned a lot about caring and compassion, and a lot about reaching out to people who are quite ill, or frightened, or feeling alone. I have learned the importance of knowing about resources that are available for persons with AIDS and how and when to present such information. I have grown tremendously from the experience.*

Contact your local hospital or a volunteer agency and ask about opportunities to volunteer.

▶ **Volunteer as a recorder for the blind.** Volunteers are needed by organizations such as the Braille Institute, which records books for blind people and makes them available in an expansive library network. Volunteers come in for an hour or two at a time to a nearby center to record books. (Refer to "Blindness and Other Vision Problems" in the Health Problems section for more information.)

▶ **Volunteer your time and services helping people with disabilities.** There are many different ways you can help. One way is to volunteer to work at a developmental center in your community. For example, the Kerby Sisters of Troy, Michigan, play with physically challenged children at a nearby center.

Or if you have a particular expertise in a certain

Simple Acts of Kindness, The United Hospital Fund, 1989.

Reprinted with permission from the White House Office of National Service.

✪ THE KERBY SISTERS ✪

Troy, MI
DAILY POINT OF LIGHT RECIPIENT: JANUARY 25, 1990

"We did this for experience and to give back to society a portion of the wonderful things we have received."—Beth Kerby

Beth, 13, Kerry, 10, and Megan, 7, have made community service a central part of their lives.

The sisters volunteer at the Wing Lake Development Center in West Bloomfield Township, which provides education and recreation to severely physically and mentally disabled children. Their responsibilities include playing with the children and assisting them in activities. The Kerby's volunteer work gives the disabled children an opportunity to interact with their peers, while bringing friendship and joy into their lives.

356

area, you could share your knowledge with others. Dr. Julius Glass donates his skills to those with disabilities.

✪ JULIUS GLASS ✪

Forest Hills, NY
DAILY POINT OF LIGHT RECIPIENT: DECEMBER 28, 1989

Julius Glass, 73, is committed to enhancing and enriching the lives of physically disabled individuals with mental retardation.

Mr. Glass, a retired psychologist, devotes his skills to helping the residents and staff at the Bernard Fineson Development Center, a residential home for the mentally disabled. He provides counseling, administers diagnostic exams, and helps the staff create therapy programs. He also trains staff members and confers with them on difficult cases. Mr. Glass has used the knowledge gained from 50 years of practice to help a new generation of mental health professionals.

Reprinted with permission from the White House Office of National Service.

Another suggestion is to join an organization such as Special Olympics and Best Buddies, which link volunteers with mentally and physically retarded children.

Organizations

Special Olympics
202-628-3630

Started by Eunice Kennedy Shriver in the early 1960s, Special Olympics is an international movement which, through year-round sports training and competition in the Olympic tradition, gives people with mental retardation the chance to strengthen their character, develop their physical skills, display their talents, and fulfill their human potential. Since 1968 more than 1 million children and adults with mental retardation have participated. Today there are Special Olympics programs in 25,000 U.S. communities, representing 97 percent of the counties in the U.S. and in nearly 80 countries worldwide.

Best Buddies
202-347-7265

A nonprofit volunteer organization whose purpose is to enhance the social and recreational lives of individuals with mental retardation, bringing them into mainstream America by uniting university students with mentally retarded persons.

Created by The Associate Trustees of The Joseph P. Kennedy Jr. Foundation for the Benefit of Citizens with Mental Retardation.

For additional information about organizations that help people with disabilities, see the "People with Disabilities" section (page 350).

▶ **Utilize your knowledge to help others.** If you have a particular medical expertise, seek ways to volunteer your services to those in need. For instance, William and Sandra Hale utilize their medical skills helping poor people in their community. They received a Daily Point of Light for their efforts.

❂ WILLIAM AND SANDRA HALE ❂

Oklahoma City, OK
DAILY POINT OF LIGHT RECIPIENT: NOVEMBER 27, 1989

The Hales, a doctor and nurse team, both afflicted with multiple sclerosis, operate a free medical clinic. For 15 years, the clinic has been located at the Baptist Mission Center in the crumbling neighborhood of Packingtown. Economically disadvantaged people live there out of necessity; Dr. and Mrs. Hale work there out of choice.

The all-volunteer clinic, open two nights a week, has treated nearly 43,000 indigent people since it opened. It consists of a network of medical specialists to whom patients are referred for free treatment. After finding a crumpled prescription outside the mission one night and realizing the patients could not afford medicine, the Hales arranged for donations from local pharmacies, doctors, and hospitals.

Reprinted with permission from the White House Office of National Service.

▶ **Volunteer your time and resources to groups that help children who have life-threatening illnesses.** Make-A-Wish Foundation of America (800-722-WISH) is a group dedicated to granting the special wishes of children up to the age of 18 who have life-threatening illnesses.

The types of wishes are as diverse as the thousands of children who make them. For example, Make-A-Wish volunteers "have persuaded Stevie Wonder to visit a young lady in her Chicago apartment and sing her a special song . . . have arranged balloon, raft, and helicopter flights . . . had a miniature 18-wheel tractor-trailer rig built . . . have made arrangements for visits with NBA basketball stars, NFL football heroes, and major league baseball figures . . . have persuaded airlines to let kids 'fly' their flight simulators."*

A.J., of Waukesha, Wisc., loved spaceships and coins. After he was diagnosed with leukemia at age 11, he told the Make-A-Wish Foundation his wish was to go to Washington, D.C., to visit both the Air and Space Museum at the Smithsonian Institution and the Treasury and to tour the White House. He did it, too. He also wanted to see the first puppies, which he did courtesy of Barbara Bush, who handed A.J. a two-week pup for his inspection. Mrs. Bush asked him if he wanted to name the pup, and A.J. did, "Brandy," after a family dog who had died.**

*Excerpt from *Make-A-Wish Foundation*® *of America 1989 Annual Report.*

**Printed with permission from *Make-A-Wish Foundation*® *of America.*

Groups such as Make-A-Wish understand the importance of granting these wishes. "What all these wishes do, these diverse dreams, is singular: It supplants, for the child and the family, the everyday regimen of medical visits, hospital tests, daily treatment, with a special, happy day or two."*

Organizations

Children's Wish Foundation, Intl.
800-323-9474

**Make-A-Wish Foundation®
of America**
800-722-WISH

Starlight Foundation
213-208-5885

Sunshine Foundation
215-335-2622

MAKE-A-WISH
FOUNDATION®

THE GIFT OF LIFE

▶ **Learn standard first aid.** You never know when you may have to help someone who requires medical assistance. Rather than standing by helplessly when a person is choking, having a heart attack, or is injured in an accident, you could utilize some critical knowledge to save a life.

*Excerpt from *Make-A-Wish Foundation® of America 1989 Annual Report.*

ORDINARY PEOPLE—EXTRAORDINARY ACTIONS
SAM DIAMOND

Sam Diamond is as valuable to Braille Institute as his name suggests. Born and raised in Los Angeles, he has spent 13 years with the Los Angeles Police Department, attaining the rank of sergeant. He "retired" in 1955, but inactivity held no attraction for him. He went into the importing business, but even this was not enough to keep him fully occupied.

About 11 years ago, Diamond answered a Braille Institute ad for the Friendly Visitor Program and began volunteering to read for a blind law student. Diamond's consistent help enabled the student to graduate from law school.

After this, Diamond became involved in the Recording Program, reading books onto tape and working one-on-one with blind individuals.

"I enjoy coming here five days a week," Diamond said. "I've met some of the nicest people here I've ever met."

In addition to reading, Diamond also teaches a weekly class that is among the most popular offered. "People and Places" features an array of interesting and colorful guest speakers from all walks of life, and Diamond spends several hours scheduling his guests and preparing for the class.

Diamond cannot imagine not spending his mornings at Braille Institute. "Volunteering has become part of my life," he said. "Every day I look forward to coming down here."

Courtesy of Braille Institute of America, Inc.

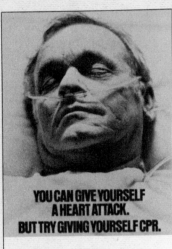

YOU CAN GIVE YOURSELF A HEART ATTACK. BUT TRY GIVING YOURSELF CPR.

Your heart suddenly gives out. You have no pulse. You can no longer breathe.

Even if you know CPR, there's one person you can't give it to. Yourself.

This man got help from someone at work who learned CPR at the Red Cross. They got help from the United Way. Thank God the United Way got help from you.

Your single contribution helps provide therapy for a handicapped child, a warm coat for a homeless man, counseling for a rape victim, job training for a former drug abuser.

Or, in this case, CPR training for this man's co-workers. Otherwise, he might have ended up somewhere other than a hospital.

United Way
It brings out the best in all of us.

Reprinted by permission, United Way of America.

The American Red Cross offers a comprehensive 8-hour course that covers the essentials about Red Cross CPR as well as Red Cross Standard First Aid. The course will teach you how to respond to such emergencies as heart attack, poisoning, diabetic coma, internal and external bleeding, and rescues.

Contact your local American Red Cross or another such organization and ask about this essential, and possibly life-saving program.

Organizations

The American Red Cross
Contact your local chapter or call 202-737-8300.

The United Way
Contact your local chapter.

▶ **Give blood.** Each year the American Red Cross collects more than 6 million units of blood donated by more than 4 million volunteers. These donations amount to nearly half the nation's blood supply and help save countless lives. The American Medical Association describes the blood-donating procedure:

> To give blood, a donor visits a blood center or hospital, where a blood test is carried out to determine the strength (hemoglobin level) of the donor's blood. If this is satisfactory, about one pint of blood is removed using an intravenous needle. This procedure, which takes only a few minutes, is virtually painless and totally safe. Giving blood cannot expose the donor to the AIDS virus or to any other disease.*

Organizations

American Association of Blood Banks
703-528-8200

American Red Cross
Contact your local chapter

Blood Systems, Inc.
602-946-4201

Central Blood Bank
412-456-1900

Council of Community Blood Centers
202-393-5725

New York Blood Center
212-590-3000

▶ **Donate your organs.** Medical science has become very proficient in transplanting organs. Almost 13,400 organ transplants were performed in 1989, including such organs as the heart, liver, lung, kidney, and pancreas. More than 22,500 people currently await such transplants.

Your final gift of life could be an organ for someone in grave need. According to the United Network of Organ Shar-

*J. Kunz, M.D., and A. Finkel, M.D., *American Medical Association Family Medical Guide* (New York: Random House, 1987), 435.

ing, one-third of the people waiting for a liver or heart will die before getting one.

DEAR ABBY:

Last May, our 22-year-old son, Michael, was involved in a motorcycle accident. He was pronounced brain dead three days later. Because of an article he had read in your column, he carried an organ donor card in his wallet.

The Lord took our precious son 10 days later, but we were comforted knowing that Michael gave two blind people the gift of sight, and a young father who had been on a kidney machine for three years is now living a normal life.

Abby, please let your readers know how to will their organs after death.
—MICHAEL'S FATHER

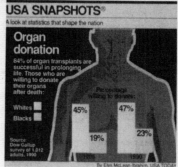

"Copyright 1990, *USA Today*. Reprinted with permission."

From the "Dear Abby" column by Abigail Van Buren copyright 1990. Reprinted with permission of Universal Press Syndicate. All rights reserved.

More than 95 percent of Americans know about organ transplants, but only 20 percent have actually signed organ donor cards. Helping is easy! All you have to do is sign an organ donor card. Many states print the donor card on the back of the driver's license.

If there is a particular organ you wish to donate, contact a health organization that deals with diseases of that organ. For instance, to donate your kidneys after death, contact the National Kidney Foundation for a donor card.

Organizations

United Network of Organ Sharing
800-666-1884

American Red Cross Transplantation Services
202-737-8300 (or your local chapter)

National Kidney Foundation
212-889-2210

Deafness Research Foundation
212-684-6556/212-684-6559 (TTY)

The Living Bank
(for donor forms)
713-528-2971

▶ Get registered! Become a potential bone marrow donor. The gift of a sample of your bone marrow may indeed be the gift of life for the thousands of people with leukemia, lymphoma, Hodgkin's disease, and other serious blood disorders. A marrow transplant replaces the diseased leukemic cells with healthy ones. If a correct match is found for someone who is

ORDINARY PEOPLE—EXTRAORDINARY ACTIONS

Two years ago Diana Brutoco, a 38-year-old mother of four young children, was diagnosed with CML, a deadly form of leukemia. Her only chance for survival was a marrow transplant.

When Diana announced to her community that she was dying of leukemia and her only chance to live meant finding an unrelated marrow donor, she became the pivotal force of a local grass-roots effort that became the signature of volunteer marrow donor recruitment that has characterized Life-Savers Foundation of America.

Diana found her life-saving marrow donor on Thanksgiving 1988. Today she is cancer free. In her typical open style, Diana admits to the fear of facing a marrow transplant and the prolonged pain of the treatment, but says, "I wanted to live for my children and for my husband. Then, I realized I could help others like myself by surviving."

Diana says that the arduous 100 day marrow transplant recuperation period became a time of meditation and much of that time was spent reflecting on her unknown donor. "He gave me the future, and I came to realize that a big part of that future was for me to do all I could to pass on the miracle of life by telling people how important it is to become a marrow donor. A day doesn't go by that I don't think about the goodness of the stranger who saved my life."

To become a volunteer marrow donor call Life-Savers hotline 800-654-1247

Reprinted with permission from Life-Savers Foundation of America.

suffering from such a disease, they have a good chance of being cured.

Finding a perfect match is extremely difficult; the odds of finding a match between unrelated individuals is about 1 in 15,000. That is why it is so important to be tested. The Life-Savers Foundation helps recruit potential donors and pays for the test if necessary. In early 1990 more than 4,000 people from San Diego were tested in order to save the life of a young boy with leukemia. Happily, the drive to find a matching donor was successful. The child received a bone marrow transplant and has beaten the cancer.

Life-Savers Foundation feels that the best of all possible worlds would be to have 1 million donors on all registries, so that everyone who needs a transplant has a chance to live. By early 1991 the National Bone Marrow Donor Program had approximately 300,000 names on the registry.

Donating a sample of your bone marrow is easy, safe, and relatively painless. A potential donor gives a sample of his or her blood to be tested. The National Bone Marrow Donor Registry (or another registry) then monitors the test results and if your marrow type matches someone in need, you will be asked to become a donor. The actual transplant lasts about 45 minutes and is performed in a hospital. The amount of marrow taken is only about a tablespoonful. The body replenishes the donated marrow within a few weeks.

Organizations

Life-Savers Foundation of America
818-967-8425

800-654-1247 (national donor line)
A nonprofit foundation

dedicated to saving lives by recruiting potential donors and by raising funds necessary to pay for the testing. In 1991 it merged with the National Bone Marrow Registry.

National Bone Marrow Donor Registry
800-654-1247
612-291-6789
800-526-7809

Matches bone marrow donors with people who are stricken by diseases that can only be cured with a bone marrow transplant.

American Red Cross Transplantation Services
202-737-8300 (or your local chapter)

National Marrow Donor Program
1-800-654-1247

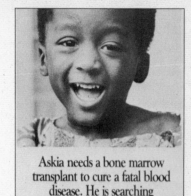

Askia needs a bone marrow transplant to cure a fatal blood disease. He is searching for a matched donor who can offer him the Chance of a Lifetime.

HEALTH ORGANIZATIONS

AIDS Action Council
223 M ST., NW, Suite 802
Washington, DC 20030
202-293-2886

AIDS Project Los Angeles (APLA)
6721 Romaine St.
Los Angeles, CA 90038
213-962-1600

ACTION
Drug Prevention Program
806 Connecticut Ave., NW
Washington, DC 20525

Alcoholics Anonymous
PO Box 459
Grand Central Station
New York, NY 10163
212-686-1100

Al-Anon/Alateen
P.O. Box 862
Midtown Station
New York, NY 10018
212-302-7240

The Alexander Graham Bell Association for the Deaf
3417 Volta Place, NW

Washington, DC 20007-2778
202-337-5220 (Voice/TTD)

The ALS Association
185 Madison Ave.
New York, NY 10016
212-755-2921

Alzheimer's Disease and Related Disorders Association (ADRA)
70 East Lake St.
Chicago, IL 60601-5997
312-853-3060/
800-621-0379

American Association of Blood Banks
1117 N. 19th St., Suite 600
Arlington, VA 22209
703-528-8200

American Association of Physicians for Human Rights
2940 16th St., Suite 105
San Francisco, CA 94103
415-255-4547

American Brotherhood for the Blind
1800 Johnson St.

Baltimore, MD 21230
301-659-9314

American Cancer Society
National Headquarters
1599 Clifton Rd., NE
Atlanta, GA 30329
800-227-2345

American Council on Alcoholism (ACA)
5024 H Campbell Blvd.
Baltimore, MD 21236
301-931-9393

American Council of the Blind
1211 Connecticut Ave., NW
Washington, DC 20036
800-424-8666

American Council for Drug Education
204 Monroe St., Suite 110
Rockville, MD 20850
301-294-0600

American Diabetes Association
1660 Duke St.
Alexandria, VA 22314
703-549-1500/ 800-232-3472

American Foundation for AIDS Research
5900 Wilshire Blvd.,
2nd floor E.
Los Angeles, CA 90036
213-857-5900

American Foundation for the Blind
15 W. 16th St.
New York, NY 10011
212-620-2000

American Heart Association
7320 Greenville Ave.
Dallas, TX 75231
214-373-6300
800-527-6941

American Horticultural Therapy Association
"Horticulture Hiring the Disabled"
9220 Wightman Rd.,
Suite 300
Gaithersburg, MD 20879
301-948-3010

American Hospital Association
840 North Lake Shore Dr.
Chicago, IL 60611
312-280-6000
800-621-6712, ext. 6436

American Institute for Cancer Research
1759 R St., NW
Washington, DC 20069-2012
202-328-7744

American Kidney Fund
6110 Executive Blvd.,
Suite 1010
Rockville, MD. 20852
800-638-8299
800-492-8361 (MD)

American Lung Association
1740 Broadway
New York, NY 10019
212-315-8700

The American Lupus Society
23751 Madison St.

Torrance, CA 90505
213-542-8891

American Medical Association
535 Dearborn St.
Chicago, IL 60610
312-464-5000

American Mental Health Fund
P.O. Box 17839
Washington, DC 20041
703-573-2200

American Parkinson's Disease Association
60 Bay St.
Staten Island, NY 10301
718-981-8891

American Printing House for the Blind
P.O. Box 6085
Louisville, KY 40206
502-895-2405

American Red Cross AIDS Education Office
1730 D St., NW
Washington, DC 20006
202-737-8300
202-639-3223

American Red Cross
National Headquarters
Washington, DC 20006
202-737-8300

American Social Health Association
P.O. Box 13827
R.T.P., NC 27709
800-342-2437

American Society for Deaf Children
814 Thayer Ave.
Silver Spring, MD 20910
301-585-5400

The Arthritis Foundation
1314 Spring St., NW
Atlanta, GA 30309
404-872-7100

Arthritis Institute
2465 Army Navy Drive
Arlington, VA 22206
703-553-2431

Association for Brain Tumor Research
6232 N. Pulaski Rd.,
Suite 200
Chicago, IL 60646
312-286-5571

Association for Care of Children's Health
3615 Wisconsin Ave., NW
Washington, DC 20016
202-244-1801

Association for Children and Adults with Learning Disabilities
4156 Library Rd.
Pittsburgh, PA 15234
412-341-1515

Association for Hearing and Speech Action
10801 Rockville Pike
Rockville, MD 20852
800-638-8255

Association for Retarded Citizens of the United States
P.O. Box 1047
Arlington, TX 76004
817-261-6003

Blind Outdoor Leisure Development
533 E. Main St.
Aspen, CO 81611
303-925-8922

Blood Systems, Inc.
6220 East Oak St.
Scottsdale, AR 85257
602-946-4201

Braille Institute
741 North Vermont Ave.
Los Angeles, CA 90029-3594
213-663-1111

Best Buddies
1350 New York Ave., NW
Suite 500
Washington, DC 20005
202-347-7265

Cancer Research Institute
133 E. 58th St.
New York, NY 10022

212-688-7515
800-99-CANCER

Central Blood Bank
812 Fifth Ave.
Pittsburgh, PA 15219
412-456-1900

Children of Alcoholics Foundation, Inc.
PO Box 4185, Dept. O
Grand Central Station
New York, NY 10163
212-754-0656

Children's Wish Foundation, Intl.
32 Perimeter Center E., NE
Suite 100
Atlanta, GA 30346
800-323-9474

Christian Record Braille Foundation
4444 S. 52nd St.
Lincoln, NE 68506
402-488-0981

Citizens Commission on AIDS
51 Madison Ave., Room 3008
New York, NY 10010
212-779-0311

City of Hope
208 W. 8th St.
Los Angeles, CA 90014
213-626-4611

Cleftline
1218 Grandview Ave.
Pittsburgh, PA 15212
800-242-5338
800-24-CLEFT

Compassionate Friends
P.O. Box 3696
Oak Brook, IL 60522
312-990-0010

The Coronary Club, Inc.
Cleveland Clinic Educational
Foundation
9500 Euclid Ave.
Cleveland, OH 44120
216-292-7120

Council of Community Blood Centers
725 15th St., NW
Washington, DC 20005
202-393-5725

Crones and Colitas Foundation of America
444 Park Ave. South
NY, NY 10016-7374
800-343-3637

The Cystic Fibrosis Foundation
6931 Arlington Rd.
Bethesda, MD 29814
301-951-4422
800-FIGHT-CF
800-344-4823

Deafness Research Foundation
55 E. 34th St.
New York, NY 10016
212-684-6556
212-684-6559(TTY)

Drug Abuse Resistance Education (D.A.R.E.)
KFC-DARE
211 East Ontario St.,
Suite 1300
Chicago, IL 60611
800-TALK-KFC

Epilepsy Foundation of America
4351 Garden City Dr.
Landover, MD 20785
301-459-3700

Families Anonymous
PO Box 528
Van Nuys, CA 91408
818-989-7841

Federation for Children with Special Needs
313 Stuart St., 2nd floor
Boston, MA 02116
617-482-2915

The Gay and Lesbian Community Services Center/AIDS ACTION Programs
1213 North Highland
Los Angeles, CA 90038
213-464-7400

Gay Men's Health Crisis
P.O. Box 274
132 West 24th St.
New York, NY 10011
212-807-6655
212-807-6664

Guide Dog Foundation for the Blind, Inc.
371 East Jericho Turnpike
Smithtown, NY 11787-2976
516-265-2121
800-548-4337

Guide Dogs for the Blind
P.O. Box 1200
San Rafael, CA 94915
415-499-4000

Hearing Dog, Inc.
5901 E. 89th Ave.
Henderson, CO 80640
303-287-EARS

Hispanic AIDS Forum c/o APRED
121 Avenue of the Americas
Room 505
New York, NY 10012
212-966-6336

Huntington's Disease Society of America
140 W. 22nd St.
New York, NY 10040
212-242-1968

Institute for a Drug Free Workplace
1701 Pennsylvania Ave., NW
Suite 950
Washington, DC 20006
202-828-4590

Jewish Guild for the Blind
15 W. 65th St.
New York, NY 10023
212-769-6200

Joslin Diabetes Center
1 Joslin Place
Boston, MA 02215
617-732-2400

Just Say No Foundation
1777 N. California Blvd.
Room 200
Walnut Creek, CA 94596
415-939-6666

Juvenile Diabetes Foundation
432 Park Ave. South
New York, NY 10010
212-889-7575
800-223-1138

Leukemia Society of America
733 Third Ave.
New York, NY 10017
212-573-8484

Life-Savers
529 South Second Ave.
Covina, CA 91723
818-967-8425
800-654-1247

The Living Bank
P.O. Box 6725
Houston, TX 77265
713-528-2971

Los Angeles AIDS Project
1362 Santa Monica Blvd.
Los Angeles, CA 90046
213-871-AIDS

The Lupus Foundation of America
4 Research Place, Suite 180
Rockville, MD 20850
301-670-9292
800-558-0121

Make-A-Wish Foundation of America
2600 N. Central Ave.,
Suite 936
Phoenix, AZ 85004
800-722-WISH

March of Dimes Birth Defects Foundation
1275 Mamaroneck Ave.
White Plains, NY 10605
914-428-7100

The Mended Hearts
7320 Greenville Ave.
Dallas, TX 75231
214-750-5442

Minority Task Force on AIDS c/o New York City Council of Churches
475 Riverside Dr, Room 456
New York, NY 10115
212-749-1214

Mothers Against Drunk Driving (MADD)
511 East John Carpenter
Freeway, Suite 700
Irving, TX 75062
800-438-MADD

Muscular Dystrophy Association
3561 E. Sunrise Drive
Tuscon, AR 85718
602-529-2000
800-223-6666

Narcotics Anonymous
16155 Wyandotte St.
Van Nuys, CA 91406
818-780-3951

National AIDS Commission
1730 K St., NW, Suite 815
Washington, DC 20006
202-254-5125

National AIDS Information Clearinghouse
Box 6003
Rockville, MD 20850

National Alliance for the Mentally Ill (NAMI)
P.O. Box NAMI-USA
Arlington, VA 22216
703-524-7600

National Association of Alcoholism Treatment Programs, Inc.
25201 Paseo de Alicia
Suite 100
Laguna Hills, CA 92653
714-837-3038

National Association for Children of Alcoholics (NACoA)
31582 Coast Highway, Suite B
South Laguna, CA 92677
714-499-3889

National Association of the Deaf
814 Thayer Ave.
Silver Spring, MD 20910
301-587-1788 (voice/TTY)

National Association for Hearing and Speech Action
10801 Rockville Pike
Rockville, MD 20852
800-638-8255
301-897-8682 (voice/TTY)

National Association of Patients on Hemodialysis and Transplantation
150 Nassau St.
New York, NY 10038
212-619-2727

National Association of People with AIDS
P.O. Box 34056
Washington, DC 20043
202-898-0414

National Association for the Visually Handicapped, Inc.
305 E. 24th St.
New York, NY 10010
212-889-3141

National Ataxia Foundation
600 Twelve Oaks Center
15500 Wayzata Blvd.
Wayzata, MN 55391
612-473-7666

National Bone Marrow Donor Registry
100 S. Robert St.
St. Paul, MN 55107
800-654-1247
612-291-6789

National Camps for Blind Children
4444 S. 52nd St.
Lincoln, NE 68506
402-488-0981

National Cancer Institute
c/o The National Institutes of Health
9000 Rockville Pike, Bldg. 31,
10A18
Bethesda, MD 20892
301-496-5583
800-4-CANCER

National Clearinghouse for Alcohol and Drug Information (NCADI)
P.O. Box 2345
Rockville, MD 20852
301-468-2600

National Council on Alcoholism (NCA)
(also the National Council on Alcoholism and Drug Dependence [NCADD])
12 W. 21st St.
New York, NY 10010
212-206-6770
800-NCA-CALL

National Council of Churches/AIDS Task Force
475 Riverside Dr., Room 572
New York, NY 10115
212 870-2421

National Coalition Against Domestic Violence
P.O. Box 34103
Washington, DC 20043-4103
202-638-6388

National Depression and Manic Depression Association
P.O. Box 3395
Merchandise Mart
Chicago, IL 60654
312-642-0049

National Diabetes Information Clearinghouse
Box NDIC
Bethesda, MD 20892
301-468-2162

National Down Syndrome Congress
1800 Dempster St.
Park Ridge, IL 60068
800-232-6372
708-823-7550

National Down Syndrome Society
666 Broadway
New York, NY 10012
800-221-4602
212-460-9330

National Easter Seal Society, Inc.
70 East Lake St.
Chicago, IL 60601
312-726-6200
800-221-6827

National Federation of the Blind
1800 Johnson St.
Baltimore, MD 21230
301-659-9314

National Federation of Parents for Drug-Free Youth (NFP)
P.O. Box 3878
St. Louis, MO 63122
314-968-1322

National Foundation for Cancer Research
7315 Wisconsin Ave.,
Suite 332W
Bethesda, MD 2081
301-654-1250

National Gay and Lesbian Task Force
1517 U St., NW
Washington, DC 20009
202-332-6483

National Handicapped Sports and Recreation Association (NHSRA)
1145 19th St., NW, Suite 717
Washington, DC 20036
301-652-7505

National Health Care Campaign
P.O. Box 27434
Washington, DC 20038
202-639-8833

National Heart, Lung and Blood Institute
National Institutes of Health
9000 Rockville Pike, Bldg. 31
Room 4A21
Bethesda, MD 20892
301-496-4236

National Information Center on Deafness
Gallaudet Univ.
800 Florida Ave., NE

Washington, DC 20002
202-651-5051
202-651-0505 (TTY)

National Information Center for Handicapped Children and Youth
P.O. Box 1492
Washington, DC 20013
703-893-6061

National Institute on Alcohol Abuse and Alcoholism (NIAAA)
Parklawn Bldg.
5600 Fishers Lane
Rockville, MD 20852
301-443-3885
800-729-6686

The National Institute of Arthritis and Musculoskeletal and Skin Diseases
9000 Rockville Pike
Bldg. 31, Room 4C05
Bethesda, MD 20892
301-496-8188

National Institute of Diabetes, Digestive, and Kidney Diseases
9000 Rockville Pike
Bldg. 31 Room 9A04
Bethesda, MD 20892
301-496-3583

National Institute on Drug Abuse
Room 11A-33
5600 Fishers Lane
Rockville, MD 20857

National Institute of Mental Health
Consumer Information Center
Pueblo, CO 81009
301-443-4513

National Institute on the Aging
9000 Rockville Pike
Bldg. 31, Room 5C35
Bethesda, MD 20892
301-496-1752

National Kidney Foundation
Two Park Ave.
New York, NY 10016
212-889-2210

National Leukemia Association
Roosevelt Field, Lower Concourse
Garden City, NY 11530
516-741-1190

National Mental Health Association
1021 Prince St.
Alexandria, VA 22314
703-684-7722

National Multiple Sclerosis Society
205 E. 42nd St.
New York, NY 10017
212-986-3240
800-624-8236

National Prevention Network
444 N. Capitol St., NW, Suite 530
Washington, DC 20001
202-783-6868

National Safety Council
444 N. Michigan Ave.
Chicago, IL 60611
312-527-4800

The National Society for Children and Adults with Autism
8601 Georgia Ave., Suite 503
Silver Spring, MD 20910
301-565-0433

National Society to Prevent Blindness
500 E. Remington Rd.
Schaumburg, IL 60173
800-221-3004

National Spinal Cord Injury Association
600 West Cummings Park
Suite 2000
Wolburn, MA 01801
800-962-9629
617-935-2722

New York Blood Center
310 E. 67th St.
New York, NY 10021
212-570-3000

North American Riding for the Handicapped
P.O. Box 33150
Denver, CO 80233
303-452-1212

The Orton Dyslexia Society
724 York Rd.
Baltimore, MD 21204
301-296-0232
800-ABC-D123

Paget's Disease Foundation
P.O. Box 2772
Brooklyn, NY 11202
718-596-1043

Parents Resources Institute on Drug Education (PRIDE)
The Hurt Building, Suite 210
50 Hurt Plaza
Atlanta, GA 30303
800-67-PRIDE

Parkinson's Disease Foundation
Columbia University Medical Center
650 W. 168th St.
New York, NY 10032
212-923-4700

Parkinson's Educational Program USA
1800 Park Newport, Suite 302
Newport Beach, CA 92660
800-344-7872

Pediatric AIDS Foundation
2407 Wilshire Blvd., #613
Santa Monica, CA 90403
213-395-9051
800-488-5000

Perkins School for the Blind
175 N. Beacon St.
Watertown, MA 02172
617-924-3434

Phoenix House
164 W. 74th St.
New York, NY 10023
212-595-5810

Recording for the Blind
20 Roszel Rd.
Princeton, NJ 08540
609-452-0606

Robert Wood Johnson Foundation
P.O. Box 2316
Princeton, NJ 08543-2316
609-452-8701

Ronald McDonald House
3101 Berger Ave.
San Diego, CA 92123
619-292-7413

RP Foundation Fighting Blindness
1401 Mt. Royal Ave.
Baltimore, MD 21217
301-225-9400/9409(TDD)
800-638-2300

Ryan White National Fund
c/o Athletes and Entertainers for Kids
8961 Sunset Dr.
Los Angeles, CA 90069
213-276-5437

San Francisco AIDS Foundation
P.O. Box 6182
San Francisco, CA 94101-6182
415-864-5855

Seeing Eye, Inc.
P.O. Box 375
Morristown, NJ 07960
201-539-4425

Shriners Hospitals for Crippled Children
2900 Rocky Point Drive
Tampa, FL 33607
813-281-0300

Sickle Cell Disease Branch
Division of Blood Diseases and Resources, National Heart, Lung and Blood Institute
Bethesda, MD 20892
301-496-6931

Special Olympics Intl.
1350 New York Ave, NW
Suite 500
Washington, DC 20005
202-628-3630

Spina Bifida Association of America
1700 Rockville Pike, Suite 540
Rockville, MD 20852
800-621-3141

Starlight Foundation
10920 Wilshire Blvd.,
Suite 1640
Los Angeles, CA 90067
213-208-5885

Stifel Paralysis Research Foundation
P.O. Box 207
Short Hills, NJ 07078
201-467-5915

St. Jude's Children's Research Hospital
c/o American Lebanese Syrian
Associated Charities
301 St. Jude Place
Memphis, TN 38105

Sunshine Foundation
4010 Levick St.
Philadelphia, PA 19135
215-335-2622

Toughlove
P.O. Box 1069
Doylestown, PA 18901
215-348-7090

United Cerebral Palsy Association, Inc.
1522 K St., NW
Washington, DC 20005
202-842-1266
800-872-5827

United Hospital Fund
55 Fifth Avenue
New York, NY 10003

United Network of Organ Sharing
1100 Boulders Parkway,
Suite 500
P.O. Box 13770
Richmond, VA
804-330-8500
800-666-1884

United Parkinson Foundation
360 W. Superior St.
Chicago, IL 60610
312-664-2344

United Scleroderma Foundation
PO Box 350
Watsonville, CA 95077
408-728-2202
800-722-HOPE

Women for Sobriety
P.O. Box 618
Quakertown, PA 18951
215-536-8026

•••

**For it isn't enough to talk about peace.
One must believe in it. And it isn't enough
to believe in it. One must work for it.**

•••

—ELEANOR ROOSEVELT

Toward Peace

■ ■

• • •

We are just at the very beginning of our road, a long road, to a long-lasting peaceful period.

• • •

—SOVIET PRESIDENT MIKHAIL GORBACHEV

MEND

CREATION OF A MONSTER

In the past century, and most notably in the last thirty to forty years, conflicts throughout the world, fueled by internal strife and external intervention, have created massive military buildups. Spurred by fears of communist aggression, capitalistic imperialism, and religious domination, the world military "monster" has grown to earth-ending proportions.

And, like the fabled Dr. Frankenstein, the world leaders lost control of their creature. As the monster grew bigger, wars escalated—leading to incredible losses of human lives. Enormous amounts of money and resources went to sustaining the war effort, crippling economies with colossal amounts of debt and robbing social programs of much needed funds.

Armageddon became no longer a warning in the book of Revelations, but also a distinct and very real possibility as lethal weaponry and arms production threatened the existence of the planet.

TAMING THE BEAST

Recognizing that the worldwide military monster had gotten out of control, the world took steps to "tame the beast" during the late 1980s. Until the Persian Gulf crisis, the last few years have signaled a considerable reduction in worldwide conflicts. Many wars either ended or showed signs of peaceful resolution. The Soviet Union pulled its troops out of Afghanistan. Iran and Iraq laid down their arms after eight years of intense battling that took countless lives. In Angola, Cambodia, El Salvador, Cambodia, and Sri Lanka armed clashes diminished and/or turned toward resolution.

Many countries also showed signs of democracy by challenging the authority of restrictive governments. This quest for peace involved surges of freedom, independence, and democracy across the world. The Communist stronghold in Eastern Europe faded as the Berlin Wall crumbled and the Czechs, Poles, and Romanians toppled their governments. Violeta Chamorro led a Nicaraguan democratic movement and defeated Sandinista President Daniel Ortega. The world watched in hope and then sorrow as Chinese students stood up to oppression in a call for democracy. And in the summer of 1991 the world rejoiced when the people of the Soviet Union stood up for democracy, foiled a coup attempt and set out to disband communism.

As the Cold War draws to an end, the USSR, the Eastern bloc and Warsaw Pact nations, and the Western alliance seek to convert minds and muscle to more peaceful endeavors, including the redeployment of funds toward social and economic necessities.

TO END THE NUCLEAR ARMS RACE

Council For A Livable World

PAYING FOR PAST MISTAKES

The war in the Persian Gulf dramatically disrupted this peaceful trend. Saddam Hussein's brutal tactics, coupled with his formidable forces and lethal weaponry, harshly reminded the world that it still can suffer the consequences for its past policies. Fed by the technology, hardware, and services of many countries around the globe, Hussein's military forces grew to monstrous proportions. And after its brutal assault on Kuwait, the Iraqi "monster" threatened the stability of the region and the world.

The world quickly responded, though. President Bush's "line in the sand" policy, coupled with worldwide economic sanctions against Iraq, met with almost universal support among the United Nations members. And the Allied coalition, made up of more than a half million men and women from 27 countries, defeated the Iraqi army and took back Kuwait in a matter of weeks.

LEARNING FROM OUR MISTAKES

Indeed, the unprecedented worldwide effort to free Kuwait serves as a vivid example of the overwhelming desire for peace and freedom throughout the world. However, the Persian Gulf war has also allowed world leaders the chance to think seriously about their actions of the past, the present, and the future. It stands as a reminder of the costs—human, environmental, and economic—of war. It teaches them about the danger of letting too much power fall into the wrong hands. And it gives them the opportunity to redirect future policies toward more peaceful purposes.

WORLDWIDE CONFLICTS

...

.... Did you know?

▶ Since 1945, 120 armed conflicts have killed 20 million people. A total of 22 wars were fought in the 1980s.

▶ In 1987, 42 countries engaged in armed conflicts. Total estimated deaths from these conflicts, not including famine-related deaths, were 260,000.

The positive steps toward peace at the end of the 1980s could not have come at a better time.

Interestingly enough, although military buildups have occurred mainly among the industrialized nations, the majority of these wars were fought in third world countries. About 75 percent of these conflicts were caused by civil wars in which six had foreign troop involvement.*

FUELING AGGRESSION

Military intervention, foreign military aid, and arms exports all play a significant role in worldwide aggression. The United States and the Soviet Union have been involved directly and indirectly in many conflicts since World War II. Notable examples of military intervention by these two countries include Vietnam, Korea, Grenada, and Panama by the United States; and Hungary and Czechoslovakia by the Soviets.

Military aid—in terms of dollars, goods, and services by the United States, USSR, and many other countries has also helped fuel conflicts throughout the world, including the Middle East, Africa, and Central America. For example, Israel receives $3 billion and Egypt gets $2.26 billion in U.S. foreign aid. More than half of this allotment to both recipients goes toward their expenditures.

THE MILITARY INDUSTRY

*On Beyond War, Bob Stevens Special Report, April 1988.

**Worldwatch Papers #89. National Security: The Economic and Environmental Dimensions, Michael Renner, The Worldwatch Institute, May 1989. Note: The author includes these countries in the third world category for the "sake of simplicity" although they have fairly advanced industrial and technological capabilities.

Military spending from foreign and internal sources helps make the military industry one of the largest in many countries. The production and exportation of arms has proved to be big business. India, Israel, and Brazil comprise more than 60 percent of the third world arms-manufacturing community.**

Weapons manufacturing capabilities among these and

other countries is becoming highly sophisticated. Countries such as India, Pakistan, Israel, South Africa, South Korea, Taiwan, Argentina, and Brazil either have nuclear weapons or are close to developing them.

If a nation cannot develop its own sophisticated fire-power, it will seek from other countries. Iraq was charged with purchasing supplies to build nuclear weapons and Libya built a chemical weapons facility with the help of foreign technology.

THE STAKES ARE STILL HIGH

Although some progress has been made in reducing the number of conflicts throughout the world, the stakes are still high.

Did you know? ··········

▶ Since 1986, approximately 20 million people became refugees as a result of wars and other tyranny.

ON BEYOND WAR-SPECIAL REPORT

April 1988

Patterns of War and Resolution

Some say that there are more wars going on now than at any time in history. Bob Stevens, a real estate developer in Northern California and a Beyond War volunteer, wondered what could be learned from them about the process of ending war and building peace. He wanted to find out where the wars are, who is fighting whom, why they fight, and what are the positive steps being taken around the world to bring these wars to an end. For the past six months, Bob has spent about half of his business day reading everything he could find on the subject and building a computer data bank.

On Beyond War presents Bob's overview of the wars now raging, and the major efforts to end them.

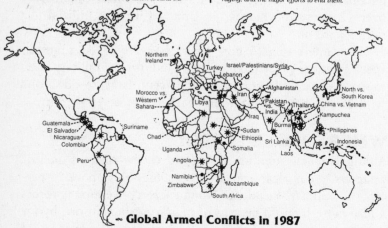

~ Global Armed Conflicts in 1987

●	Armed conflicts with 50 – 1000 deaths (Multiple conflicts within a country counted as one conflict)	14	Estimated deaths from armed conflicts (Famine-related deaths not included)	260,000
✳	Armed conflicts with more than 1000 deaths	20	Refugees as of 1986 (People internally displaced or taking refuge in other countries)	20,000,000
	Countries fighting in armed conflicts	42		

PATTERNS OF WAR

The wars being fought are essentially in the poorer Third World countries.

27 of the 34 armed conflicts are internal (civil) wars.

A clash of East–West ideologies has a major role in 13 of the 34 conflicts.

Ethnic or religious differences have a dominant role in 6 of the conflicts.

In 6 of the internal wars, foreign troops have a major role in the fighting.

PATTERNS OF RESOLUTION

A peace process has begun in at least 18 conflicts.

Significant progress towards ending 11 of these conflicts was made in 1987.

The UN is playing a leading role in efforts to resolve many of the conflicts.

Regional pressure is important in the process of resolving these conflicts.

Resolution of these conflicts has been a slow, step-by-step process.

Bob Stevens. "On Beyond War" Newsletter, Beyond War Foundation.

Easy access to advanced weaponry makes any conflict a threat to entire regions, if not to the whole world. Iraq's massive military and deadly firepower has sent shock waves across the planet. The devastation that resulted from the massive oil spill in the Persian Gulf, and the many oil-well fires in Kuwait will be felt throughout much of the world for years to come.

MILITARY MIGHT

■ ■ ■

.... Did you know?

In 1990 U.S. military expenditures were:
$818 million . . . a day
$34 million . . . an hour
$568,104 . . . a minute

MASSIVE SPENDING

Since World War II a total of $17.5 trillion has been spent throughout for the world for military purposes. In 1987, total world military spending surpassed $1 trillion. Most of that money is spent by industrialized nations.

Besides aggregate spending, military expenditures must be viewed in terms of their percentage of Gross National Product. The countries of the world spend an average of 6 percent of total production on the military. In 1985, the United States allocated approximately 6.6 percent of its total national productivity to the Pentagon. The Soviet Union spent over 12 percent, whereas the United Kingdom utilized just over 5 percent.*

It is interesting to note that lesser developed countries spent a greater percentage of their GNP for the military. Iraq topped the list with more than 40 percent, Israel stood second with 25 percent, and Ethiopia reached almost 10 percent.

WHERE DOES IT GO?

Although much attention is devoted to the costs of nuclear weapons, the nuclear arms race consumes only about 15 percent of military spending. Nonnuclear conventional forces utilize more than 80 percent of military expenditures, by far the greatest portion of the military spending allotment.

Nuclear weaponry. What does the world get for these trillions of dollars? By the late 1980s the world was equipped with approximately 50,000 nuclear weapons. The two superpowers dominate nuclear ownership with control of 96 percent of these weapons. Five other powerful nations including the United Kingdom, France, and China control 4 percent.

*The 1990 estimate of military spending as a percent of GNP is lower than the 1985 figure, standing at 5.7 percent. Defense expenditures of NATO Europe in 1990 are expected to be 3 percent of the total GNP.

The "firepower" of these weapons is almost unimaginable. The total explosive power of all bombs dropped in World War II was 3 megatons. Today, the world's nuclear arsenal amounts to 16,000 megatons, or the firepower of 5,300 World War II's. A single U.S. 10-warhead MX strategic missile's destructive capabilities equal that of 200 Hiroshima bombs. In less than 30 minutes this warhead or others like it can be fired from underground silos and travel more than 10,000 miles and strike within 300 feet of its target.*

Conventional forces. Conventional forces, including troops, comprise the largest portion of world military expenditures.

▶ The total number of armed forces in the world is approximately 29 million. Another 16 million people work in defense industries.

▶ In the United States, defense-related employment exceeds 6.5 million. This includes 3.3 million employed in arms producing industries, 1.1 million Department of Defense civil servants, and 2.2 million military personnel.

Did you know? ⋯⋯⋯

▶ The U.S. and the USSR comprise two-thirds of world military expenditures by spending about $300 billion a year each on the military.

*Worldwatch Papers #89, National Security, Michael Renner, May 1989; *Peace Resource Book,* The Institute for Defense and Disarmament Studies; SANE/FREEZE.

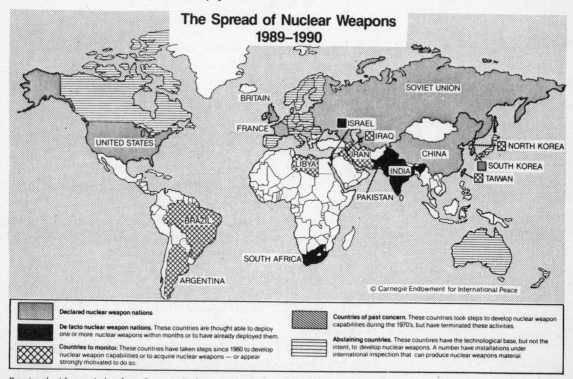

The Spread of Nuclear Weapons 1989–1990

SOVIET UNION · BRITAIN · FRANCE · ISRAEL · IRAQ · IRAN · LIBYA · CHINA · NORTH KOREA · SOUTH KOREA · TAIWAN · INDIA · PAKISTAN · UNITED STATES · BRAZIL · SOUTH AFRICA · ARGENTINA

© Carnegie Endowment for International Peace

Declared nuclear weapon nations

De facto nuclear weapon nations. These countries are thought able to deploy one or more nuclear weapons within months or to have already deployed them.

Countries to monitor. These countries have taken steps since 1980 to develop nuclear weapon capabilities or to acquire nuclear weapons — or appear strongly motivated to do so.

Countries of past concern. These countries took steps to develop nuclear weapon capabilities during the 1970's, but have terminated these activities.

Abstaining countries. These countries have the technological base, but not the intent, to develop nuclear weapons. A number have installations under international inspection that can produce nuclear weapons material.

Reprinted with permission from Carnegie Endowment for International Peace

▶ The total Soviet military personnel is approximately 5 million, with estimates of 4.5 million as actual military personnel employed by natural defense industries.

Other costs. Out of that $1 trillion military spending bill, approximately $80 to $100 billion goes toward research and development, whereas $200 billion goes toward military arms production. Besides nuclear weaponry and manpower, $1 trillion buys weapons systems, such as planes and tanks. Ships, submarines, and bombers are very expensive to build and maintain. For example, B-2 Stealth bombers cost $540 million apiece, and a Seawolf submarine costs $3.5 billion. The high price tags of these items make it easy to see how these costs add up to the almost $300 billion a year U.S. military budget.

ARMS CONTROL

∎∎∎

The United States strongly seeks a lasting agreement for the discontinuance of nuclear weapons tests. We believe that this would be an important step toward reduction of international tensions and would open the way to further agreement on substantial measures of disarmament.

—PRESIDENT DWIGHT D. EISENHOWER, April 13, 1959

The huge amounts of money and resources allocated to the military have served to thwart many other important programs in society, frequently leading to massive economic problems. In order to curb the military's negative effect on growth, as well as reduce the threat of a potential nuclear doomsday, the superpowers have engaged in arms control discussions, agreements, and treaties.

For more than 30 years the United States and the Soviet Union have been meeting to discuss reductions and/or total elimination of nuclear arms, including launchers and warheads; chemical and biological weapons; nonnuclear forces and troops; nuclear weapons testing; and strategic defense programs.

THE ARMS BUILDUP: NO LONGER A RACE

The end of the Cold War prompted new arms control talks between the two superpowers and their allies. Most noticeable are the dramatic proposals and agreements by the Americans and Soviets to reduce arms production, disarm some existing weapons, and cut troops and other conventional forces.

A number of other countries have also taken positive steps toward a more peaceful existence by reassessing their defense programs, closing army bases, and decreasing military expenditures. According to the Swedish Peace Institute (SIPRP), defense spending among the 16 NATO countries declined by 3 percent at the end of the decade. These numbers are expected to decline further into the 1990s.

A LOOK AHEAD

Although recent positive developments in the arms negotiations between the superpowers have allayed some fears of impending nuclear destruction among the world's "mighty," there is still much work to be done. Vladimir Petrovsky, Soviet vice minister of foreign affairs, explains, "I see first of all disarmament, which needs to keep the momentum and go further. In conflict resolution, I think it's a world situation where actually almost all the crisis situations are the subject of negotiations."*

The United States and the Soviet Union should use the period ahead not only to breathe a sigh of relief, but they must also attempt to take negotiations to even more lofty levels.

CONVERSION

■ ■ ■

CONVERSION—A DIVIDEND FOR PEACE

For years, many concerned people have argued that less money should be spent for military purposes and more should go toward social and environmental needs. The effective ending to the Cold War has now prompted more intense discussion about "conversion."

Did you know? ▪▪▪▪▪▪▪▪▪▪

▶ West Germany expects to drop defense spending by .8 percent in real terms in 1990.

▶ The British government's $33.5 billion defense bill could drop 3 percent a year, inflation adjusted, with Italy's dropping similarly.

▶ The Dutch announced a cut of $1.5 billion by 1995 and the Belgians discuss the withdrawal of 25,000 troops from Germany.

Michael Renner and the Worldwatch Institute, *State of the World 1990*, (New York: W. W. Norton, 1990).

*"Eastern Europeans Will Decide Their Own Policies," *USA Today*, 16 October 1989.

Conversion is the process of taking money and other resources that formerly went to military expenditures and reallotting it to other uses, such as social programs. Michael Renner of the Worldwatch Institute explains the benefits of economic conversion, or as some call it, a peace dividend. "By releasing resources now absorbed by the military, conversion can make an important contribution to the social and economic regeneration of urban areas, particularly benefiting disadvantaged inner-city residents. . . . Conversion could release desperately needed funds to clean up the planet."*

With the U.S. annual military budget at $300 billion, reductions in that category could provide sizable sums for some other humanitarian purposes. For instance, cutting the Pentagon budget in half would reduce the military's share of GNP to about 3 percent, freeing up $150 billion for other purposes.

WHO GETS THE PEACE DIVIDEND?

Just where that money will go is a subject of considerable debate, however. Helping the homeless, improving the na-

*The Bulletin of Atomic Scientists 312-702-2555

From Worldwatch Papers #89, National Security: The Economic and Environmental Dimensions, Michael Renner, the Worldwatch Institute, May 1989.

OTHER NEEDS BESIDE THE MILITARY

In order to understand the peace dividend a comparison of costs between military programs and social and environmental programs is necessary:

$100 billion	*Trident II and F-16 Jet Fighter Programs* Estimated clean-up cost for the 3,000 worst hazardous waste dumps in the U.S.
$68 billion	*Stealth Bomber Program* Two-thirds estimated costs to meet U.S. clean water goals by the year 2000.
$8 billion	*Approximately 4 days of global military spending* Action Plan over 5 years to save the world's tropical forests.
$1.4 billion	*1 Trident Submarine* 5-year child immunization program against 6 deadly diseases, preventing 1 million deaths a year.
$12 million	*1 Nuclear Weapons test* Installation of 80,000 hand pumps to give third world villages access to safe water.

tion's educational system, funding the war on drugs are a few social and human interest programs that could be funded. Environmental concerns such as cleaning the air, the water, and the polluted land cry out for extra monetary support. The nation's deteriorating infrastructure—its roads, bridges, mass transit, and other facilities require an urgent facelift. Finally, the country's massive deficit would benefit highly by a reduction in one of its greatest expenditures.

Obviously, many important projects and programs need more funding and the debt level of the country must decline. The positive trend toward peace in recent years may serve to provide a much needed shot in the arm. Richard Hornik of *Time* magazine aptly describes the nation's potential windfall. "Despite America's fiscal recklessness in the 1980s, the sudden end of the cold war has provided the nation at least a modest opportunity to improve its economic health without raising taxes or cutting already anemic social spending."*

With time, it is hoped that the movement toward peace will continue, so each and every group may receive its share of a progressively larger peace dividend.

IF A FREE SOCIETY CANNOT HELP THE MANY WHO ARE POOR, IT CANNOT SAVE THE FEW WHO ARE RICH —JOHN F. KENNEDY

Original linoleum block print by David Adams, 1986.

CONVERTING THE ECONOMY FROM WAR TO PEACE

Conversion is also the process of shifting the elements of the military sector—jobs, production, and research—to activities and occupations designed for peaceful purposes. For instance, how does a society reemploy its military personnel? If a soldier no longer has a job, can he or she find a similar or better paying occupation elsewhere? Will a military research scientist be able to take his or her knowledge to a corporation outside of the military industry? Also, can the nation effectively and smoothly retool factories that make weapons, planes, and tanks to produce automobiles, tractors, and television sets?

Although it is beneficial to contemplate and discuss conversion, the actual process is highly complex. This is due to the extensive integration of the military in this country and in many others, as well.

Redeploying funds. Approximately $120 billion a year is spent in this country to employ and outfit the military. The programs and people benefiting from this massive amount of funds must be redeployed elsewhere.

*"The Peace Dividend: Myth and Reality," *Time*, 12 February 1990.

Get Credit for Helping the Cause of Peace

Sane freeze

SANE/FREEZE Campaign for Global Security

Military customers. Many industries rely heavily on the military to buy their goods and services. More than 250,000 businesses in 215 industries rely on the military. For example, the U.S. military consumes 93 percent of the industrial output of the shipbuilding industry, 66 percent of the aircraft industry, and 20 percent of the electronic components industry.*

These industries would lose a very big customer if the military went out of business tomorrow.

The Research and Development (R&D) industry would suffer as well from a loss of the military as a client. According to the Council on Economic Priorities, R&D expenditures are close to 45 percent of total government and private spending. In the United States, an estimated 27 percent of all scientists and engineers are engaged in military-related work.**

Imagine the future. Obviously, many groups—including those employed by the military, have a vested interest in keeping their jobs or at least having the opportunity to shift careers. This is not to say that our nation's massive investment in the military is good and should not change. Just imagine a society that utilizes all of its resources toward peaceful ventures.

Budgeting a "Peace Dividend"

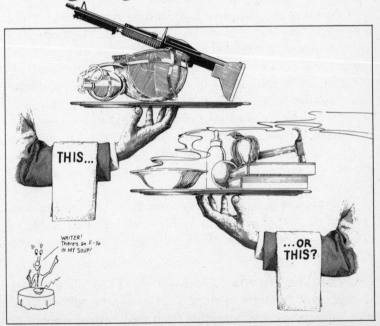

Tim Achor-Hock/Bread for the World

*"The Defense Buildup," 1977–1985, U.S. Department of Labor; Janice Castro, "Biting the Bullets," *Time,* 30 April 1990.

**Worldwatch Papers #89, National Security: The Economic and Environmental Dimensions, Michael Renner, the Worldwatch Institute, May 1989.

▶ Manpower could build new bridges and roads instead of submarines.

▶ Brainpower could create beneficial drugs rather than chemical weapons.

▶ Money spent accommodating the troops could be transferred to housing the poor.

What this discussion implies, however, is that conversion from a warring society to a peaceful one requires considerate thought—translated into manageable and equitable action.

THE THREAT OF AN EXPANDING "NUCLEAR CLUB"

● ● ●

CONFLICT AND RESOLUTION

In the summer of 1988 The Windstar Foundation, a research and education organization founded by John Denver and Tom Crum, conducted a fascinating weekend seminar about "Choices" for the future.

During one evening presentation Tom Crum discussed the topic of conflict and resolution. In a thought-provoking demonstration Tom pretended to hold a gun to the head of Vevgeni Velikhov, vice president of the Soviet Academy of Sciences and a member of the Supreme Soviet, the country's principal legislative body. Mr. Velikhov attended the seminar, during which he received the 1988 Windstar Award.

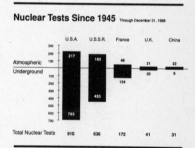

SANE/FREEZE Campaign for Global Security

Tom stood facing Mr. Velikhov with his arm wrapped around his neck as he held the imaginary gun to his head. He asked the Soviet gentleman to imitate him by pretending to point his own gun at Tom.

Then Tom asked the Soviet dignitary an interesting question.

"What type of man would Mr. Velikhov want to be holding such a weapon? A strong and mentally stable fellow, or a insecure, weak, and desperate man?"

To further illustrate the point, Tom tilted backwards and put both of them off balance. Tom then asked the same question.

The point became rather clear by the performance. Of course, neither wanted to be in a position in which one held a gun and the other did not. Both felt more comfortable if the stakes were equal. If one of the men stood off balance, however, it put both men at jeopardy.

STRENGTH VERSUS AGGRESSION

This illustration raises two important issues. First, it is important that the U.S. and the USSR retain their stability—economic and political. Not only must they both feel secure about each other, but they also must appear strong to the rest of the world.

It should be noted that there is a difference between strength and aggression. A strong country is comfortable with its current power, whereas an aggressive country desires more.

It is critical that countries holding weapons remain stable and strong, because nuclear weaponry does not allow room for error. The stakes have become too great—one mistake and everybody suffers drastically. In this age, stability and security are imperative.

CONTROLLING STRENGTH

The second topic evolves from a discussion of the first. Not only is it crucial that the two superpowers remain strong, it is also essential that all nations with the capacity of developing or purchasing nuclear bombs treat these weapons with the utmost respect and safety.

In the early 1980s many Americans worried about the threat of nuclear war. Communism was strong and still spreading. The Soviet Union was considered "evil." Both the Soviets and the Americans were aggressively increasing their doomsday arsenal.

As the decade went on both parties not only realized the danger of their mistrustful arms buildup, but they also did something about it by meeting face to face and subsequently reducing their weaponry.

Another element, however, crept into the picture. Lethal arms technology spread from the more industrialized nations to third world and other "less-developed" countries—making the issue of stability critically tested once again. And the stakes may be much higher because many of the emerging nuclear and chemical weapons players are in regions of instability, such as the Middle East and Asia. Libya, led by a dubious general, is manufacturing chemical bombs. The tension between the neighboring countries of India and Pakistan grows, along with their ability to produce deadly weapons. The Persian Gulf War proved how one man, Saddam Hussein, used dangerous weapons and the world's fourth largest army to put the region, and the world, in jeopardy.

Unfortunately, the list of countries with advanced arms-producing capabilities is growing, together with the number of areas in the world considered "hotspots" of conflict. It is interesting that although most of the world's military bill is spent by the superpowers, the majority of the more recent conflicts have occurred outside the backyard of these countries. Moreover, as NATO and the Warsaw Pact appear headed toward arms reduction, other lesser-developed countries seek to increase their weapons capability. The Institute for Defense and Disarmament Studies points out the danger of such a trend:

> As more and more countries gain access to nuclear and high technology conventional weapons systems, and their own independent military industries, the ability of today's major powers to reduce the arms race decreases. More actors create a more complex system. The utility of military powers, already declining, will diminish further still as retaliatory capabilities increase. But the world will be on more of a hair trigger, wired to an ever greater number of detonators arising from regional conflicts. In effect, the world's nations, led by the superpowers, will spend tens of trillions of dollars to create an ever more dangerous situation.*

*Peace Resource book 1988–89, Institute for Defense and Disarmament Studies.

Each superpower must concentrate not only on defusing its own immediate situation but also on potential tragedies outside its own backyard. And it is the realization of this emerging di-

Carnegie Endowment for International Peace

THE "NUCLEAR CLUB"

···

Declared Nuclear Weapon Countries
China
France
Soviet Union
Great Britain
United States

"de facto" Nuclear Weapon Countries
India
Israel
Pakistan
South Africa

Countries of Proliferation Concern
Iran, Iraq
Argentina
North Korea
Libya, Brazil

---

lemma that strikes fear into the minds and hearts of our leaders, motivating them not only to remain stable, but also to assure stability throughout the world.

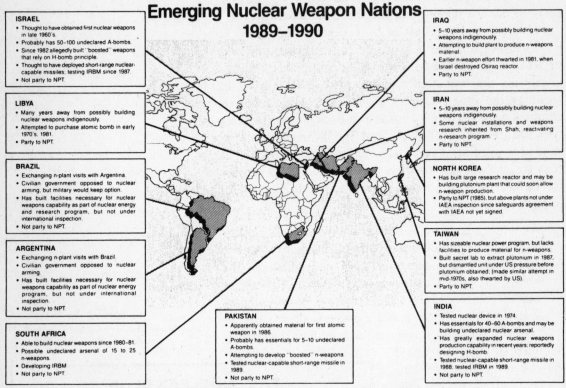

Emerging Nuclear Weapon Nations 1989–1990

ISRAEL
- Thought to have obtained first nuclear weapons in late 1960's.
- Probably has 50–100 undeclared A-bombs.
- Since 1982 allegedly built "boosted" weapons that rely on H-bomb principle.
- Thought to have deployed short-range nuclear-capable missiles; testing IRBM since 1987.
- Not party to NPT.

LIBYA
- Many years away from possibly building nuclear weapons indigenously.
- Attempted to purchase atomic bomb in early 1970's, 1981.
- Party to NPT.

BRAZIL
- Exchanging n-plant visits with Argentina.
- Civilian government opposed to nuclear arming, but military would keep option.
- Has built facilities necessary for nuclear weapons capability as part of nuclear energy and research program, but not under international inspection.
- Not party to NPT.

ARGENTINA
- Exchanging n-plant visits with Brazil.
- Civilian government opposed to nuclear arming.
- Has built facilities necessary for nuclear weapons capability as part of nuclear energy program, but not under international inspection.
- Not party to NPT.

SOUTH AFRICA
- Able to build nuclear weapons since 1980–81.
- Possible undeclared arsenal of 15 to 25 n-weapons.
- Developing IRBM.
- Not party to NPT.

IRAQ
- 5–10 years away from possibly building nuclear weapons indigenously.
- Attempting to build plant to produce n-weapons material.
- Earlier n-weapon effort thwarted in 1981, when Israel destroyed Osiraq reactor.
- Party to NPT.

IRAN
- 5–10 years away from possibly building nuclear weapons indigenously.
- Some nuclear installations and weapons research inherited from Shah; reactivating n-research program.
- Party to NPT.

NORTH KOREA
- Has built large research reactor and may be building plutonium plant that could soon allow n-weapon production.
- Party to NPT (1985), but above plants not under IAEA inspection since safeguards agreement with IAEA not yet signed.

TAIWAN
- Has sizeable nuclear power program, but lacks facilities to produce material for n-weapons.
- Built secret lab to extract plutonium in 1987, but dismantled unit under US pressure before plutonium obtained. (made similar attempt in mid-1970s, also thwarted by US).
- Party to NPT.

INDIA
- Tested nuclear device in 1974.
- Has essentials for 40–60 A-bombs and may be building undeclared nuclear arsenal.
- Has greatly expanded nuclear weapons production capability in recent years; reportedly designing H-bomb.
- Tested nuclear-capable short-range missile in 1988, tested IRBM in 1989.
- Not party to NPT.

PAKISTAN
- Apparently obtained material for first atomic weapon in 1986.
- Probably has essentials for 5–10 undeclared A-bombs.
- Attempting to develop "boosted" n-weapons.
- Tested nuclear-capable short-range missile in 1989.
- Not party to NPT.

NPT—The Nuclear Non-Proliferation Treaty. Requires all nuclear installations in a signatory country to be placed under International Atomic Energy Agency inspection.

Reprinted with permission from Carnegie Endowment for International Peace

WHAT CAN I DO?

. . . .

▶ **Support peace organizations and their activities.** Peace organizations pursue countless activities to promote their cause. These activities range from organizing community chapters to meeting with political leaders.

    ▶ For detailed information about the types of peace groups and their missions, refer to *The Peace Resource Book: A Comprehensive Guide to the Issues, Organizations, and Literature,* published by The Institute for Defense and Disarmament Studies.

▶ **Vote for peace!** Learn the past record and promises by political candidates on issues of peace:

    ▶ Contact Peace Links for their Vote Peace Kit.

▶ The Council for a Livable World publishes profiles of political officials and candidates and lobbies extensively for peace issues.

▶ **Learn about peace issues.** The reference materials listed at the end of this section provide much information about peace issues. Many peace organizations publish educational materials as well.

▶ The Union of Concerned Scientist's Voter Education Project provides arms control and energy information to 2 million voters.

▶ The National Security Archive, a division of the Fund for Peace, makes available the internal government documentation that is indispensable for research and informed public debate on important issues of foreign intelligence, defense, and international economic policy.

▶ The Nuclear Age Peace Foundation, an educational organization, publishes books and newsletters such as "Waging Peace," "Nuclear Alert," and "Global Security Studies."

▶ The Arms Control Association provides in-depth articles on arms control issues written by experts in the field of arms control and national security policy.

▶ The Better World Society offers videos on peace such as "Disarmament and Beyond," "Behind the Threat," and "Are We Winning, Mommy?" Show the BWS videos to your friends and organizations.

▶ **Promote peace curriculum in our schools and teach your children about issues of war and peace.** The best way to foster peace throughout the world is to educate our children about issues of war and peace and give them ideas and actions they can take to help bring about peace on the planet.

▶ Contact Peace Links for their information kits: Talking to Your Children Kit; Celebrate Peace-Elementary School Kit; Reach for Peace-High School Kit.

▶ Refer to *Working for Peace,* by the Fund for Peace, for more resources on peace issues and children. Some of the books include *What About the Children?,* by the Parents and Teachers for Social Responsibility; *A Manual on Non-Violence and Children,* by Stephanie Judson; and *How to Talk to Your Children About Nuclear War,* by Peace Links and Women Against Nuclear War.

▶ Mothers Embracing Nuclear Disarmament (MEND) educates people about peace issues and helps them teach

When people lead, eventually the leaders will follow.

Did you know? ··········

▶ The Council for a Livable World publishes *How to Lobby Congress for an End to the Nuclear Arms Race,* a citizen's guide to lobbying Congress, which provides practical advice on the most effective methods of constituent lobbying and describes how Congress acts on the military budget and shapes nuclear arm policies.

If we wish to create a lasting peace, . . . we must begin with the children.

—MAHATMA GANDHI

what they have learned to their children. Ask for their "Children's Wish for Peace" brochure, which deals with children's fear of nuclear war and explains what children can do for peace.

What children can do to make a difference.

- Ask yourself: "What can I do to make peace in my family or at school? Are there ways I can solve problems better with my brothers and sisters or with friends?"
- Demonstrate good sportsmanship. Promote cooperative rather than competitive games.
- Learn about the variety of cultures in this country – and around the world. Become a pen pal.
- Read or tell stories that illustrate themes of cooperation, respect for others, and peaceful conflict resolution. Talk about these stories; draw, paint or sculpt something to illustrate these ideas.

- Ask for assembly speakers or school programs related to peace or international friendship and understanding.
- Do study projects at school related to the concept of peace.
- Work on peace-related programs and projects within your school, church or community.
- Become informed. Read newspapers, magazines and books, watch TV programs that discuss current events and the past. Talk about these events with your parents, teachers, clergy and friends.
- Write to elected officials and local and national newspapers to express your feelings.
- Get involved and work for a peace organization.

This brochure was produced by Mothers Embracing Nuclear Disarmament (MEND), a national, nonprofit, educational organization. MEND's mission is to inspire mothers and other nurturers with the hope, the means, and the belief in their own ability to take actions that reduce the risk of nuclear war.

MEND supports multilateral, verifiable nuclear arms reductions and other efforts to promote understanding among the people and nations of the world. We recognize the need for a strong defense, but believe that our survival depends on taking a new approach to national security.

Mothers Embracing Nuclear Disarmament
National Office: P. O. Box 2309 La Jolla, CA 92038 ■ (619) 454-3343
Washington Office: 1801 18th Street Washington, D.C. 20009 ■ (202) 232-0418

·········· Did you know?

▶ A nine-month campaign by SANE/FREEZE and other peace groups for ratification of the Intermediate Nuclear Forces Treaty (INF) culminated in an overwhelming Senate vote in favor of the Treaty.

▶ The 20/20 National Vision Project provides resources necessary to write letters to members of Congress.

▶ Bread for the World provides information about legislative issues related to peace and offers profiles of politicians.

▶ **Promote a school trip to Washington or to a local political office.** For instance, the Fund for Peace launched a "Days in D.C." program, which brought New York City schoolchildren to Washington, DC.

▶ **Get involved with Peace Child.** Since 1982, the Peace Child Foundation has utilized the performing arts and international exchanges to promote cultural understanding.

The main vehicle for its programs, PEACE CHILD is a musical fantasy based on *The Peace Book* by Bernard S. Benson, which tells how children bring peace to the world. The Peace Child Foundation has been set up to promote that fantasy and play a part in making it a reality.

There have been in excess of 1,000 presentations of PEACE CHILD in the USA and around the world, involving approximately 15,000 children and seen by almost one million people.

▶ Call 703-385-4494 for more information.

▶ **Let your voice be heard!** If you are concerned about issues such as military costs, the arms buildup, and the safety of nuclear weapon testing, let your voice be heard! For instance, Barbara Wiedner worried about the future welfare of her grandchildren so she started Grandmothers for Peace.

ORDINARY PEOPLE—EXTRAORDINARY ACTIONS
BARBARA WIEDNER—GRANDMOTHER FOR PEACE

Barbara Wiedner, of Sacramento, Calif., was just like many other grandmothers throughout the country. Her main concerns were the welfare and lives of her children and grandchildren. However, in 1982 her world of concerns expanded as she discovered that the nearby Mather Air Force Base housed nuclear weapons.

"I suddenly realized the horrible thought that the generation of grandchildren could well end up as the last generation on earth."

Determined to do something about it, Wiedner participated in a protest at the air force base where she and others were arrested. That experience only firmed her resolve to seek peace and so she started Grandmothers for Peace, an organization of over 20,000 grandmothers and others committed to peace in this lifetime.

Since 1982, Mrs. Wiedner has participated in demonstrations and other activities for peace in many parts of the country and abroad—highlighted by five trips to the Soviet Union, including a meeting with Mrs. Gorbachev. And as further proof of her continued resolve for peace she has been arrested a total of fifteen times—one for each of her grandchildren!

For more information about Grandmothers for Peace, call 916-444-5080.

▶ **If you are concerned about nuclear weapons testing, let your feelings be known.** The creation and testing of nuclear weapons not only costs millions of dollars that could be spent for other human needs programs, it also harms the environment. There are reports of increased cancer rates among the population living near nuclear production facilities and incidence of leakages of radioactive poisons into the air, water, and soil. Clean-up costs may be as high as $110 billion.

For these reasons, many of the first and most notable peace groups concentrate on nonviolent demonstrations against the nuclear weaponry and testing. Protests at test sites, missile launch pads, and political offices are some of the areas where these groups voice their feelings.

Did you know? ▪▪▪▪▪▪▪▪▪

▶ Since 1985, the American Peace Test, SANE/FREEZE, and other groups have organized some of the largest demonstrations of nonviolent resistance with their "Reclaim the Test Site" demonstration. Protesters meet at a Nevada nuclear test location. Participants have included elected officials, labor and religious leaders, students and seniors, including representation by every ethnic, sexual, and political segment of the peace movement.

▶ SANE/FREEZE, Greenpeace, and other U.S., European, and Asian groups joined together for an International Test Ban Campaign, which included a worldwide program of action and education on Hiroshima Day, August 6.

> ▶ **Contact your legislators.** If you are concerned about issues of peace, let your political representatives know. They often will have to vote on issues such as the funding of a particular weapon and the allocation of certain moneys. Pressure from constituents will help them decide.

> ▶ To learn more about contacting your legislators, refer to "Writing Letters" (page 13) and "Your Political Representative Works for You!" (page 18).

▶ **Become a citizen diplomat.** Many citizens of this country and others join together in various worldwide forums. These meetings include camps, educational programs, and rehabilitation projects.

Albert Einstein once said that "peace cannot be kept by force. It can only be achieved by understanding." Citizen diplomats believe that everyone has the ability and the responsibility to foster peace in the world.

A citizen diplomat participates in programs that bring people together from around the world to unique forums for the development of creative solutions to current global challenges.

▶ **Open to all ages.** Citizen diplomat programs involve people of all ages, including children. In fact, there are many opportunities for children to connect with their counterparts across the world. In 1983, 10-year-old Samantha Smith wrote a letter to the Soviet government about peace between our nations. As perhaps our youngest goodwill ambassador she went to a Soviet youth camp at the invitation Premier Yuri Andropov and paved the way for many other peace activists to visit and learn about other countries and their citizens.

Now, children throughout the world write letters to each other, join student exchange programs, and meet in conferences and camps. Their experiences serve to show the adults of the world that we can all live together. As President Gorbachev points out, "Children show

---

EXAMPLE:

Feb. 1, 1969

The Hon. Glenn Anderson
House of Representatives
Washington, D.C., 30618

Dear Rep. Anderson,

I urge you to vote against the [XXX] system, Bill [No. YYY]. I believe it is a dangerous nuclear weapon, which threatens our safety and increases the likelihood of war.

How are you planning to vote on this issue?

Sincerely,

Jane Q. Public
222 Main St.
Yosemite, CA 90900

SANE/FREEZE Campaign for Global Security

Adapted from Fund for Peace article, by Karin von Hippel, assistant to the director, Fund for Peace.

STUDENTS FOR PEACE

During the spring of 1989 more than 350 schoolchildren traveled to the nation's capital to participate in "Days in D.C.," a program on conflict resolution sponsored by the Fund for Peace.

A total of seven classes from New York schools met with members of Congress, sat in on Congressional proceedings, and toured some of Washington's important museums and attractions.

The Fund for Peace, a private, nonprofit educational organization dedicated to the preservation of peace and human rights, paid all expenses for the trip.

to us an example of how one should get rid of prejudices and boring stereotypes."

Youth diplomacy programs offer some effective ways to achieve world peace because they help to build a foundation of acceptance and friendship rather than prejudice and distrust with our future leaders.

INTERNATIONAL WORKCAMPS

International workcamps are like a fully internationalized short-term "peace corps." For more than 70 years, workcamps have brought people from different countries together to engage in projects such as construction, restoration, environmental, social, agricultural, and maintenance.

For example, volunteers from the Soviet Union, Czechoslovakia, France, West Germany, Finland, Canada, and Turkey met for three weeks in Harlem to help feed and house the homeless. Working with the Emmaus House, the Volunteers for Peace participants renovated an old woodshop for use as a shelter for the homeless. Workcamp volunteers from Costa Rica, the United States, and the Soviet Union planted trees in several regions of Costa Rica during a workcamp organized by Earthstewards.

Workcamp volunteers live together, share experiences, and in turn gain a greater understanding of each other.

▶ For more information about International Workcamps, contact the Volunteers for Peace and ask for the International Workcamp directory which contains over 800 listings of workcamp opportunities in 33 countries throughout Europe.

▶ If you would like to host international workcamp participants while they are in the United States, contact Volunteers for Peace.

THE ONLY REQUIREMENT— FRIENDSHIP AND UNDERSTANDING

Citizen diplomacy programs bring so much enrichment and understanding to the lives of their participants. President Ronald Reagan noted to a group of Soviet Youth Ambassadors that "when individual citizens in diverse nations are exposed to each other's way of life, their philosophies and opinions come into clearer view and a friendly discourse can ensue."*

Did you know? ▪▪▪▪▪▪▪▪▪▪▪

▶ The International Youth Ambassadors offer programs such as leadership and international diplomacy training experiences and other educational summits where one learns about other parts of the world and meets people from those areas.

▶ The Earthstewards Network sponsors exchanges to the Soviet Union by American youth and adults.

▶ The Volunteers for Peace organizes international work camps where people from four or five different countries participate in a community project together, such as the planting of trees in India or building of low-income homes in Connecticut.

▶ Connect US-USSR creates linkages between Soviet and American organizations through such programs as youth soccer exchanges with teams in Kimre, Soviet Union, and Minneapolis.

*From the *International Workcamper* 1990, the annual newsletter of the Volunteers for Peace.

I don't know of any other way I could have gotten a more genuine look at Soviet life and the Soviet people.

—RACHEL HASTINGS, 1989 volunteer in the Soviet Union

Until we meet in Pereslavl

"Goodbye, my new friend"

The most cherished moment I had with my Soviet friends was the day we said goodbye. Natalie Velikhov and I stood holding each other in the church patio. We each had a white helium balloon and we tied the two balloons together, kissed them and let them go. The balloons together symbolized our love for each other and our commitment to our friendship and peace.

—Ginna Swavely, age 13

Youth Ambassadors International 202-734-6132

As we break down the barriers of ignorance we begin to realize that everyone has the same questions, fears, and hopes and through that understanding we can step forward into a world of peace.

Organizations for Citizen Diplomacy

Center for U.S.-U.S.S.R. Initiatives
415-346-1875
Citizen Diplomacy travel, hosting Soviets, and Educational Outreach.

Connect US-USSR
612-333-1962
A nonprofit Minneapolis organization that arranges sister-city projects between the Twin Cities and Novosibirsk, a Soviet city of 1.5 million people. They also develop projects for other Americans and Soviets seeking exchanges and relationships.

Earthstewards Network
206-842-7986
A Washington-based group that sponsors dozens of citizen diplomacy trips to the Soviet Union, northern Ireland, and elsewhere.

Institute for Soviet American Relations (ISAR)
202-387-3034
ISAR serves as a clearinghouse for Soviet-American exchange, providing information and answering questions from organizations, individuals, government offices, and the press. It is the hope of ISAR, that by making connections between people, ideas, and systems, we can help build a network of greater understanding and cooperation in Soviet-American relations. Ask for a copy of *Hosting Soviet Visitors: A Handbook* and about *Surviving Together:*

A Journal of Soviet-American Relations.

The Peace Child Foundation
703-385-4494
Since 1982, the Peace Child Foundation has utilized the performing arts and international exchanges to promote cultural understanding. The main vehicle for its programs, PEACE CHILD, is a musical fantasy based on *The Peace Book* by Bernard S. Benson, which tells how children bring peace to the world. The Peace Child Foundation has been set up to promote that fantasy and play a part in making it a reality. There have been more than 1,000 presentations of PEACE CHILD in the United States and around the world, involving approximately 15,000 children and seen by almost 1 million people.

Peace Corps
800-424-8580
Peace Corps volunteers help people in developing countries learn new ways to fight hunger, disease, poverty, and lack of opportunity.

Peace Links
202-544-0805
Contact them about the US/USSR Letter Links, which organizes people from those countries to write and receive letters.

Volunteers for Peace (VFP)
802-259-2759
VFP operates under the aegis of UNESCO. One of their main programs is the coordination of International Workcamps. International workcamps are like a fully internationalized short-term "peace corps." In the summer of 1989 VFP coordinated 25 workcamps in 13 states involving more than 325 foreign volunteers from 25 countries. VFP also placed more than 400 Americans in 600 workcamps abroad. Ask them for a copy of the 1990 *International Workcamp Directory* (112 pages), which contains over 800 listings of workcamp opportunities in 33 countries throughout Europe.

Youth Exchange Service (YES)
800-848-2121/714-955-2030
An international teenage exchange student program dedicated to world peace. If you are interested in hosting an international teenage "ambassador" contact this group.

OTHER COMMITTED ORGANIZATIONS

▶ For more information about citizen diplomacy between the United States and the Soviet Union, refer to *Working for Peace,* by the Fund for Peace, a book that lists resources and organizations on this subject.

American Field Service Intercultural Programs
212-949-4242

Center for Innovative Diplomacy
714-250-1296

Citizen Exchange Council
212-643-1985

Experiment in International Living
802-257-7751

A REPRESENTATIVE SAMPLING OF PEACE ORGANIZATIONS

■ ■ ■

Citizen mobilization for peace has been around as long as the threat of war. Today, there are thousands of peace organizations throughout the world that concentrate on a wide variety of issues. Some groups are more general in nature, providing information or promoting action in topics ranging from defense cuts to citizen diplomacy. Other organizations specialize on issues such as citizen defense, war-tax resistance, or economic conversion.

"Never doubt that a small group of thoughtful, committed citizens can change the world. Indeed, it's the only thing that ever has."

—MARGARET MEAD

Organizations and Resources

The Arms Control Association
202-797-4626

A non-partisan national organization founded in 1971 by a group of experts in the field of arms control and national security policy. The purpose of the Association is to promote understanding of arms control and its contribution to national security. Among the Association's programs are the publication of ARMS CONTROL TODAY, a monthly compendium of opinion, analysis and factual information.

Beyond War
415-328-7756

Focuses on the questions of what life would be like in the world if we did not have any war. Publishes "On Beyond War."

Concerned Educators Allied for a Safe Environment (CEASE)
617-628-9030

A national network of parents, teachers, and other advocates of young children who work toward the elimination of nuclear power, the abolition of all nuclear weapons, and the end to their production and stockpiling. They also work for the redirection of funds from the military to human service programs for young children and their families. Ask for a copy of *Learning to Be Peaceful Together: A Handbook for Teachers and Parents of Young Children* ($12.50).

Council on Economic Priorities
212-420-1133/800-822-6435

Founded almost 20 years ago to promote corporate responsibility, they rate corporate America on its performance in environmental impact, military weapon involvement, and community participation. Ask about their publications *Shopping for a Better World* and *Rating America's Corporate Conscience.*

Council for a Livable World
617-542-2282

A nonpartisan political action committee devoted solely to the prevention of nuclear war. The Council publishes profiles of political officials and candidates and lobbies extensively for peace issues. Ask for a copy of *How to Lobby Congress for an End to the Nuclear Arms Race.*

Fellowship of Reconciliation (FOR)
914-358-4601

An interfaith peacemaking organization, FOP has carried out programs and educational projects concerned with racial justice, ending violence against women, disarmament, nonviolent alternatives to conflict, and rights of conscience.

Fund for Peace
212-661-5900

The Fund for Peace has developed a number of independent, semi-independent, and in-house projects representing a variety of approaches to peace. These include CDI, the National Security Archive, and the US-Soviet Scholar Exchange. Ask for a copy of *Working for Peace,* an annotated resource guide on issues ranging from arms control to peace studies and careers.

Grandmothers for Peace
916-444-5080

A grass-roots, all-volunteer organization whose primary focus has been to halt the nuclear arms race and violence in all its forms around the globe.

Institute for Defense and Disarmament Studies (IDDS)
617-734-4216

A research and education organization committed to the abolition of nuclear arms. Provides information on subjects ranging from military escalation to arms control treaties.

International Physicians for the Prevention of Nuclear War
617-868-5050

A federation of national groups dedicated to mobilizing the influence of the medical profession against the threat of nuclear weapons.

Jobs with Peace
617-338-5783

Concerned with the issues of converting military resources to other very important spending areas, such as social programs.

Mothers Embracing Nuclear Disarmament (MEND)
619-454-3343

A national, nonprofit educational organization whose mission is to inspire mothers and other nurturers with the hope, the means, and the belief in their own ability to take actions that reduce the threat of nuclear war.

Nuclear Age Peace Foundation
805-965-3443
A nonprofit and nonpartisan educational organization. The Foundation develops and supports innovative, action-oriented ideas to reverse the nuclear arms race, and find nonviolent solutions to international conflicts. They publish "Waging Peace," a series of booklets that explore the nuclear weapons dilemma from different viewpoints, and offer positive steps for reversing the nuclear arms race.

Peace Links
202-544-0805
A nationwide network of citizens who are committed to the prevention of nuclear war. Founded in 1982 by Betty Bumpers, wife of Senator Dale Bumpers of Arkansas. Ask for publications such as "Global Awareness Kit" and "Reach for Peace: High School Kit."

SANE/FREEZE
202-862-9740
SANE/FREEZE is a nonprofit peace organization dedicated to nuclear disarmament, nonintervention, and controlled military spending. The largest national peace organization with membership over 170,000, SANE/FREEZE results from the merging of two organizations in 1987: SANE (The Committee for a Sane Nuclear Policy) and the National Nuclear Weapons Freeze Campaign.

Union of Concerned Scientists
617-547-5552
An independent, nonprofit organization of scientists and other citizens concerned about the impact of advanced technology on society. UCS is committed to national security policies that reduce the threat of nuclear war. UCS also works for an environmentally sound energy policy and for nuclear power safety.

War Resisters League
212-228-0450
A group concerned with complete disarmament, nonintervention, and war-tax resistance.

World Federalist Association
800-HATE-WAR
An organization which stresses a world government as the solution to the many problems to today. Advocates strengthening the United Nations and convening a World Constitutional Convention.

World Policy Institute
212-490-0010
An organization concerned with creating security for all nations, including the United States. Promotes improving political relationships and publishes information on issues such as disarmament and social justice.

Worldwatch Institute
202-638-6300
A research and education organization concerned with issues such as the environment, global poverty, and peace. Publishes *Worldwatch*, a bimonthly magazine reporting on important topics and *The State of the World*, an annual book on important planetary concerns. Ask for a copy of Worldwatch Paper #89, "National Security: The Economic and Environmental Dimensions."

...I PUT EVERYTHING I HAD IN WAR BONDS,... AND THEN PEACE BROKE OUT!

ZiGGY®

PEACE ORGANIZATIONS

ACCESS
1730 M St., #605
Washington, DC 20036
202-785-6630

American Committee on US-Soviet Relations
109 Eleventh St., SE
Washington, DC 20003
202-546-1700

American Field Service Intercultural Programs
313 E. 43rd St.
New York, NY 10017
212-949-4242

American Friends Service Committee/NARMIC
1501 Cherry St.
Philadelphia, PA 19102
215-241-7000

The Arms Control Association
11 Dupont Circle, NW
Washington, DC 20036
202-797-4626

The Better World Society
1100 Seventeenth St., NW
Suite 502
Washington, DC 20036

Beyond War
222 High St.
Palo Alto, CA 94301
415-328-7756

Bikes Not Bombs
P.O. Box 56538
Brightwood Station
Washington, DC 20011
202-589-1810

Bulletin of Atomic Scientists
6042 S. Kimbark Ave.

Chicago, IL 61637
312-702-2555

Business Executives for National Security
600 Pennsylvania Ave., NW
Washington, DC 20004
202-737-1090

Carnegie Endowment for International Peace
11 DuPont Circle, NW, #900
Washington, DC 20036
202-797-6400

CEASE
P.O. Box 44-456
Somerville, MA 02144
617-628-9030

Center for Defense Information
1500 Massachusetts Ave., NW
Washington, DC 20005
202-862-0700

Center for Development Policy
731 Eighth St., SE
Washington, DC 20003
202-547-3800

Center for Economic Conversion
222 View St.
Mountain View, CA 94041
415-968-8798

Center for Innovative Diplomacy
17931 Sky Park Circle, #F
Irvine, CA 92714
714-250-1296

Center for International Policy
1755 Massachusetts Ave., NW
Washington, DC 20036
202-232-3317

Center for National Security Studies
122 Maryland Ave., NE
Washington, DC 20002
202-544-5380

Center for U.S.-U.S.S.R. Initiatives
3268 Sacramento St.
San Francisco, CA 94115
415-346-1875

Center on Budge and Policy Priorities
236 Massachusetts Ave., NE
Washington, DC 20002
202-546-9737

Citizen Exchange Council
12 West 31st St.
New York, NY 10001-4415
212-643-1985

Citizens Against Nuclear War
1616 P St., NW, #320
Washington, DC 20036
202-322-4823

Committee for National Security
1601 Connecticut Ave., NW
Washington, DC 20009
202-745-2450

Common Cause
2030 M. St., NW
Washington, DC 20036
202-833-1200

Connect US-USSR
2225 E. Franklin St.
Minneapolis, MN 55409
612-333-1962

Consortium on Peace Research, Education and Development (COPRED)
Center for Conflict Resolution

George Mason University
4400 University Drive
Fairfax, VA 22030
703-323-2806

Council for a Livable World
20 Park Plaza
Boston, MA 02116
617-542-2282

Council on Economic Priorities
30 Irving Place
New York, NY 10003
212-420-1133

EarthStewards Network
P.O. Box 10697
Bainbridge Island, WA 98110
206-842-7986

Experiment in International Living
Black Mountain Rd.
Brattleboro, VT 05301
802-257-7751

Fellowship of Reconciliation
P.O. Box 271
Nyack, NY 10960
914-358-4601

Foreign Policy Association
729 Seventh Ave.
New York, NY 10019
212-764-4050

The Fund for Peace
345 E. 46th St.
New York, NY 10017
212-661-5900

Global Education Associates
475 Riverside Drive
Suite 456
New York, NY 10115
212-870-3290

Grandmothers for Peace
909 12th St., Suite 118
Sacramento CA 95814
916-444-5080

Institute for Defense and Disarmament Studies
2001 Beacon St.

Brookline, MA 02146
617-734-4216

Institute for Peace and Justice
4144 Lindell, #122
St. Louis, MO 63108
314-533-4445

Institute for Policy Studies
1601 Connecticut Ave., NW
Washington, DC 20009
202-234-9382

Institute for Soviet-American Relations (ISAR)
1608 New Hampshire Ave., NW
Washington, DC 20009
202-387-3034

Jobs with Peace Campaign
76 Summer St.
Boston, MA 02110
617-338-5783

Mothers Embracing Nuclear Disarmament (MEND)
P.O. Box 2309
La Jolla, CA 92038
619-454-3343

National Peace Institute Foundation
1100 Maryland Ave., NW
#409
Washington, DC 20002
202-546-9500

Nuclear Age Peace Foundation
1187 Coast Billage Rd. #123
Santa Barbara, CA 93108
805-969-9137

Nuclear Information and Resource Service
1424 16th St., NW #601
Washington, DC 20036
202-328-0002

Nukewatch
2206 Fox Ave.
Madison, WI 53711
608-256-4146

Pacific Peace Fund
5516 Roosevelt Way, NE

Seattle, WA 98105
206-525-0025

Peace Development Fund
P.O. Box 270
Amherst, MA 01004
413-256-8306

Peace Child Foundation
3977 Chain Bridge Road, Suite 204
Fairfax, VA 22030
703-385-4494

Peace Corps
P-301
Washington, DC 20526
800-424-8580

Peace Links
747 Eighth St., SE, Dept. L
Washington, DC 20003
202-544-0805

Peacenet/Institute for Global Communications
3228 Sacramento St.
San Francisco, CA 94115
415-923-0900

Physicians for Social Responsibility
1601 Connecticut Ave., NW
Washington, DC 20009
202-939-5750

Promoting World Peace
P.O. Box 5103
112 Beach Ave.
Woodmont, CT 06460
203-878-4769

Quixote Center
P.O. Box 5206
Hyattsville, MD 20782

Resource Center for Nonviolence
515 Broadway
Santa Cruz, CA 95060
408-423-1626

SANE/FREEZE
1819 H St., NW, Suite 1000
Washington, DC 20006-3603
202-862-9740

20/20 Vision National Project
69 South Pleasant St., #203

Amherst, MA 01002
413-253-2939

Union of Concerned Scientists
26 Church St.
Cambridge, MA 02238
617-547-5552

United Nations Association—USA
485 Fifth Ave., 2nd floor
New York, NY 10017
212-697-3232

United States Institute of Peace
1550 M St., NW, #700
Washington, DC 20005
202-457-1700

US-USSR Bridges for Peace
The Norwich Center, Inc.
P.O. Box 710
Norwich, VT 05055
802-649-1000

Volunteers for Peace (VFP), Inc.
43 Tiffany Rd.

Belmont, VT 05730
802-259-2759

War Resisters League
33 Lafayette St.
New York, NY 10012
212-228-0450

Woman's Action for Nuclear Disarmament (WAND)
691 Massachusetts Ave.
Arlington, MA 02174
617-643-6740

Women's International League for Peace and Freedom
1213 Race St.
Philadelphia, PA 19107
215-563-7110

Women Strike for Peace
145 S. 13th St., Room 706
Philadelphia, PA 19107
215-923-0681

World Federalist Association
418 Seventh St., SE

Washington, DC 20003
202-546-3950

World Peacemakers, Inc.
2025 Massachusetts Ave. NW
Washington, DC 20036
202-265-7582

World Policy Institute
777 UN Plaza, 5th floor
New York, NY 10017
212-490-0010

World Priorities, Inc.
P.O. Box 25140
Washington, DC 20007
202-965-1661

World Without War Council
1730 M.L. King Jr. Way
Berkeley, CA 94709
415-845-1992

Youth Exchange Service (YES)
4675 MacArthur Court, Suite 830
Newport Beach, CA 92660
800-848-2121
714-955-2030

A FINAL NOTE

Creating
a Better World

▪▪▪

• • •

Knowing is not enough; we must apply. Willing is not enough; we must do.

• • •

—GOETHE

Volunteers for Peace

Perhaps the most surprising thing I learned while writing this book is that every great challenge we face has an answer. Pollution, animal cruelty, hunger, inadequate education, racism, and oppression are all complicated issues, but they are not problems that lack solutions. We know what causes these dilemmas and we know what it will take to correct them.

We have identified which chemicals eat holes in the ozone. We realize what air pollutants do to our atmosphere and our lungs. We understand what the excessive use of dangerous pesticides does to our topsoil and our bodies. We see the gap widening between the rich and the poor. We watch as hatred and discrimination rule our lives and wreck many others.

This knowledge has led to many ingenious solutions. The technology already exists to make more fuel-efficient cars, energy-efficient homes, and water-saving devices. Different farming methods will save our soil. New types of laboratory testing allow us to test drugs, cosmetics and medical breakthroughs without hurting animals. Greater resources devoted to our children will help them become better educated and less likely to fall into the deadly rut of crime and substance addiction.

The answers to these problems, however, are not only found in research and development departments; many can be solved by simple actions taken by everyone. Simple conservation measures save water and energy and alleviate the strain on the environment. A change in eating habits will make us healthier, create more efficiency in farming, and help the environment. A call to a politician will influence a vote. A letter to a corporate chief will affect policy. A meal delivery will brighten the day for an elderly person. Spending time as a tutor will help someone learn to read. Mentoring a teenager will improve his or her life.

What is knowledge without application? Knowing what causes the greenhouse effect will not cure it. But cutting down on carbon emissions, planting trees, and writing letters to politicians will most certainly help. Understanding the origins of homelessness will not get people off the streets. But donating food and clothing to a shelter may make life easier for a homeless person, while political pressure will help create better low-income housing projects and job programs. Sympathizing with a political prisoner will not free him. But a letter-writing campaign may improve his situation and perhaps even secure his release.

Hope for a future

It is our task, therefore, not only to gain awareness of the many problems facing the world today. We must also realize that the answers to these problems lie within each of us. So instead of just asking, "What can be done?" we must now focus on the question, "What can I do to make a difference?"